CHINA'S OLD DWELLINGS

CHINA'S OLD DWELLINGS

RONALD G. KNAPP

UNIVERSITY OF HAWAI'I PRESS, HONOLULU

Publication of this book has been assisted by grants from the following organizations:

Furthermore, the publication program of The J. M. Kaplan Fund
The Graham Foundation for Advance Studies in the Fine Arts
The Pacific Cultural Foundation

05   04   03   02   01   00   5   4   3   2   1

Library of Congress Cataloging-in-Publication Data

Knapp, Ronald G., 1940–
    China's old dwellings / Ronald G. Knapp.
      p.   cm.
    Includes bibliographical references and index.
    ISBN 0-8248-2075-4 (cloth :alk. paper). —ISBN 0-8248-2214-5 (pbk. : alk. paper)
    1. Architecture, Domestic—China. 2. Farmhouses—China.
    3. Vernacular architecture—China. I. Title
    NA7448.K567   1999
    728'.0951—dc21   99-20353
                                                  CIP

Designed by Kenneth Miyamoto

Printed by Friesens

For May, Too

CONTENTS

ACKNOWLEDGMENTS

THIS SURVEY OF OLD Chinese houses represents more than the fruits of my own fieldwork over the past thirty years. Equally important, as readers will note especially from the notes and figure captions, *China's Old Dwellings* draws upon the broad range of published and unpublished materials by Chinese scholars, architects, and amateurs, as well as a small number of non-Chinese, who are struggling to validate and document vernacular building forms that are rapidly being dismantled. My debt to individuals and institutions is indeed substantial. These include financial support that made possible extensive travel and photographic documentation, valuable materials shared by scholars from all over the world, invitations to conferences in which I was the only non-Chinese present, and the kindnesses of countless villagers who opened their homes to the intrusions of a curious foreigner.

Although I have acknowledged in earlier publications the small and larger grants that made it possible for me to persevere in my quest to understand Chinese vernacular architecture over a long period of time, I feel a need to reiterate my appreciation to the Association of American Geographers, SUNY Research Foundation, National Endowment for the Humanities, National Geographic Society, and SUNY New Paltz Grants for Research and Creative Projects for their support. Although this book has evolved from earlier work, it was completed during a year's leave in 1996 made possible by a Senior Scholar Research Grant from the Chiang Ching-kuo Foundation that was matched by Title F Funds from the State University of New York. The funded project "China's

Folk Architecture: Aesthetic, Architectonic, and Ecological Traditions" was intended to lead to a single book that would reconceptualize the approach used in my now out-of-print book *China's Traditional Rural Architecture* (1986). A pair of companion volumes, however, resulted instead: *China's Living Houses: Folk Beliefs, Symbols, and Household Ornamentation*, published also by University of Hawai'i Press in 1999, and this volume, *China's Old Houses.* Some of the illustrations and text in both of these new volumes appeared in my earlier University of Hawai'i books, but the range of subjects and regions covered in the companion volumes is more comprehensive and interdisciplinary.

Thirty years of fieldwork and extensive travel have provided abundant opportunities for interaction with Chinese and other scholars who have been generous in sharing field notes, publications, drawings, and photographs. In the preparation of this manuscript, the incisive criticism of many colleagues is appreciated, especially Jeffrey Cody, Joseph Wang, and Xu Yinong, who reviewed the whole manuscript, as well as Nancy Berliner, Hsu Min-fu, and David Lung, who commented on parts. Although most of the 500 photographs appearing in *China's Old Dwellings* were taken by me over the past thirty years, I have been able to supplement them with the original photographs and drawings of a number of scholars from around the world who have responded with enthusiasm to my requests for help. I am especially appreciative of the following scholars who generously gave permission to include their valuable original photographs to fill gaps in my coverage of China: Arthur J. Van Alstyne, Lawrence Crissman, Catherine Enderton, China Culture Center of San Francisco, Uli Franz, Jonathan Hammond, Puay-peng Ho, Huang Hanmin, Huang Yungsung, Elizabeth Knight of *Orientations*, Oliver Laude, Lee Chien-lang, Elizabeth Leppman, Andrew Li, Li Yuxiang, Liang Qi, Jay Manzo, Charles McKhann, Asakawa Shigeo, Shin Hada, Joseph Chuo Wang, Wu Meiyun and *Hansheng zazhi*, Wu Xiujie, Yang Liming, Kentaro Yamada, and Zhu Chengliang. In addition, the original drawings by Jonathan Hammond, Hsu Min-fu, Huang Hanmin, Liu Ming-chou, Liu Xin, Bonnie Shemie, Shen Dongqi, Paul Sun, and Wang Qijun add creative dimensions and detail to the book that go far beyond my own artistic abilities.

Over the years, the capable assistance of Corinne Nyquist and staff at the Interlibrary Loan office of Sojourner Truth Library, SUNY New Paltz, has meant a great deal to me in searching out and locating difficult-to-find materials. Marleigh Grayer Ryan's help with the transliteration of Japanese titles is much appreciated.

At the University of Hawai'i Press, the continuing encouragement of Patricia Crosby, executive editor and commissioning editor of three of my previous books, is much valued. Her willingness to write successful proposals in order to secure publication subventions has helped enhance the final appearance of the book and lowered costs. Robyn Sweesy's copyediting has helped improve style and presentation. I am appreciative of Masako Ikeda's careful guidance of this complicated manuscript with its high ratio of illustrations to text through the production process.

A NOTE ON CHINESE NAMES AND TERMS

PERSONAL AND PLACE NAMES as well as technical terms are given using the *pinyin* system of romanization. This applies even when describing the dwellings and settlements of minority nationalities in China where it may appear to have been more accurate to use a non-Chinese spelling.

The references section includes Chinese language materials published in many parts of the world. Chinese characters appear as they do on the actual title page of a book or article, with full-form characters generally for books published in Taiwan and in Hong Kong. Although simplified characters are generally employed in books and articles published in the People's Republic of China, increasing numbers are being published there using full-form characters. The names of Chinese authors are generally romanized according to *pinyin*, except where a cited author has published in both Chinese and English and uses a romanization form that differs from *pinyin*.

In the figure captions, romanized Chinese terms for administrative units are used: *cun,* village; *xiang,* rural township; *zhen,* urban township; *qu,* district; *shi,* city; and *xian,* county.

Introduction

THE RICHLY DIVERSE VERNACULAR architectural traditions of China are unrivaled in the world. No nation has as long an unbroken tradition, and, with the dissolution of the former Soviet Union, none is as ethnically diverse. China, a nation of fifty-six nationalities living in disparate natural landscapes with widely varying climatic conditions, is certainly more varied in its housing patterns than is the single nation United States or even multinational Europe. China's folk architectural forms, even as they portray common elements, clearly reveal the broad range of solutions that humans are capable of in providing basic shelter and creating homes for their families. The hierarchically ordered quadrangular residence in Beijing, the imposing silhouette of a circular Hakka fortress in Fujian, the subdued grandeur of a cubelike Huizhou merchant's manse in Anhui, the graceful "swallow's tail" ridgeline of a Taiwan farmer's house, the compact and utilitarian shape of a Mongol yurt, and the stark functionality of an underground dwelling in the loessial uplands of northern China are but a few of the notable examples of China's diverse dwelling types that can still be seen today. Each emerged out of specific environmental and social conditions characteristic of China at different times in the past and in the different regions of the country's vast space.

Bracketing the two major sections of this book, which focus on spaces and structures and places and regions, are a look backward and a look forward. Chapter 1 examines retrospectively the slow emergence of interest in Chinese vernacular buildings during the course of the twentieth century. It emphasizes the impact of war and politics on frustrating the efforts of individuals to document and contextualize building traditions across time and space. Chapter 7, an epilogue, explores China's surviving old dwellings in the context of contemporary rapid economic and social development that is destroying so many of them. Among issues that are addressed are questions of how Chinese architects and others are struggling to document and preserve representative building types and to maintain and restore historic homes of famous individuals.

No single explanation suffices to tell us how Chinese dwelling space is conceptualized and given external form, the diversity of which is the subject of two chapters in Part II: Spaces and Structures. As elsewhere in the world, Chinese dwellings protect their inhabitants from the elements of weather—cold and heat, rain and snow, humidity and wind—yet sheltering is but one factor in determining the makeup of a Chinese house. Chapter 2 details how space is composed in order to give Chinese dwellings their plan and shape, emphasizing common spatial denominators. Enclosed spaces that are built and open spaces that are framed by buildings are axiomatic components of most Chinese structures. Whether dwellings, palaces, halls, or temples, all Chinese structures share a relatively common set of conventional spatial forms as well as a repertoire of building components. Especially notable structural configurations, as described in Chapter 3, are the intricate and unique timber framing systems, the dimensioning and assembly of which represent skills and wisdom transmitted and shared over many centuries. In addition to utilizing molded bricks of many types, tamped earth wall construction and the excavation of cave dwellings (some 40 million Chinese even today live below ground in such dwellings) represent sophisticated treatments of a very common building material, the earth. This chapter also surveys the broad range of striking roof structures that distinguish Chinese architecture. An effort is made throughout Part II to relate building spaces and structures to the quite different physical geographic environments of China. Both Chapters 2 and 3 emphasize vernacular architectonics—the basic building principles and the interrelationship of building parts—that together comprise the structural unity of Chinese folk buildings.

After presenting the common ways in which building spaces are given shape throughout China, Part III: Places and Regions examines representative housing types in the three broad regions into which China may be divided. Besides discussing the different types of houses built by China's predominant Han nationality, who comprise 94 percent of China's population, these chapters also survey representative examples of the dwellings of most of the fifty-five minority nationalities, who together have a population totaling some 72 million. Although the non-Han ethnic minorities principally inhabit areas along China's western periphery, significant numbers are also found in the northern and southern parts of the country. While Part III emphasizes external appearance and form, excursions are made into building structure, materials, environmental adaptation, domestic routines, and social organization, among other topics, and assessing the influence of the dominant Han culture on ethnic minority folk/ vernacular housing patterns.

A seemingly bewildering variety of rural settlement forms are encountered in China, ranging from isolated farmsteads to extensive compact villages with populations that exceed two thousand households. Chinese architects, architectural historians, and cultural geographers have attempted to organize the seemingly disparate dwelling types found within China into a set of regional types and patterns that are based on a range of criteria, including building plan, external form, building structure, and building materials. Establishing a reasonable classification system is frustrated not only because of the degree to which dwelling types are commingled throughout the country but also because common and distinctive elements are shared between humble dwellings and palaces from preimperial times to the imperial past. Distilling a complex set of criteria that reflect environmental and human considerations, the geographer Jin Qiming has differentiated three basic cultural realms with eleven distinct regions and twenty-five subregions (Jin 1989, 128-312; Jin, Dong, and Lu 1990, 486-503; Jin and Li 1992, 20-34). The northern, southern, and western cultural realms, as seen in Map 1, provide a useful, if imperfect, guide for discussing the variety of dwelling and settlement forms found throughout China.

In early times, climatic elements as well as available building materials presented a limited range of possible construction options within which humans experimented. In some places this range must have been quite restrictive, but in other places there were fewer limitations. For example, when a migrating

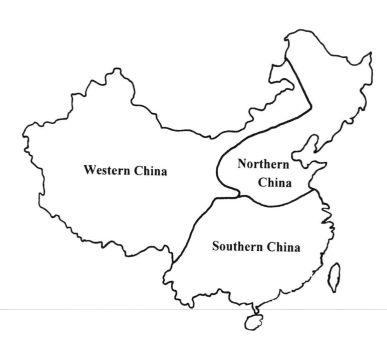

Map 1. The northern, southern, and western cultural realms, based on settlement types, provide a first-order division for examining house types in China.

group took a well-established housing form into a region that was climatically quite different, fundamental transformations of local patterns frequently emerged. Yet, while pervasive Han forms—themselves quite diverse—obviously were adopted by ethnic minority groups along China's periphery via acculturation processes that are difficult to document, migrating Han also adapted to local conditions. Examples of these interactions will appear throughout the book. Available materials and the level of knowledge of construction techniques and technologies certainly play modifying roles in guiding the diverse building configurations that dwellings ultimately take. Yet, as Rapoport has persuasively argued, a "house is an institution, not just a structure, created for a complex set of purposes," resulting from a multifaceted interplay of a broad range of sociocultural factors (1969, 46).

Dwellings are more than buildings sheltering humans from the harshness of natural forces. They are indeed humanized space, structured to express and shape family organization and guide the web of social and ethical norms, beliefs, and values that are distinctly Chinese. They thus express the vitality of sociocultural circumstances derived not only from Confucianism but also from areas of Chinese cosmological traditions, encoding and transmitting Chinese social norms and values. Chinese architecture—whether vernacular or monumental—communicates elements of Chinese cosmology and folk beliefs in building form and ornamentation.

Building sites traditionally were selected based on shared assumptions concerning an organic view of the cosmos, binding individuals, families, and society at large to the past and future. Chinese households even today continue to employ the somewhat esoteric but widely held beliefs concerning *fengshui*, or geomancy, to insure prosperity and guard against misfortune. Not incidentally, *fengshui* practices reveal a sensitivity to recurring patterns of nature, an environmental awareness that has its roots in China's past. Vernacular architecture in much of the world has been seen as an "unselfconscious" expression of people's ideas. Increasingly, however, in the case of Chinese structures—common or otherwise—one must acknowledge the *selfconscious* way in which peo-

ple have traditionally given shape to space using *yin-yang* cosmology, *wuxing* correlative principles, and cosmic paradigms. While apparently mute structures of matter, Chinese dwellings nonetheless reveal and communicate important aspects of Chinese culture. The significance of sociocultural factors of this sort in shaping building space and generating house forms is explored in a companion volume, *China's Living Houses: Folk Beliefs, Symbols, and Household Ornamentation* (Knapp 1999).

Economic development in China over the past decade and a half has brought in its wake the wholesale destruction of many of China's historic structures as well as more humble, yet important and representative buildings. As discussed throughout the book, many fine large residences, temples, and lineage halls indeed have been razed, abandoned, or turned to alternative uses in the wake of destructive political movements since the founding of the People's Republic of China. Destruction in Taiwan and Hong Kong in recent decades, while not the direct result of political movements, reflects the power of economic development (Knapp 1996). As in other areas of the world, the Chinese appreciation of their rural built heritage has come about only slowly and unevenly—a striking contrast to the well-known Chinese reverence for their imperial architectural inheritance. Chinese architects and others have helped to stimulate interest in the documentation or preservation of the country's architectural patrimony. Nevertheless, many unnoticed and unheralded dwellings, it is sad to say, continue to be destroyed because their residents and others regard them as too ordinary, outdated, and dysfunctional to maintain.

This book attempts to understand environmental "design" in rural China from an architectural, geographical, historical, and broad cultural perspective. It makes an effort to merge Chinese and western traditions of scholarship in pursuit of the study of a dominant and important component of Chinese material culture, folk architecture. China's position as a hearth area for cultural traditions that subsequently were disseminated to Japan, Korea, and Southeast Asia, moreover, underscores the value of this study in explaining and evaluating building traditions that involve nearly a quarter of the population of the world. As a work of synthesis, it attempts to go beyond the mere description and documentation of China's folk architecture that has been characteristic of most of the work in China and the west on the topic up to now. The traditional empirical methodology of the past that focused on recording with measured drawings and photographs continues in the research of countless local fieldworkers in China who take an interest in vernacular forms that all too often are on the threshold of destruction. While their efforts are heroic in that they preserve at least a record on paper of artifacts of material culture that once destroyed are irretrievable, their efforts must be seen as only a first step. What is needed to elevate their—and this—work beyond mere observation and compilation is critical collation, a nuanced consideration of many variables within an interdisciplinary and comparative framework. For the most part, as a review of relevant publications in the Chinese language reveals, few professional architects or amateurs have made more than preliminary attempts at examining dwellings comprehensively as vectors for understanding broader issues of Chinese culture.

Part I

PROLOGUE

CHAPTER 1

Looking Back: Appreciating China's Folk Architecture

WHILE CHINESE, JAPANESE, AND WESTERN scholars have had a longtime interest in Chinese monumental architecture, interest in and appreciation of Chinese folk architecture has developed slowly and rather recently—as has been the case with other aspects of Chinese material culture. There is increasing evidence, however, that folk architecture has, as do other areas of popular material culture, the potential to inform us of matters that texts and monuments cannot about common people in the past and in the present.

In the 1920s, German, Swedish, and Japanese scholars published a small number of extensively illustrated books that depicted examples of China's historically significant monumental architectural tradition. The formal study of this tradition, however, was left to Chinese pioneers of architectural history. Sponsored by the Society (later Institute) for Research in Chinese Architecture, which formed in 1929, various expeditions in the 1930s and 1940s were carried out under the leadership of Liang Sicheng, Liu Dunzhen, and others and focused on monuments—principally temples, halls, pagodas, tombs, gardens, and bridges—that hitherto had never been adequately described or rendered in measured drawings.

Because the intent of the Society was "aimed at discovering the stages of evolution of Chinese architecture as evident in building that had survived through the centuries," little attention was directed toward common dwellings (Fairbank 1994, 109-110). Zhu Qiqian, the Society's founder and first president, however, offered in his inaugural address tantalizingly prescient comments about the significance of Chinese dwellings (Zhu 1930, 1-2; Knapp 1999, 1-2). Indeed, among the many detailed articles on monuments published in the Society's quarterly bulletin, *Zhongguo yingzao xueshe huikan* [Bulletin of the Society for the Research in Chinese Architecture], there are abundant casual observations about and sometimes photographs of common dwellings seen during fieldwork in remote villages and towns.

Perhaps the first academic treatment of Chinese vernacular dwellings by an architect in a Chinese journal was a brief report by Long Feiliao in 1934 on the relationship between recent archaeological excavations, textual references, and existing cave dwellings. Through the efforts of these pioneers in the emerging field of Chinese architectural history, the seeds for the study of vernacular architecture were sown.

With the invasion of China by Japan in 1937, the extraordinary and intrepid migration of government, academia, and industry from the developed areas of northern and eastern China to the less developed mountain-ringed redoubts of China's southwest brought about also an altering of research agendas that hitherto had focused on the core areas of Chinese civilization and history. In the field of Chinese architecture, "the difficult and exhausting conditions of travel from Peking to Kunming across fifteen hundred miles of back country, putting up at night in villages, had opened the eyes of the Institute staff to the special architectural significance of Chinese dwellings. The distinct features of such dwellings, their relationship to the life-styles of the occupants, and their variations in different areas of the country were suddenly obvious and interesting" (Fairbank 1994, 110).

In spite of efforts expended, knowledge gained, and documentation completed, few articles were published in the Society's bulletin that suggested the richness of vernacular forms in southwest China during this period. Notable is the unpublished survey report by Liu Dunzhen that attempted to differentiate Chinese dwellings according to building types and Liu Zhiping's lengthy handwritten discussion of "seal-type" dwellings in Yunnan (1944). Liu Dunzhen's efforts set the stage for his major contributions in the 1950s to the study of Chinese vernacular architecture, but they sadly failed to have the intended impact, again because of political conditions.

Because of wartime conditions throughout most of the 1940s, many reports were lost and never published. One that survived was the manuscript of Liu Zhiping's 1941 survey in western Sichuan of some 200 examples of domestic architecture, more than sixty of which were detailed in measured drawings; however, Liu's manuscript was not published for nearly a half-century after it was completed. It was delayed first by the impediments of China's war with Japan and then by the severe restraints on scholarship due to vacillating movements of Chinese domestic politics after 1949. After the establishment of the People's Republic of China in 1949, Liu, then at Qinghua University as a junior associate to Liang Sicheng, reworked his manuscript, titled "Residential Architecture of Sichuan," and had it ready for publication in 1954. In addition, he prepared a manuscript titled "A Brief History of Chinese Residential Architecture." Unforeseen circumstances intervened so neither was published as planned, even though Liu was successful in having a comprehensive work concerning Chinese architectural types and structures published in 1957. It was not until 1990 that Liu Zhiping's Sichuan manuscript was

"attached" to his brief history of residential architecture. This long overdue publication of Liu's texts, however, had to be carried out without the benefit of his photographs and drawings, all of which unfortunately had been destroyed in the turmoil of the Cultural Revolution in the late 1960s. The reassembling of fragments of Liu's important scholarship was accomplished through the efforts of his colleagues and students. They and others worked diligently to bring forth the work of several of China's trailblazing scholars of architectural history, some of whom had died under conditions of torment in the preceding decade and a half, or, having survived the political upheavals, indeed lay dying as the editorial work was being carried out. The loss of scholarly momentum and fragile photographs and drawings was repeated time and again over the decades.

Liu Dunzhen, who pioneered work on domestic architecture in southwest China in the early 1940s, was invited to head the Department of Architecture at Nanjing College of Engineering. There his research turned to Chinese vernacular architecture in its many forms. In 1956, he published a lengthy article on Chinese dwellings that was expanded into a pathbreaking book. With the appearance of *Zhongguo zhuzhai gaishuo* [Introduction to Chinese dwellings] in 1957, it seemed as if the study of vernacular architecture had become an accepted academic field with tentative steps away from mere description toward an assessment of building types. In the preface to the book, Liu informed readers that his travels in southwestern China (Yunnan, Guizhou, and Sichuan) during the Anti-Japanese War (1937–1945) had opened his eyes to vernacular architecture, but it was not until the formation of the Chinese Architectural Research Unit by the Nanjing College of Engineering and the former East China Architectural Design Company in 1953 that it was possible to carry out systematic surveys. Liu unapologetically admitted that his book was preliminary and that the story of vernacular architecture in China could not be adequately told until a comprehensive countrywide survey was completed. His book was an appeal for such an effort. Liu's book presented a brief historical summary of the development of the Chinese house from neolithic times through the Qing dynasty. While the book focused on dwellings he had visited that reached back to the Ming dynasty, his approach was less historical than morphological. He organized dwellings into nine categories according to their plans and shapes. The book is replete with useful measured drawings and photographs.

In 1957, in addition to the publication of Liu Dunzhen's book on Chinese dwellings and Liu Zhiping's on architectural types and structural forms, a third important book appeared. *Huizhou Mingdai zhuzhai* [Ming dynasty houses in Huizhou] by Zhang Zhongyi and cohorts focused on the dwellings of wealthy merchants of southern Anhui province, many of which had been standing for more than three hundred years. In contrast to the simplicity of folk architecture, this book revealed the simple elegance of merchant's mansions, none of which had ever been documented in such detail. Flush with original drawings and photographs, this book still stands as an outstanding source on these magnificent dwellings, many of which have disappeared over the past forty years. Some illustrations as well as fragmentary translations from these books found their way into English language treatments of Chinese architecture, unfortunately all too often without proper attribution to the Chinese architects who made them.

International events, Chinese politics, and the limited circulation of these few books in China and abroad clearly restricted their impact. In the West, note was made of Liu Dunzhen's book by R. T. F. Skinner in the *Journal of the Royal Institute of British Architects:* "it is perhaps difficult for us in Europe, where at least all the main types of domestic architecture have been studied and presented in innumerable excellent publications, to realize how important it is that this research work has started in China, where the material is quite as rich as in Europe, and almost entirely unrecorded" (1958, 431). An abridged English language typescript of Liu's book was prepared in England and had limited circulation and impact. This mimeographed typescript as well as the Chinese language edition of the book found their way onto the shelves of some libraries in the West, but, with one noteworthy exception, little attention was paid to Liu's pathbreaking contribution in the West. In 1962, the British architect Andrew Boyd published *Chinese Architecture and Town Planning,* "a very small book on a very large subject." Depending principally on Chinese materials published in the 1950s for its text, drawings, and photographs, this book sadly and carelessly did not clearly acknowledge the origins as the work of specific Chinese architects and architectural historians. Because of this negligence, many of the photographs and drawings in Boyd's book subsequently were credited in other publications to Boyd rather than to the Chinese researchers who had produced them. Boyd's generously illustrated volume became in time a standard reference in the West on the subject of Chinese architecture.

Throughout the 1950s and, to a lesser degree, into the early 1960s, fieldwork continued in China by architects and others in order to survey, document, measure, and assess common dwellings as well as the magnificent dwellings of gentry and merchants, many of which had historical significance. Between 1956 and 1964, nearly twenty articles dealing with *minjian jianzhu* [folk architecture] appeared in *Jianzhu xuebao* [Architectural journal], mere glimpses of the heterogeneity of Chinese vernacular dwellings and boldly suggestive of future research needs. Some architectural research reports with limited circulation within China, such as one on dwellings in Zhejiang province, were issued, but these focused essentially on structural and spatial elements of interest to architects. Very little attention was drawn to the influence of historical, cultural, environmental, and social factors in the formation of vernacular dwellings (Lu 1996, 2). The periodic mention in Western architectural publications of Chinese conference reports, writings, and drawings aroused some hope that documenting Chinese architecture was well under way. Unfortunately, as the decade of the 1960s began, the study of vernacular architecture in China was already entering a stage of relative dormancy, striking and melancholy inactivity, rather than the period of vigorous and healthy development hoped for by Liu Dunzhen and others just a short time before.

For the most part, what research work was being done on the subject in China—drawings, photographs, and texts—was not being published. Even in cases where ongoing editorial work was being carried out on joint projects, scholarship was frustrated by politics, especially the onset of the Great Proletarian Cultural Revolution in 1966. A striking example of this was *The History of Ancient Architecture* [*Zhongguo gudai jianzhu shi*] under the general editorship of Liu Dunzhen. Between 1959 and 1965, the manuscript for this comprehensive history that placed "dwellings" [*zhuzhai* 住宅] among the generally acknowledged monuments that were the nation's patrimony had gone through six revisions involving scholars throughout the country. However, this important book lay unpublished until 1980 when changes in the political environment made its publication possible. As with other scholarship, it was unappreciated, held hostage to the convulsions of the Cultural Revolution that engulfed China between 1966 and 1976. The public humiliation of academics like Liu Dunzhen and Liang Sicheng tragically led to their untimely deaths, Liu in 1968 and Liang in 1972. Beyond the personal and professional adversities of individuals and their life work, the Cultural Revolution impacted the country's cultural landscape as historical monuments as well as dwellings of all types were destroyed. Aspects of this destruction appear throughout this book.

The languished state of China's architectural studies, as with other aspects of academic life, was invigorated by the political events of the late 1970s, leading eventually in the 1980s and 1990s to a resurgence of activity and an avalanche of publications relating to vernacular architecture. Over the past two decades, in addition to substantial increases in the quantity and quality of publications, there have been increasingly collegial and collaborative efforts at studying China's vernacular architectural traditions. A turning point was the publication of *Zhejiang minju* [Folk dwellings of Zhejiang] in 1984, and the revelation that fieldwork for the book had begun in 1961, a draft manuscript had been completed by 1963, but that "political events" had aborted the project. This book's drawings, photographs, and text clearly enriched the earlier countrywide observations of Liu Dunzhen, providing a link with the work of Liu and others in the 1950s. Prior to the publication of *Zhejiang minju*, supplementary fieldwork, several new chapters, and overall reorganization were carried out to update the manuscript. The authorship of the book was officially collective, an ex-

pression not only of the lingering political atmosphere at this time of transition but the fact that several generations of Chinese architects and architectural historians had played a role in its eventual appearance. Concentrating on a single province, this book examines building materials and structure as well as the climatic, topographic, social, and historical contexts in which one of China's most important vernacular traditions emerged.

The next year another volume appeared, *Jilin minju* [Folk houses of Jilin] (1985), in which the author Zhang Yuhuan revealed that fieldwork had been carried out in 1956-1957 and the manuscript completed in 1958. The preface noted somewhat elliptically and with an implied sense of sadness that publication had been delayed "for various reasons." The manuscript was supplemented as a result of recent prepublication fieldwork, but unfortunately there was no differentiation made between information and illustrations pertinent to the late 1950s or early 1980s. While stressing Han vernacular architectural forms, Zhang also presents useful information about the folk dwellings of the Manchu, Korean, and Mongol ethnic minorities who also populate Jilin province.

With the publication in 1986 of *Yunnan minju* [Vernacular dwellings of Yunnan], under the joint authorship of the Yunnan Provincial Design Institute, it appeared as if there was an annual schedule planned for this building series by the China Architecture and Building Press. As with its two recent precursors, this volume under the general guidance of Wang Cuilan and Zhao Qin had its origins decades earlier in the 1960s and had benefited from recent revisions. Altogether ten field expeditions involving more than twenty individuals contributed to the breadth of this book. More explicitly than the others, the book's purpose was to go beyond mere documentation and analysis of building traditions to "make the past serve the present" [*gu wei jin yong* 古为今用]. This notion of a need for practical relevance rather than mere scholarship had come to characterize much academic work in socialist China in many fields. While Yunnan province is the most ethnically diverse area in China, *Yunnan minju* focuses on only nine of the largest minority groups: Bai, Naxi, Hani,

Yi, Dai, Jingpo, De'ang, Va, and Lahu. Peculiarly, little mention is made of Han house forms in the province, although the book offers a rich resource for making comparisons across cultural boundaries.

Jointly authored by Gao Zhenming, Wang Naixiang, and Chen Yu, who took responsibility for different sections, *Fujian minju* [Vernacular dwellings of Fujian] was published in the series in 1987. The preface does not indicate that the research for the book had been completed decades earlier. While the volume surveys overall settlement patterns, housing plans, building structure, construction materials, and architectural details in some fifty locations around the province, the bulk of the book focuses its drawings and photographs on nearly ninety individual dwellings.

Although 1988 passed without an addition to the series, the inclusion of the *Vernacular Architecture* volume as one of the six volumes on Chinese architecture that were part of the encyclopedic *Zhongguo meishu quanji* [Arts of China series] was a heralded event. This beautifully produced volume included a brief but wide ranging introduction by Lu Yuanding and Yang Gusheng as well as 175 annotated color photographs selectively depicting the aesthetic elements of China's rich regional and ethnic vernacular architecture. By the end of 1995, this volume had been reprinted four times. Using traditional Chinese characters in order to bring the subject to a larger Chinese audience beyond the mainland, vernacular architecture was being shown as no longer peripheral to Chinese architecture or outside the realm of Chinese arts.

By the end of 1988 more than a hundred articles had appeared in various academic journals, including *Jianzhu xuebao* [Architectural journal], *Jianzhu shi* [The architect], *Jianzhu lishi yu lilun* [Architectural history and theory], *Jianzhu shilun wenji* [Treatises on the history of architecture], *Keji shi wenji* [Collection on the history of science and technology], *Gu jian yuanlin jishu* [Technology of ancient architecture and gardens], *Huazhong jianzhu* [Huazhong architecture China], *Xin jianzhu* [New architecture], *Nanfang jianzhu* [Architecture of south China], *Shidai jianzhu* [Architectural times], *Zhongguo gudai jianzhu shihua* [Historical notes on China's ancient architecture],

and *Fujian jianzhu* [Architecture of Fujian]. A number of specialized monographs, such as Zhu Liangwen's richly detailed study of the Naxi ethnic minority group's vernacular architecture, also appeared during this time. A host of sketchbooks, pamphlets, news articles, architectural surveys, and preservation studies, as well as several somewhat idiosyncratic books appeared, which further enrich our knowledge of the country's diverse vernacular building traditions. (A list of Chinese periodical articles and books on "traditional dwellings" published between 1949 and 1991 appears in Lu 1992, 190–196 and an examination of materials in Chinese as well as western languages appears in Knapp 1994).

Recognizing the increasing interest in local architectural traditions, a National Conference on Chinese Vernacular Dwellings was held in Guangzhou in November 1988. Hosted by the South China University of Technology's Department of Architecture under the leadership of Professor Lu Yuanding, this successful conference set the stage for a continuing series of others whose avowed purpose has been to promote vernacular architecture and to bring veteran scholars into contact with a younger generation. Half of the papers presented at the initial conference subsequently appeared in a 1991 volume titled *Zhongguo chuantong minju yu wenhua* [China's traditional vernacular dwellings and culture]. From this inaugural conference, nine other national conferences have followed—Yunnan in 1990, Guangxi in 1991, Jiangxi in 1992, Sichuan in 1994, Xinjiang in 1995, Shanxi in 1996, Hong Kong in 1997, Guizhou in 1998, and Beijing in 2000. The publication of conference papers in subsequent issues of *Zhongguo chuantong minju yu wenhua* has enriched the field and given clear evidence of a maturation of approaches to the topic that increasingly have moved away from pure architecture to embrace historical, cultural, linguistic, geographic, and aesthetic approaches to the subject.

Under the auspices of several organizations, South China University of Technology convened an International Conference on Chinese Traditional Houses in 1993 and a Cross Straits Symposium on Traditional Vernacular geared to young scholars in 1995. A selection of papers presented at the 1993 conference was published as *Minju shilun yu wenhua* [History and culture of vernacular architecture] in 1995. The papers from the Cross-Straits conference appeared in 1996 in a special issue of the journal *Huazhong jianzhu.*

The China Architecture and Building Press series was restarted again in 1989 and has continued to publish at least one book a year since. Virtually each of these new surveys broke new ground in one way or another, such as expanding the unit of analysis from single dwellings to whole villages and searching for ways in which traditional housing design could help meet current needs. The quality of photography and printing generally has improved each year. At a time of increasing commercialization in Chinese publishing, it was not surprising that the smaller print runs of titles in the series obviously reflect some concerns about their marketability. All titles, however, quickly sell out and are difficult to find in bookshops. The first book to go beyond a single province was *Yaodong minju* [Vernacular cave dwellings] by Hou Jiyao, Ren Zhiyuan, Zhou Peinan, and Li Zhuanze (1989). In 1990, Lu Yuanding and Wei Yanjun's *Guangdong minju* [Folk houses of Guangdong] broached new topics such as historical context, cultural factors important in site selection, measurements and proportions, as well as detailed comparative tables of building terminology. No book in the series before or since has surpassed *Guibei minjian jianzhu* [The folk architecture of northern Guangxi], edited by Li Changjie, in terms of artistic quality and size. Emphasizing the *ganlan* [pile or stilt-supported] dwellings, bridges, drum towers, and other wooden structures of the Zhuang, Dong, Yao, and Miao minority nationalities, this volume portrays the highly developed carpentry skills of non-Han groups along China's periphery.

Books focusing on dwellings in urban areas appeared in 1991 and 1993. *Suzhou minju* [The vernacular dwellings of Suzhou], edited by Xu Minsu and others, illustrates Jiangnan architecture, including the gardens, and examples of fine furniture found within many of them. *Shanghai lilong minju* [Vernacular dwellings of Shanghai's neighborhoods], edited by Shen Hua, depicted the chronological development of urban dwellings under the influence of Chinese and foreign styles from the early nineteenth century to the present.

Zhang Bitian and Liu Zhenya's *Shaanxi minju* [Vernacular dwellings of Shaanxi] in 1993 brought a return to province-wide surveys. In the same year, Wang Cuilan and Chen Moude edited *Yunnan minju xubian* [Vernacular dwellings of Yunnan, continued], which expanded the coverage of the 1986 volume on Yunnan province. This new volume provides further information for three groups covered initially in the 1986 book (Hani, Va, and Lahu) and for an additional seven groups (Drung, Jinuo, Blang, Lisu, Nu, Pumi, and Achang). These sixteen groups, each of which is concentrated in Yunnan, represent some two-thirds of all minority nationality groups in the province. The remaining nine minority nationality groups found in Yunnan (Zhuang, Miao, Hui, Yao, Zang [Tibetan], Buyi [Bouyei], Mongol, Shui, and Manchu) spill over from concentrations in adjacent provinces, such as Guizhou and Tibet, or are migrants from areas farther afield, such as Northern and Northeast China. Living mixed among other groups whose architecture they often share, few of these remaining nine minority groups have populations in Yunnan that exceed 10,000. Again, the dwellings of the Han majority who account for nearly two-thirds of the province's population are not treated.

Beijing *siheyuan*, also known as courtyard or quadrangle-style houses, were the subject of books in both 1994 and 1996. Although many of the publications discussed earlier had compared vernacular dwellings within their geographical realm with Beijing *siheyuan*, this quintessential Chinese vernacular dwelling form itself hitherto had not been studied systematically. Although both Wu Liangyong's *Beijing jiu cheng yu Ju'er hutong* [The old city of Beijing and Ju'er Lane] and Lu Shan and Wang Qiming's *Beijing siheyuan* [Beijing courtyards] provide insights into the historical background and contemporary relevance of *siheyuan*, neither book unfortunately is sufficiently comprehensive to do justice to this archetypical housing form. The city of Beijing has undergone a rapid transformation over the past decade with much destruction of its historic form including not only buildings but also the scale and character of its neighborhoods. Much of the city's structure historically was related to a grid and cellular system based upon the architectural grouping of courtyard forms at many scales. In searching for a means to bring about an "organic renewal" of Beijing's residential areas, Wu Liangyong and his design team proposed a planning process for the replacement of dilapidated single-story *siheyuan* with modern multistoried structures reminiscent of traditional styles. It is this design process over a decade and a half and its lessons for the future that are the focus of Wu's book. Lu and Wang's objective is more limited, simply a broad survey of Beijing courtyard dwellings. Included in an appendix is a useful list of 102 historically important courtyard houses found throughout Beijing. The definitive study of *siheyuan* has yet to be written.

The publication of *Xinjiang minju* [Vernacular dwellings of Xinjiang], edited by Yan Dachun, was timed to coincide with a National Conference on Chinese Vernacular Dwellings held in Xinjiang in the summer of 1995. Emphasizing the variations of Uygur dwellings in different portions of an area that is three times the size of France, the volume also surveys Han, Kazak, Hui, Kirgiz, Mongol, and Tajik vernacular dwellings. At a significantly smaller scale, He Zhongyi examines Han dwellings as well as those of Tujia, Miao, and Dong minority nationalities in western Hunan province in *Xiangxi minju* [Vernacular dwellings of western Hunan]. Both volumes are rather straightforward architectural treatments of the subject matter with only incidental references to the social, environmental, and economic factors that have contributed to the variant forms found in the two areas.

Unrelated to these conferences and the books published by China Architecture and Building Press, journal articles and conference papers on relevant topics also increased in number throughout the 1980s and 1990s. Many have enriched the evolution of this field of study, but all too many more are descriptive, idiosyncratic in content and approach, and extremely brief. A few represent rather sophisticated but brief excursions by Chinese architects into traditional symbolism (Xu Yinong 1989-1990), phenomenology (Miao Po 1989-1991), architectonics (Lu Yuanding 1990), diffusion and cultural adaptation (Pan An 1994-1995), as approaches to the study of the vernacular in the context of other Chinese architectural forms (Chen Zhihua 1997), among other

more orthodox descriptive architectural topics focusing on individual ancestral halls, opera stages, dwellings, and other structures.

The 1980s, especially, was a time in which there was a great building boom in rural China, with an unprecedented and widespread destruction of traditional rural houses as new construction took place. This "new look to peasant houses" and their relationship to vernacular traditions was engagingly examined by Frances Wood (1987). In many cases, the published works of Chinese architects during this period are not only valiant and important efforts at documenting structures slated for destruction, they provide significant raw material that can contribute toward contemporary design solutions. Throughout this period and even to the present, thoughtful Chinese architects are striving to make stylistic and functional connections between new forms and traditional patterns.

Two creative series that document vernacular architecture throughout China appeared in the 1990s, both resulting from the intrepid fieldwork of several individuals who endured great hardship in acquiring their images. The first is a remarkable set of photographic surveys of "China's Old Houses" carried out under the general editorship of Zhu Chengliang of the Jiangsu Fine Arts Publishing House. Based principally on the work of Li Yuxiang and other photographers, eleven large volumes of black and white prints have already been published that capture the beauty of China's remaining old houses: southern Anhui (1993) with an essay by Yu Hongli, the Jiangnan canal country with an essay by Zheng Guangfu (1993), Shanxi with an essay by Wang Qijun (1994), Fujian with an essay by Huang Hanmin (1994), Tujia minority nationality architecture with an essay by Zhang Liangnie (1994), Dong minority nationality architecture with an essay by Chen Shouxiang (1996), and Beijing *siheyuan* by Wang Qijun (1998). More than a melancholy record of sad and decaying structures, these photographic folios capture the essence of the Chinese aesthetic sense in architecture as they provide detail and context.

The pen and ink portrayals of Chinese structures by Wang Qijun represent a different type of record. Trained in art before becoming an architect and architectural historian, Wang has at his fingertips the necessary tools for capturing the many facets of buildings, among which are their structure, materials, detail, and proportions. Over the decades, other Chinese architects have compensated for their lack of recording equipment by using their pens to sketch architectural forms. All too often, however, the work is seen as formalistic, exact, and embellished, without giving a full sense of the actual state of existing buildings as they survive. Wang Qijun, however, has succeeded in securing fine representations that match well the high-quality photographs that sometimes accompany his work (1991b, 1993a, 1993b, 1994, 1996a, 1996b, 1996c). While there are other capable individuals pursuing similar efforts with a degree of success, the work of these individuals deserves special mention because they have brought forth an abundant body of rich materials that will stand as enduring records and as fine art. With the kind permission of Zhu Chengliang, Li Yuxiang, and Wang Qijun, I have been able to include some of their work in this volume.

Glimpses of Chinese vernacular architectural traditions can be found in the writings of Westerners who visited or lived in China during the nineteenth and early twentieth centuries. As fragmentary records of housing conditions encountered during a tumultuous century and a half of China's history, these drawings, photographs, and descriptions rarely hint at the craftsmanship and meaning associated with common dwellings. The first broad academic article concerning "the houses of the Chinese" appeared in 1947 and was written by a geographer. Although this survey was admittedly "preliminary observations," Joseph E. Spencer spelled out important research themes concerning regional differences in Chinese folk architecture that required comprehensive and comparative study. Spencer faulted earlier observers of Chinese rural architecture who unsatisfactorily "generalized into a relatively uniform 'Chinese' pattern, a single simplified style somewhat at variance with the facts" (1947, 254). Unfortunately, it was not possible in subsequent decades for any foreign researcher to build on Spencer's work because of China's isolation from the world from the late 1940s well into the late 1970s.

Accompanying recent Chinese efforts at understanding their own folk/vernacular architectural forms over the past two decades, there has been a growing parallel interest by American, European, and Japanese researchers as well as specialists in Taiwan and Hong Kong who increasingly are focusing on mainland forms. Theses and dissertations on Chinese vernacular architecture have appeared in recent years in Germany, Italy, Japan, Switzerland, the United Kingdom, the United States, and, as one would expect, in China, Hong Kong, and Taiwan. As international contact has expanded and field study opportunities have materialized, there have been increasing levels of cooperation and sharing among many individuals and organizations. While some of this work is idiosyncratic in approach and content, a great deal of it is mutually supporting and helping to bring China's vernacular architectural traditions to a field that has generally ignored it in the past. The reinforcing efforts of scholars all over the world who focus on China can be seen in the masterfully comprehensive *Encyclopedia of World Vernacular Architecture* edited by Paul Oliver (1997). Since 1988, the International Association for the Study of Traditional Environments (IASTE), with headquarters at the University of California, Berkeley, has played a key role in promoting comparative and interdisciplinary studies of vernacular architecture. Increasingly, research relating to China appears in the society's journal, *Traditional Dwellings and Settlements Review*, its working paper series, and is presented at the biennial IASTE conferences.

Liu Dunzhen's pathbreaking 1957 book was translated into Japanese as *Chūgoku no jūtaku* in 1976 and into French as *La Maison Chinoise* in 1980. Although the book was never translated into English, its approach provided much of the structure for this author's *China's Traditional Rural Architecture: A Cultural Geography of the Common House*. Published in 1986, this book was the first in English to survey the evolution, variety, construction techniques, social context, and contemporary transformations of Chinese dwellings. Its nearly 200 photographs and drawings drew attention to the richness of Chinese folk traditions, but the book is a preliminary glimpse, not a definitive treatment, of the topic. Unlike similar surveys in China for

Chinese audiences, *China's Traditional Rural Architecture*, written to introduce the subject to Western readers, explores the ways in which Chinese dwellings communicate folk beliefs and employ geomancy [*fengshui*], almanacs, and charms in house construction. An even briefer introductory treatment for a general audience was published by this author as *The Chinese House* in 1990, the manuscript of which was translated into Japanese as *Chūgoku no sumai* in 1996.

This author's 1989 book *China's Vernacular Architecture: House Form and Culture* turned inward to a single province to explore in detail the sensitivity to the natural environment, the use of space, construction principles and techniques, exterior and interior ornamentation, and folk traditions associated with the building of and living within rural dwellings. Each chapter also examines the ways in which these elements are changing, the ways in which rural housing resonates the tensions between continuity and innovation as rapid economic change subjects rural China to a stressful transformation unparalleled in Chinese history.

Specific Chinese house types have been explored in English by others, such as Gideon Golany's books on earth-sheltered dwellings (1989, 1990, 1992). Golany's books, while doing a masterful job of documenting architectural detail, fail to examine the cultural context within which the structures took form. Jean-Paul Loubes' study of "troglodyte architecture" is a fine survey of the origins, distributions, and construction of these underground dwelling forms (1988). In 1979, Werner Blaser described well the archetypical Beijing courtyard house and brought the subject up to date in 1995. David Ping-yee Lung published a bilingual Chinese/English book, *Chinese Traditional Rural Architecture*, in 1991, which accompanied an important multimedia exhibition in Hong Kong. Field research by Lung and his students is tied to the only college-level course on Chinese vernacular architecture offered in the world in English. In 1995, Puay-peng Ho published a broad ranging compendium titled *The Living Building: Vernacular Environments of South China*.

Drawing on Chinese materials and the fruits of intensive study expeditions in the 1980s and early 1990s involving Japanese scholars and their students, a number of important Japanese publications document Chinese vernacular architectural traditions. These include a study of Jiangnan waterside and Hakka fortress architecture by Mogi Keiichiro, Inaji Toshiro, and Katayama Kazutoshi (1991); stilt housing of ethnic minority nationalities in Guizhou with contributions by Tanaka Tan and others in the journal *Chutaku kenchiku* [Residential architecture]; subterranean dwellings (1993) and Naxi dwellings in Yunnan by Asakawa Shigeo (1996); and an exploration of possible Chinese origins for Japanese dwellings by Sugimoto Hisatsugu (1984).

Traditional construction materials and technologies are explored in many of the Chinese and Western language studies of Chinese houses, but none examines the tools used by carpenters and masons as thoroughly as does Rudolf Hommel (1937). This subject is worthy of further attention. Klaas Ruitenbeek, based on research on the fifteenth-century carpenter's manual *Lu Ban jing*, has documented well the interplay of craft and ritual used by builders in Chinese house construction (1986, 1993). His scholarly research goes far beyond the efforts of the folklorist Wolfram Eberhard (1970) in documenting the ways in which house construction was more than mere building. Ruitenbeek's textual work is enriched by contemporary fieldwork on the mainland and in Taiwan.

There are several accessible studies of general geomantic theory (Feuchtwang 1974; Bennett 1978), but Richard J. Smith's comprehensive and informed survey of divination in traditional China should lead researchers to examine further the role of *fengshui* in site selection for dwellings (1991). The unpublished dissertations of Sang Hae Lee (1986) and Xu Ping (1990) are useful treatments of the topic. Sophie Clément, Pierre Clément, and Shin Yong-hak (1987) explore the spread of these geomantic ideas elsewhere in East Asia. Rolf Stein's study of "the religious role of the dwelling place in China," published in French in 1957 and in English in 1990, examines the ways in which Chinese cosmological speculations were given material form in their dwellings.

Over the years, a number of Western scholars have written about the forms and rich symbolic vocabulary of ornamentation found on and about Chinese dwellings: Daniel Sheets Dye's *A Grammar of Chinese Lattice* (1937) and Clarence Burton Day's *Chinese Peasant*

Cults: Being a Study of Chinese Paper Gods (1940), and, more recently, Nancy Zeng Berliner's *Chinese Folk Art: The Small Skills of Carving Insects* (1986), Po Sung-nien's and David Johnson's *Domesticated Deities and Auspicious Emblems: The Iconography of Everyday Life in Village China* (1992), John Lust's *Chinese Popular Prints* (1996), and Francesca Bray's *Technology and Gender: Fabrics of Power in Late Imperial China* (1997). Valuable information and insights that help inform our understanding of these subjects still rely to some degree on books written a century ago: Henry Doré's *Researches into Chinese Superstitions* (1917), J. J. M. deGroot's *The Religious System of China* (1892–1910), and Edouard Chavannes' *The Five Happinesses: Symbolism in Chinese Popular Art* (1901). Mary Fong's treatment of the iconography of popular gods and other art historical studies are quite valuable (1983, 1989). The many works of Wang Shucun in Chinese, English, and other Western languages provide comprehensive treatments of the history and production of New Year's pictures and other folk prints. With examples drawn from the collections of scholars living in Taiwan, the catalog titled *The Art of the Traditional Chinese New Year Print* by Chen Chi-lu and others is lavishly printed and useful to Chinese and Western readers alike (1992). For western readers, Eberhard's *Dictionary of Chinese Symbols: Hidden Symbols in Chinese Life and Thought* (1986) and C. A. S. Williams' *Outlines of Chinese Symbolism and Art Motifs* (1932) remain remarkably handy reference tools for examining this topic. An imaginative and useful excursion into the manner in which human activities, including shelter, were given form in the Chinese written language has been written by Cecilia Lindqvist (1991). Robert Chard's textual and field-based research on the Cult of the Stove has brought attention to this important subject (1990a, 1990b, 1995). Many of these themes are explored in this book's companion volume *China's Living Houses: Folk Beliefs, Symbols, and Household Ornamentation* (Knapp 1999).

Although a great deal of substantial research has been completed concerning high-style Chinese furniture by Wang Shixiang (1986) and others, only a few books, such as *Friends of the House: Furniture from China's Towns and Villages* by Nancy Berliner and Sarah Handler (1995) and *Classical and Vernacular Chi-*

nese Furniture in the Living Environment—Examples from the Kai-yin Lo Collection (Zhongguo gudian 1998), treat the furnishing found in common dwellings. Ellen Johnson Laing's interesting article (1989) concerning the "correct" arrangement of furniture and selection of decorative paintings points clearly to the persistence of traditional attitudes concerning what is proper in contemporary Chinese households. Deborah Davis (1989) shows how urban apartment dwellers use interior space in ways that clearly distinguish private and public domains. Laing (1988–1989) also has imaginatively used Jin dynasty (1115–1234) period paintings, tomb murals, and decorated ceramics to assess the increasing ornateness of household decoration and furnishings.

While most of the research described above focuses on individual dwellings, it is increasingly clear that understanding may be augmented if one changes the scale of inquiry and examines settlement ensembles, such as villages. One recent edited collection, *Chinese Landscapes: The Village as Place* (Knapp 1992), draws upon the perspectives of anthropologists, architects, geographers, historians, a sociologist, and a veterinary ecologist in examining the various settings of habitation, work, and leisure of China's village population. The book includes general discussions of regional differences in size and morphology of villages, traditional principles used in siting villages, and the impact of politics on contemporary village form. Except for tantalizing articles in the *Journal of the Royal Asiatic Society, Hong Kong Branch* over the years, the vernacular architectural traditions of that dynamic region have not been well studied, although *Rural Architecture in Hong Kong* (1979) provided glimpses of these vital traditions. *Beyond the Metropolis: Villages in Hong Kong*, edited by P. H. Hase and Elizabeth Sinn (1995), and *Hong Kong Architecture: Contemporary and Past* by David Lung (1992) document in text and photographs the survival of substantial vestiges of traditional China in the New Territories even as they have been fundamentally transformed.

Although the political factors that slowed the development of vernacular architecture studies on the China mainland did not affect Taiwan, the field developed slowly there as well. A small number of very useful publications came early, but it was not until recently that the field became vigorous. Reed Dillingham and Chang-lin Dillingham's *Taiwan chuantong jianzhu zhi kaocha* [A survey of traditional architecture of Taiwan] (1971), with its excellent measured drawings and photographs, documented traditional farmhouses and other rural structures at a time when many of these were being destroyed or renovated as Taiwan developed. Many useful observations concerning the historical, social, and structural aspects of these dwellings were discussed in a notes section. The book acknowledges the research of Chinese scholars on these topics, especially that of Lin Hengdao and Shao Mei, but it does not call attention to numerous articles in Japanese completed during the Japanese occupation of Taiwan between 1895 and 1945.

An early source for insightful and richly illustrated articles on folk culture, broadly, and vernacular architecture, in particular, was *ECHO of Things Chinese* magazine in the 1970s and 1980s and subsequently in its Chinese edition *Hansheng*. Under the editorship and artistic guidance of Huang Yung-sung and Wu Mei-yun (Linda Wu), these articles called early attention to the importance of material culture in understanding broader issues of Chinese society and culture. Their work over three decades clearly reveals the vast resources available for such efforts, even though many researchers are yet to appreciate them. More recently, *Hansheng* has published high-quality books on mainland vernacular architectural traditions by mainland scholars (Huang 1994c, Ji 1994, Chen, Lou, and Li 1996). The addition of imaginative line drawings and other artwork by the talented staff of *Hansheng* significantly enriches the research efforts of these mainland scholars. *Da di* [The Earth], a Chinese language geographic monthly that began publishing in 1988, has been an important vehicle for promoting knowledge and appreciation of China's vernacular architecture. Published by Hsu Chung-jung, *Da di* has become an important publication for high-quality photographic documentation of Chinese cultural landscapes.

Beginning with several early attempts to preserve historic structures, such as the Lin family villa in Banqiao (Han 1973, 1983), increasing attention was paid by departments of architecture and architectural

firms to documenting structures and recommending directions for preservation. A small number of anthropologists increasingly called attention to domestic space. Wang Sung-hsing's "Taiwanese Architecture and the Supernatural" (1974) was especially significant in moving researchers away from focusing on mere form to considering meaning. Emily M. Ahearn looked at continuity and change in some of these patterns (1979). General articles by Knapp (1981, 1982, 1986) examined the emergence of rural housing forms under frontier conditions and warned of the difficulty of generalizing about Chinese vernacular patterns before the completion of extensive fieldwork on the mainland.

Liu Dunzhen's work entered academic discourse in Taiwan through the thesis written by Chang Wen-jui (1976). Kwan Hwa-san (1980) extended the discussion with an examination of the components of "space conceptualization" in traditional folk architecture. Chinese domestic architecture of the pre-Qin period has been studied by Lin Huicheng (1984), who has also authored a very useful handbook focusing on Taiwan's traditional architecture, which should be a model for others on mainland areas (1990). The impact of changing forms of the family on contemporary housing in Taiwan was examined by John K. C. Liu (1980) in a way that has not yet been applied elsewhere in China. The work of Hsu Min-fu (1986, 1990a) combines theory and fieldwork in a way that promises further advances in the development of a comprehensive understanding of folk architecture by using local historical materials. Kao Ts'an-jung's study of the structural, ornamental, and symbolic meanings of the roofs of Taiwan dwellings (1989, 1993) focuses on details that heretofore had only been generally studied. The working papers appearing in the journal *Wenhua yu jianzhu yanjiu jikan* [C+A culture and architecture research], edited by Hsu Min-fu at Cheng-kung University, reveal the broadening interests of architects as they explore topics at the intersection of structure and culture.

No individual has carried out more research and has had a greater impact on understanding Taiwan's architecture than Lee Chien-lang. His early and detailed bilingual study of rural architecture (1978) on the island of Jinmen, just off the coast of the mainland city of Xiamen, clearly suggested that the island was a link between mainland and Taiwan patterns. Lee placed vernacular patterns within the context of overall architectural developments on Taiwan from 1600 to 1945 in a comprehensive architectural history (1980). Over the years, numerous surveys, reports, and booklets by Lee have not only documented a broad range of vernacular patterns in Taiwan but have also served as models that stimulate a general concern for historical preservation. Lee's wide-ranging role in nurturing popular appreciation of Taiwan's architectural heritage was underscored by the publication of a richly illustrated children's book by Liu Siyuan (1989). More recently, Lee has authored books on the art of craftsmen in Taiwan (1995) and, with Yan Ya-ning and Shyu Yu-chien, has carried out an exemplary study combining textual and field-based research concerning a late Qing master carpenter from Fujian (1996).

Over the millennia, the architecture of China's villages—whether one calls it vernacular, folk, or popular—changed slowly. Each generation bequeathed cultural landscapes not too different from the ones they themselves inherited. Besides a tendency for cultural conservatism, the slow pace of technological change no doubt contributed to the maintenance of old dwelling forms. Many such forms have been carried even to the end of the twentieth century and are only now undergoing accelerated change. Much has been destroyed over the decades—by war, neglect, overuse, abuse, political movements, and natural disasters—but there is a remarkable resilience of traditional patterns. Throughout China today, one sees a melange of hybrid patterns, an intermixing of the old and the new. In the fifty years since 1949, political movements and then economic development brought about the razing and scarring of many fine large residences, temples, and lineage halls. As population grew, doubling between 1949 and 1990, common dwellings that were originally built for a household of one size were divided and subdivided with destructive consequences in order to provide housing for new residents. As the new century begins, there is a sense of both despair and joy as far as China's vernacular dwellings are concerned. Much of value has been destroyed, yet common Chinese today live in better housing than at any time in history.

Part II

SPACES AND STRUCTURES

CHAPTER 2

Composing Space

WHATEVER THE LINKAGES AMONG environmental, sociocultural, and technical factors, Chinese houses share common and distinctive spatial compositions. The patterns and vocabulary used to characterize these conventional and characteristic spaces—the plan and general layout—are the subject of this chapter. Whether a dwelling is built to endure the bitterly cold winters of the northeast, the high humidity and heat of the southeast or southwest, or the extremes characteristic of the arid interior, standard spatial forms are shared among virtually all Chinese structures, whether modest or imposing. This is true whether one is examining a palace or a humble dwelling, an ancient building or a modern one, and to some degree the dwellings of minority nationalities. Even dwellings with apparently striking contrasts and unique building styles, such as the enormous multistory round or square Hakka complexes of Fujian, Guangdong, and Jiangxi provinces or the sometimes complicated cavelike dwellings of Henan, Shanxi, and Shaanxi, embrace the same fundamental building elements used in much simpler structures. Chinese builders, whether consciously or unconsciously, do not conceal the standard expressions of space and form that are rooted so deeply in Chinese building traditions. Indeed, the enduring utility of Chinese notions of space and form has carried them into the spatial conceptualization and building traditions of the Japanese and Koreans as well. As Chinese build, they are attentive not only to erecting enclosed and roofed structures but also to defining open spaces. While roofed and enclosed structures are clearly buildings and thus an outcome of architectural design, the meaningful voids—open spaces—placed within the structures must also be seen as a product of conscious architectural conception. Chapter 3 examines the various building materials and structural systems that give these forms shape, while chapters 4 through 6 present the myriad ways in which these components are combined in order to produce regional dwelling types that vary somewhat in external form.

Jian, Kaijian, and *Jia:* Divisions of Structural Space

Chinese structures begin with the common denominators *jian, kaijian,* and *jia.* These spatial units of measurement give buildings their plan and shape. As a fundamental measure of width, a *jian* 间 is the span between two lateral columns or pillars that constitutes a bay. *Jian* can also be viewed as the expanse between four columns, comprising both the two-dimensional floor space and the volumetric measure of the void defined by the floor and the walls (Figure 2.1). A *jian* sometimes constitutes a room, although often a room is made up of several structural *jian.* The term *"kaijian"* 开间 is sometimes used synonymously with the single character *jian* in describing the horizontal compartmentalization or sectioning of building space across the facade. While the depth of a dwelling's bay can be expressed in terms of the receding two-dimensionality of *jian* or *kaijian,* depth is normally specified in terms

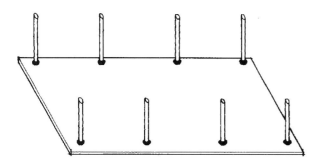

Figure 2.1. *Jian*, a fundamental measure of width, is the distance between two columns and is used synonymously with *kaijian*. It also connotes the floor space between four columns and is sometimes used to express the volumetric measurement.

of *jia* 架. Each *jia* refers to one of the stepped roof purlins, the horizontal longitudinal timbers needed to support the common rafters of a rising roof. The slope and curvature of a roof ultimately depend upon the relative *vertical* placement of purlins, yet it is the *horizontal* relationship among them, expressed in terms of *jia*, that is ordinarily used to define the depth of a bay. Linked together in a series to form the geometric grid of a plan or layout, these divisions of structural space lay bare the scaled three-dimensional proportions of any Chinese structure because of the intimate interrelationships among the ratios involving *jian*, *kaijian*, and *jia*. Except for wealthy families, whose dwellings may have been designed and built as an integrated complex, the majority of Chinese have always lived in houses in which modular form responded relatively easily to modification and growth as a family's circumstances and resources changed over several generations.

A single *jian* represents a nucleus of habitation in the smallest dwelling, providing common space for living, sleeping, and other activities, which could be expanded to meet a household's changing circumstances. Single *jian* dwellings have always been the homes of relatively poor villagers or workers with insufficient resources to meet larger housing needs. Single *jian* structures sometimes represent a household in an early stage of family formation or one recently moved into an area. If such a small box-shaped dwelling continues to serve a rural family over several generations, it is a sure sign of economic stagnation.

Most Chinese dwellings, however, are horizontal I-shaped structures comprised of at least three *jian* linked laterally along a transverse line, which is sometimes referred to as "a dragon" [*yitiao long* 一条龙] to emphasize its linearity. The width of each *jian* in north China generally ranges between 3.3 and 3.6 meters, while those in south China are typically between 3.6 and 3.9 meters. The depth of bays is usually also deeper in southern China, reaching as much as 6.6 meters; those in the north rarely exceed 4.8 meters (Figure 2.2). In southern China, as seen in Figures 2.3 and 2.4, overall depth is usually increased by adding at least a *jian*, with the result that the space beneath the rafters is tripled as the number of *jia* increases. *Jian* and *jia* normally are found in odd multiples, such as three, five, or seven. Chinese generally believe that odd numbers of units provide balance and symmetry to a building. In general, odd numbers are considered lucky numbers, while even numbers are inauspicious, according to the *Huitu Lu Ban jing* 绘图鲁班经, a fifteenth-century carpenter's

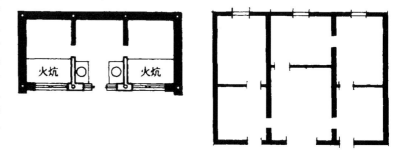

Figure 2.2. Comparison of rectangular three-*jian* dwellings in north China (left) and south China (right). Wrapped with solid weight-bearing walls on the side and back walls, the tight northern structures rarely exceed 4.8 meters in depth, while the width of each of the three *jian* range between 3.3 and 3.6 meters. A brick bed, called a *kang* or *huokang*, is connected to round stoves in the central bay and dominates each of the side bays in the left figure. Southern dwellings are generally much deeper, reaching as much as 6.6 meters, while the width of *jian* are usually a little more than those in the north. The walls of these deep structures are usually curtain walls that are placed between the load-bearing wooden framework.

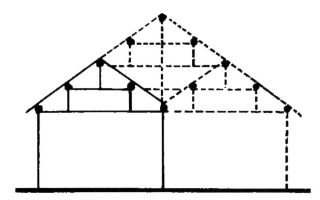

Figure 2.3. Throughout southern China, the depth of dwellings is often at least double that of northern patterns, thus allowing for a loft in the raised space beneath the rafters.

manual that had its roots in the Song dynasty (1983, 11). Four- or six-*jian* dwellings traditionally were avoided, since even numbers were regarded as asymmetrical and inauspicious. Two bays were judged "neutral," according to manuals, perhaps as a practical consideration in that "among poorer people houses of two bays are very common. It would be too harsh to condemn their houses as unfavorable" (Ruitenbeek 1993, 168). Four bays were avoided, since the word for "four" [*si* 四] is a homonym for the word "death."

Sumptuary regulations, while formulated to preserve Confucian status distinctions, also contributed to the standardization, modularization, and stylization of Chinese houses. Employed as early as the Tang and flourishing during the Ming and Qing dynasties, sumptuary regulations attempted to control socially inappropriate consumption. Sumptuary regulations stipulated, for example, that houses of common people [*shumin* 庶民] could not exceed three *jian* in width and five *jia* in depth [三间五架] with an exterior gate only a single *jian* wide. According to decrees in 1393, during the Ming dynasty, aimed at affirming social status and limiting expenditures, officials from the sixth through ninth ranks were limited to three bays and seven purlins, while those of the first and second ranks were permitted to have longer and deeper dwellings with five bays and nine purlins (Zhang 1985b, 123; Ch'ü 1965, 141–142).

Temples might reach an alignment of nine and palaces even eleven *jian*, as in the Hall of Supreme Harmony in Beijing's Forbidden City. Later in the Qing dynasty these rules were altered, but stratified gradations according to hierarchical rank continued. Prescribed widths governed the dimensions of timber and set proportional heights, in the process declaring the occupant's social status. Decorative details and colors found along the roof ridge, under the eaves, or on the gate were similarly described in sumptuary regulations and differentiated with a striking diligence. Penalties were fixed for violations, with scholars and officials liable for greater publishment than commoners because they presumably understood better the status distinctions that undergirded the codes. Enforcement of sumptuary codes in late imperial China, however, was often lax, perhaps because "enforcing rules was not as crucial as having rules," according to Patricia Ebrey (1991b, 36). Furthermore, there is clear evidence that the wealthy and those enjoying higher status were able to indulge their tastes to a greater extent than those of lesser means, often resulting in grander dwellings than their ascribed status would allow.

Variations in width and depth of *jian* across China not only reflect the simplicity or grandeur of

Figure 2.4. By tripling the depth of a dwelling and increasing the height of columns, a second floor is made possible. The wooden framework structure of this dwelling, clearly evident because the building is being dismantled, is discussed in Chapter 3. Lubucun, Shuidong *xiang*, Lishui *xian*, Zhejiang. [RGK photograph 1987.]

Figure 2.5. The open doorway into the wide central *jian* of this three-bay dwelling leads to the ceremonial room and then into adjacent bedrooms on either side. As will be discussed later, this longitudinal structure is accompanied by two wings to form a U-shaped dwelling. Deng Xiaoping was born in a bedroom in the north wing in 1904. When the dwelling was visited in 1986 by a German writer, it was occupied by some twelve families, only one of which was related to Deng. As some later illustrations will show, when the author visited the house in 1994, it had been emptied of residents and had become a destination for Chinese tourists. Paifang *cun*, Xiexing *xiang*, Guang'an *xian*, Sichuan. [Original photograph used with the permission of Uli Franz. Source: Franz 1988, 12.]

a dwelling but also the successful management of space as a means of dealing with the forces of nature. Intercolumnar spacing governs the kind of wood necessary for structural columns and beams. Narrow spans are more forgiving of material quality than broader ones and thus allow for the use of smaller, less costly timber, a subject discussed at length in Chapter 3.

The central *jian* of a three- or five-bay rectangular dwelling typically is wider than flanking *jian*, since it is often the principal ceremonial or utility "room," but its functions and names vary from one part of the country to another. Among the names used to describe this central *jian* are *zhengwu* 正屋 , *tangwu* 堂屋, *gongting* 公厅, and *tingtang* 厅堂 , all of which connote "hall" or "main room" (Figures 2.5 and 2.6). In most of southern China, the central *jian* is symbolic of unity and continuity—a significance heightened by the traditional placement of a long table facing the door upon which are placed ancestral tablets, images of gods and goddesses, family mementos, and ceremonial paraphernalia (Figure 2.7). This central space is flanked by a pair of *cijian* 次间 [secondary bays], which serve usually as bedrooms; and, if the building has five *jian*, there is a pair of "end bays," or "outer bays," [*shaojian* 梢间] for sleeping or storage. If the structure has seven bays, the end bay is called *jinjian* 尽间, with the *shaojian* then becoming "intermediate bays." Flanking bays

Figure 2.6 (above). This rectangular three-bay southern dwelling has two additional lower bays added to it. The central bay is somewhat wider than the adjacent ones and it lacks an exterior wall in the front, creating an "open room," or *changting*, which will be discussed later. Shuitou *xiang*, Cangnan *xian*, Zhejiang. [RGK photograph 1988.]

Figure 2.7 (below). With a central bay containing the ancestral hall, this rather complex courtyard-style dwelling has two parallel three-bay structures, each with a flanking pair of *cijian* ["secondary rooms"] and connecting halls. The courtyard and outer wings will be discussed later. Built in the early nineteenth century and known as the Antai Lin dwelling, it was dismantled in 1978 and then reconstructed in Binjiang Park in Taipei, Taiwan, in 1985. [Original drawing used with the permission of Lee Chien-lang.]

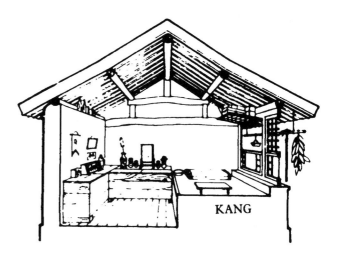

Figure 2.10 (above). Section view from the central hall into the eastern bedroom shows the dominance of the *kang* just inside the southern windows. [Source: Jing 1985, 65.]

Figure 2.8 (above). This common three-bay *yiming liangan*-type dwelling, found throughout northern and northeastern China, is identified as a Manchu farmer's residence. Entry is into a central room, which includes stoves for cooking and heating the *kang* beds found in adjacent bedrooms. Xinglong *xian*, Hebei. [Source: Adapted from Liu 1957, 82.]

Figure 2.9 (below). Viewed from the back wall, the central *jian* of this three-bay dwelling is narrower than those adjacent to it. The south-facing door leads to the cooking stoves that are connected to the *kang*. Qiqiha'er, Heilongjiang. [Source: Zhou 1992, 142.]

Figure 2.11. With lattice windows across its south-facing facade, this three-*jian* dwelling has an entry into the central room. The placement of only a single chimney indicates the presence of only one *kang* in the westernmost *jian*. Central Shanxi. [Original photograph courtesy of Arthur J. Van Alstyne.]

are known by a variety of regional names. (For terms used in Taiwan, see Lin 1990, 33). Throughout northern China, a common three-bay configuration is colloquially termed *yiming liangan* 一明两暗 [one bright, two dark or one opened, two closed]. Here the central room serves as corridor, kitchen, and common utility room (Figures 2.8, 2.9, 2.10, and 2.11). It links the adjacent bedrooms and provides the location for the low brick stoves used for cooking as well as heating the elevated bed platforms called *kang* 炕 or *huokang* 火炕 found in the adjacent *ci-jian*. Access to the flanking rooms is almost always through the central *jian* and then from one adjacent *jian* to another.

As a measurement unit employed by builders and as a structural unit itself, a *jian* thus becomes a design module that can be duplicated in a series to give overall two-dimensional and three-dimensional shape to an expanding dwelling. The use of *jian* enforces a discipline, an order, on a building's construction. Building modules have made possible a high degree of standardization in the timber components used in the actual construction of all types of Chinese structures. For many country builders, dwellings could simply be "assembled" from rather predictable prescribed modular wooden building materials. Rules observed by carpenters were passed down orally or transmitted through manuals, such as the *Lu Ban jing*, and served to confirm traditional choices that had arisen out of pragmatic considerations. While expressing a building plan in two-dimensional terms using *jian* and *jia*, Chinese carpenters typically also depicted dwellings in cross-section that emphasized the columns and cross members (Ruitenbeek 1993, 50). Plan and cross-section together successfully revealed the three-dimensionality of a structure. Employing a repertoire of standardized geometrical units, peasants and others could build even on rough terrain because *jian* can be so easily linked on different planes of a building site. Because different size *jian* necessitated dissimilar proportions in building materials, it was possible to erect even complicated earthen dwelling complexes. For example, in remote areas of southeastern China, some complexes were constructed of as many as 100 *jian* on four or five levels by simply following the specifications of *jian* size and without the guidance of measured drawings.

Divisions of Exterior Space

In Chinese architecture, exterior open spaces are necessarily pivotal spatial forms that complement the structures enclosing them or sited adjacent to them. Uncovered open areas, whether termed "courtyards" [*yuanzi* 院子, *yuanluo* 院落, or *tingyuan* 庭院] when they are large or "skywells" [*tianjing* 天井] when they are relatively small, render Chinese rural or urban dwelling compounds whole in that they function as important supplementary locations for productive work, storage, and leisure. They serve also to bring the natural world beyond the walls of the structure into its domain. In "composing a house," to use Nelson Wu's felicitous phrase, open spaces must be recognized as part of a "house-yard" complex: "the student of Chinese architecture will miss the point if he does not focus his attention on the space and the impalpable relationships between members of this complex, but, rather, fixes his eyes on the solids of the building alone" (1963, 32). The framing of exterior space by inward-facing structures arranged both at right angles to and parallel with the facades of other buildings creates a configuration strikingly similar to the character 井, a well or open vertical passage sunk into the confining earth. The encircling walls create an "implicit paradox of a rigid boundary versus an open sky" within (Wu 1963, 32).

The complementary bipolarity of the open and closed elements that give shape to a well are often expressed also in spatial terms relating to Chinese architecture. They express the balanced dualistic relationships of *yin* and *yang* cosmological thinking as well as the aesthetic concepts of *xu* and *shi*. The significance of *yin* 阴 and *yang* 阳 within Chinese correlative thinking is well known; thus, the use of balanced paired concepts in expressing spatial relationships within residences is not surprising (Graham 1986). While both *yin* and *yang* elements are essential and complementary, mutually dependent and producing harmony, *yang* is implicitly hierarchically dominant over *yin* as well as dynamically interrelated. *Xu* 虚 and *shi* 实 , as expressions of Chinese aesthetics, express the interdependence of the intangible and the tangible in which both the objects and the voids have meaning whether it is a painting or a building. As in a Chinese painting, the areas without black brushstrokes are as much a part of the composition as the pigmented lines and dots. The interplay between the white walls of southern dwellings, which can be seen to represent a void, serve to anchor tangible windows and doors, which are themselves openings in a solid just as are enclosed and open spaces. Interior and exterior, above and below, host and guest, light and shade, active and passive, as well

as solid and void are but several of the correlative associations relating to domestic spatial compositions involving structures and courtyards. The dwelling is a microcosm in which there is an implicit parallel correlative syntax with that of Chinese cosmological thinking.

While open spaces are axiomatic elements of Chinese domestic space, their composition and scale differ to such a degree across China that the common term "courtyard" and its Chinese language equivalents do not suffice to differentiate them clearly. As seen in Figure 2.12, the proportion of open space to structural space diminishes significantly from northeast to southeast China. Further, from northern to southern China there is an increasing ratio of transitional "gray" or "shaded" spaces, which are neither interior nor exterior. Similar progressions occur as one moves from northern China toward the northwest and southwest. While there are no sharp distinctions in terminology as these progressions take place over great distances, the Chinese language does clearly differentiate the northern prototypical *yuanzi* courtyard-type open space from its condensed southern cousins, the *tianjing*, or "skywell type," and its variant the compact *yikeyin*, or "seal style." While open spaces can be designed into a dwelling's plan and built as part of it, many emerge rather from the expansion of common three-*jian* structures as a family becomes more prosperous over time. Figure 2.13 portrays conceptual progressions of building form and plan in northern and southern China, the first resulting from "enclosing" [*wei* 围] and the second from "excavating" [*wa* 挖] open space. Adding a perpendicular wing sometimes is accompanied by the creation of an open corner space that may be duplicated as the dwelling becomes an inverted U-shaped structure with an embracing but unenclosed courtyard. The addition of a structure along the exposed fourth side creates a complete quadrangular dwelling common in northern China. Similar three-*jian* longitudinal units in southern China are more likely to expand toward the front or the back, with a doubling of enclosed space. The opening of a "well" in the interior of the building's mass may emerge as a true skywell and be duplicated as the dwelling grows. Figure 2.14 deline-

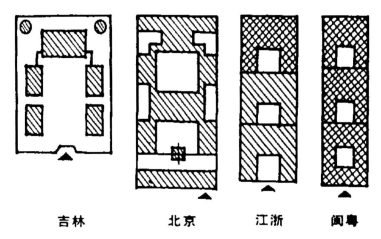

吉林　　　　　北京　　　　江浙　　　　闽粤

Figure 2.12. The ratio of open spaces to enclosed spaces generally decreases from northeast to southeast as expansive courtyards are transformed into diminutive skywells. From left to right, this progression shows a walled courtyard complex in Jilin, a double quadrangle courtyard dwelling *(siheyuan)* in Beijing, a three-skywell, U-shaped residence with a two-story innermost structure in Zhejiang, and finally a composite two-story structure made up of a quadrangle and two inverted U-shaped forms placed back-to-back in Guangdong. [Source: Huang et al. 1992, 13.]

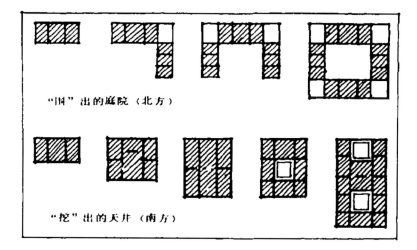

"围" 出的庭院（北方）

"挖" 出的天井（南方）

Figure 2.13. As a household becomes prosperous, its dwelling may grow from a simple three-*jian* rectangle to shapes that include open spaces. In northern China, according to the hypothetical progression shown across the top, the "enclosing" of open space begins with the addition of a wing and continues until a complete quadrangular dwelling, termed *siheyuan*, takes shape. In southern China, as shown in the bottom series, open space results from "excavating" a "well" in the interior, which may eventually emerge as a true skywell and then be duplicated as the dwelling grows. [Source: Huang et al. 1992, 5.]

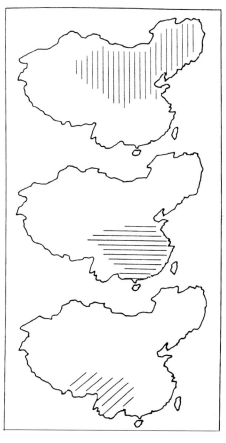

Figure 2.14. Northern *yuanzi*-type courtyards (top), southern *tianjing*-type skywells (middle), and southwestern *yikeyin* (bottom) each has a clearly defined regional distribution, although there are areas of overlap where intermixing of building forms occur. These maps show the late Qing dynasty boundaries of China. [Source: After Lu and Wang 1996, 38.]

Figure 2.15. Surrounded by a wall, generous *yuanzi*, or courtyards, in northeast China provide storage areas for farm tools and harvested crops. [Source: "Agriculture" 1927, 1045.]

ates the regional distributions of northern *yuanzi*-type courtyards, southern *tianjing*-type skywells, and southwestern *yikeyin*.

Yuanzi: *Expansive Courtyards*

Some *yuanzi* courtyards in northeast China, as seen in Figure 2.15, are clearly a major part of a farmstead, which is itself wrapped by a demarcating wall. Within the wall, each of the structures is positioned in a standard way that becomes increasingly formalized, as discussed later. The three-*jian* rectangular residence faces south and has an unconnected accessory residential building to its east. Directly across the approximately square courtyard is a matched building, similar in shape and size, that serves as a farm workshop. On one side of the main house, grain is stored in a cylindrical silo. On the other side of the main house there is a covered pen for domestic fowl. Firewood, tools, and carts are left in locations throughout the courtyard where they can be accessed easily and taken through the center gate.

Large walled enclosures are sometimes found on southern dwellings as well. The imposing gate at the entrance of the Zhejiang dwelling shown in Figure 2.16 leads to what is most likely a temporary courtyard, since the blocked doorway on the gable wall suggests that the owners anticipate building wings to the main structure, which inevitably will lead to a more complex courtyard form. Any open area fronting a Chinese dwelling, which in English might simply be called a "yard," is usually called a "*yuanzi*" in Chinese. Conventional courtyards and skywells that are contained open spaces with multiple buildings or walls framing them are integral elements of the *siheyuan* and *sanheyuan*.

Siheyuan: *A Quadrangle of Buildings Enclosing a Courtyard*

Archaeological excavations reveal that the tight enclosure of a courtyard within a quadrangular building has been a common core element of Chinese dwellings since at least the Western Zhou period, be-

Figure 2.16. The walled courtyard of this rectangular two-story dwelling is entered through an imposing gate. The presence of a bricked-in doorway on the end of the structure suggests the anticipation of an additional bay or perpendicular wing. Nantang *xiang*, Dongyang *xian*, Zhejiang. [RGK photograph 1987.]

guided inner movement through the placement of building components, created a central gathering place for ritual, and communicated hierarchical relationships via the sequencing of spaces (Thorpe 1984, 62).

A similar front-to-back courtyard composition is seen on an engraved stone of the Han dynasty (206 B.C.–A.D. 220) discovered at the Wuliang burial chamber of the Yinan tomb in Shandong. Reflecting changes in building materials and technologies, the complex is clearly an upper-class residence comprising open courtyards encompassed by rooms and walled enclosures (Figure 2.18). Here gates and corridors are supplemented with external watchtowers. As is true with most courtyard houses that followed in later centuries, the overall composition of this *tingyuan* 庭院 is

tween the eleventh and tenth centuries B.C. (Zhang 1986b, 35; Thorpe 1983, 26–31). A sophisticated ground plan fitted within a 45-by-33-meter oblong containing flanking rectangular structures around three sets of open spaces, which may be called "courtyards," can be seen in an excavated building complex at Fengchu 风雏, about 100 kilometers west of Xi'an in Shaanxi province (Figure 2.17). This Bronze Age structural complex has been identified as a well-developed palace [*gongdian* 宫殿] rather than a dwelling, and it is strikingly different from rather open walled compounds excavated at earlier Shang sites (Hsu 1986, 121–128, 189–193). Made up of integrated elements in a self-contained building unit, this early courtyard plan at Fengchu removed private activities from the view of outsiders,

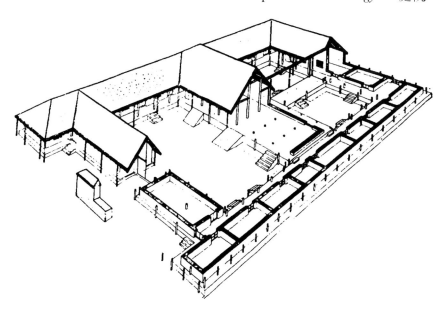

Figure 2.17. This reconstruction of the rectangular walled compound at Fengchu, Shaanxi, includes a raised platform of pounded earth and three courtyards. Excavated in 1976, the original compound was probably built in the eleventh century B.C. [Source: Yang 1981, 25.]

Figure 2.18. Built during the Han dynasty, this upper-class residential complex comprises a walled enclosure with encircling rooms around open courtyards. Inward facing and cut off from the outside, the complex includes gates and watchtowers. Yinan *xian*, Shandong. [Source: Zhongguo kexueyuan 1957, 11.]

inward facing, with halls adjacent to courtyards, and closed off to the outside world by walls with limited fenestration. There is, in addition, clear orientation to the cardinal directions, axiality, balanced side-to-side symmetry, and an implied hierarchical organization of space, all subsequently canonical elements of *siheyuan*. Sited so that the main halls face toward the south [*zuobei chaonan* 座北朝南, having its back to the north and facing south], the dwelling maintains a preferred siting principle that protects its inhabitants from fierce winds yet welcomes the heat of the sun during the winter season. A bisecting axis passes from the south gate through the first courtyard, middle hall, second courtyard, and on to the center of the back hall. It is likely that the central hall is an ancestral hall and that the back hall is a residential space for the senior generation of the household. Rooms along the side wall are for sleeping, and those at the entry are for storage and for the use of servants. Except for the entrance gate, the demarcated threshold of the dwelling, no other doors or windows cut the outer walls. Doors and windows open only to the courtyards within. Throughout northern China, each of the enclosing buildings of this type is made up of single-story structures constructed in multiple *jian* modules. Narrow verandas provide a protected circuit for movement within the complex.

Notwithstanding the differences in materials and

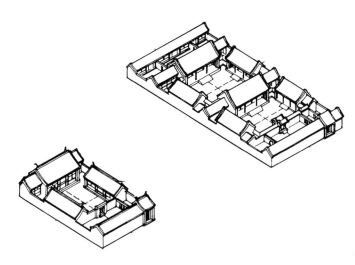

Figure 2.19. On the left is a one-*jin* quadrangle *siheyuan* and on the right a two-*jin siheyuan*. When referring to traditional *siheyuan*, each of the horizontal buildings facing south is considered a *jin* 进 except for the horizontally placed entry structure. [Source: Fu 1984, 28.]

for example the homes of gentry and especially imperial palaces, longitudinal routes from front to back are designated to reinforce a spatial hierarchical layering of etiquette as one moves from front to rear or to the side. Gradations in the progression of horizontal and vertical space create "graduated privacy," a term coined by Nelson Wu, in which "the dual quality of the house, as a setting for ceremony and as a home, is a most important characteristic of the house as an image of human relationship" (1963, 32–34). The world of strangers is beyond the walls and gate, while within is the realm of the family (Figure 2.21). Casual visitors may be invited into the entry vestibule, while friends and relatives are welcomed into the courtyard and into at least the first level of adjacent halls. Further inward is a realm of privacy for women in the family. The cacophony of sounds beyond the perimeter walls of a courtyard house are muted by the en-

detail, the building components—gates, screen walls, steps, corridors, platforms, halls, wings, side chambers, courtyards—of these early courtyard forms clearly foreshadow the classical residential courtyard type known as *siheyuan*, which has flourished over the centuries in northern China (Figures 2.19 and 2.20). When referring to traditional *siheyuan* courtyard quadrangles, each of the parallel halls—horizontal buildings facing south—is considered a *jin* 进 , so that a dwelling with two horizontal units and associated courtyards will be termed a "two-*jin* courtyard quadrangle" [*liangjin siheyuan* 两进四合院]. The horizontally placed entry building along the south wall is not counted. A two-*jin* courtyard quadrangle thus is actually made up of a pair of hall-courtyard components that together form a relatively large *siheyuan*. In order to expand a dwelling by duplicating hall-courtyard modules, each component can be placed front to back or side to side. As larger structures are composed in this way,

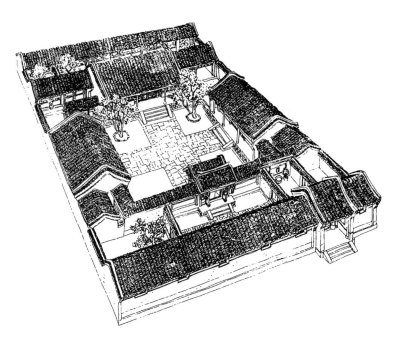

Figure 2.20. Perspective drawing of a Beijing *siheyuan*. The complex includes an entryway along the southeastern wall, an outer entry yard, and a formal gate that leads to the core courtyard with its south-facing main structure and two wing structures. [Original artwork used with the permission of Wang Qijun.]

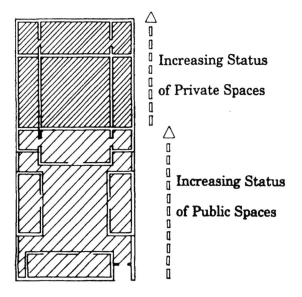

Increasing Status
of Private Spaces

Increasing Status
of Public Spaces

Figure 2.21. "Graduated privacy" leads from public to private space as one moves from the southern courtyard to the northern courtyard. This hierarchical gradient is reflected in the nature of the rooms and their function, each of which is mediated by a sequence of gates and walls. Casual visitors only traverse the public spaces, while the private spaces are reserved for family and friends. [Source: Cheu 1993, 47.]

closing walls, manifesting relative quiet within.

Within hall-courtyard complexes, even the elevation of structures a few steps above the courtyard provides a vertical differentiation analogous to the gradations across horizontal space. As elaborated by Nelson Wu, "the raised terraces exercise yet another tyranny. They dictate the path for movement, and the statements of their inviting stairways and prohibitive corners are firm and final" (1963, 33–34). Within the cellular form of a *siheyuan*, the spatial manifestations of open or closed, front or back, and above or below not only echoed but also helped regulate traditional Chinese social relationships.

Open spaces were generous portions of early hall-courtyard dwellings, and this pattern continues to the present in *siheyuan* in northern China. Representing as much as 40 percent of the total ground area, courtyards thus encompass more floor space than any one of the surrounding structures. Seclusion is ensured by the bordering walls and single gate, yet

from any position in the courtyard the sky appears to reach to distant horizons unobstructed either by the dwelling itself or by neighboring buildings that are of the same height. The symmetrical placement of trees, walkways, and gateways complements the balanced proportions of the quadrangle itself.

Siheyuan-style dwellings vary somewhat in the form of enclosure. Although there are some regional differences, generally one of two configurations can be seen throughout China. In northern China, each of the four buildings of the *siheyuan* is separate, and they are joined only by their connection to the outer walls between them. The gaps between buildings form open outliers of the central courtyard. Sometimes the outliers are covered with partial roofs, but some are left open in order to maintain their connection with the adjacent courtyard. In southern China, the roof lines and ends of each of the four enclosing structures actually intersect at right angles in order to bring about a complete enclosure of the courtyard by buildings. One corner space in the southwest frequently provides a location for the household's latrine, while other corner spaces are used for storage.

Regional variations in the shapes of the courtyards of *siheyuan* abound throughout the provinces of northern China. In central Shanxi province, courtyards are elongated and narrow, yet other elements of the complex echo Beijing-type *siheyuan*. Henan province, climatically a transitional region between north and south China that straddles the Huanghe River, displays a range of *siheyuan* patterns. Corresponding to the marked climatic variations from north to south, there is a gradual reduction in the size of open space of the courtyard. North of the Huanghe River there are expansive *yuanluo* courtyards reminiscent of Beijing *siheyuan* and representative of the culture of the Central Plains, but south of the river open spaces become increasingly constricted, even though the rectangular shape and order of the prototypical *siheyuan* is preserved (Figure 2.22). True *tianjing* and other architectural features emerge in the Xinyang area of southern Henan in order to restrict the infiltration of the intense direct rays of the sun and to facilitate ventilation (Hu 1995, 74).

Each of the three natural regions of Shaanxi province in northwest China is similarly character-

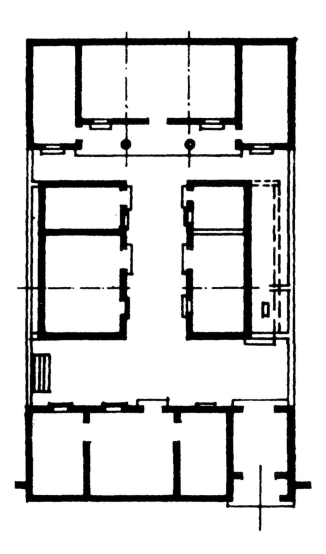

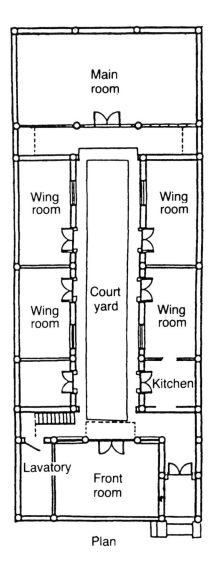

Plan

Figure 2.22. Regional differences in the form of *siheyuan* are found throughout northern China. In Zhengzhou, Henan, basic bilateral symmetry is apparent, but the courtyard has become narrowed. [Source: Hu 1995, 70.]

Figure 2.23. The plan of this dwelling in Dangjia, Shaanxi, maintains all the elements of a northern *siheyuan*, but the shape of the courtyard is a slender rectangle. [Source: Liu 1992, 134.]

ized by a variety of *siheyuan* courtyard patterns that can be differentiated on the basis of one environmental element being more prominent than the others. The Guanzhong region, centering on Xi'an, and some areas farther north are well known for long and narrow courtyards (Figure 2.23). Preserving the spatial elements of a traditional *siheyuan*, Guanzhong dwellings nonetheless are much tighter

structures. Due to hot summers and severe winters, the placement of buildings and open spaces effectively blocks direct sunlight from entering rooms except in the early morning and late afternoon in summer and mitigates the intrusion of cold winds in winter. Unlike Beijing-style *siheyuan* courtyards, which are often as wide as the principal three-*jian* building on its north side, courtyards in Guanzhong

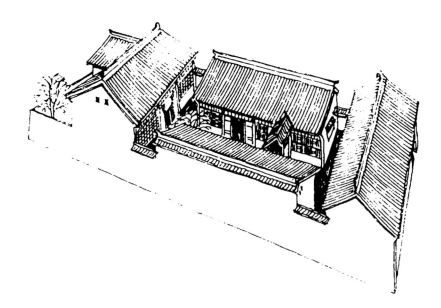

Figure 2.24. The narrow courtyard of this dwelling in the Xi'an area of the Guanzhong region of Shaanxi province is no wider than the center *jian* of the principal building on the left. Entry into the dwelling from the lane is from the upper right into a generally east-west oriented open area. This open area leads to a gate held between the two wing structures—*shafang*—that then opens into the inner courtyard. [Source: Zhang and Liu 1993, 6.]

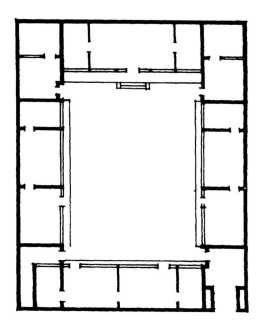

rarely exceed the width of the central *jian* of the northern structure. On the other hand, the length of the courtyard typically exceeds that of the facing side buildings (Figure 2.24). Called *xiangfang* 厢房, or "wing rooms," in much of China, these long side buildings framing the courtyard are called *shafang* 厦房 in the Guanzhong region, using a character that elsewhere in China would emphasize the verticality of a structure.

There are generally great differences between dwellings to the north and south of the Guanzhong region. Southern Shaanxi lies to the south of the Qinling mountain range in the upper reaches of the south-flowing Hanshui River. Heavy rains, hot and humid summers, and relatively moderate winters provide striking contrasts with the rest of Shaanxi. Because the region is less populated and more remote than other areas of the province, dwellings are

Figure 2.25. Although many of the *siheyuan* in northern Shaanxi are long and narrow, the plan of some are quite similar to those found in the Beijing area. Shenmu *xian*. [Source; Zhang and Liu 1993, 71.]

generally simpler and more open. While northern-style *siheyuan* are found, most dwellings are simply multi-*jian* rectangular structures with numerous windows placed to take advantage of prevailing winds throughout the year. Northern Shaanxi, on the other hand, is a relatively poor region characterized by harsh winters, limited rainfall, thick loessial soil, and a virtual absence of trees. While much of the settlement here is in subterranean dwellings, there are many *siheyuan*. Some have narrow courtyards, while the plan of others, such as a *siheyuan* complex in Shenmu *xian* shown in Figure 2.25, maintains all of the essential characteristics of those found in the Beijing area (Zhang and Liu 1993).

Clearly reminiscent of classic *siheyuan* courtyard houses are the sunken courtyards carved into the earth in Henan and Shanxi provinces. While the typical courtyard of a *siheyuan* results from the structures built to enclose it, the courtyard of a subterranean dwelling is in fact formed first, and it becomes the initial "constructed" component of the dwelling complex whose "walls" provide the exposed surfaces for facades into which the flanking residential "structures" are then hewn. Excavated from the loessial soil, the sunken courtyard thus becomes a "walled" compound with significant outdoor living space open to the sky (Figures 2.26 and 2.27), a subject that will be explored further in Chapter 4.

While courtyards are almost always square or rectangular as part of quadrangular plans, the open courtyards of round earthen fortresses in Fujian and Guangdong usually take the shape of the encircling walls, just as the modular *jian* units deviate from rectilinearity. When rectangular structures are built within the circular courtyard, the *yuanzi* or *tianjing* may be rectangular, trapezoidal, or semicircular (Figures 2.28, 2.29 and 2.30). Octagonal courtyards have been documented in several areas of China, includ-

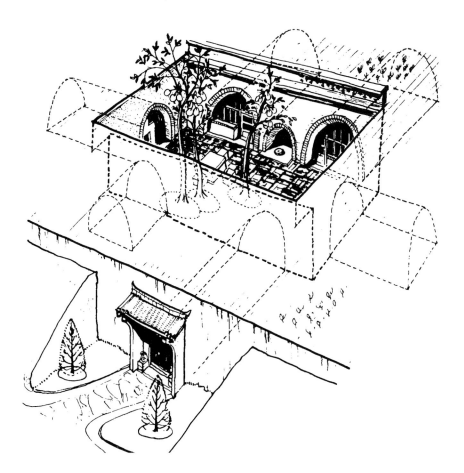

Figure 2.26. Three-dimensional view of an excavated sunken courtyard complex. Entry is via a gated sloping ramp in the southeast corner that tunnels to the courtyard. Arcuate rooms are hewn into the sides of the courtyard. [Source: Hou, Ren, Zhou, and Li 1989, 30.]

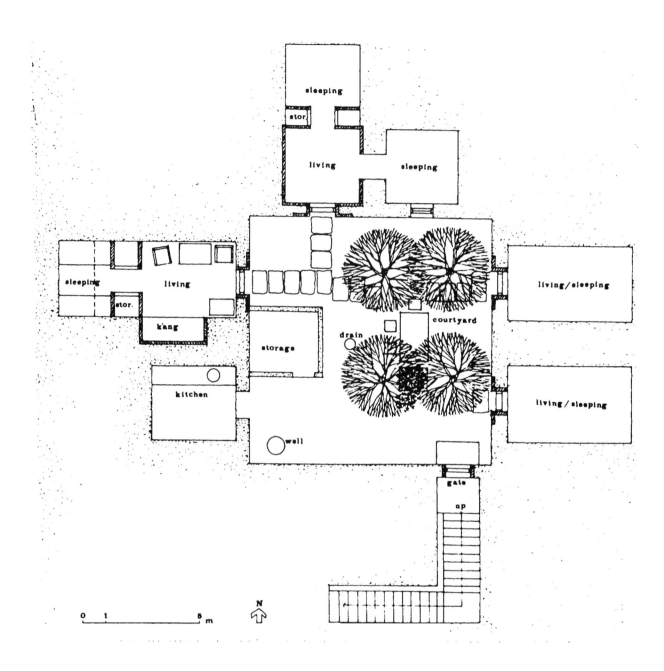

sleeping

stor.

living

sleeping

sleeping

living

stor.

living/sleeping

k'ang

courtyard

drain

storage

kitchen

living/sleeping

well

gate

up

0   1   5 m

N

Figure 2.27. Plan view of a rectangular courtyard complex dug into the soil to form a dwelling. Entry to the courtyard is from the southeast. The principal rooms are dug into the northern wall and face south. Subsidiary living space is built into the side walls. Henan. [Original drawing used with the permission of the family of the late Paul Sun.]

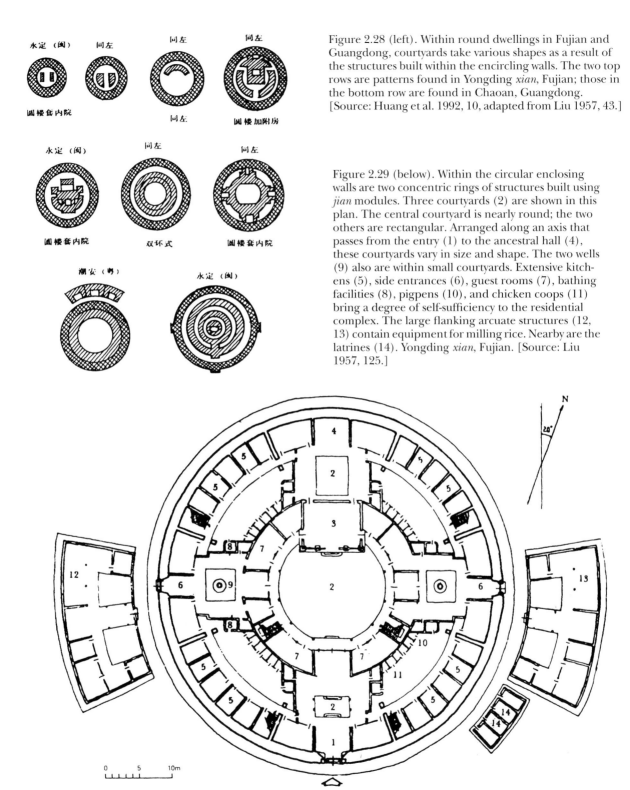

Figure 2.28 (left). Within round dwellings in Fujian and Guangdong, courtyards take various shapes as a result of the structures built within the encircling walls. The two top rows are patterns found in Yongding *xian*, Fujian; those in the bottom row are found in Chaoan, Guangdong. [Source: Huang et al. 1992, 10, adapted from Liu 1957, 43.]

Figure 2.29 (below). Within the circular enclosing walls are two concentric rings of structures built using *jian* modules. Three courtyards (2) are shown in this plan. The central courtyard is nearly round; the two others are rectangular. Arranged along an axis that passes from the entry (1) to the ancestral hall (4), these courtyards vary in size and shape. The two wells (9) also are within small courtyards. Extensive kitchens (5), side entrances (6), guest rooms (7), bathing facilities (8), pigpens (10), and chicken coops (11) bring a degree of self-sufficiency to the residential complex. The large flanking arcuate structures (12, 13) contain equipment for milling rice. Nearby are the latrines (14). Yongding *xian*, Fujian. [Source: Liu 1957, 125.]

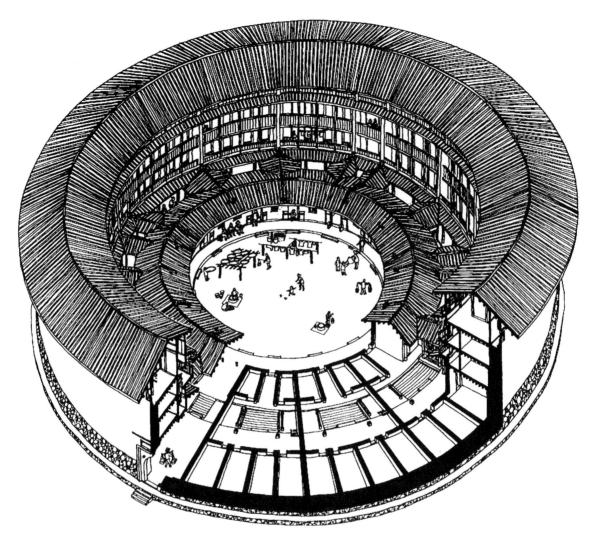

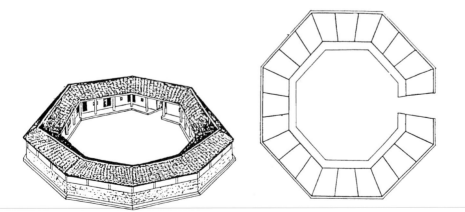

Figure 2.30 (above). The common core courtyard at the center of this dwelling complex is round, yet within each of the encircling apartment units smaller rectangular "skywells" are placed between the structures. Additional details of this complex are provided in Chapter 4. Eryilou, Zhaoan *xian*, Fujian. [Source: Huang, 1994c, vol. I, 18.]

Figure 2.31 (left). Octagonal-shaped courtyards illustrate the cosmic diagram known as *Bagua*, or Eight Trigrams. Xinkai *cun*, Gongyi *xiang*, Pengshan *xian*, Sichuan. [Source: Ji 1993b, 5.]

ing western Sichuan, as seen in Figure 2.31, where 6.4-meter-long interior segments are divided on one side into modular residential units three *jian* wide. The eight side walls together frame an expansive 170-square-meter courtyard (Ji 1993b). The spatial structuring of octagonal courtyard space goes beyond the general criteria relating to common quadrangular forms to represent emblematically the cosmic diagram called Eight Trigrams [*Bagua* 八卦].

Sanheyuan: *Three Buildings and a Wall Enclosing a Courtyard*

Sometimes structures are found only along three sides of a courtyard in order to form an inverted U-shape building plan, which looks like the Chinese character 凹. Termed *sanheyuan* 三合院 [three buildings joining a courtyard], enclosure is normally completed by a wall linking the two forward-thrusting side wings called *xiangfang* 廂房, just as with the wings of a *siheyuan. Sanheyuan* may be single- or multiple-story structures and take square and rectangular shapes (Figures 2.32, 2.33, and 2.34). Sometimes the rear structure is

two stories, while the flanking structures are single story. In Taiwan and Fujian, however, the enclosure of the open side of a U-shaped complex is often marked only by a low wall (Figure 2.35). In many parts of Fujian, the roofs of the flanking side structures are flat, so they can be used for drying purposes. In the Jiangnan region of central China, the front wall is as high or higher than the side walls so that the inside is completely hidden from the outside, creating an interior

Figure 2.32 (below, left). Each of these three U-shaped *sanheyuan* plans has a longitudinal structure with a central bay somewhat wider than the adjacent ones. While the perpendicular wings are essentially the same in these three plans, the alignment of the three-bay main structure varies. Xinpu, Taiwan. [Original drawing used with the permission of Hsu Min-fu and Chang Sheng-shou.]

Figure 2.33 (below, right). Seen in plan view, a high wall connects the two wings of this symmetrical single-story *sanheyuan*. Just inside the gates is a substantial courtyard, and toward the back there are two narrow skywells, providing shafts of air and light. Courtyard/Skywell (1); Veranda (2); Main Hall (3); Bedroom (4); Kitchen (5). Baidan *xiang*, Dongyang *xian*, Zhejiang. [Original drawing used with the permission of Shen Dongqi.]

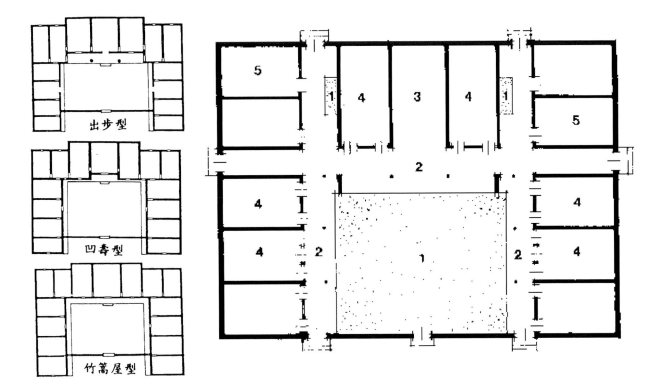

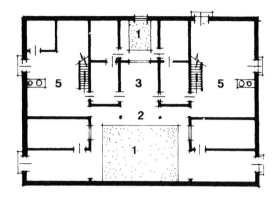

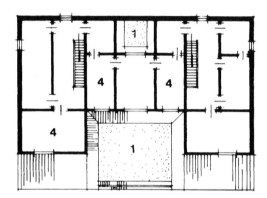

environment very much like that of a secluded *sihe-yuan* (Figure 2.36). With any of these patterns, the entry gate may be in the center or at one end of the front wall and sometimes along a side wall. The building components of any mature *sanheyuan* typically form a bilaterally symmetrical plan. Chinese architects generally consider any U-shaped residential plan a *sanheyuan* even in the absence of a connecting wall.

Mao Zedong's ancestral home at Shaoshan in Hunan province, built during the late Qing period, is basically a U-shaped *sanheyuan* without a wall across the front (Figures 2.37 and 2.38). Contrasting with standard siting practices, the dwelling is situated so that the main hall and courtyard face north [*zuonan chaobei* 座南朝北, having its back to the south and facing north]. The wooded hills to the rear and the pond to the front satisfy the dictates of good *fengshui* even

Figure 2.34 (left). Side gates lead to a 40-square-meter courtyard within this two-story *sanheyuan* house. A smaller 7.5-square-meter utility skywell is found in the rear. On the first floor (top), there are two large kitchens and an ancestral hall. Bedrooms are located on the second floor (bottom). Courtyard/Skywell (1); Veranda (2); Main Hall (3); Bedroom (4); Kitchen (5). Bacun, Yunhe *xiang*, Tiantai *xian*, Zhejiang. [Original drawing used with the permission of Shen Dongqi.]

Figure 2.35. The courtyard contained within this inverted U-shaped *sanheyuan* is defined by a low wall, which is entered through a central gate. A new three-story dwelling rises beyond the dilapidated and abandoned traditional farmhouse. Zhanghua *xian*, Taiwan. [RGK photograph 1993.]

Figure 2.36. With a pair of two-story wings connected by a high wall between them, this *sanheyuan* presents a nearly blank facade to the lane in front. Only a plain entryway and two small hexagonal windows interrupt the wall. Behind the wall is a small courtyard. Xinye *cun*, Tancun *xiang*, Jiande *xian*, Zhejiang. [RGK photograph 1987.]

Figure 2.37. Mao Zedong's birthplace is basically a U-shaped *sanheyuan* without a wall across the front. Built during the late Qing dynasty, an addition added in the early twentieth century disturbs its symmetry. Shaoshan *cun*, Xiangtan *xian*, Hunan. [Source: Yang Shenchu 1993, 180.]

Figure 2.38. With a hill, bamboo, and other vegetation as backdrops, Mao Zedong's *sanheyuan* embraces an open courtyard that slopes down to a pond. To the left is an addition that is arrayed around a small enclosed *tianjing*. [Source: Zhongguo kexueyuan 1957, 142.]

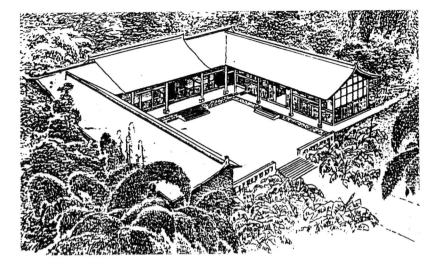

Figure 2.39. Steps lead up to the open courtyard fronting Deng Xiaoping's birthplace. Three sets of additional steps rise to the main structure and wings of the *sanheyuan* U-shaped dwelling. Paifang *cun*, Xiexing *xiang*, Guang'an *xian*, Sichuan. [Source: Ji 1993a, 3.]

though the compass directions are inverted. The symmetrical U-shaped plan includes a central hall in the middle *jian*, with a *tianjing* behind it, and a small projection across the back wall to accommodate it.

Mao was born here in 1893, remaining until he was thirteen, when he left to study in a school in Xiangtan. As his father became more prosperous, changes were made to the dwelling. Sometime during the early Republic, Mao's family added a substantial addition on the side of the dwelling that incorporated a large kitchen, stables, bathing facilities, and space for additional storage. Although undermining its symmetrical shape, an inner courtyard was created, which transformed a modest structure into a spacious dwelling. According to various reports, the house was burned and ravaged in 1929 by Mao's Kuomintang adversaries. After 1949, it was rebuilt so that by the time Mao visited his birthplace in 1959, the house was much as he had remembered it as a child. In 1961, the State Council placed it under national protection as a cultural site of historic significance. Mao's adobe brick house subsequently became a shrine during the Cultural Revolution and was visited by millions of Red Guards and others, who as pilgrims came to seek revolutionary inspiration from his humble peasant origins.

Surrounded by subtropical vegetation, a spacious U-shaped *sanheyuan* embraces a large open courtyard at Deng Xiaoping's birthplace north of Chongqing in Guang'an *xian*, Sichuan province (Figure 2.39). Born here in 1904, the son of a comfortably prosperous

small-scale landlord, Deng left the village in 1920 and never returned. By the early 1990s, local authorities began refurbishing the farmstead in the hope that Chinese tourists would bring some measure of prosperity to the county.

Although the basic floor plans of *sanheyuan* vary little throughout China, the names applied to them do, as several earlier references suggest. Typically, there are three structural divisions—three "rooms" or bays—in the horizontal main building; thus, the unit is termed a "three-*jian* building" [*sanjianwu* 三间屋]. In many respects this is quite similar to the *yiming liangan* [one bright, two dark] three-*jian* form described earlier for northern Chinese dwellings. In southern China, however, each *jian* is typically narrower across its face than it is deep. The central room is a hall serving ceremonial purposes, and it is bounded on each side by a bedroom. The pair of wings that juts out from the main building may be short or long, a condition that varies widely according to need. These wings provide room for kitchens, toilets, storage, and additional bedrooms. In central Guangdong, each of the wings is referred to as *lang* 廊, a term normally used to describe an arcade. The full structure is called a *sanjian lianglangwu* 三间两廊屋 [building with three *jian* and a pair of *lang*] (Lu and Wei 1990, 48). This pattern is employed not only with small dwellings but also with larger ones. Each of the jutting wings of the modest dwelling shown in Figure 2.40 serves as a kitchen, one of which leads to the main door of the dwelling on its side.

In Taiwan, the wings of *sanheyuan* are called "protecting dragons" [*hulong* 护龙]. It is sometimes the case that only one *hulong* is built perpendicular to the main building, thus creating an L-shaped form that is not a true *sanheyuan*. With the completion of a facing pair of *hulong*, however, a true *sanheyuan* is formed because they embrace an open area. In northern Taiwan, the courtyard is usually not bounded on the fourth side by a wall, but in central and southern Taiwan the unity of the compound is completed with the addition of a waist-high wall. In both cases, the courtyard functions as the accessway to and from each component of the dwelling, provides space for carrying out household chores outside, and serves as drying space for agricultural products. Each *hulong* serves purposes that are subsidiary to those found in the rooms of the horizontal structure: bedrooms for younger members of a family, storage, and for kitchens. Typically erected first to stage left and then to stage right, each wing typically has accordant rooflines somewhat lower than the main body of the dwelling (Figure 2.41). As large households grew, the U-shaped form of a *sanheyuan* could be extended either laterally or crosswise, depending on socioeconomic circumstances. The compounds of farm households normally grew laterally, while the dwellings of ambitious gentry and others of wealth stretched to greater depth. Additional *hulong* were typically added in pairs and placed parallel to the first set and then duplicated as necessary. The initial or

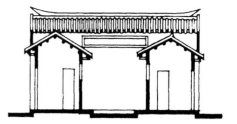

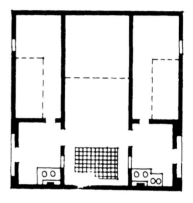

Figure 2.40. Essentially square in plan, this *sanheyuan* is called a *sanjian lianglangwu* [building with three *jian* and a pair of *lang*] in central Guangdong. The main hall at the back is higher than the protruding wings, each of which includes a kitchen at the front. Doors are located on the side walls and lead into the kitchens. See also Figure 2.43. [Source: Lu and Wei 1990, 48.]

Figure 2.41. Arrayed laterally in order to expand a *sanheyuan*, *hulong* are added in pairs, each placed parallel to the first set and then duplicated as necessary: the *neihu* [inner protectors], *waihu* [outer protectors], and *waiwaihu* [outer outer protectors]. Two threshing grounds are marked in the plan, one in the central courtyard and another between the low wall and the pond. This is a scaled model of Jiaxing mansion, built between 1847–1877, on display at the theme park Window on China, Taoyuan, Taiwan. Taizhong, Taiwan. [RGK photograph 1988.]

Figure 2.42. When viewed from above the roof, *tianjing* appear as voids in various shapes that penetrate the building's mass. Within generous roof overhang, it is possible to dry laundry and have privacy within the protected dwelling. Top, southern Jiangxi, bottom, Langzhong, Sichuan. [RGK photograph 1993, 1994, respectively.]

inner pair traditionally was called *neihu* 内护 [inner protectors], the second *waihu* 外护 [outer protectors], and the next *waiwaihu* 外外护 [outer outer protectors]. Embraced within the *neihu* and marked by a low wall was an "inner threshing ground" [*neicheng* 内埕] and between it and the pond was an "outer threshing ground" [*waicheng* 外埕]. Qing dynasty dwellings with three pairs of *hulong* still can be seen in Beipu and in Toufen in central Taiwan (Lin 1990, 25). In the past, the expansion of dwellings vertically in Taiwan was quite rare, resulting in urban and rural landscapes that were for the most part low and horizontal. Throughout China, *sanheyuan* and *siheyuan* are combined as building modules in an unlimited number of configurations to create impressively large residences for extended families. Most of these include multiple courtyards of varying sizes, including the very compact courtyards called *tianjing*, or "skywells," throughout southern China.

Tianjing: *Compact Courtyards*

Tianjing 天井 are literally "skywells" or "heavenly wells," abbreviated rectangular open spaces or voids found within structures. They are so small and compact that they do not qualify as true courtyards. While even a single courtyard of a northern *siheyuan* may exceed 40 percent of a dwelling's total area, *tianjing* rarely exceed 20 percent even when they are a dominant forecourt of a *sanheyuan*. Most *tianjing* are indeed much smaller. As ingenious sunken interior cavities whose scale restricts the degree of openness to the broad sky above, *tianjing* are useful in the hot and humid conditions characteristic of much of southern China for catching passing breezes and evacuating interior heat. Within southern dwellings, there are often multiple *tianjing*, each being an atriumlike enclosed vertical space whose size, shape, and number varies according to the scale of the residence. Many are no larger than a mere shaft or well, only several meters across, while others are long and narrow slivers running the breadth of the dwelling (Figures 2.42, 2.43, 2.44, and 2.45). Standing in the center of most *tianjing*, described in Chinese as *jingdi zhi wa* 井底之蛙 [a frog at the bottom of a well], one

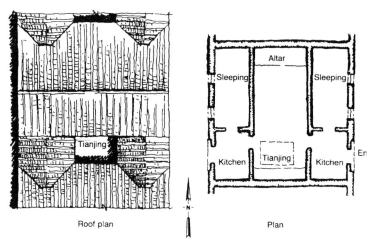

Roof plan

Plan

Figure 2.43 (left and above). The small *tianjing* near the front of this compact single-story dwelling is tightly framed by the intersecting and sloping roof lines but opens below to the kitchens and main ceremonial hall. Tiled roofs slope to bring rainwater into the *tianjing*, where it is stored in large vats. Xiqi village, Taishan *xian*, Guangdong, 1989. [Source: Hammond 1992, 99–100. Original drawings and photograph used with the permission of Jonathan Hammond.]

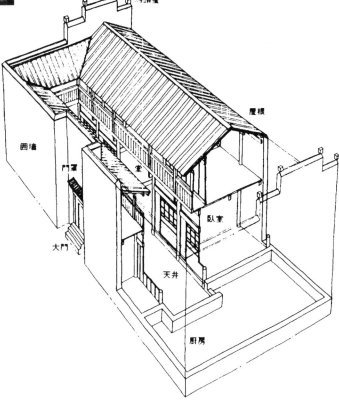

Figure 2.44 (right). *Tianjing* are sometimes a mere sliver of open space several meters across and running the breadth of the structure. Placed just inside the gate and high perimeter wall, this *tianjing* serves to open the main structure to light and air. [Source: Mogi, Inaji, and Katayama 1991, 57.]

Figure 2.45. Between the high outer wall and the wooden galleries surrounding it, this *tianjing* is narrowest at the top, where the overhanging roofline foreshortens it. The volume of open space within is quite substantial, serving to augment fresh air and diffused light within the dwelling. Xidi *cun*, Yixian, Anhui. [RGK photograph 1987.]

Figure 2.46 (above). Although only a mere patch of the sky above is visible, the open space within the dwelling is quite generous. Chengcun, Xingtian, Wuyishan, Fujian. [Original photograph used with the permission of Li Yuxiang.]

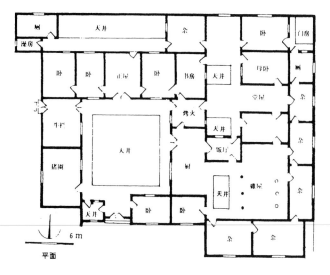

Figure 2.47 (left). Surrounded on four sides by rooms, the main portion of this late Qing residence, Liu Shaoqi's birthplace, is a *siheyuan* with five small *tianjing* of various sizes. Ningxiang *xian*, Hunan. [Source: Yang Shenchu. 1993, 278.]

Figure 2.48. With massive brick walls that are painted white, this Ming dynasty dwelling appears compact and squat and somewhat box-like. Its height is enhanced by black coping tiles that rise on the ends. Limited fenestration reinforces a sense of enclosure. *Zhelin xiang*, Shexian, Anhui. [Source: Zhang et al., 1957, plate 26.]

to the rear or along the side wall of two-story southern dwellings.

Among the most distinctive *tianjing*-style dwellings are two-story dwellings that survive from the Ming dynasty (1368–1644) in the region where Anhui, Jiangxi, and Zhejiang provinces come together. Some of these remarkable dwellings were built in towns and villages, but many were built alone in the midst of the verdant countryside. Most were constructed in the Huizhou region of southern Anhui by merchants whose commercial activities were far beyond their home districts but who expended large amounts of money to build multistory dwellings as well as memorial arches, temples, and bridges in their native places. Appearing like squat boxes or elongated loaves with solid walls and limited windows, these Ming dynasty dwellings in the Huizhou region maintain design features similar to northern courtyard-style *siheyuan*: axiality, symmetry, hierarchy, orientation to the cardinal directions, and enclosure behind walls to ensure privacy. Unlike northern structures, which emphasize horizontality and openness within to the sky above, Huizhou houses rise to two stories, emphasize verticality, and are constructed on relatively small building lots (Figure 2.48). While appearing modest from the outside in terms of building materials, inside the brick walls expensive woods are used structurally as well as ornamentally. *Tianjing* are integral parts of virtually all plans, with forecourts, posterior courts, and central courts.

Throughout Guangdong province, there is a close relationship between the open space of *tianjing* and the enclosure of main halls, or *tingtang*. In the Chaoan and Shantou area in the eastern part of the province, both compact *sanheyuan*- and *siheyuan*-style dwellings are found either standing alone or duplicated to form a larger structure to meet the needs of prosperous ex-

typically has only a limited outlook and can see merely a patch of the sky directly above (Figure 2.46). In southern China, larger residences sometimes have skywells that approximate northern courtyards in extent even though they are referred to locally as *tianjing*. For example, Liu Shaoqi's birthplace in Ningxiang *xian*, Hunan province, includes a large 64-square-meter courtyard that is locally termed a *"tianjing,"* even though in northern China it might be called a "courtyard" (Figure 2.47). It is surrounded on four sides by rooms and thus forms a *siheyuan*. Five smaller *tianjing* punctuate the surrounding building mass. Liu lived in this prosperous residence from the time of his birth in 1898 through 1916.

Many southern dwellings with *tianjing* are inverted U-shaped or H-shaped *sanheyuan* with the skywell fitting within the open space of the U or H plan. Entry thus is directly into a forecourt-type *tianjing* through a singular gate along the southern wall. When viewed from inside, the exterior wall of this initial *tianjing* is usually painted white in order to reflect light across the *tianjing* into the adjacent rooms. This reflecting surface simultaneously absorbs much of the heat of the sun's rays while scattering visible light at a much lower and tolerable intensity. In the forecourt, there sometimes is a well and almost always several stone stands to hold potted plants as well as pottery cisterns in which to collect water led into the *tianjing* by the inward slope of the roof. Smaller elongated *tianjing* are frequently found

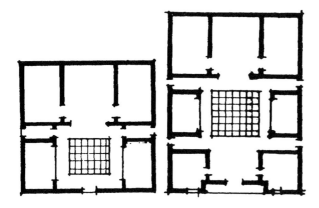

Figure 2.49. Compact three-*jian sanheyuan*-style and *siheyuan*-style dwellings are found throughout Guangdong. The plan on the left is a *sanheyuan* and is locally called a "crouching lion" [*pashi* 爬狮]. On the right is a "four metal points" [*sidianjin* 四点金] *siheyuan*, so called because each of the gable walls has the slope profile of the Chinese character for "metal." Chaoan and Shantou, Guangdong. [Source: Lu and Wei 1982, 141.]

tended families. As seen in Figure 2.49, each is typically a three-*jian* form with entry through a *jian*-wide central gate. The *sanheyuan*-style dwelling opens directly into the *tianjing*, while the *siheyuan*-style dwelling possesses a foyer-passageway that leads to an interior *tianjing*. Multiple side gates are found along the east and west walls, but rarely are openings placed along the back, or northern, wall. According to architectural surveys in this region, the dimensions of both types are quite standardized. However, there is a remarkable degree of flexibility once smaller modular units are linked together into a larger residential complex (Lu and Wei 1982, 141–142). Xiangpuzhai 象埔寨 in Chaoan, Guangdong, for example, contains within it nineteen variations of *sanheyuan*- and *siheyuan*-style modules, even though almost all of them maintain a width

Figure 2.50. A total of 122 *tianjing* of various sizes are contained with the nineteen variations of *sanheyuan*- and *siheyuan*-style modules. This plan of the 162.4 meter by 154.4 meter fortress called Xiangpuzhai houses 317 households in 72 dwelling units. Chaoan, Guangdong. [Source: Hui 1996, 156.]

of five *jian* or less (Figure 2.50). With an overall breadth of 162.4 meters and a depth of 154.4 meters, this large square fortress provides seventy-two dwelling units with at least 122 *tianjing* of various sizes for more than 317 households (Lu and Wei 1995, 1–5). Where dwellings expand laterally from three to nine *jian* in width, the number, size, and placement of *tianjing* increase as well (Figure 2.51).

Very compact two-story *sanheyuan* are found throughout Nanhai *xian*, Guangdong. They are somewhat more complex than the relatively simple Guangdong-style *sanjian lianglang* dwellings described earlier. Appearing like tall, nearly square boxes with massive decorative gable walls, each preserves the standard Chinese three-bay pattern with a large central hall and flanking bedrooms. Placed above these, however, is a loft and two subsidiary rooms for storage or for sleeping. As can be seen in the home of the late imperial period reformer Kang Youwei (Figure 2.52), each of the rooms is substantially deeper than it is wide. Fronting this two-story space is a single-story rectangle that incorporates a central *tianjing* and a pair of roofed cubes called *lang* 廊, the term normally used elsewhere in China to describe an arcade but here simply referring to a trun-

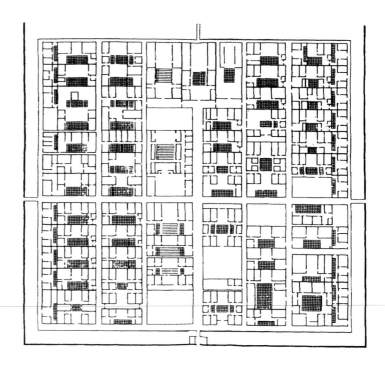

cated wing. One square *lang* serves as the kitchen and the other a vestibule. Both include side doors into the dwelling. The massive lobate gable walls of these dwellings are locally called *ao'erwu* 鳌耳屋 [sea tortoise ear buildings], which Chinese architects liken to the "handles of a large cauldron" [*huo'er* 镬耳, cauldron ears] (Lin and Li 1992, 57 ff.).

Besides multiple *tianjing*, some larger dwellings of the rich in southern China were also built with walled flower gardens [*tingyuan* 庭园 or *huayuan* 花园] attached to them. For the most part, *tingyuan* are quite different from the classical gentry gardens [*yuanlin* 园林], which are clearly the product of sophisticated Chinese landscape design found throughout the Jiangnan region and especially in Suzhou (Liu 1993; Wang 1998). While not drawing fully upon the art and philosophy that inspire *yuanlin*, some attempt is typically made to create "nature in miniature" within flower gardens through the planting of shrubs and trees and the naturalistic layout of paths. Flower gardens are generally located at the rear or backside of large dwelling complexes for extended families (Figure 2.53). In a large dwelling, a *tianjing* sometimes is occupied by a pond of circulating water, which brings the natural world into the dwelling and allows those within to

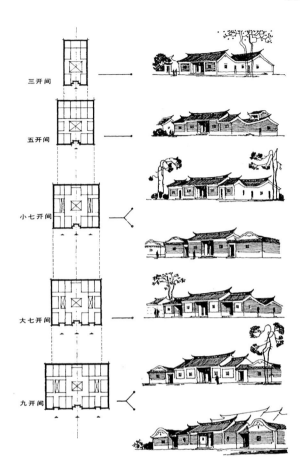

Figure 2.51 (above). The number of *tianjing* typically increase as the breadth of a dwelling expands. Various plans ranging from three- to nine-*jian* wide are shown with the placement, size, and shape of *tianjing*. Jinjiang *xian*, Fujian. [Source: Huang et al. 1992, 46.]

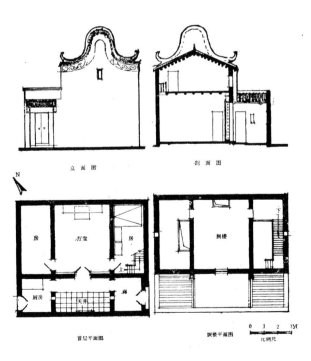

Figure 2.52 (left). With dominating gable walls, this tall, nearly square boxlike dwelling is the ancestral home of the late imperial period reformer Kang Youwei. As seen in the bottom plans, the three-*jian* unit in the rear includes a hall and two bedrooms on the first level and a loft and two utility rooms on the second. Each room is deeper than it is wide. A pair of truncated single-story wings jut from the rear structure with a *tianjing* held between them. The wings are called *lang*, one a kitchen and the other a vestibule, and each has a side door into the dwelling. The lobate gable walls seen in the upper elevation and section views have given rise to these dwellings being called "sea tortoise ear buildings" or *ao'erwu*. Sucun, Danzao yintang *xiang*, Nanhai *xian*, Guangdong. [Source: Lin and Li 1991, 58.]

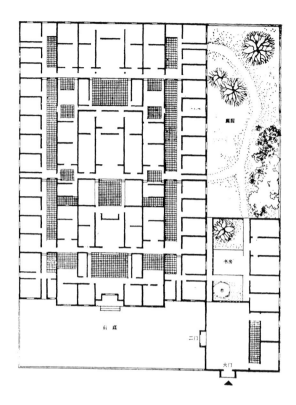

experience the world outside from either adjacent rooms or overhanging seats (Figure 2.54). Even within the confines of a town, such as the small charming residence of the celebrated Ming dynasty calligrapher and painter Xu Wei, space is composed for maximum effect. Xu's dwelling includes a front courtyard with benches, leafy vegetation, and a stone path that leads through a moon gate to a small *tianjing*. Visible from his study through a simple lattice window are a pool of water, rockery, and more vegetation (Figure 2.55).

Figure 2.54. *Tianjing* in larger dwellings in Anhui, Jiangxi, and Zhejiang sometimes include a pond of circulating water, which brings the natural world into the dwelling for those using an overhanging bench. When the lattice frames are removed, exterior and interior spaces are interconnected. Hongcun, Yixian, Anhui. [Source: Shan 1992, 126.]

Figure 2.53 (left). In the Wan family mansion in southeastern China, the *tingyuan*, or flower garden, is located at the rear side of the dwelling. Quanzhou, Fujian. [Source: Dai 1991, 164.]

Yikeyin 一颗印 [seal or chop style] dwellings in the Kunming area of Yunnan province are square and squat two-story *siheyuan*-style structures that look like a common Chinese seal (Figure 2.56, 2.57, and 2.58). Instead of a broad courtyard, a single focal *tianjing* is wrapped by structures: a three-*jian* main building along the back, a pair of slender symmetrical wings called *erfang* [耳房 ear rooms, or flanking rooms], and an entry portico [门廊 *menlang*] that leads immediately to the *tianjing*. A double layer of overhanging eaves helps to further shade the *tianjing* without significantly reducing the open space. While the *tangwu*, or main hall, faces the *tianjing* of a *yikeyin* dwelling, other spaces on the ground floor are more utilitarian: a stable for animals and a room for storage are to the side of the *tangwu*, and two kitchens are usually found within the jutting wings at the front. Family bedrooms and storage are above on the second story. While *yikeyin* are similar to the *sanjian lianglangwu* in central Guangdong discussed earlier, they differ in the location and style of their entry, the number of stories, the stabling of animals, and other details.

Figure 2.55 (above). The elegantly small dwelling built by the celebrated calligrapher and painter Xu Wei includes a front courtyard (left) that, through the moon gate on the side, connects with a small *tianjing* (right) with a pool of water, rockery, and vegetation. The lattice window connects the study and living space. Shaoxing *shi*, Zhejiang. [RGK photograph 1987.]

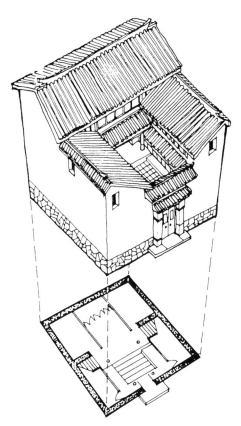

Figure 2.56. In this *yikeyin*, a single *tianjing* is wrapped by a three-*jian* main building along the back and a pair of slender symmetrical wings called *erfang* ["ear rooms," or "flanking rooms"] on the sides. Dominating the front facade is a gate whose expanse usually fills the distance between the two wings. Kunming, Yunnan. [Source: Rao and Yu 1994, 150.]

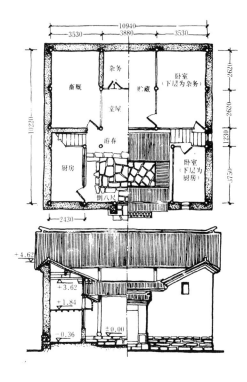

Figure 2.57. Measured elevation, section, and plan of a *yikeyin*. Two kitchens are found in the jutting wings just inside the gate on the right and left. Facing the *tianjing* is a *tangwu*, or "main hall," with a stable for animals and storage to its side. Bedrooms and storage are reserved for the second story. Haizi *cun*, Ala *xiang*, Gongdu *qu*, Kunming, Yunnan. [Source: Li Xingfa 1992, 175.]

Figure 2.58. View of the facade of a *yikeyin* in the country-side near Kunming, Yunnan. Constructed of adobe bricks, wooden frame, and fired tiles, the dwelling provides a relatively inexpensive residence for humans and their animals. [Source: Rao and Yu 1994, 150.]

Lang: *Passageways and Transitional Spaces*

Even though translated as "veranda" or "arcade," *lang* 廊 [also *langzi* 廊子] vary in form and function from one area to another in China. As linear roofed areas under an eaves overhang, they may serve simply as covered outside corridors but in many regions they are also significant transitional or "gray" spaces between the inside and outside of a structure. As part of a *siheyuan* in northern China, they are called *langzi* 廊子, *youlang* 游廊, or *chuanlang* 穿廊, simply a covered narrow passageway that completes the circuit around the perimeter of a quadrangle's courtyard, necessary because each of the four individual buildings is usually structurally separate (Figure 2.59). Because no doorways interconnect the four buildings that comprise a *siheyuan*, each side of the quadrangle is entered and exited through a door facing the focal courtyard. Wide steps typically lead from the central *jian* of each of the flanking structures to the courtyard, so movement between buildings is often more direct across the courtyard than around it. Throughout northern China, even though *youlang* are usually so narrow that only single-file movement is possible along them and there is little room to place any furniture, family members may temporarily place a chair or stool on the *youlang* from which to chat or

carry out minor household tasks. While the courtyard functions as a principal node of passage in good weather, the encircling *youlang* offers some limited protection along a peripheral circulation route during times of inclement weather. The overhanging eaves and columns help to buffer the wind and trap the sun's heat during the course of a day. Varying somewhat in depth, the breadth of the eaves regulates the amount of direct sunlight that can reach the interior of each of the structures that abut the *youlang* and helps to protect the wooden facades of the structures from weathering.

Siheyuan found in northern Shaanxi province, unlike those in the Beijing area, do not have verandas

Figure 2.59. This *langzi*, pictured in front of a structure on the western side of the courtyard, connects with the main south-facing building. Beijing. [RGK photograph 1997.]

Figure 2.60. Some dwellings in northern Shaanxi do not have verandas around their large courtyards but instead have a linear portico *in antis* called a *baolang* [embraced veranda].
[Source: Zhang and Liu 1993, 72.]

that complete a circuit around the courtyard. As seen in Figure 2.60, covered space is limited to a location in front of the south-facing main *zhengfang* structure and is more a linear portico *in antis* than a veranda. Called a *baolang* 抱廊 [embraced veranda], it typically recedes about 1.5 meters into the middle of the three *jian* of the northernmost structure instead of running the full length of the facade. Because the distance across the slender courtyard of *siheyuan* found in the Guanzhong area of south central Shaanxi is but a few steps, there is no need for a protruding eaves overhang *lang* (Zhang and Liu 1993, 72).

Moving from northern China southward, verandas become wider as courtyards become smaller. This inverse relationship helps transform *lang* from mere pas-

sageway to roomlike utility. In some areas of southern China, the area under the overhanging eaves projection constituting the veranda can actually approximate or exceed that of the adjacent *tianjing* (Figure 2.61). As size is altered to open up space, verandas can be viewed as an extension of both interior space and exterior space, depending on the vantage point. They sometimes form a large covered "porch" that is a virtual room for many activities throughout the day.

Throughout southern China, but especially in Fujian, Guangdong, and Zhejiang, one or more of the principal rooms may be fully exposed to the *yanlang* and courtyard beyond, forming a *changting* 敞厅 [open room]. "Open rooms" are sometimes seen in rectangular rural structures, as in Figure 2.6, but they

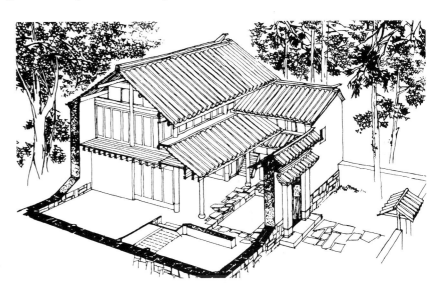

Figure 2.61. Within a *yikeyin*, the broad veranda created below the substantial roof overhang rivals in area the adjacent *tianjing.* Yunnan. [Source: Yunnan sheng 1986, 188.]

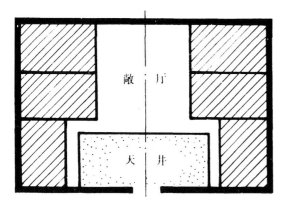

Figure 2.62. *Changting*, or "open rooms," often recede from the *tianjing* into a structure. The *changting* in this *sanheyuan* plan is nearly five meters wide, more than a third of the dwelling's breadth. [Source: Zhongguo jianzhu 1984, 94.]

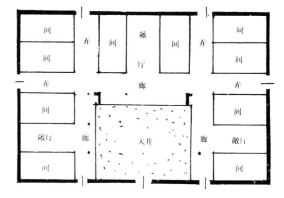

Figure 2.64. Top, view across the broad and recessed *tianjing* looking into the *changting*, here marked by a low fence to keep the pig and chickens from entering. Bottom, view across the fence into the "open room" toward what remains of the ancestral altar and other ceremonial paraphernalia. Hebian *cun*, Dagangtou *zhen*, Lishui *xian*, Zhejiang. [RGK photograph 1988.]

Figure 2.63. In this symmetrical *sanheyuan*, a *changting* occupies the central *jian* facing the rectangular *tianjing*. Raised two steps above the impluvium that collects and drains rainwater, the *changting* unites interior and exterior space. During inclement weather, it serves as a sheltered terrace for household activities, and throughout the year, it functions as a space for eating and entertaining. This is the home of the revolutionary Xu Xiling. Dongpu *zhen*, Shaoxing *shi*, Zhejiang. [RGK photograph 1987.]

Figure 2.65. This large U-shaped *sanheyuan*-type dwelling in Zhejiang includes three *changting*, each of which opens onto a *lang*, or veranda. In addition to the veranda, covered passageways or side corridors called *long* lead to side exits. The spatial composition of this dwelling complex is fragmented yet connected, open yet closed. [Source: Zhongguo jianzhu 1984, 94.]

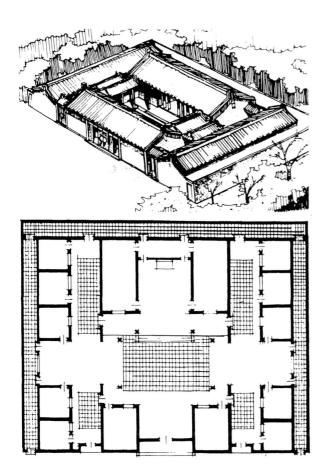

Figure 2.66. Interior, exterior, and transitional spaces are clearly presented in this southern *siheyuan* quadrangle-type dwelling called a "four halls facing each other" [*si ting xiangxiang*]. The entry leads to an open room and then to the main *tianjing*, beyond which is another *changting*. On each end of the axial *tianjing* is another *changting*. Together these serve to both fragment and open the interior, clearly dividing space for several generations yet affirming the unity of the family with its main central hall. Chaozhou, Guangdong. [Source: Lu and Wei 1990, 324.]

are more commonly seen within dwellings wrapped with high walls (Figures 2.62, 2.63, and 2.64). With the central *jian* along the back wall of a dwelling fully exposed to the *tianjing*, ventilation is enhanced into the interior, and the space between the *changting* and the *tianjing* becomes integrated. Within the U-shaped *sanheyuan*-type dwelling, shown in Figure 2.65, the connections among the single focal *tianjing*, encircling

lang, three *changting*, and two narrow and covered side corridors called *long* 弄 not only fragment the dwelling into units but also open the interior of the walled complex to the outside. The complex linkages among interior, exterior, and transitional spaces are clearly demonstrated in a *siheyuan* in Chaozhou, Guangdong province (Figure 2.66). This type of layout is known locally as "four halls facing each other" [*si ting xiangxiang* 四厅相向] because each of the *changting* found within the surrounding structures is a main room that opens on to the large axial courtyardlike central *tianjing*. The dwelling provides a clear division of space for several generations within it. The articulated areas surrounding the core of the open central hall and linked to outside spaces that reach in several directions together affirm the unity of the family by providing generous sites for ritual and household celebrations (Lu and Wei 1990, 324–325).

Throughout Anhui, Jiangxi, and Zhejiang provinces, verandas are so deep that substantial columns are needed to support the weight of the woodwork and tile above. Although some verandas are covered by the floor of rooms above, most are formed from overhanging eaves [*langyan* 廊檐] cantilevered out into a skywell within a *sanheyuan* plan, as seen in Figure 2.67. By inverting the term "*langyan*," verandas of this type are called *yanlang* 檐廊 [eaves veranda] in this region. Because many southern dwellings are multistory, upper-story *yanlang* are also common. Upper-story verandas obviously require a structurally more complex first floor veranda to lift them. The increasing width of *yanlang* in this region allows them to become important transitional spaces between enclosed rooms and open spaces. Flanking both open and closed spaces, verandas permit inside activities to spill over to the outside and allow the outdoors to be immediately visible from the inside. Whatever the weather, they serve as covered corridors and as a place to sit halfway between indoors and outdoors. The deep overhangs of the *yanlang* screen adjacent rooms from the harsh subtropical sunlight and prevent windblown rain from entering the living spaces. While light is obstructed, ventilation of the dwelling is possible even under the worst weather conditions. Figure 2.68 bares the interconnectedness of the interior/exterior spaces repre-

Figure 2.67(left). Transitional spaces between a *tianjing* and the surrounding rooms are formed by overhanging structures that create verandas. Throughout Anhui and Zhejiang, these areas are the focus of much ornamentation on heavy structural elements as well as on delicate lattice doors and windows, all made of wood. Bainiken *cun*, Huangze *zhen*, Sheng *xian*, Zhejiang. [RGK photograph 1987.]

Figure 2.68 (below). The integration of *changting*, *yanlang*, and *tianjing* is apparent in this view from the inside *changting* toward the entry. Southern Jiangxi. [RGK photograph 1993.]

Figure 2.69. Crafted from crescent-shaped timber beams and other components that carry the eaves to the outer, or peripheral, wooden columns, arcades in front of the main halls of the wealthy are functional as well as the focus of much ornamentation. Presented here are views of four verandas or arcades [*lang* or *yanlang*] in Zhejiang province (from left to right): Zhuangshi *zhen*, Zhenhai *qu*, Ningbo *shi*; Weishan *zhen*, Dongyang *xian*; Dongyang *xian*; Nanxun *zhen*, Huzhou *shi*. [Source: Zhongguo jianzhu 1984, 203.]

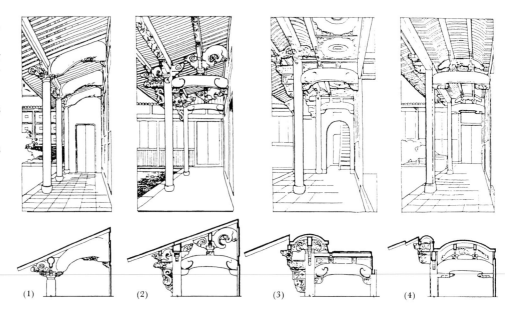

(1)   (2)   (3)   (4)

sented by *changting* [open room], *yanlang* [veranda], and *tianjing* [skywell].

Figure 2.69 illustrates four fronting verandas in large dwellings in eastern, central, and northern Zhejiang, and these reveal the significant ornamentation characteristic of this region. The crescent-shaped timber beams that carry the eaves to the outer, or peripheral, pillars [*yanzhu* 檐柱] are both functional and boldly and richly decorative. *Niutui* [牛腿 ox's flank; also called *matui* 马腿 horse's flank] traditionally were added to the upper areas of verandas in the homes of the wealthy, just as they were common features in clan halls and temples in the region (Figure 2.70). Of greater height than projection, *niutui* are solid and intricately carved consoles or brackets that extend support to the outer eaves along the exterior of a column. (Numerous examples are illustrated in Knapp 1989, 122-125). Contrasted with ceilings of the interior rooms, the ceiling of a veranda may be artistically shaped and brightly decorated. Like the center hall of a Victorian home, Zhejiang and Anhui arcades are hubs of activity. Here a household has an opportunity to display its aesthetic sense in an area visitors are likely to experience intimately. Less pretentious and more serviceable arcades are commonly seen constructed as part of canalside dwellings throughout the Jiangnan region (Figure 2.71). Many of these arcades, called

Figure 2.70 (above). Throughout western Zhejiang and the neighboring provinces of Anhui and Jiangxi, verandas often include intricately carved brackets. Many such brackets tell stories from history or literature as well as narrate didactic themes. Huilu *cun*, Huailu *xiang*, Dongyang *xian*, Zhejiang. [RGK photograph 1988.]

Figure 2.71 (right). Along the canals that thread through the villages and towns of the Jiangnan region of Jiangsu and Zhejiang provinces, simple unornamented arcades or walkways jut from the waterside dwellings, serving public and private needs. Stone steps lead to the water, providing spaces for washing clothes and vegetables as well as for taking watercraft. Nanxun *zhen*, Huzhou *shi*, Zhejiang. [RGK photograph 1988.]

Figure 2.72. Well protected from weathering by rain and sun underneath the arcades, perforated lattice doors and windows are common features of dwellings throughout southern China. The lattice patterns are sometimes simple geometric forms, but often they are rich with traditional imagery and abundant meaning. Langzhong *shi*, Sichuan. [RGK photograph 1994.]

From the inside, each perforated panel functions as a link to the outside or as a visual barrier, depending upon the density of the pattern (Figure 2.74). Whether the panels are closed or open, the tracery of lattice panels frame for the inside viewer scenes of the natural world outside in the courtyard. Decorative yet functional openwork screen walls of this type, but fashioned of bronze, stone, brick, or porcelain, have existed in China since at least the Han period, as attested by funerary objects and literary records. These panels serve as important locations for didactic ornamentation. Before glass was available, semitransparent paper was pasted on the inside of perforated surfaces to block the penetration of

qilou 骑楼 in Zhejiang, serve as public walkways while functioning as elongated covered spaces for a family's activities at the entry of its canalside dwelling.

Exterior walls of rooms facing the veranda throughout the provinces of southern China—from the coastal provinces of Fujian, Guangdong, Hainan, and Zhejiang through interior Jiangxi, Hunan, and Sichuan—are usually fitted with perforated wooden panels that screen interior space from the outside (Figures 2.72 and 2.73). Well protected against weathering from rain and sun, the detailed carpentry of the lattice patterns and exquisite carving of wooden windows and door panels are aesthetically noteworthy and functionally significant. Arranged vertically and horizontally across the opening, they can be flexibly positioned by swiveling on a center or side pivot, sliding, or swinging up, or they can be dismounted from their frames. As permeable partitions [*ge* 隔], they are also boundaries that alter the division of space. When fixed in position, they form "doors" and "windows" that filter light and air, but when dismounted they allow interior and exterior space to blend without any separation. Each lattice design responds to different requirements in terms of "shaping the wind"—regulating the direction, volume, and velocity of air flow necessary to ventilate interior space. (Many screening panels in Zhejiang are illustrated in Knapp 1989, 126-132.)

Figure 2.73. Laundry is hanging here to dry under the eaves overhang and in front of richly carved lattice door panels. The central panels swivel open, but all of the panels may be removed if there is need to join exterior and interior space. Dongyang *xian*, Zhejiang. [RGK photograph 1988.]

Figure 2.74. From inside a hall looking through the lattice doors toward the *tianjing*, interior and exterior spaces are visually and physically linked. Home of Yang Gegong, Shangjiang *zhen*, Tongnan *xian*, Sichuan. [RGK photograph 1994.]

outside air during the cold months. The contrast of wood pattern and intervening paper is sharpest at night when viewed from outside as the dim interior glow is diffused through the lattice. Left to fray during the spring, the paper traditionally was punctured to facilitate ventilation as the days got warmer. Horizontal transom lattice windows [*qichuang* 气窗] were sometimes used in the upper walls of Jiangnan dwellings, where they exhausted warm air from the ceiling area and primed the circulation of cooler air through the openwork of the lower perforated panels.

Throughout subtropical Yunnan province, "gray" or semiopen spaces [*hui kongjian* 灰空间; *bankaichang kongjian* 半开敞空间] provide important living areas for ethnic minorities as well as Han. Much more than mere transitional spaces between interior

and exterior, these include broad verandas called *shazi* 厦子, open halls of a *yikeyin* plan, and unique covered porches elevated above the ground. In the Lijiang area, as seen in Figure 2.75, verandas that are part of a *sanheyuan* are often as wide as 2.4 meters in order to create broad semiopen *shazi* galleries ringing the *tianjing*. These galleries are used as porchlike utilitarian "rooms" for entertaining guests, serving family meals, producing handicrafts, and for sleeping. Unlike verandas elsewhere in China, where furniture is placed only temporarily, *shazi* in this area of Yunnan are designed to comfortably accommodate four-sided tables and stools.

Within *yikeyin*, the compact seal-type dwellings of the Kunming area, at least one-third of the ground floor is composed on open or semi-open space (Figure 2.76). Immediately inside the gate is a *menlang* 门廊 [gate arcade], leading directly to a small *tianjing*, perhaps 4.5 by 3.8 meters, and then a central hall that is fully exposed to the *tianjing*. Besides being an entry corridor, the *menlang* is a place to store farm implements and to sit and do handicraft work. Covered by a sloping roof that leads water into the *tianjing*, the *menlang* is higher than the central hall's *changting*, facing it across the open *tianjing*, whose ceiling is formed by the floor of the rooms above. Less private than the space on the second floor, the

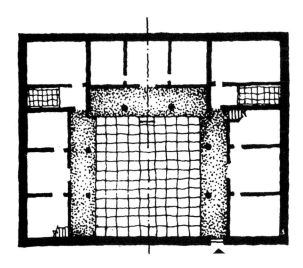

Figure 2.75. Verandas ringing a *tianjing* of *sanheyuan* in Yunnan province are often as wide as 2.4 meters in order to create broad semiopen spaces called "*shazi*." They are broad enough for furniture to be left there for daily use. [Source: Zhu 1992b, 123.]

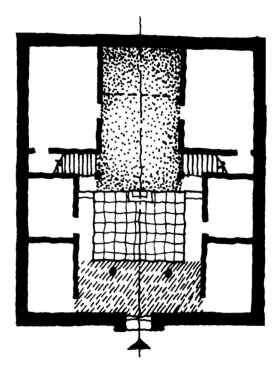

Figure 2.77. *Qianlang,* substantial porches that are breezy and cool, are built as part of Dai ethnic minority dwellings in the Dehong area of subtropical Yunnan. Elevated above the ground, they range between 10 and 30 square meters in area, occupying about a third of the total floor space. [Source: Zhu 1992b, 125.]

Figure 2.76. Compact seal-type *yikeyin* dwellings found in the Kunming area of Yunnan generally have as much as one-third of the ground floor as open or semiopen space. This "gray" space extends from directly inside the front gate, across the small *tianjing,* and into an "open room," or *changting.* [Source: Zhu 1992b, 125.]

quate protection even during heavy rains. Even though shaded, they are brighter areas for work and leisure than interior spaces and provide clear connections with the natural world beyond (Zhu 1992b, 123–127).

open and semiopen core of a *yikeyin*-style dwelling—made up of the free-flowing *menlang, tianjing,* and *changting*—represents at least a third of the ground floor area and provides abundant space for entertaining, drying herbs, working crafts, and washing clothes.

Among minority nationality groups in Yunnan, such as the Blang, Jingpo, De'ang, and some Dai, substantial porches project from their dwellings but are structurally an extension of adjacent enclosed space. With a roof supported by similar columns, as seen in Figure 2.77, these porches [*qianlang* 前廊] range between 10 and 30 square meters in floor area and about a third of the total floor space of the dwelling. Usually elevated above the ground as platforms and exposed to the outside on three sides, broad *qianlang* are breezy and cool yet offer ade-

Men: Entry, Transition, and Status

Enclosure, as this chapter has emphasized, is an intentional and meaningful spatial composition in Chinese domestic architecture. Facing inward rather than outward, the whole of a dwelling and even its subsidiary parts separate residential units from the world beyond, with only a single gate providing access into the seclusion of the bounded space of the dwelling. Even in very large dwellings, such as the Hakka fortresslike complexes in Fujian and Guangdong and the extensive ramified merchant dwellings in Shanxi or Shaanxi, only a solitary gate mediates between inside and outside. Within large or small dwellings, gateways of many types serve to separate as much as connect fragmented spaces.

The placement of the main exterior gate of dwellings varies from place to place in China. In the north,

Figure 2.78 (top left). Some gates on new and old dwellings are simply functional portals, composed of brick supports, wooden members, and modest ornamentation. A common pattern for Chinese gates is a raised doorsill, which must be stepped over. Beyond the gate is a *zhaobi*, or "spirit wall," which blocks the view of the courtyard from outside the gate even when the gate is open. Liuminying, Huairou *xian*, Beijing. [RGK photograph 1987.]

Figure 2.79 (top right). Both the top-heavy gate structure to the left and the two gates in the wall are capped with tiles. Zhaoxian, Hebei. [RGK photograph 1983.]

Figure 2.80 (bottom left). Chinese gates are usually quite generous in height even in modest dwellings. This ornamented entry to a cavelike dwelling complex is fitted into a tamped earth wall. Beyond the gate is a low *zhaobi*, a screen wall, which offers some level of privacy by limiting the view of the courtyard to passersby. Qianling, Shaanxi. [RGK photograph 1984.]

centering on the Beijing area but also including Shandong, Shanxi, Henan, and Shaanxi provinces, the preferred location for a residential gate is along the southeast wall with entry into a vestibule before another turn leads to the courtyard. Positioning the entry gate at the center of the south wall is most common in areas throughout southern China, but this pattern is found as far north as the southern banks of the Huanghe River. Central gates traditionally were also common in northeast China where the need to move large carts and agricultural equipment into the courtyard was facilitated by an opening in the middle of the wall.

While many gates are merely functional portals providing a threshold to pass between two worlds, others make grand and imposing statements about a household's status (Figures 2.78, 2.79, 2.80, 2.81,

Figure 2.81 (left). This well-built house and gate, made of fired bricks and tile, are enclosed by a crude wall. Northern Hebei. [RGK photograph 1984.]

Figure 2.83. Guided by sumptuary regulations of the late imperial period, this entry includes columns, a hooded overhang, calligraphy, a doorsill, and two substantial door panels. Dingcun, Linfen *xian*, Shanxi. [RGK photograph 1996.]

Figure 2.82. This interior gate between two small courtyards is framed with a singular motif of woody stems and leaves of a bamboo plant, unusual since the dwelling is in the semi-arid loessial plateau. Wangjia *dayuan*, Jingseng *cun*, Lingshi *xian*, Shanxi. [RGK photograph 1996.]

Figure 2.84. Leading to an urban dwelling of the Qing dynasty, this gateway includes a post-and-beam superstructure with roof elements common to a main dwelling structure. Pingyao *shi*, Shanxi. [RGK photograph 1996.]

2.82, 2.83, and 2.84). In northern China where sumptuary regulations were honored in imperial times, careful attention was paid to the scale and decoration of gates as representations of the rank or status of each head of the household. Throughout the city of Beijing, even today, two basic types of gates can be seen: relatively broad and deep gatehouses that are elaborately adorned and narrow and shallow ones whose door panels are quite ordinary. The large multicourtyard residences of imperial princes had "great gates" [王府大门], five bays across with three central doorways that could be opened. Painted red, capped with glazed tile, and embellished with ornamented brackets, these and other similar but hierarchically smaller entries echoed imperial architectural forms found within China's great palaces (Zhang 1995, 8–19).

"Broad and brilliant gates" [*guangliang* 广亮门], as seen in Figure 2.85, while less dramatic than the great gates of imperial princes, were prominent elements in the composition of large *siheyuan* built by officials and merchants. As a single portico along the southeast wall, each *guangliang* gate was raised several steps above the passing lane, then recessed at least a meter from the outer wall to which it was connected. Inside the gate was a small walled courtyard or covered space leading to less constricted space inside. Raised above the encircling outer wall, the side walls of *guangliang* gates usually duplicate those of buildings within with their grey fired brick walls and tiled roofs. A pair of relatively simple wooden panels is used to shutter each *guangliang* gate. More common among the *siheyuan* that line Beijing's lanes are relatively modest *menlou* 门楼 [gate structures or storied gateways], most of which are framed in stone and wood to heighten their prominence.

Figure 2.85. Throughout the Qing dynasty, *guangliang* gates were placed along the southeast wall of the residences of officials and merchants in Beijing. A single bay wide, they were wider than function demanded and represented the status of the owner. The door panels usually were painted red and accompanied by ornamentation mounted under the rafters that suggested the rank of the head of household within. [RGK photograph 1997.]

Inner gates of *siheyuan* and *sanheyuan* vary, depending on the overall scale of the dwelling. In fully developed *siheyuan*, a *chuihuamen* 垂花门 [festooned gate] is placed between the outer peripheral and inner central courtyard at a position along the central axis where it provides not only security but offers a focal point of ornamentation. *Chuihuamen*, as seen in Figure 2.86, are generally more resplendent than the outer gate that leads to the world outside. Less pretentious *chuihuamen* gates are also found in smaller dwellings in Beijing. Enclosed side yards are usually separated from the main courtyard by walls and connected through simple portals of many different shapes that do not have closing panels (Figure 2.87).

In central China, as in the north, the adornment of the entryway was traditionally an important statement of the status of the resident and took many forms (Figure 2.88): *menlou* [storied gateway], *menzhao* [overhanging door shade], *menlang* [horizontal portico], and *mendou* [vertical portico]. The large, multilevel arch "structures" with prominent vertical elements in raised relief called *menlou* in southern China are much larger and more distinctive than most of those called by the same name in the north. Although sometimes crafted of brick and mortar, as seen in Figure 2.89, southern *menlou* usually imitate traditional wooden architectural elements, such as posts, beams, brackets, and carved ornamentation. Each proclaims status but offers the entryway little protection from the elements. In proportion, they usually overwhelm the facade and

Figure 2.86 (left). Between the outer peripheral and inner central courtyard of a *siheyuan*, a resplendent *chuihuamen* [festooned gate] marks the transition. [Source: Ma 1995, 30.]

Figure 2.87 (below). This vase-shaped gateway leads to and from a secluded side yard in a *siheyuan*. Beijing. [RGK photograph 1988.]

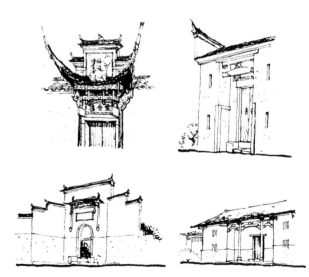

Figure 2.88. The four common gate forms found in Jiangxi, Zhejiang, and Anhui are (clockwise from the top right): *menzhao* [overhanging door shade]; *menlang* [horizontal portico]; *mendou* [vertical portico]; and *menlou* [storied doorway]. [Source: Huang, Shao, and Li 1990, 41.]

Figure 2.89. Built early in the twentieth century, conspicuous *menlou* dominate the facade of this *tianjing*-style dwelling. The carved brick and stone of this *menlou* imitate wooden structural and ornamental elements. The type of materials used is not apparent until one nears the gate. Maoping *cun*, Luci *xiang*, Tonglu *xian*, Zhejiang. [RGK photograph 1987.]

appear similar to freestanding and imposing honorific portals called *pailou* 牌楼 [memorial gateways], which are often profusely ornamented. In larger dwelling complexes in northern China, such as in Qiaojia manor and Qujia manors of central Shanxi, elaborate *menlou* are found at the main entry as well as within interior courtyards, where they draw attention to the entry of the main hall (Figures 2.90 and 2.91). Other examples of magnificent *menlou* found within northern merchants' dwellings in Shanxi and Shaanxi provinces that rival those commonly associated with southern China are illustrated in Chapter 4.

Substantial carved brick, stone, and wood "canopies" or "hoods" [*menzhao* 门罩 overhanging door shade] at a scale that also typically overwhelms the modest door opening are common in Anhui, Jiangxi, Jiangsu, Zhejiang, and adjacent provinces. Taking many forms, as seen in Figures 2.92 and 2.93, "canopies," however, offer only limited protection from pouring rain or sunlight. Both *menlang* [horizontal portico] and *mendou* [vertical portico] are identifiable, since they both recede into a wall surface, but they differ in orientation. *Menlang* typically are wider than they are high and are often accentuated with pillars to hold whatever superstructure is built above. *Mendou* are often not much wider than the gate itself, although sometimes they are broad and elaborately ornamented, as seen in Figure 2.94. *Menlang* and *mendou* are especially common in Jiangxi province and adjacent areas of Anhui and Zhejiang, but they are found elsewhere in China. The single gateway that controls access into the extensive Hakka *yuanlou* fortresses in Fujian are formidable in strength and heavily ornamented with calligraphy (Figure 2.95). Most are composed of a rectangular frame of stone structural supports into which is set a stone arch.

Many of the environmental factors considered in the composition of traditional dwelling spaces—whether

Figure 2.90 (top left). Within large manor complexes in northern China, *menlou* are sometimes found at the entry of a main hall, visible across a courtyard. Qiaojia *dayuan*, Qiaojiabao village, Qixian, Shanxi. [RGK photograph 1996.]

Figure 2.91 (bottom left). Similar to that shown in Figure 2.90, this *menlou* within the Qu family manor includes a heavy superstructure with baked tiles, intricate wooden brackets, and carved wooden ornamentation. Qujia *dayuan*, Qixian, Shanxi. [RGK photograph 1996.]

Figure 2.92 (top right). Carved brick *menzhao*, canopies or hoods above a door, accentuate the entrance, provide a location for calligraphic adornment, and create limited shade for the gateway. Xidi *cun*, Yixian, Anhui. [RGK photograph 1987.]

Figure 2.93 (bottom right). *Menzhao* heighten the verticality of an entrance, expressing with its detail the status of the dwelling owner. Zhangcun, Zhangcun *xiang*, Dongyang *xian*, Zhejiang. [RGK photograph 1987.]

Figure 2.94. Recessed entries are called *"mendou."* While many are not much wider than the doorway itself, others are broad. This entryway is heavily ornamented with carved wood, stone, and brick elements. Yang Amiao dwelling, Quanzhou, Fujian. [Source: Lu and Lu 1992, 34.]

Figure 2.95. The entry to large Hakka *yuanlou* complexes, discussed in detail in Chapter 5, is normally through a single gateway. At *Beichenlou*, the gateway is heavily fortified. Framed with granite blocks, the wooden door panels are more than ten centimeters and are encased with an iron skin and reinforced with iron rods. Above the arch-shaped portal, the entry is a focal point for calligraphy. In addition to the bold characters of the name of the complex and couplets added at the New Year, fading characters reveal the ardor of recent revolutionary times. Fujian. [RGK photograph 1990.]

in the north or south, whether *siheyuan* or *sanheyuan*, whether courtyard-style or skywell-style—have been suggested earlier in this chapter. While southern multistory dwellings can be described as compact and wasting little space, even northern *siheyuan*, with their large interior courtyards and adjacent side buildings, have been described by Chinese architects as "high density" structures, even though traditionally the actual "density of residents" was low (Shang and Yang

1982, 51). Figure 2.96 compares the spatial relationships of three dwelling types with open space, all on the same size building lot. On the top, the traditional *siheyuan* is shown with a ratio of 70 percent enclosing building space and a central courtyard representing 30 percent of the lot. Even with substantial structures, there remains extensive open space that is shared by all who live within the dwelling. The middle figure illustrates a pattern typical of an American dwelling in which the proportion of building and open space is the opposite of a Chinese *siheyuan*. Clearly serving a different social purpose, this western-style single-family detached dwelling meets other needs. Yet, if Chinese architects were to abandon the courtyard as anachronistic and replicate the same proportion of building and open space as in the western residential layout, the authors demonstrate, on the bottom, that the fringing yard becomes useless. Courtyards of various shapes and sizes are clearly preferred even today by Chinese living in rural and urban areas. Evolving over several thousand years to meet different environmental and changing social conditions, the courtyard in its many forms continues to unfold as an appropriate component in the spatial composition of Chinese residences throughout the country.

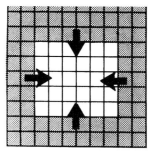

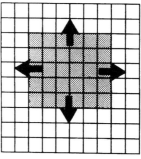

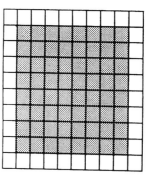

Figure 2.96. Comparison of the areal relationships among structural space and open space on building lots of the same size in China and the United States. [Source: After Shang and Yang 1982, 56.]

CHAPTER 3

Building Structures

HAN DWELLINGS THROUGHOUT CHINA share common structural forms with119 the palaces and temples that epitomize China's grand ceremonial and religious architecture. Many of these forms have also found their way into the buildings of minority nationality groups through the process of acculturation over a long period of time. Although less designed than merely built, Chinese rural and urban houses generally take shape from a set of conventional structural components that reveal an extraordinarily conservative tradition based upon building modules in which structure and space are mutually delimited. Employing standard measurements and commonly available structural elements, peasant builders and the local craftsmen who aided them have always been pragmatic, able to temper experience and skill with the practical conditions at hand. The existence of apparent structural and spatial variations throughout China, nonetheless, reflects a tolerance of conspicuous empiricism in which builders respond to local conditions even in the face of ostensibly confining construction traditions. House construction by Chinese peasants, moreover, traditionally was a long-term process, one in which building materials were accumulated piecemeal and work was accomplished stage by stage over an extended period of time, resulting often in hybrid structures. Since work was usually accomplished by oneself or with the aid of a few neighbors and kinsmen, relatively simple materials such as tamped earth, adobe brick, rough stone, and simple wooden timbers have dominated. Only at additional cost and with attention to higher levels of

skill and technology was it possible to use fired brick, quarried stone, and sophisticated carpentry. The economic circumstances of a household always have played important roles in this decision making. Common dwellings exhibit a high degree of structural flexibility based upon the manipulation of the building module known as *jian*, the bay that was discussed in Chapter 2, whose versatile form varies according to types of materials and levels of craftsmanship.

Like dwellings all over the world, those in China are composed of a conventional set of elementary building parts—foundation, walls, and roof. While there is little that is uncommon about Chinese foundations, walls and roofs are often quite distinctive. Chinese builders have devised rather unique solutions to span, enclose, and cover space that warrant detailed discussion. Particularly noteworthy is the fact that Chinese walls frequently do not directly support the weight of the roof but rather serve as "curtains" between complicated wooden framework, which lifts the roof independent of the walls.

Earlier in this century, Chinese architectural historians, such as Liang Sicheng, Liu Dunzhen, and Liu Zhiping, identified three fundamental elements or components of Chinese buildings: the platform or foundation [*taiji* 台基 and *jichu* 基础], pillars and beams skeleton [*zhuliang* 柱梁], and pitched roof [*wuding* 屋顶]. They ignored the walls as a building element. Liang Sicheng called the method of building Chinese structures an "osseous construction," analogous to the human skeleton in which the tripartite division of building elements

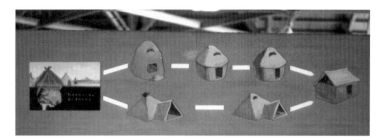

Figure 3.1. This hypothetical sequence suggests the emergence of round and square semisubterranean habitat forms that eventually merged as an elevated rectangular dwelling form during the neolithic period. Banpo, Shaanxi. [RGK photograph 1985.]

permits complete freedom in walling and fenestration and, by the simple adjustment of the proportion between walls and openings, renders a house practical and comfortable in any climate from that of tropical Indochina to that of subarctic Manchuria. Due to this extreme flexibility and adaptability, this method of construction could be employed wherever Chinese civilization spread and would effectively shelter occupants from the elements, however diverse they might be. Perhaps nothing analogous is found in Western architecture . . . until the invention of reinforced concrete and the steel framing systems of the twentieth century. (Liang 1984, 8)

As true as this is—as will be discussed in this chapter—many of the houses built by ordinary Chinese nonetheless have been built with load-bearing walls rather than a load-bearing wooden framework of pillars and beams because of cost and other factors. For the most part, this chapter focuses on Han dwellings and does not draw examples from the building traditions of minority nationalities, general aspects of which are discussed in later chapters.

Foundations and Platforms: The Base

Traditional Chinese dwellings generally rest directly on compacted earth or are slightly raised on a solid foundation made of earth, stone, or brick. Such bases serve as transitional devices to carry the substantial weight of a building safely to the ground without al-

lowing it to become deformed. Basements are rare in contemporary Chinese dwellings, but it is clear that the floors of early dwellings were excavated below ground level and were firmly tamped. Except for housing types identified with ethnic minorities in southern China, furthermore, Chinese houses today are not elevated on a platform in the manner of traditional Japanese or Southeast Asian houses, although archaeological evidence from the neolithic period clearly shows that the proto-Chinese in south central coastal areas raised their dwellings on piles above the ground. Yet, where terrain is uneven, such as along hill slopes, Han builders do construct dwellings using wooden piles of varying length to form substructural scaffolds for support from below.

Documented neolithic dwellings exhibit both semisubterranean and raised types of houses. At Banpo in Shaanxi, semisubterranean pit dwellings were dug a half-meter or so into the warm ground. They were transitional between earlier cave dwellings and later elevated structures built with post-and-beam construction, as seen in the hypothetical pro-

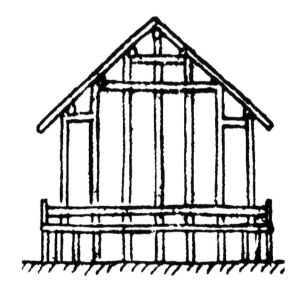

Figure 3.2. In order to reduce contact with ground moisture, neolithic dwellings near the mouth of the Changjiang were elevated above the ground on stilts or piles. Hemudu, Zhejiang. [Source: Lin Huadong 1992, 202.]

Figure 3.3. Each of the Shang dynasty oracle bone characters relates to building and give pictographic prominence to raised platforms and gabled roofs. [Source: Liu 1984, 30.]

gression in Figure 3.1. At Xiaotun and Erligang, excavated in large numbers earlier in the twentieth century in Henan province on both sides of the Huanghe River, the floors of sunken tamped earth pits were plastered with a limey clay. The Hemudu neolithic site in northeastern Zhejiang, on the other hand, revealed dwellings that had been elevated 0.8 to 1.0 meter above the ground on stilts or piles in order to reduce contact with ground moisture from the high water table and adjacent surface water (Figure 3.2). Not incidentally, increased ventilation also helped keep such dwellings dry under the rather humid conditions that prevailed at the time. Among the Han Chinese, such an elevated pile type is no longer seen, but it is not clear when raised dwellings were overtaken in primacy by on-ground foundations upon which virtually all Chinese houses have been built over the centuries.

Archaeological remains from the Shang dynasty (ca. 1700–1100 B.C.) provide substantial evidence for a progression from below-ground to above-ground tamped earthen podiums, thus increasingly reducing dampness and providing a compacted base necessary to support the often large and heavy structures that were increasingly being built at that time. Square and rectangular tamped earth podium foundations consisting of thirty discrete layers of pounded soil were excavated at sites in southern Henan province and demonstrated that dwellings were constructed as much as 3 meters above ground level (Chang 1980, 90). Shang dynasty oracle bone characters relating to buildings give pictographic prominence to raised platforms (Figure 3.3). The scale of some excavated Shang structures suggests that many were palaces—one had a length of 85 meters—yet modest above-ground houses with tamped podium foundations

have been found as well. Excavated pit house foundations, scattered beside and among the larger above-ground foundations, were probably occupied by commoners who served the Shang royal family. This mixture of foundation patterns points clearly to the continuity of a given form over time even in the face of qualitative cultural changes that would eventually overtake the earlier form. The technique of utilizing a boxlike frame to raise a load-bearing tamped earth wall, to be discussed later, had its origins during the Shang dynasty.

During the nine hundred year Zhou dynasty, which followed the Shang, the height of a building's podium was linked to the status of the occupant. Excavated dwelling sites suggest that commoners were restricted to building directly on the compacted ground. Senior officials and above, however, built dwellings on raised platforms, the height of which was regulated by a graded scale related to their position in the social hierarchy.

Coupled with crude troughs and sometimes underground conduits to drain water, tamped earth, stone, or brick foundations and podiums eventually provided dry and secure bases for many types of dwellings throughout the country. Such sensitivity to the warmth of the earth and the need to control moisture content no doubt was appropriate in neolithic and subsequent settlements on the North China plain and in many adjacent areas later occupied by peasants as Chinese civilization spread into frontier areas. Yet Chinese migrants, peculiarly, carried this predilection for construction, directly on or slightly above ground level, even to areas where its appropriateness was questionable: in areas of southern China and in peninsular Southeast Asia where the dwellings of indigenous groups were raised on piles in order to lessen humidity by providing ventilation beneath the floor. Throughout China today, tamped earth foundations are frequently confined by an encircling stone or brick buttress, which provides lateral support for the weight of wooden columns or tamped earth walls that rise above the foundation. In areas where rainfall is substantial, this stone or brick perimeter is extended well beyond the walls in order to mitigate the flow of water dripping from the roof that might otherwise undercut the foundation.

Figure 3.4. The stone podium beneath this open U-shaped *sanheyuan* extends beyond the drip line of the roof, thus leading water away from the lower walls. Shuangnushi *cun*, Wufeng *xiang*, Nanchong, Sichuan. [RGK photograph 1994.]

Classic quadrangle-shaped *siheyuan* and U-shaped *sanheyuan* courtyard-style houses are typically built on a podium that extends beyond the walls of the dwelling (Figure 3.4). At the drip line of the roof's overhang a gutter or drain may carry rainwater to a large storage vat or an exterior location beyond the walls. In some cases, the elevation of podiums beneath individual structures around the courtyard will vary so that the principal hall in the rear will be higher than either side or front halls, with the central courtyard sunken beneath all of the flanking structures (Figure 3.5). Seniority within an extended family is thus acknowledged by hierarchically distinct elevations that increase as one moves farther from the main gate. The foundation/podium that lies beneath and supports a Chinese dwelling thus customarily has a meaning that goes beyond mere utility, as will be shown further in several of the dwellings discussed in Chapters 4 and 5.

Stone foundations are found on small and large dwellings all over China, as can be seen in figures throughout this book. Usually battered and extending a meter or two above the tamped earth beneath, piled stones of various shapes and sizes are laid with and without mortar (Figures 3.6, 3.7, and 3.8). Foundations of this sort are stable enough to support tamped earth, adobe, or fired brick walls above. New construction today includes either deep footings dug into the soil, which are then filled with tightly placed stone and earth, or mortared stone walls raised above the ground (Figures 3.9 and 3.10). While rough stone collected from streambeds and hill slopes are the most common foundation materials, quarried stone is a qualitative improvement on more substantial dwellings (Figure 3.11).

Figure 3.5. Throughout the Ming and Qing dynasty courtyard units in Dingcun, the podium of the main structure is elevated above those of side halls. The drip line for each overhanging roof plane leads rainwater into the sunken courtyard. A stone slab is needed as a step from the courtyard to the podium of the three-*jian* rear hall. Dingcun, Xiangfen *xian*, Shanxi. [RGK photograph 1993.]

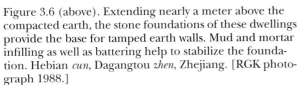

Figure 3.6 (above). Extending nearly a meter above the compacted earth, the stone foundations of these dwellings provide the base for tamped earth walls. Mud and mortar infilling as well as battering help to stabilize the foundation. Hebian *cun*, Dagangtou *zhen*, Zhejiang. [RGK photograph 1988.]

Figure 3.7 (top right). Boulders are carefully placed at the base of this Hakka fortresslike dwelling. Yanglinglou, Nanjing *xian*, Fujian. [RGK photograph 1990.]

Figure 3.8 (bottom right). Although the tamped earth walls above have begun to deteriorate, the massive stone foundation remains firm. Nanjing *xian*, Fujian. [RGK photograph 1990.]

Figure 3.9 (top left). In this recent construction, footing channels were dug into the ground and filled with stone of various sizes in order to create a firm and deep base for a structure that will be built on grade. Xishansi *cun*, Lingdong *xiang*, Lanxi *shi*, Zhejiang. [RGK photograph 1988.]

Figure 3.10 (top right). Raised a half-meter above ground level to protect the dwelling from heavy rains characteristic of this area of southeastern China, this mortared stone foundation also provides sufficient support for the heavy walls of fired brick around the outside as well as those used to form the inner walls. Near Guilin, Guangxi Zhuang Autonomous Region. [RGK photograph 1985.]

Figure 3.11 (bottom left). Quarried stones cut in various sizes were laid as the foundation beneath the brick walls of this large Hakka fortress. The raised aperture is a drain, leading water from the courtyard within to the walls outside. Yanyiwei, Yangcun, Longnan *xian*, Jiangxi. [RGK photograph 1993.]

Wood Framework Construction: Support without Enclosure

In enclosing and spanning the space found above a foundation/podium and beneath the roof, Chinese builders confront universal problems: "In the same way that the house responds to the physical stresses of climate—heat, cold, humidity, radiation, and light—it must respond structurally to the mechanical stresses—gravity, wind, rain, and snow" (Rapoport 1969, 104). The builders' responses to these problems have always been governed by the range of available materials as well as technical skills, the inherited craftsmanship derived from pragmatic trial and error over a long period of time.

The building form that links the foundation and the roof usually depends on either walls that bear the load or another mechanism of uplift for the upper exterior surface and its interior supporting structure. For traditional palaces, temples, and large residences, which epitomize Chinese architecture, walls were not normally load bearing. Instead, a wooden skeleton of structural pillars and beams was used to lift the roof. Employing an upright timber skeleton to support the roof is indeed a traditional Chinese structural solution, with walls treated as mere "curtains" without bearing any load. Such a structural system is a clear precursor of contemporary skyscraper construction, which is generally viewed as a modern innovation, with the mass carried by multistory steel framing and wrapping window-walls attached as "curtains." The non-load-bearing walls in Chinese building are added so as to either surround the framework as a continuous mass or infill between the wooden uprights. The various materials used in the construction of load-bearing and non-load-bearing walls will be discussed following the treatment of the wooden skeletal framework, which emerged so early in Chinese history and became a paramount characteristic of Chinese architecture throughout the country.

Wooden framework construction [*mugoujia jiegou* 木构架结构] is an axiomatic element of the Chinese architectural tradition and is well documented in monumental buildings at various scales. While there are different forms in which vertical pillars/columns and horizontal beams made of wood can be related, one can differentiate two basic wooden framework systems: *tailiang* 抬梁 [also called *liangzhu* 梁柱], or pillars and beams, and *chuandou* 穿斗 [also 穿逗], or pillars and transverse tie beams. The repertoire of elements utilizing these framing systems in fashioning the roof structures of temples and other types of monumental architecture is well described (Steinhardt 1984; Glahn 1981; Liang 1984, 11–12; Zhang 1985b, 57–166; Guo 1995).

Wood framework systems found in Chinese dwellings are generally simple, ranging from elementary pillar-and-beam construction to quite elaborate structural ensembles that clearly mimic those of temples and palaces. Whatever the form, timber structures are essentially assembled from standard modular parts rather than being "constructed" using building materials. In Figure 3.12, a Qing dynasty woodblock print contrasts a heavy

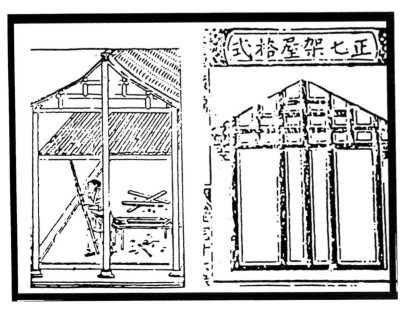

Figure 3.12. These traditional woodblock prints show two wood framing systems: pillars and beams [*tailiang*] (left) and pillars and transverse tie beams [*chuandou*] (right). [Source: Lu Ban jing. After Ruitenbeek 1993, I53, 16:3a.]

Figure 3.13 (above). Supporting a wooden pillar holding up a roof overhang, this simple stone base rests on a thin piece of square stone set into the earthen floor of this modest dwelling. A matching base along the wall is just beyond the pig's head. Shuitou *xiang*, Cangnan *xian*, Zhejiang. [RGK photograph 1988.]

Figure 3.14 (above). Both the carved stone column base and pedestal beneath are set on a raised stone podium. Zhiyan *xiang*, Lanxi *shi*, Zhejiang. [RGK photograph 1987.]

Figure 3.15 (above). A variety of stone column bases from various provinces (clockwise from top right): Zhuangshi *zhen*, Zhenhai *qu*, Ningbo *shi*, Zhejiang; Huailu *cun*, Huailu *xiang*, Dongyang *xian*, Zhejiang; Fenghuo *xiang*, Liquan *xian*, Shaanxi; Wangjia *dayuan*, Lingshi *xian*, Shanxi. [RGK photograph 1990.]

three-column *tailiang* framing system with the lighter seven-pillar *chuandou* frame. In no other feature of Chinese housing is the prosperity of the owner so clearly expressed than that of the wooden frame, since the cost of timber always far exceeds that of the earth required to compose the walls even when fired bricks are used. Besides these two principal framing systems, *tailiang* and *chuandou*, this section will also cover *ganlan*, so-called pile or stilt structures, which can be traced to China's prehistory and are still being built today not only by numerous minority nationalities in Yunnan, Guizhou, Guangxi, Hunan, and Sichuan but also by Han in the rugged areas of southeastern China.

Each of the pillars that forms a vertical element of either of the two wooden superstructure types is set on a pedestal [*zhuchu* 柱础 or *zhuzuo* 柱座] instead of being anchored in the tamped foundation. This attention to the base support helps reduce the transmission of moisture into the columns and makes it difficult for termites to move from the ground below into the vulnerable wood supports above. Pedestals range from rough-hewn stone blocks chamfered along the top edges to elaborately carved shapes—drums, octagons, and lotus (Figures 3.13, 3.14, and 3.15; for a selection of others, see Knapp 1989, 135-137). Throughout southern China, the beams, pillars, and pedestals permit a resonance to the structure while providing substantial stability and strength. In contrast to Japanese vernacular structures, most Chinese dwellings do not have ground sills to tie the columns together at the base and steady the structure (Kawashima 1986, 77-79). Still, Chinese dwellings without ground sills function well in areas of earthquakes, amid the "falling heavens and cracking earth." Horizontal movements are easily countered by flexible *chuandou* structures, since the pillars are not anchored to the ground and are thus able to move with the tremors rather than against them. Although the pillars might shift off the pedestals, or the walls themselves might fall, the integrity of the *mugoujia jiegou*, "wooden framework," would most likely be maintained. For any Chinese household, the framework represents the most costly and difficult building component to be replaced, while the intervening walls—whatever they are made of—could be reconstructed fairly easily from less costly local ma-terials. The many types of exterior walling—tamped earth, adobe brick, fired brick, stone, wooden logs or planks, bamboo, wattle and daub—that are employed with Chinese timber framing systems to enclose and protect interior space will be discussed later.

Tailiang *Framing System*

Tailiang framing is essentially trabeated or post-and-beam construction, such as that found in the West. Yet the Chinese form often differs significantly from Western structures in the treatment of the roof line. At its simplest, only a pair of pillars [*zhuzi* 柱子 or *zhu* 柱]—often only corner posts—support a beam [*liang* 梁], either laid perpendicular to the pillars or slightly inclined to create a shedlike roof with endwall-to-endwall running purlins. This simple dwelling type has a long history throughout northern China. In Jilin province in northeastern China, simple *tailiang* frames supported by posts of varying length, with the longest in the center and diminishing lengths toward the walls, have made possible the construction of barrel-shaped roofs, as seen in Figure 3.16. Where wood is not available, some of these dwellings actually lack corner pillars, and instead the single beam is seated on the front and back walls with the purlins extending through the surface of the walls (Zhang 1985b,

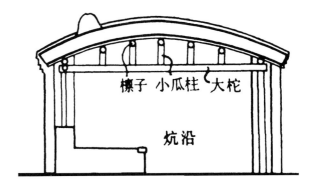

Figure 3.16. Two corner posts support a long beam or girder upon which five short posts of varying length are arrayed in a symmetrical pattern in order to support circular purlins that lift a barrel-shaped roof. Qingshanbao, Baicheng *xian*, Jilin. [Source: Zhang 1985a, 120.]

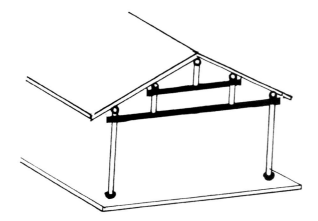

Figure 3.17. The simplest *tailiang* framework comprises pairs of corner pillars that each support a long beam upon which are raised two small posts that lift another beam on which is set a central crown king-post that holds a ridgepole. Purlins—horizontal longitudinal timbers—are set directly upon a beam above a pillar below. At the other end of the dwelling, the purlins rest on a matching setup. [Original drawing used with permission of Shen Dongqi.]

119-130). In general, the longer the beam, the less load it can carry. Doubling the length of a beam reduces its capacity to support weight by half. On the other hand, by doubling the cross section dimensions of a beam, its overall strength is quadrupled (Oliver 1987, 92).

Fully developed *tailiang* structures, however, are much more complex than the simple forms just de-

scribed. They usually rise to a central peak to produce either a symmetrical or asymmetrical double sloping roof. To accomplish this, two squat queen posts [*guazhu* 瓜柱, *duanzhu* 短柱, or *tongzhu* 童柱] are set symmetrically upon a beam and are used to lift one or two shorter beams that hold a final short post (Figures 3.17 and 3.18). At the apex, a longitudinal ridgepole [*jilin* 脊檩] defines the peak of the triangular roof. The ends of each beam provide seats for four additional transverse purlins [*lin* 檩, *lintiao* 檩条, or *hengtiao* 桁条] that lie parallel to the ridgepole and, with the ridgepole, define the slope of the roof. The details of *tailiang* structures vary from building to building, as seen in Figures 3.19 and 3.20, sometimes depending on the carpenter's decisions concerning available timber. A middle pillar running from the ground up to the ridgepole may be placed between the corner columns to support the weight of especially heavy beams or where beams of sufficient length are not available. In the last case, each of the cross beams is truncated and secured to the middle column. Cross beams may be finished to a rectangular shape or may retain their natural arcuate shape. When there is a curvature to the beam, it is generally placed in a downward concave position to utilize its greatest strength. Instead of placing squat posts between beams for support, slablike piers [*tuodun* 柁 礅], which accentuate the horizontality of the upper structure, are used by the Bai nationality in Yunnan

Figure 3.18. The components of a simple *tailiang* frame found in common three-*jian* northern Chinese dwellings are indicated on this drawing: *zhuzi* [pillar], *liang* [beam], *lin* [purlin], *jilin* [ridgepole]. Other components of dwellings that will be discussed later are also indicated.

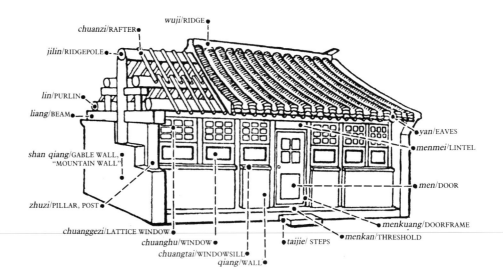

Figure 3.19. Because of the width and depth of this dwelling, several adjustments have been made to the *tailiang* framework: purlins rest directly on the brick gable walls and short beams have been tenoned into queen posts in order to support an additional set of purlins. Beijing area. [RGK photograph 1987.]

Figure 3.20. The massive timbers used in this structure include all common elements of a *tailiang* framework except that, instead of a single ridgepole, a pair of ridgepoles are used in order to make possible a slight roll to the crown of the roof. Xuanwumen Park, Beijing. [RGK photograph 1984.]

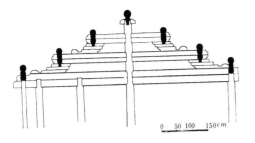

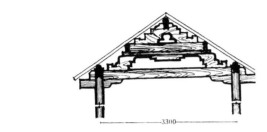

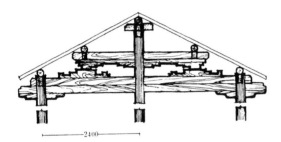

Figure 3.22 (above). Inclined rafters that are slight in diameter are laid across the purlins—from the ridgepole down to the top of the wall—to support the roof covering. Huairou *xian*, Beijing. [RGK photograph 1987.]

Figure 3.23 (below). In some northern structures, *tailiang* timbers are embedded within the gable endwall, providing a striking contrast of textures and colors. Lugouqiao area, Beijing. [RGK photograph 1983.]

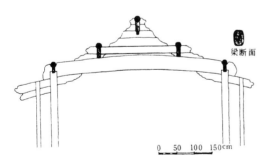

Figure 3.21. Among the Bai in Yunnan, both *tailiang* and *chuandou* frames are used. Ornamented slablike piers instead of squat queen posts are placed between some of the beams for support. The lateral shifting that is possible with these slablike piers dampens the effect of earthquake activity and high winds. Various locations in Yunnan. [Source: Yunnan sheng 1986, 41.]

province (Figure 3.21). The lateral shifting that is possible with slablike piers between beams seems to be an innovative response in areas of great earthquake activity and high winds (Yunnan sheng 1986, 39-41). Whatever the positioning of the purlins, short crosswise roof rafters, as seen in Figure 3.22, are laid across them in a sloping fashion in order to support the overlapping layers of roof tile. Sometimes a roof board is also needed atop the rafters to hold the tiles. When necessary for stability, pillars, beams, and posts can be embedded within the endwall, creating a juxtaposition of textures and colors (Figure 3.23).

The profiles of houses constructed throughout China using the *tailiang* system appear similar to those in the west that result from using truss systems. However, unlike the rigid roof truss which is based upon triangularly positioned segments, the cross section of the developed *tailiang* structure is a composition of only vertical and horizontal elements that may be flexibly positioned to introduce a degree of curvature into the roof line for functional and aesthetic reasons. In Zhejiang province, for example, reducing the height of the symmetrically paired queen posts in comparison to the single uppermost one creates a break in slope that introduces a pleasing curve to the profile while helping to facilitate the shedding of copious summer rainfall characteristic of the region. The substantial weight of the roof is indirectly carried to the pillars by the horizontal beams which span the space between. Chinese builders traditionally believed that the sturdiness of a structure was ensured by placing great weight on it; hence, the *tailiang* beams and purlins are often far heavier than would seem necessary to carry even the weight of unusually massive tile roofs.

Chuandou *Framing System*

The *chuandou* framing system, especially common throughout southern China, permits a much higher degree of roof curvature and differs from the *tailiang* system in three important ways: the pillars directly support the roof purlins; the number of pillars is greater; and the horizontal tie beam members [*chuanfang* 椽枋] are mortised directly into or tenoned through the pillars to form an interlocking ma-

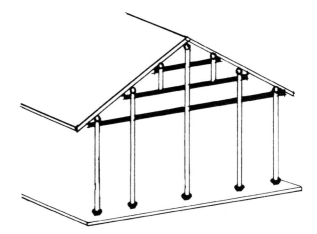

Figure 3.24. *Chuandou* frames differ from *tailiang* frames in three important ways: the pillars directly support the roof purlins; the number of pillars is greater; and the horizontal tie beam members or *chuanfang* are mortised directly into or tenoned through the multiple pillars to form an interlocked matrix that inhibits skewing of the frame. [Original drawing used with the permission of Shen Dongqi.]

trix that inhibits skewing of the relatively pliable frame (Figure 3.24). The weight of the roof is carried directly to the ground by the notched pillars upon which the roof purlins rest. The horizontal tie beam members serve only to stabilize the structural framework. In some cases, perhaps because of material shortages and the need to cut costs, short posts that do not reach the ground are seated on mortised *chuanfang*—some full length and others shorter—in order to support the purlins above (Figure 3.25). There are extraordinary variations in the forms that these long and short posts take. Modified *chuandou* frames built by the Bai nationality in Yunnan province have at least five vertical members running from the ground to a roof purlin. To counter the strong earthquakes in the Dali and Jianchuan areas, a large number of short beams are mortised and tenoned to the multiple pillars. Shortcomings of these frames with multiple pillars are the higher overall cost of the finished building and the fact that interior floor space is usually divided into relatively small units (Si 1992, 158).

Five pillars with only a pair of lateral tie beams is often sufficient for a *chuandou* framework, but one

can encounter structures with more than nine pillars and multiple linking tie beams. The distance between pillars is termed a *bu* 步 [a pace], and thus a five-pillar *chuandou* frame is called "a four pace structure" [*sibu chuandou* 四步穿斗] and a nine-pillar frame is "an eight pace structure" [*babu chuandou* 八步穿斗]. It is easy to vary basic patterns, depending on the quality of available timber and other needs. For example, short posts resting on tie beams may be added to support additional purlins or horizontal beams, which may support floor boards for a loft (Figure 3.26). While the lower wall of a two-story dwelling may be solid masonry, the upper story reaching to the roof may be a *chuandou* structure (Figure 3.27). Where a substantial eaves overhang is needed for protection from heavy rainfall, it is possible to extend tie beams of various lengths beyond the facade of a dwelling without needing a corbeled bracket (Figure 3.28). Greater depth of the eaves overhang to form a veranda necessitates a tier of pro-

Figure 3.25 (above). In the process of being demolished, the internal *chuandou* frame of this two-story structure with a loft is apparent. Five thin pillars run from the ground to the roof purlins and are assisted by six shorter posts that do not reach the ground but are instead tied to principal load-bearing pillars by mortised and tenoned tie beams. Lubu *cun*, Shuidong *xiang*, Lishui *xian*, Zhejiang. [RGK photograph 1988.]

Figure 3.26 (below). For additional support of the purlins in this wide dwelling, short posts have been tenoned into a cross timber that is braced from below. Each of the posts supports a roof purlin that is embedded in the endwall. The posts are mortised and tenoned to each other via the tie beams. Wooden pegs secure the connections. Yangmeiwan *cun*, Yanxi *xiang*, Jiande *xian*, Zhejiang. [RGK photograph 1987.]

Figure 3.27. It is clear that the five thin pillars rising along the lower wall of this two-story dwelling cannot support the heavy weight above and that the weight is being carried by a load-bearing wall, probably of adobe or fired brick upon which a strong girder has been raised. The upper story is clearly a *chuandou* framework, with five major pillars and eight minor ones and tie beams in the understory below the eaves. Cangpo *cun*, Gangtou *xiang*, Yongjia *xian*, Zhejiang. [RGK photograph 1990.]

jecting tie beams of different lengths. While a single projecting tie beam might extend 1 meter from the wall, a 3-meter-deep eaves overhang can be attained only if a tier of at least three tie beams is used. Projecting eaves formed in this way dictate at least one and sometimes as many as three additional purlins, all of which can be supported by struts and/or cantilevering rather than by peristyle pillars (Figure 3.29).

The spacing and elevation of each roof purlin, of course, is directly related to the progressively different heights of pillar sets. As a result, the relative positions of purlins define the roof's slope and make it possible to give it curvature. Where the relative position of the purlins remains fixed, the roof slope itself maintains a constant downward slope without a break. If the pitch is varied in a regular mathematical relationship from one purlin to another, the changing relative elevations institute a curved roof line. While manuals provided guidance for building the roofs of palaces and temples, local carpenters drew from their experience rather than the written word for the ratios that determine the pitch and curvature of a roof, termed "sloping and folding" [*juzhe* 举折]. Mnemonic verses committed to memory allowed traditional carpenters to recall readily a list of the varied structural components needed for a design and to recapitulate the necessary formulas for required sizes and shapes. In this fashion, carpenters were able to transmit effectively what knowledge and experience they had to their

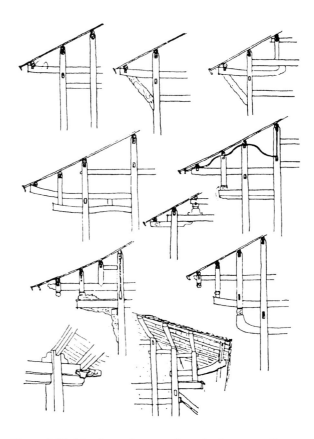

Figure 3.28. Mortise and tenon *chuandou* frames easily accommodate the extension necessary to project substantial eaves overhangs in areas of heavy rainfall. Sichuan. [Source: Liu Zhiping 1957, 295.]

Figure 3.29. The two-story main hall at Deng Xiaoping's birthplace includes a high and deep eaves projection that creates a broad veranda across the front of the dwelling. Between the outer column and that embedded in the wall of the facade, two short posts rise to provide support for additional purlins. The natural patina of the wooden columns, exterior wainscoat, and lattice windows contrast with the whitewashed infilling between the columns. Paifang *cun*, Xiexing *xiang*, Guang'an *xian*, Sichuan. [RGK photograph 1994.]

apprentices. The importance of memorized verses in guiding woodworking has been recently described by an American who had been apprenticed to Huizhou carpenters in Anhui province (Geisler 1995). As observed in the rural areas of Hong Kong, carpenters sometimes even sketch on the ground adjacent to a building site a full-scale patterned outline of an assembled building module composed of pillars, tie beams, and short posts. Klaas Ruitenbeek, drawing on information provided in various editions of the *Lu Ban jing*, provides numerous examples of roof-shaping rules, building verses, and rituals involved in the building of dwellings (1993, 62–76).

The larger number of full-length pillars and even truncated posts in *chuandou* versus *tailiang* structures is necessitated by the fact that each pillar is of small diameter, often only 20 to 30 centimeters. Further, the grooves and slots mortised into pillars in order to hold horizontal tie beams weaken each of the individual pierced pillars. With a larger number of pillars, the spacing of pillars for a *chuandou* frame is also closer together than is generally found in *tailiang* frames. It may be that *chuandou* framework evolved in response to a shortage of timber of sufficient size to construct dwellings according to the pillar-and-beam principles. Trees as young as five years old can be used for *chuandou* pillars, purlins, and tie beams, but it takes trees at least a generation old for pillars and beams of *tailiang* structures. Further, *chuandou*-type frames can be assembled even from pieces of timber of various sizes by cleverly jointing and fitting them together.

The construction of a dwelling using a *chuandou* framework is accomplished as a series of linked modules. Figure 3.30 shows the completed end of a large farmhouse in western Sichuan. Beneath the broad overhang of the gable end, seven sturdy pillars rise directly to the purlins. The three center pillars are tied together with a transverse tie beam high in the frame; four transverse tie beams beneath link up two additional pillars. On the other end of the rising dwelling, as seen in Figures 3.31 and 3.32, each of the *chuandou* skeletal upright panels stands alone yet is linked to others by longitudinal timber members in order to maintain a common depth, width, and height. Mor-

Figure 3.30. Viewed from the completed gable end, this large farmhouse has a *chuandou* framework comprising seven sturdy pillars that rise to support the roof purlins. Three center pillars are stabilized via a transverse tie beam high in the frame while four transverse tie beams beneath link the two additional pillars. Foothills of Emeishan, Sichuan. [RGK photograph 1984.]

tised, tenoned, and notched joinery is apparent. The abundance of large trees on the nearby hill slopes provides an extraordinary range of building materials for the carpenters to choose from. Timbers are dressed on the building site using a trestle sawhorse (Figures 3.33 and 3.34). Using a simple adze, the carpenter is able to dress the log to a smoothness that does not require planing and cut a needed notch in the end. The places that are to become either a mortise or tenon are marked with a carpenter's square, rule, and red or black chalk before being chiseled to shape. All of the elements of a *chuandou* segment are replicated as a module before being assembled into a unit on the ground. Each assembled segment is then raised to its final upright location, propped, and secured to adjacent segments by longitudinal cross members that are assembled and raised the same way. The raising of the ridgepole as well as some of the columns is an especially important phase in Chinese housebuilding, a subject discussed in *China's Living Houses* (Knapp 1999b, 41–48). The ridgepole and purlins connect all the vertical segments and thus play critical roles in stabilizing the "osseous" structure. Wooden or bamboo

Figure 3.31 (top left). Completed in a series of modular segments, each of the front-to-back and side-to-side building elements is tied together with wooden members. As this photograph demonstrates, the heavy tiled roof surface is completed well before the enclosing curtain walls are raised. Foothills of Emeishan, Sichuan. [RGK photograph 1984.]

Figure 3.32 (top right). Each of these four stepped pillars is notched at the top in order to provide a seat for a purlin. Three additional pillars toward the rear match the three in the front. Mortised, tenoned, and notched transverse tie beams stabilize the upright panel, which is linked to a matching panel with threaded longitudinal timbers. Foothills of Emeishan, Sichuan. [RGK photograph 1984.]

Figure 3.33 (above). With a timber set on a trestle sawhorse, the carpenter is dressing the log with an adze to a smoothness that does not require planing and is cutting a notch in the end. Foothills of Emeishan, Sichuan. [RGK photograph 1984.]

Figure 3.34 (left). Carefully measuring each of the longitudinal timber elements with a rule, the carpenters are also cutting exact notches into each of the ends. Foothills of Emeishan, Sichuan. [RGK photograph 1984.]

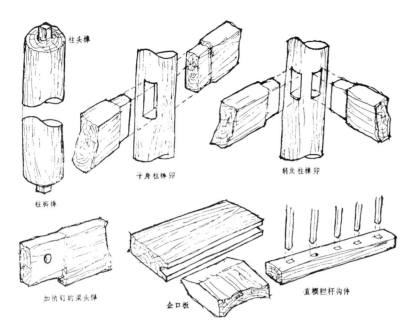

Figure 3.35. Mortise and tenon joinery has a history of at least seven thousand years in China. The earliest examples were discovered in the mid-1970s at the Hemudu neolithic site, Yuyao *xian*, Zhejiang. [Source: Yang 1980a, 70.]

roof rafters are laid crosswise between the purlins to serve as the base for layers of roof tiles. Supported by the wooden framework, the mass of the heavy roof helps anchor the structure even before the wall infilling is put into place.

Conventional traditional wooden frameworks—whether *tailiang* or *chuandou*, simple or complex—were rarely secured with metal fittings such as nails and clamps. *Tailiang* frames depend only on dead weight and wooden dowels and wedges to ensure a snug fit. The basic fitting together of the components of *chuandou* frames obviously is more elaborate, relying on precisely chiseled mortise and tenon [*maosun* 卯榫] connections—complex joinery that can be traced in China back to the neolithic period at the Hemudu neolithic site in Zhejiang province on the lower reaches of the Changjiang River. As depicted in Figure 3.35, the ancient techniques used to notch or mortise pillars holding tenon beams or purlins do not differ much from those seen today. In making doors, windows, and partition walls—considered like furniture making, or *xiaomu* 小木 [minor woodwork], compared with the carpentry of the building itself, *damu* 大木 [major woodwork]—carpenters could give full play to even somewhat eccentric joinery techniques. "Mortises," Rudolf Hommel observed

sixty years ago, "are an infatuation of the Chinese carpenter," a statement that is still valid today (1937, 299). *Chuandou* frames with infilled panels of tamped earth are discernible in many of the Han dynasty funerary models, or *mingqi*, that have been uncovered from tombs in Guangdong province.

Ganlan *Framing System*

Ganlan 干栏, stilt or pile dwellings, are associated with numerous minority nationalities in Yunnan, Guizhou, Guangxi, Hunan, and Sichuan, but they are also built by Han in rugged areas throughout southeastern China. The origins of this structural form have been traced through archaeological evidence to the middle reaches of the Yangzi River in the Chu 楚 region. Various ethnic minority groups throughout southwestern China, as will be discussed in Chapter 4, have a long history of constructing stilt dwellings even as they have also adopted *tailiang* and *chuandou* structures brought into the region over the centuries by Han settlers. While it is not always apparent whether a *tailiang* or *chuandou* dwelling is inhabited by one of the minority groups or by Han, there is no such doubt about a *ganlan* dwelling in southwestern China. Arguably, the most developed *ganlan*

Figure 3.36. Dai *zhulou* are among the best examples of *ganlan* stilt-type structures. Xishuangbanna, southwestern Yunnan. [Source: Yunnan sheng 1986, 238.]

dwellings are made of bamboo, so-called *zhulou* 竹楼 by the Dai, who are found principally along the border with Myanmar in the Xishuangbanna area of southwestern Yunnan (Figure 3.36). The Jingpo, De'ang, Blang, Pumi, Drung, Jino, Lisu, Nu, Bai, and Hani who live along the upland hill slopes of Yunnan province build in this style, although they also construct other structural forms (Yunnan sheng 1986; Wang and Chen 1993). Among the minority nationality groups in neighboring Guizhou and the Guangxi Zhuang Autonomous Region, there are substantial differences in dwelling styles, ranging from timbered *ganlan* to houses of adobe and brick built on grade. Storied *ganlan* dwellings are commonly built on hill slopes by Miao, Buyi/Bouyei, Zhuang, Dong, Yao, and Maonan. The Tujia, who live on the slopes of the Wuling Mountains in southeastern Hunan and western Hubei, and the Buyi/Bouyei, who live in southwestern Guizhou, build dwellings on piles as well as other structural forms of stone, adobe, and brick. The Shui, Mulam, Jing, and Gelo, who live dispersed among many of these groups, however, usually do not build *ganlan* dwellings but single-story adobe, bamboo, or stone houses directly on the ground (Guangxi minzu 1991).

Varying greatly in size, *ganlan* dwellings elevated above ground level are an ancient structural type in Yunnan and are crudely similar to those found in the neolithic excavations at Hemudu and other sites in the lower and middle Changjiang River areas. Raised approximately 2 meters above the ground on bamboo piles, which today are more likely timber piles, are a floor and side walls made of sawn timber or woven bamboo. The open space beneath the floor, used to coop domestic animals and for storage, traditionally also served as a cool, although somewhat dark, space for women to work. Raised above the ground in order to reduce the intrusion of insects, snakes, and wild animals as well as limit the impact of periodic mountain flooding, above-ground space is residential, with separate but unpartitioned spaces for daily living and sleeping. Although the walls are without windows, *zhulou* are built loosely so that air flows readily through them in order to reduce humidity, dissipate heat from outside, and evacuate heat and smoke from the inside fire pit cooking area. Dai structures are oriented so that different areas are shaded from the heat of the sun as the day progresses. In addition to the utilitarian open underpart and the enclosed living space, an encircling covered veranda and open balcony extend the available options for living and working. The floor of a *ganlan* dwelling serves as both an enclosing and a loading component of the structure. Traditionally the floor was made of split bamboo with many gaps and was intended to be somewhat flexible. Sawn planks are widely employed today. While the roof cover of *ganlan* dwellings was traditionally thatching and today is usually flat earthen tile, the form of the roof itself is commonly a relatively elaborate combined gable and hipped *xie-shan*-style roof (Yunnan sheng, 1986, 213–215).

Ganlan dwellings of the Dong nationality, who live in the rugged areas straddling the borders of Guangxi, Guizhou, and Hunan, provide fine examples of complicated and sophisticated structural carpentry. Timbered houses often overhang streams, where they are supported by columns set on stone blocks resting in the shallows. The versatility of *ganlan* structures that are built along hill slopes can be seen in Figures 3.37 and 3.38, where terracing allows complex configurations of timbers in a variety of stilt-building forms. Sometimes referred to as a "hanging pillar dwelling" [*diaozhu lou* 吊柱楼], "projecting footed dwelling" [*diaojiao lou* 吊脚楼], or a "half-landed dwelling" [*banbian lou* 半边楼], Dong tim-

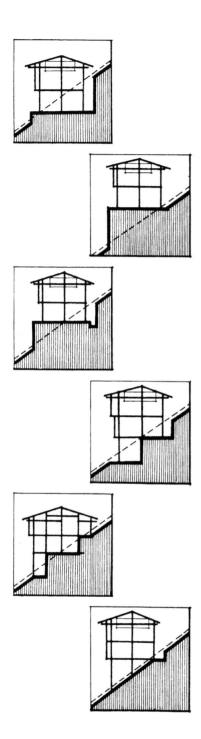

bered houses are lifted above ingenious scaffolding systems (Chen Shouxiang 1997).

Built on level ground, a Zhuang nationality *ganlan* dwelling includes stables for cattle and horses below and living space above (Figure 3.39). The living area is elevated 1.8 meters above the ground and includes a broad veranda across the front, a large common room, four bedrooms, and a large kitchen. With six sets of seven pillars and countless crossbeams, the upper portion is clearly a *chuandou* frame.

Adaptability of Wooden Frameworks in Han Dwellings

Earlier in this chapter it was demonstrated that there is greater standardization in the form and structure of northern dwellings than in southern dwellings.

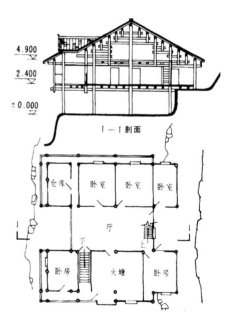

Figure 3.38. Resting on a narrow upper terrace, this dwelling is thrust out over another wider one and is supported by a set of four pillars that rise from the ground to the roof purlins. Shorter pillars and transverse tie beams tie the structure together. As shown in the lower plan, a hall is placed at the center of the dwelling and is surrounded by five bedrooms, a storage room in the left rear, and a kitchen along the front adjacent to the stairs. [Source: Guangxi minzu 1991, 63.]

Figure 3.37. The terracing of hill slopes creates a variety of building sites, making possible various *ganlan* structural forms for two- and three-story minority nationality dwellings in the northern portions of the Guangxi Zhuang Autonomous Region. [Source: Li 1990, 363.]

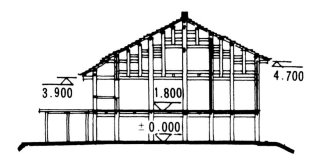

Figure 3.39. Elevated 1.8 meters above the level ground, the living area above includes a broad veranda, a large common room, four bedrooms, and a large kitchen. The ground level is used to stable cattle and horses. [Source: Guangxi minzu 1991, 19.]

This contrast, however, should not simply be seen as one of northern Han dwellings versus southern minority nationality dwellings, since even southern Han dwellings have been adapted well to irregular topography and varying building materials. Northern dwellings are usually longer than they are deep in order to create spaces that will be exposed to the winter sun yet will be protected from the summer sun (Figure 3.40). Built on level ground and utilizing relatively simple pillar and post *tailiang* frames, northern houses share similarities in form and structure even though they vary in how they are composed around open courtyard spaces. Yet, when *tailiang* structures are built in central and southern China, as can be seen in Figure 3.41, they do vary in depth according to the number of pillars and purlins.

However, in southern China, where no attempt is made to "capture" the sun at any season, Han and minority nationality dwellings often have substantial depths that equal or exceed their frontal width and frequently rise several levels above the ground. As a general rule, an increase in the depth of a dwelling is reflected also in increasing height. In a *chuandou* structure, extending the depth from a single to a double bay augments the potentially usable space beneath the rafters by a factor of 3. As shown in Figure 3.42 and as is apparent in a number of the plans and elevations seen earlier, this expansion creates an elevated open space for a loft [*gelou* 阁楼], which may be used for secure and safe storage as well as for sleeping. Ancillary lofts are usually set on joists that have been notched into the frames. Depth is fixed by the number of purlins and the pitch of the roof. With *chuandou* frames, the number of pillars increases to match the number of purlins, as the depth of the dwelling is increased. Throughout Anhui and Zhejiang provinces and in other areas of southern China, depths of Han dwellings often reach 10 meters, making it possible for interior space to be divided into front and back rooms, a layout rarely encountered in the north. Southern Han *chuandou* structures also permit building extensions, such as verandas and sheds under the eaves, the edges of which are supported by peristyle pillars.

The adaptability of the *chuandou* frame to hill slopes and riverbanks is seen clearly in the two- and three-story dwellings found in southern China, a number of which were discussed earlier. Here individual rooms often exceed 4 meters in height to improve

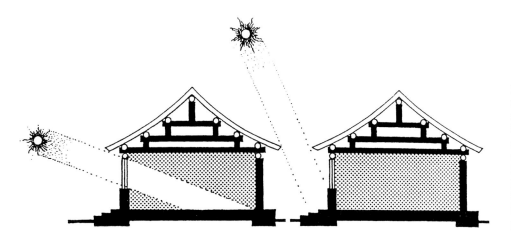

Figure 3.40. The depth of northern *tailiang* structures, when combined with broad windows across the front, allow the low winter sun to penetrate and offer passive solar heating while in summer the higher sun is unable to penetrate the dwelling.

Figure 3.41. Common *tailiang* framing systems used in Zhejiang in central China reveal the increasing depth that is possible when using long timber beams supplemented with additional wooden columns. In these *tailiang* structures, purlins rest upon beams instead of the pillars themselves, which is characteristic of *chuandou* frames. [Original drawing used with the permission of Shen Dongqi.]

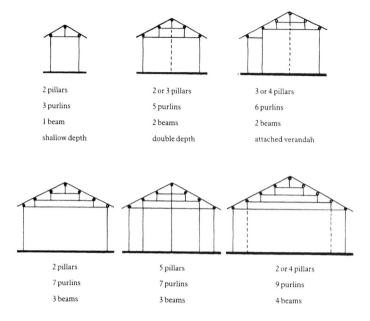

2 pillars	2 or 3 pillars	3 or 4 pillars
3 purlins	5 purlins	6 purlins
1 beam	2 beams	2 beams
shallow depth	double depth	attached verandah

2 pillars	5 pillars	2 or 4 pillars
7 purlins	7 purlins	9 purlins
3 beams	3 beams	4 beams

ventilation and compensate for critically limited building space. As seen in Figure 3.43, a center column of the *chuandou* frame of the dwelling may be nearly 10 meters in height from floor to ridgepole. With other relatively thin pillars also rising through the two stories and supporting a heavy superstructure of roof supports and tile, the overall building is top-heavy. In these cases, a jutting colonnaded veranda, perhaps even on both sides, is added usually to serve as a buttress (Figure 3.44). Stairways in such dwellings usually rise at a steep pitch, rarely break angles, and contribute to the stabilization of top-heavy dwellings. Constructing *chuandou* frameworks as a series of stepped units that link pillars and beams on different planes has made it possible for Han and nationality minority builders to utilize uneven terrain along hill slopes and along streambanks throughout southern China without compromising the integrity of their structures.

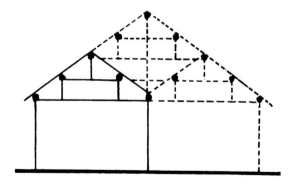

Figure 3.42. Doubling the depth of a dwelling, whether the structure is *tailiang* or *chuandou*, triples the space beneath the rafters and allows room for a loft or *gelou*, a common feature of many southern dwellings.

Non-Load-Bearing Curtain Walls

Once *tailiang*, *chuandou*, or *ganlan* wooden frameworks are completed, it is necessary to create walls that enclose and surround the space as well as protect and divide it. Walls of any type are in direct contact with the raw elements of the outside world and must withstand the scouring of wind and cycles of heat and cold, wet and dry, shrinking and expanding as well as shed rainwater. When a wooden framework supports the roof, walls are normally nonload-bearing and are constructed so as to completely encase the wooden skeleton or to simply fill the gaps between the pillars. In most cases, substantial load-bearing building materials, such as tamped earth, adobe brick, fired brick, stone, logs, or rubble of various sorts are employed to create such walls. Each of these building materials and forms will be discussed once the more fragile non-load-bearing walling is described. In southern China, non-load-bearing walling is often of vegetative origin and relatively weak. Except for sawn timber and bamboo, which are strong, grasses, grain stalks, and even cob walls mixed with sand and straw are usually not even capable of supporting any mass other than their own. Because infilling walls and those placed outside the timber framework are actually cur-

Figure 3.43. Reaching more than 8 meters from floor to ridgepole, this center column of a *chuandou* frame is a substantial and costly timber. Only the upper half of the timber column is visible. Near the bottom, floor joists have been added to make possible a second floor. Changle *cun*, Zhuge *xiang*, Lanxi *shi*, Zhejiang. [RGK photograph 1987.]

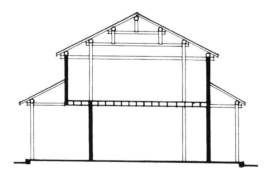

Figure 3.44. Many southern dwellings are relatively top-heavy so that jutting colonnaded verandas are sometimes added to both the front and back as a kind of buttress. [Original drawing used with the permission of Shen Dongqi.]

tain walls that serve only to enclose, they allow relative freedom in the placement of windows and doors.

Bamboo

Perhaps the most versatile of all plant materials used in building is bamboo. A multipurpose grass that grows rapidly and in many forms, bamboo has many good structural qualities: it is strong yet light, rigid yet pliant. Bamboo also has a few shortcomings: it is difficult to join, and it is vulnerable to splitting, rotting, and burning. Bamboo typically grows quickly by extending each of the sections between every pair of nodes. It is not unusual for some bamboo to grow as much as 30 centimeters a day. *Mao* bamboo 毛竹, an extraordinarily versatile building material that reaches 15 meters in length and 20 centimeters in diameter, is widely used in southeastern China. A shorter type, reaching only perhaps 10 meters, called *nan* bamboo 南竹, is exploited for building purposes from Sichuan through Hunan and Hubei in the middle reaches of the Yangzi River.

Bamboo can be easily cut, split, and worked with simple tools. Because the cylindrical shells come in different sizes, bamboo is an all-purpose building material that can be used for framing members and floor joists, for roof components such as rafters, purlins, and ridgepoles, and for a variety of walling forms. When split and with their inner diaphragms scooped out, half rounds of bamboo can be laid as a roof covering, either side by side with the open face up or overlapping as roof "tiles."

For walling, bamboo culms are split into thin splines and interlaced at a 90-degree angle to form a kind of woven lattice or lathing that occupies either all or part of the wall between pillars. This type of simple woven reed or finely split bamboo matting [*zhuxi* 竹席] is sufficient to screen the elements and provide a modicum of privacy for the poor as well as to enhance the ventilation of higher quality dwellings in humid areas of southern China (Figures 3.45, 3.46, and 3.47). Bamboo plaited curtain walls are often sealed with a mud or mud-and-lime plaster on both sides to make the wall impervious to air and water, as can be seen in Figures 3.48, 3.49, and 3.50. Plastered dwellings of this type, seen in Sichuan and Jiangxi es-

Figure 3.45. Among the most common bamboo walling used to fill the spaces between pillars and beams of *chuandou* frames are panels made of split bamboo culms. Each of the splines is interlaced at a 90-degree angle to form a woven lattice or lathing. Zhuangyuan area, Langzhong *shi*, Sichuan. [RGK photograph 1994.]

Figure 3.46. Split bamboo panels in various sizes and shapes are cut to fit the upper interpillar spaces where their light weight and porosity are advantageous. Wanyao *cun*, Zhuxi *xiang*, Cangnan *xian*. [RGK photograph 1988.]

Figure 3.47. The lower walls of this humble thatched dwelling are made of tamped earth, while the upper areas are of plaited bamboo splines. Zhuangyuan area, Langzhong *shi*, Sichuan. [RGK photograph 1994.]

Figure 3.48. Sealed first with a mud or mud-and-lime plaster before being whitewashed, each of the bamboo panels becomes impervious to air and moisture. Over time, spalling occurs, as portions break up into fragments that then fall from the wall. Cangpo *cun*, Gangtou *xiang*, Yongjia *xian*, Zhejiang. [RGK photograph 1990.]

Figure 3.49. The plaited bamboo panels on this structure are hung from the frame rather than placed between the members. Although covered with a whitewashed mud plaster, the protective coating is spalling off in areas that are exposed most often to the elements. Xikou *zhen*, Fenghua *xian*, Zhejiang. [RGK photograph 1987.]

Figure 3.50. When well maintained, the whitewashed nonstructural and cellular wall panels appear to some western visitors to be reminiscent of vernacular half-timbered dwellings in England and southern Germany. Luo Ruiqing's late nineteenth-century birthplace. Shuangnushi *cun*, Wufeng *xiang*, Nanchong *shi*, Sichuan. [RGK photograph 1994.]

Figure 3.51. Finely split bamboo is woven into broad bands to form artful patterns in this walling of a reconstructed Hani *ganlan* structure. Chinese Ethnic Culture Park, Beijing. [RGK photograph 1993.]

pecially, have been described as reminiscent of simple vernacular half-timbered dwellings in England and Germany (Spencer 1947, 262). Among the Hani and other minority nationalities in Yunnan, finely split bamboo is woven into artful bamboo panels and used as walling (Figure 3.51). Buck's survey of sixty years ago showed that nearly 30 percent of houses countrywide had woven plant walls of various types. Nearly two-thirds of all dwellings in the southwestern portions of the country were of plant origin (Buck 1937, 443). Even in moderately prosperous Taiwan, as recently as 1958, dwellings that included substantial amounts of bamboo, rather than adobe or fired brick, represented 40 percent of sampled rural dwellings (Kirby 1960, 149).

Despite its widespread and versatile use as a building material, however, bamboo rots easily, especially in contact with damp soil. It is also vulnerable to insects, such as termites, and is also highly inflammable. As a result, bamboo paneling is usually found in higher locations on a wall rather than nearer the ground. Although most stilt dwellings in southwestern China were once true *zhulou* [bamboo dwellings], today they are actually *mulou*, or "wood dwellings," instead. Because of the extensive range of tree species in the subtropics, the increasing familiarity with the strengths and weaknesses of each species, and the new knowledge of effective methods to season wood in order to forestall rotting, builders of all ethnic nationality groups are now able to select from a broad range of wood materials. Yet, even as wood has become the material of choice instead of bamboo, the use of the term "stilt bamboo house" continues in the Chinese literature to describe a housing type that is rarely being built today (Zhu 1992a, 98, 103–104).

Sorghum and Corn Stalks

Sorghum, also called *"kaoliang,"* and corn stalks, which have more of the weaknesses than the strengths of bamboo, also have been used as walling materials in China. In the northeast and north, poor peasants generally tied *kaoliang* and corn stalks closely together, stood them on end against an unfinished wall frame, and crudely plastered walls with mud as a kind of daub. Sometimes a second

Figure 3.52 (top left). In the forested areas of central and southern China, sawn timber is used to form the non-load-bearing walls of hillside dwellings, *diaojiao lou*, which are supported by wooden scaffoldlike understructures. Wanyao *cun*, Zhuxi *xiang*, Cangnan *xian*, Zhejiang. [RGK photograph 1988.]

Figure 3.53 (top right). Seen from below, the *ganlan* dwelling shown in Figure 3.52, includes the extensive use of sawn wood for flooring, walling, and ornamental carpentry. Wanyao *cun*, Zhuxi *xiang*, Cangnan *xian*, Zhejiang. [RGK photograph 1988.]

Figure 3.54 (bottom left). The *chuandou* structure of this row of shops employs only sawn timber between the pillars. Removable wooden panels are located in both the upper and lower stories. Wanyao *cun*, Zhuxi *xiang*, Cangnan *xian*, Zhejiang. [RGK photograph 1988.]

Figure 3.55 (bottom right). Although on the opposite side of Zhejiang province, this series of row houses is quite similar to the row of shops shown in Figure 3.54. Except for the columns, none of the sawn wood is load-bearing. Doors and window panels are either removable or can be swiveled. Shetou *cun*, Shifu *xiang*, Lanxi *shi*, Zhejiang. [RGK photograph 1987.]

layer of stalks was placed inside the house, which, after being plastered, would serve as insulation between the inside and outside walls (King 1927, 144). While commonly used by poor peasants in the past, huts of this type are rarely seen today.

Sawn Wood

Although sawn wood has never been widely used to form exterior walls in humble dwellings, it continues to be employed in structures throughout many of the mountainous areas of central and southern China, where timber is readily available (Figures 3.52, 3.53, 3.54, and 3.55). Moreover, the plain and unpretentious exterior walls surrounding northern courtyard-type or southern *tianjing*-type dwellings typically masquerade substantial wood, brick, and tile ornamentation found within the quadrangles. In inward-facing residences of the wealthy and even some of lesser

Figure 3.56. The inward-facing structures around *tianjing* in southern China usually have carved wooden door panels between the columns. Upper panels usually have lattice patterns, while the lower ones are solid. Langzhong *shi*, Sichuan. [RGK photograph 1994.]

Figure 3.57. Within the Wang family manor, some of the structures appear cavelike, with wooden frame facades holding the door and window panels. Carved ornamental wood is used lavishly throughout this complex. Jingshang *cun*, Lingshi *xian*, Shanxi. [RGK photograph 1993.]

Figure 3.58. Each of the four structures surrounding this narrow courtyard of the Cao family is composed of wooden lattice panels and doors set between the columns. The square pattern of the lattice panels is papered on the inside. Caojia manor, Taigu, Shanxi. [RGK photograph 1996.]

means, the facades facing open areas are usually completely of sawn lumber that has been fashioned by carpenters into exquisite wooden latticework door and window panels (Figures 3.56, 3.57, and 3.58). Because they do not need to be load-bearing, wood panels are usually light and sometimes intricately carved, especially in southern China. *Chuandou* wooden frameworks are usually found within Hakka and Hokkien fortresses in southwestern Fujian with wooden panel infilling used between the columns (Figure 3.59).

With most any type of curtain wall, no attempt is made to conceal the wooden framework. The natural lines of the wooden pillars and beams and the various infill between them that are employed throughout China in *tailiang*, *chuandou*, or *ganlan* structures are considered beautifying aspects of houses that convey a distinctive regional character. Vernacular dwellings in south central and southwestern China typically have white plaster walls of brick between the wooden parts of the *chuandou* frame. Horizontally mortised *chuanfang* in prosperous dwellings, temples, and clan halls frequently are seated completely within the walls, where their crescent shape, rich carving, and rhythmic rise are focal points of ornamentation. Perhaps because less skill is necessary in the raising curtain walls of bamboo and sawn wood, many are rather ordinary. On the other hand, even though less care can be paid to the sturdiness of such enclosing walls than is necessary with load-bearing walls, many are heavily ornamented and sometimes quite costly because of the artistry of the carpentry.

Solid Walls: Load-Bearing and Non-Load-Bearing

In addition to pliant plant materials, non-load-bearing curtain walls throughout China are constructed of solid materials such as earth, brick, and stone. Thus, they appear quite similar to load-bearing walls in terms of matter and means of construction, but they carry no load. Although one must clearly differentiate them in terms of their functions, non-load-bearing and load-bearing walls of these materials can be discussed together. The mass of a non-load-bear-

Figure 3.59. Although the exterior walls of Hakka and Hokkien fortresses are massive, the interiors are all made of wood. At whatever level, the space between the columns is filled with similar modular wooden open or closed panels. Hekeng *cun*, Shuyang *xiang*, Nanjing *xian*, Fujian. [RGK photograph 1990.]

Figure 3.60 (top). Continuous walls placed outside the pillars of the wooden framework are non-load-bearing, even when massive, and serve only to enclose.

Figure 3.62 (right). Viewed from inside the tamped wall, a solitary corner pillar rises from its stone base to lift the roof structure in conjunction with other pillars and transverse tie beams. Fenglin *cun*, Luci *xiang*, Tonglu *xian*, Zhejiang. [RGK photograph 1987.]

Figure 3.61 (bottom). These masons are raising a brick curtain wall around the outside of a load-bearing *chuandou* wooden framework that is supporting the roof structure. Changle *cun*, Zhuge *xiang*, Lanxi *shi*, Zhejiang. [RGK photograph 1987.]

ing wall indeed sometimes is even as great as that of a load-bearing wall when the wall is continuous and placed beyond the pillars (Figures 3.60, 3.61, and 3.62). Whether load-bearing or non-load-bearing, sturdy walls provide protection and insulation from cold and heat.

Solid, load-bearing walls have a long history of use in the construction of Chinese dwellings and are far more common even today than is generally acknowledged in studies of Chinese buildings. Sturdy walls that directly bear the weight of horizontal roofing timbers and other components, carrying the mass to the ground, are made of a variety of materials, which may be tamped, formed, or hewn. Tamped materials include mixtures of clay-textured soils, generically called *nitu* 泥土, and amalgams of other substances. The fundamental limitations of tamped walls gave rise to use of formed clay bricks—sun-dried and kiln-dried—which not only offered greater compression, enabling the direct support of increased dead loads, but also made possible more flexible building shapes. Hewn stone or timber may be shaped with tools into manageable units. Load-bearing walls are often made of combinations of these materials as well as naturally occurring solids, such as gathered rocks. Substantial, load-bearing walls were integral components of Qin and Han dynasty palaces, even as builders were beginning to successfully employ timber frameworks in order to span greater distances than had previously been feasible (Thorpe 1986, 368–369).

In time, economical and readily available building materials—tamped earthen segments, bricks of various types, logs, and stone—came to be widely used to fill the gaps *between* supporting columns and beams of fully developed wooden frameworks. Even though such walls might be massive and capable of substantial support, they were non-load-bearing curtain walls that provided a weather protective envelope for interior space.

Hangtu: *Tamped Earth Walls*

The tamping or pounding of clay soil or other materials into solid walls—called the *hangtu* 夯土, *zhuangtu* 桩土, and *banzhu* 版筑 method of construction—has been used for much of Chinese history in raising the walls of houses and other buildings, en-

closing compounds and open areas, and fortifying villages and cities. Even before China was unified in the third century B.C. under the Qin, high tamped earth walls were used to demarcate the borders of regional states. The emperor of Qin is credited with supervising the construction of an immense range of tamped earthen walls, precursor forms of what today is called China's "ten thousand *li*-long wall" [*wanli changcheng*], the legendary Great Wall.

Archaeological excavations, bronze mirror depictions, wall paintings, literary notes from periods that span Chinese history, and countless extant walls from China's dynastic past attest to the widespread application of *hangtu* techniques to building structures of all types. Impressive 9-meter high sections of a 7-kilometer-long wall that was raised between the eighteenth and twelfth centuries B.C. still survive at the Erligang archaeological site in Henan province. Chinese excavation reports continue to affirm the existence of tamped earth walls hitherto only known from early textual references.

Just as with tamped foundations, the *hangtu* technique continues to be employed even today in erecting solid, strong walls in virtually every province. Tamped earth walls are especially well documented in the less humid areas of northern China, where neither timber nor bamboo are readily available for building. The drier climate clearly helps preserve earthen walls from possible surface erosion from rain splash, a condition that is quite likely in areas of substantial rainfall throughout southern China. Nonetheless, tamped walls are even common in villages throughout south China where precipitation is abundant. In these areas, broad roof overhangs as well as plaster help mitigate the deterioration of the tamped earth walls. Arising out of an economy of scarcity, the simple *hangtu* method makes it possible for builders to tap the ubiquity of accessible clay soil and other earthen materials in order to create a product that is remarkably durable. This notion of depending on local resources, *jiudi qucai* 就地取材, persists today as a characteristic of vernacular construction throughout China. Because soil is an infinitely varying mixture of inorganic and organic ingredients, formed from complex soil-forming processes that exhibit the qualities of underlying rock and the impact of climate, it can be transformed

Figure 3.63. Seventeenth-century drawing of the tamped earth method of raising a wall. Walls of this type are called *hangtu* walls. [Source: *Er ya, juan* 2, 6b. After Needham 1971, 39.]

through compaction. Clay, the smallest soil particle, differs in color from place to place: it is black in the northeast, yellow or light brown in the loessial and alluvial areas of the north, and red in many areas of the southeast and southwest. In some areas, clay has been finely graded and sorted by the action of wind or water. In other areas, clay, silt, and sand are so integrated that they cannot be easily separated from one another. The myriad differences in soil properties and mixtures contribute to the apparent variety of tamped earth walling throughout the country. Some local soils are ideal for tamping, but they cannot be easily moved from one place to another. On the other hand, there are satisfactory soils for tamping everywhere in China—except perhaps the deserts. The ubiquity of suitable soils is an important consideration and has led to the fact that most earth used in the tamping of walls is removed directly from areas adjacent to the building site. There is no need to transport heavy building materials over any distance.

The *Shijing* 诗经 [Book of Songs], dating from the early Zhou dynasty, vividly portrays the *hangtu* wall building process (Waley 1937, 248-249):

Dead straight was the plumb line.
The planks were lashed to hold the earth;
. . . .
They tilted in the earth with a rattling,
They pounded it with a dull thud,
They beat the walls with a loud clang,
They pared and chiseled them with a faint *p'ing, p'ing;*
The hundred cubits all rose.

Known in the west as *pisé de terre,* or "rammed earth," the *hangtu* method generally involves piling various sorts of freshly dug earth [*shengtu* 生土] or mixtures involving less soil than other materials, such as for the *sanhetu* 三合土 method discussed later, into a slightly battered caisson before it is pounded firmly. Varying somewhat from place to place but similar to forms used elsewhere in the world, the confining framework form has changed little over time, as can be seen in comparing Figures 3.63 and 3.64. The ba-

Figure 3.64. Using a sloping frame like the one shown in Figure 3.63, the shuttering on each side is comprised of small-diameter round logs that leave the outer surface corrugated. Each of the men standing on the earth is holding a stone rammer. Xi'an area, Shaanxi. [RGK photograph 1984.]

Figure 3.65. With the corrugated wall behind him, this worker is using a rope to scrape accumulated earth from one of the shuttering poles in order to create a tight fit. A stone rammer with its wooden handle rests on the earth. Xi'an area, Shaanxi. [RGK photograph 1984.]

sic frame used throughout northern China is fundamentally a confining shutter mold consisting of a pair of H-shaped supports reaching perhaps 4 meters in height that are framed on their long sides by movable wooden poles lashed together with thin rope or held by dowels. The thin poles can be quickly and easily raised up the sloping supports, level by level, as the ramming takes place. Each of the poles must be periodically removed and cleaned of clinging earth (Figure 3.65). Throughout southern China, shuttering boards are used instead of timber poles in order to fashion a formwork frame that is a three-sided box without a cover or bottom. Rectangular formwork frames [*moban* 模版 or 模板, *qiangban* 墙版, *jiaban* 夾版, *qiangshai* 墙筛, and *qiangfang* 墙枋] vary in size from 1.3 to 2 meters long and 0.32 to 0.5 meters high and wide (Figures 3.66, 3.67, and 3.68). An end board with projecting tenons secured by wooden pegs holds the flanking boards together on one end. The other end is held by an easily manipulated crosspiece, which grips the bottom flanks of the frame and passes through the rising wall. An end clamp or a set of braces tightens the frame. A plumb line weighted with a stone serves as a simple level. Between the cavity of the timber or board shutters, freshly dug earth or a composite material—perhaps 10 centimeters thick at a time—is mixed with a small amount of broken grain stalks, paper, lime, and sometimes water or oil.

In order to increase the bearing strength of this earthen composition filling, it is pounded or tamped with a stone or wooden rammer until it is uniformly compacted with all air pockets eliminated. A typical rammer is made of heavy stone head, perhaps 25 centimeters wide, that is rounded on the bottom and attached to a projecting wooden rod. Sometimes a transverse handle is threaded through the top of the wooden rod to ease the lifting and dropping of the rammer. Some rammers in central China are made of a single piece of hardwood with a large wooden block carved into one end and a smaller one chiseled on the other end; in fact, they are similar to the pestles used to husk rice. These dual shapes enable the worker to better manipulate the soil into the corners of the frame.

A range of smaller tools of various sizes are used as well to insure that the soil mixture is firmly packed. The soil is compacted until it is sufficiently dense to support the tamping of other layers above it. Before the movable shutters of the frame are raised, leveled, clamped into place, to begin the process anew, a thin layer of bamboo strips or stone rubble may be laid to encourage drying of the earthen core. This sequence is repeated until the desired height is reached.

Wooden window and door frames may be set into the wall and once the wall is completed openings are carved out of the compacted soil. Because the wall is weakened by the opening of such voids, care is taken to limit their number and size.

Once the frame is removed, the wall is left with a rough, even corrugated, surface from the impression of the timber or moldboards. Depending on the weather, the full drying of the exterior surface may take months. Small holes left when the brace rods are dislodged are typically left in view, although some at-

Figure 3.66 (top). Used throughout southern China, a three-sided formwork box frame that is open on one end holds the soil mixture that is to be tamped. Shang-shan *cun*, Yangcunqiao *xiang*, Jiande *xian*, Zhejiang. [RGK photograph 1987.]

Figure 3.67 (left). Here one man adds the soil mixture while the other tamps it firmly. Shangshan *cun*, Yangcun-qiao *xiang*, Jiande *xian*, Zhejiang. [RGK photograph 1987.]

Figure 3.68 (bottom). A drawing prepared by the architect Liu Zhiping in the 1930s details the names and measurements of the box frame and the principal tools used in raising a tamped wall. [Liu 1957, 378.]

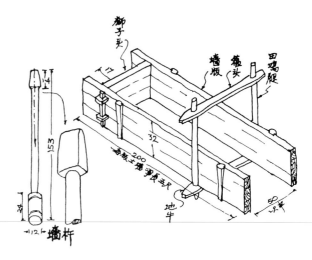

tempt is generally made to plug them (Figure 3.69). Boards typically leave smoother surfaces than poles, but in both cases the irregularities facilitate the adherence of a lime or a soil slurry plaster once the wall cures completely (Figure 3.70).

In Zhejiang, Jiangxi, Anhui, and Fujian provinces, while the walls of poorer houses may be of common soil, most other walls comprise only a small proportion of soil and depend upon greater amounts of more durable sand and lime to form a mortarlike composite (Figure 3.71). The availability of limestone or oyster shells, the need to overcome possible destruction from greater precipitation, and better economic conditions

have made such variants possible. Although differing in proportion from place to place, a common mixture is 60 percent fine sand, 30 percent lime, and 10 percent earth. Called *sanhetu* 三合土 [triple soils], this wall building method, utilizing only locally available resources mixed with a small amount of water and often a little gravel before being pounded firmly into the wooden frame, produces walls of strength akin to those formed using concrete. Sometimes corner braces of thin stone, serving as quoins, are placed within the rising wall to stabilize it. As seen in Figure 3.72, additional flat stones set at intervals within the wall, serve the same purpose. Rudolf Hommel, who chronicled building practices in China in the 1920s, noted that only thin bamboo rods were used to facilitate the drying of *hangtu* walls in Zhejiang. He claims to have suggested the use of flat stones, "foreign to Chinese practice," as an improvement over perishable bamboo (1937, 296), but this pattern has been observed in recent fieldwork in very old buildings as well. A course or two of bricks may then be added along the top of the

Figure 3.70. Although many tamped earth walls are left a tawny color without any coating, some are spread with a lime or a soil slurry plaster once the wall cures. White walls reflect, rather than absorb solar energy and thus contribute somewhat to limiting a heat buildup. Changle *cun*, Zhuge *xiang*, Lanxi *shi*, Zhejiang. [RGK photograph 1987.]

Figure 3.71. This high outer wall of six layers of tamped *sanhetu* was raised above a below-ground stone foundation, atop which six courses of layered stone have been placed. A tile coping caps the wall and the entry is framed with fired bricks. Shetou *cun*, Shifu *xiang*, Lanxi *shi*, Zhejiang. [RGK photograph 1987.]

Figure 3.72. In this decaying wall, small stones and other substances are sometimes placed within the rising wall to stabilize it as well as to facilitate the drying of the various layers. Moganshan, Jiaxing *xian*, Zhejiang. [RGK photograph 1983.]

Figure 3.73. Multistory fortified complexes come in various shapes and sizes and will be described in Chapter 5. So-called *yuanlou*, or "round buildings," are mixed among square, rectangular, and elliptical shapes. Most are constructed using tamped earth technologies and include a stone base as well as overhanging tile roof. Huanxinglou, Fujian. [RGK photograph 1990.]

Figure 3.74. A broad stone podium provides a stable foundation ring, and this is supplemented by a piled stone base before any tamping is carried out. Yongding *xian,* Fujian. [RGK photograph 1990.]

completed earthen or *sanhetu* load-bearing wall to retard rotting of the roof purlins, which are set directly on the wall, or embedded in the walls themselves.

In Heilongjiang province in northeastern China, a type of millet or rice stalk braid called *laha* 拉哈, perhaps an approximation of a Manchu word, is embedded in the black clay *hangtu* walls as reinforcement. Cut to a length of 60 to 80 centimeters, the braided *laha* is softened in water, mixed with mud, and then laid horizontally within the rising courses of 30-to-40-centimeters-thick tamped earth. *Laha* braids are hung in the interior to partition space and are used to cover roof boarding (Zhang 1985b, 55).

While it might appear that only straight walls could emerge from using shuttering boards with the *hangtu* technique, the remarkable and unique circular *yuan-lou* 圆楼 [round dwellings] found in Fujian and Guangdong prove otherwise. Described in Chapter 5 as veritable multistory fortifications, the number of stories and their varying dimensions attest to the flexibility of structural shapes and the capacity of Hakka builders to improvise (Figure 3.73). Ranging in diameter from 11 to 86 meters, some include an interior ring or two of structures. While they vary from two to five stories in height, over two-thirds are three stories, with an average of twenty related households living within. *Yuanlou* are mixed among other *tulou* "earthen dwellings," which include square, rectangular, and elliptical shapes, each similarly constructed though the geometrical requirements differ. Although the general means of raising walls with these structures is quite similar to that of smaller dwellings, the scale at which it takes place justifies a relatively detailed look at this remarkable form of *hangtu* building.

Prior to construction of Fujian fortresses, extreme care is taken in selecting and preparing a building site. (A detailed illustrated examination of this building process appears in Huang 1994b, 79-98). Critical measurements are made to determine the placement of the entry and the axis of the overall structure and to locate the midpoint and radius of the intended circular wall. Once an outline is sketched on the ground, efforts turn toward securing a firm base, first by digging out a foundation trench (*jicao* 基槽) to a depth of at least a meter. This trench may be tamped before being filled with tightly packed stone and rubble (Figure 3.74). On top of these substantial circular footings, a battered and mortared stone wall is raised to a height that is at least equal to the depth of the foundation trench. Unless the base of the footings is compacted well, the weight of the stone foundation and wall above will cause settling and cracking. A broad yet shallow bed is dug inside and outside the wall of the packed stone foundation trench. This concentric zone is first tamped firm, lined with stones, and filled with compacted earth to form a raised podium that will extend beyond the roofline of the wooden structure that will eventually be attached to the wall and raised above it.

Once the stone base is completed, the forming and pounding of the walls can begin. Throughout the "wall forming" [*xing qiang* 行墙] process, careful attention is paid to maintaining both a horizontal level and a slight battering to the outside surface of the rising wall. The interior side of the wall is kept perpendicular. At the base, tamped walls are typically 1 to 2 meters thick, depending on the projected height of the structure, and gradually diminishing to a thickness at the top of only one-half or two-thirds of that at ground level. Much care is expended on the

Figure 3.75. Wall ramming boards in southwestern Fujian are usually rectangular in shape and are similar to those used in Zhejiang. Both stone and wooden rammers are used as compacting tools in order to insure firm compaction in the high walls. Source: Huang 1994a, 82. [Original photograph used with the permission of *Han-sheng zazhi* and Huang Yung-sung.]

laying out of the first layer. It must be completed as a continuous ring before moving on to the next higher level. The stability of each level is a critical precondition for successfully completing the wall.

The arcuate walls are fashioned section by section using forming frames, locally called *qiangtuiban* 墙推板 or *qiangfang* 墙枋 [wall ramming boards], that are straight and not curved as one might expect. Each relatively short forming frame acts as a chord that can be flexibly adjusted to approximate a section of a circle as the circumference takes shape (Figure 3.75). The movable frame is first filled only a third full with a mixture of earth and other raw materials. This mixture, termed *sanhetu* and similar to that used in neighboring Zhejiang province, includes fine sand, lime, and soil in different ratios. In southwestern Fujian, the proportions vary significantly from village to village; some areas even use a greater proportion of soil than either sand or lime. The *sanhetu* mixture may be tamped dry or it may be moistened with the addition of water. Countering the supposition that the sand, lime, and soil are relatively cheap is the fact that it has been reported that some ten egg whites as well as 500 grams of both brown sugar and cooked glutinous rice are used per cubic meter of rising wall

in some areas in order to increase the durability of the composition (Lin and Lin 1992, 140). Bamboo slips are placed between the pounded levels, as in other areas of the south where tamping is employed, to help bond the tamped layers. In addition, small-diameter bamboo rods or pine saplings are sometimes

Figure 3.76. Small vents from the kitchen stoves inside are cut through the lower wall without substantially weakening it. Gaobei *cun*, Guzhu *xiang*, Yongding *xian*, Fujian. [RGK photograph 1990.]

laid lengthwise between tamped layers to connect the horizontally abutting units in a chainlike fashion. Depending on the size of the frame, teams of two or four workers utilize various rammers and other tools to spread the mixture, paying special attention to the corners, and to insure adequate and even compaction of the *sanhetu* mixture.

Large structures of this type take several seasons to complete, so much care must be expended to keep rain from falling on the rising wall over a considerable period of time. Once the shuttered frames are removed as each section of the wall is completed, careful attention is paid to filling in gaps, patching cracks, and finishing the surface. The first story of *tulou* always lacks exterior windows so as to maintain the strength of the base structure and, not incidentally, to heighten security. In some cases, however, small vents from the kitchen stoves will pierce the lower wall without weakening it (Figure 3.76). Upper-level windows, seen in Figure 3.73, are not usually staggered but are aligned one directly atop the other in order to minimize weaknesses in the wall. In some cases, the width of openings increases from lower to upper stories as the load to be carried decreases (Figure 3.77). The rather random placement of what appear to be new window openings in older structures throughout southwestern Fujian is evidence of recent decisions to meet new needs without considering possible structural consequences (Figure 3.78). Wooden or stone lintels are always placed atop the span of each narrow opening and vertical supports are sometimes added as well as a surround to the opening. Because a *tulou* is first of all a secure fortification, each without exception has only a single entry. Most entries are framed in granite stone, which can withstand the massive weight above.

To counteract the lateral thrust of the battered wall and to transform the edifice from mere fortification to inhabitable dwelling, a complex wooden structure that gives shape to rooms is built into the *hangtu* walls as

Figure 3.77. Along the wall of this square rammed *sanhetu* fortress structure built in 1806, windows are aligned one above the other, with the size of the openings increasing from bottom to top. Horizontal braces stabilize each of the openings. Yijinglou, Shangyang *cun*, Gaopi *xiang*, Yongding *xian*, Fujian. [Source: Mogi, Inaji, and Katayama 1991, 141.]

Figure 3.78. To increase ventilation, new window openings are sometimes cut into the thick lower walls of older structures. The rather random patterns apparently disregard the diminishing of structural stability. Nanjing *xian*, Fujian. [RGK photograph 1990.]

they are constructed (Figure 3.79). At an appropriate level representing a "floor," the ends of timber beams are laid atop the wall with the other ends set on a post-and-beam structure that is concentric with the encircling outer wall. Once these beams are all in place, an additional layer of tamped earth is added to the wall that effectively secures the timbers within it. As each new floor level is reached, another set of wooden timbers is set on top of the wall and linked to the rising wooden framework. This process continues until the desired height of the structure is reached. Even though no formal separate scaffold is used in raising walls to heights of as much as six stories, the interior wooden framework not only appears scaffoldlike, it actually functions as one. While the ultimate purpose of the timber framework is to create interior living space, the encircling interlocked wooden structure also clearly serves to buttress and reinforce the massive walls. The placement of load-bearing and non-load-bearing partition walls, floorboards, doors, windows, and stairs completes the creation of individual apartment units within. New rectangular structures, as seen in Figure 3.80, maintain the form and structure of the residential portions of fortresses. Throughout southwestern Fujian, the wooden frameworks are usually constructed of relatively thin pillars and transverse tie beams interlocked with mortises and tenons in a *chuandou* framing system. Both the wooden interior structure and the earthen or *sanhetu* encircling wall are always capped by a prominent tiled roof with generous exterior and interior overhangs, which keep all but blowing rain from hitting and wearing away the walls.

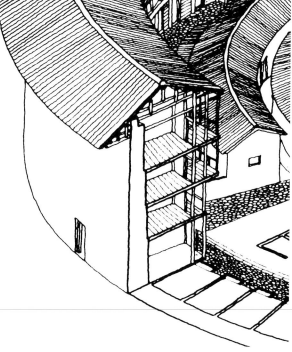

Figure 3.79. As the outer walls are being raised, a complex wooden framework is added to the inside. This structure shows four floors with an arcade overlooking the central circular courtyard, where single-story structures are found. The interior wooden framework buttresses the battered walls. Atop the elongated *chuandou* wooden framework is a prominent tiled roof with generous interior and exterior overhang. Chengqilou, Gaobei *cun*, Guzhu *xiang*, Yongding *xian*, Fujian. [Source: Adapted from Mogi, Inaji, and Katayama 1991, 194.]

With careful construction and ongoing mainte-nance, *tulou* will last for many decades, and some may endure for centuries. Most of the 698 *tulou* seen to-day in Nanjing *xian* in Fujian were built prior to 1949. More than a third were built prior to 1900, with a handful reputedly surviving since the thirteenth cen-tury. As large as *tulou* are and whatever their shape, they have proved remarkably resistant to ravages of gravity as well as periodic earthquakes, even though some spalling may occur on their outer surfaces.

Sun-Dried and Kiln-Dried Bricks

Sun-Dried Bricks. While possessing the economic ad-vantages and technical characteristics of tamped earth, sun-dried, or adobe, bricks [*tupi* 土坯, *zhuanpi* 砖坯, or *nipi* 泥坯] make possible greater flexibility in building form. Sun-dried clay bricks, actually clay slabs, have been excavated from houses in Henan province built as early as the Longshan period, ap-proximately 2500 B.C. The early use of adobe brick ap-pears to have been simply a supplement to *hangtu* wall construction, as such bricks were used primarily to build stairs, frame gateways, form interior partition walls, and constitute *kang*, the heatable beds found throughout northern China. Their earliest use typi-cally was for halls, pagodas, and other larger struc-tures before being more widely used in common construction. Parallel innovations in both tamping and adobe brick making techniques, however, appear to have been promoted more by the development of fortifications rather than ordinary buildings, espe-cially houses (Zhang 1985b, 51-52). Over time, the making of sun-dried bricks expanded as the simple tools for their manufacture became readily available.

The variability of local soil types has led inevitably to a range of methods for utilizing this most ubiqui-tous building material. Together with tamped earth walls, adobe bricks constituted nearly 50 percent of all farm buildings in China in the early 1930s, most of them in the north. At the same time, these materials in Zhejiang province, in the relatively prosperous rice- and tea-producing region of the south, constituted slightly more than 20 percent of farm building, the lowest percentage in the country (Buck 1937, 443). Even today, new houses in many villages throughout

Figure 3.80. New rectangular tamped earth structures are built in similar ways as the larger round and square fortress structures. Their high tamped earth walls are joined to a wooden framework that is connected to tall brick columns on the front of the building that reach upward to the trian-gular roof framework. Gaobei *cun*, Guzhu *xiang*, Yongding *xian*, Fujian. [RGK photograph 1990.]

rural China are being built at relatively low cost of adobe brick as well as tamped earth (Figures 3.81 and 3.82). Such use of earth, even where wood is relatively common, reflects uneven economic development and a persisting level of penury in pockets of rural China. When poorly formed, both adobe brick and tamped earth walls have been known to "melt down over night" from the washing of a heavy downpour or from flooding, according to observations in Sichuan prov-ince (Spencer 1947, 261). Whenever possible, an earthen wall traditionally has a simple stone or brick foundation, its most vulnerable location, where water

Figure 3.81. Recently constructed of adobe brick with a wooden *tailiang* frame, this massive two-story dwelling lacks windows on the back and sides. A wall across the middle of the facade stops short of the eaves to let in some light and air and complements the two low windows and upper ventilation ports. Fenghuo *xiang*, Liquan *xian*, Shaanxi. [RGK photograph 1991.]

Figure 3.82. The weighty adobe brick walls are mere curtain walls in this large dwelling, as a *chuandou* frame is lifting the roof structure. Guanxi *xiang*, Longnan *xian*, Jiangxi. [RGK photograph 1993.]

Figure 3.83. As with tamped earth walls, adobe brick walls are often covered with a mud plaster and whitewashed. Here much of the plaster has loosened, exposing the adobe bricks beneath. Guanxi *xiang*, Longnan *xian*, Jiangxi. [RGK photograph 1993.]

Figure 3.84. The seventeenth-century technical manual *Tiangong kaiwu* [The creations of nature and man] illustrates the use of wooden frames to mold bricks and a wire-strung bow to cut them evenly. [Source: Sung 1966, 139.]

might easily soften the lower portion and lead to the collapse of the house. News reports in recent years also underscore the vulnerability of earthen construction to earthquakes throughout China.

If compacted well and dried completely, adobe brick can become relatively stonelike and is suitable for heavy load-bearing walls or for infilling between columns or pillars of both *tailiang* and *chuandou* frames. If sun-dried bricks are sometimes improperly cured, they may become brittle, leading to failure of a wall. Freezing and thawing in northern and northeastern China also contribute to the weakening. Because the surfaces of adobe brick walls are subject to spalling and flaking due to natural deterioration and weathering, just as with tamped earth walls, they too are sometimes plastered with a mud slurry and whitewashed if resources permit (Figure 3.83). Tamped or molded earthen bricks—unlike fired bricks discussed later—can be reused in case of damage from flood or other causes by crushing and then reforming their remains.

Whether bricks are sun- or kiln-dried, they are similarly fashioned using relatively common techniques applied to locally available soils near a building site, just as is the case with *hangtu* walls. The seventeenth-century manual *Tiangong kaiwu* 天工开物 [The creations of nature and man] depicts techniques of brick manufacture still encountered throughout China today (Figure 3.84). Figure 3.85 illustrates this process of using nonreleasable molds with a wire cutter in western Shanxi.

Figure 3.85. Using techniques similar to those shown in Figure 3.84, workers in western Shanxi province place moistened loessial soil into a double nonreleasable mold (top left), smoothening it with the hands before trimming it with a bow-shaped wire cutter (top right). Two uniform bricks are dumped from the frame and left to cure in the April sun (bottom). Lishi *xian*, Shanxi. [Original photographs used with the permission of Arthur J. Van Alstyne 1982.]

Other simple and common practices of brick-making include packing earth in a mold and shaping it by hand or with the feet without the use of a bow or using a stone pestle to firmly compact the soil in a mold. The hand-shaping of bricks in Xinjiang, as seen in Figure 3.86, is accomplished using small rudimentary molds on level ground. Made of coal dust and soil, these thin bricks are of relatively poor quality and are used only for low walls and floors.

The pounding of earth in releasable molds using hand rammers—similar to the *hangtu* wall building technique described earlier—produces strong bricks with improved compression (Figure 3.87). Bricks formed in this manner in Gansu province are produced in the fall at a time when the heat is less intense, thus allowing the bricks to cure slowly. The

Figure 3.86. Thin bricks of coal dust and mud are formed in small molds. The hand-shaping of bricks in Xinjiang is accomplished with small rudimentary molds on level ground. The poor quality thin brick product is typically used only for low walls, foundations, and floors throughout northwestern China. Xinjiang Uygur Autonomous Region. [RGK photograph 1985.]

Figure 3.87. Similar to the tamping of earthen walls, bricks can be formed in releasable molds using the pressure of the feet or stone hand rammers. West of Lanzhou, Gansu. [RGK photograph 1985.]

soil used is either completely dry or slightly moistened, conditions which contribute to variations in sizes. Bricks made from moistened soil are usually thicker and broader but shorter than those made from completely dry earth. All bricks are stacked for curing and usually capped with a sloping cover of straw to keep them from getting wet from passing showers. Once stacked to form a wall using one or more bonding patterns, adobe bricks are almost always coated with a slurry of soil and/or lime. In Jilin province, bluish-white alkaline earth that forms on the surface in the spring is collected and especially prized for its durability. The clumps of concentrated alkaline soil are both pounded into bricks and used for waterproofing of the roof (Zhang 1985b, 55).

Sometimes adobe bricks are simply cut out of the fields. In Jilin province, when the water recedes from low-lying marshy areas, square segments, including roots and other vegetative matter, are cut. The roots of grasses, which are naturally woven into a dense web, are believed to impart strength to the bricks once they are dry (Zhang 1985a, 5-6). Paddy fields also serve as borrow pits for adobe bricks in many areas of southern China, from Sichuan eastward to Guangdong and northward to Jiangxi. In the Guangxi Zhuang Autonomous Region, as shown in Figure 3.88, brick-making from paddy fields not only produces a necessary building material but provides a means to correct the natural siltation of fields. Considerable silt is carried in the water that inundates paddy fields in the life-cycle of rice growing. As a result, eventually the depth of the alluvial silt elevates the bottom of the paddy to unacceptable levels. If the silt is not removed the surrounding embankments would have to be raised in order to confine water to an acceptable depth. Such an adjustment is necessary every ten years or so. Carried out usually during the fall, a newly harvested rice field is plowed, harrowed, and compressed with a stone roller. Then the field is either flooded from canals or allowed to become puddled from a heavy rain. Once evaporation has reduced the moisture content of the soil to a dense yet

Figure 3.88. Bricks cut from paddy fields not only produce a necessary building material but provide a means to correct the natural siltation of fields. Baisha *xiang*, Lipu *xian*, Guangxi Zhuang Autonomous Region. [RGK photograph 1984.]

viscous consistency, brick-size sections of earth, approximately 15 centimeters thick, are sliced and lifted from the floor of the field with a spade. Here, too, the roots of paddy rice serve as a natural reinforcement within the adobe brick. Although in some areas, the roughly cut bricks are simply stacked to dry, in Guangxi each segment of paddy floor is placed into a simple wooden and bamboo frame in which the soil is then tamped with the feet to a common shape. Once the brick is molded, the bamboo handle of the shaping frame is lifted and the brick is allowed to dry *in situ* adjacent to other bricks for several days. After restacking and curing for several weeks under a straw cap, the adobe bricks are ready for use. Unlike the heat of summer, which would dry the bricks too quickly and cause cracks and brittleness, the less intense sun of autumn assures a more satisfactory product. Peasants in the past were aware of the corresponding need to address the reduced fertility of fields as a result of these brick-making practices, which removed nutrient-rich alluvial silt from the paddy.

Adobe brick exterior walls are usually left bare with a rather unfinished natural appearance in many of the semiarid areas of northern China. The resulting tawny look presents a soft brown tone that links the genuine earth beneath to the fabricated building above. When mud and lime plasters of various types are applied, as discussed earlier, they too are normally left in a natural earthen shade throughout the north and in many areas of the south. Generally in southern China, however, the mud plaster applied to the exterior walls is usually whitewashed in order to function as a thermal regulator by reflecting the sun.

Kiln-Dried Bricks. When the firing of bricks in kilns began is not clear, but the practice was common by the Han dynasty in the third century B.C. It was not until the Ming dynasty in the fourteenth century, however, that fired bricks became widely used as they became relatively inexpensive. Kiln-dried bricks [*zhuan* 砖 or *zhuantou* 砖头] were clearly a qualitative improvement over inferior adobe in terms of durability, imperviousness to water, and fire-resistance, but they have always been significantly more costly due to the extraordinary amounts of fuel necessary to bake them. The firing of bricks at temperatures that reach 1150°C materially changes the raw soil that constitutes them, as sintering and partial vitrification take place. As a result, once baked, bricks cannot be pulverized, reconstituted, and reused as is the case with adobe bricks. Throughout China, fired bricks vary significantly in color as a consequence of the differ-

ent types of soils used to make them as well as the techniques employed in firing and cooling them.

Chinese architectural historians view the early mastery and refinement of pottery-making in the kiln as the precursor of similar specialized craft technologies used to strengthen earthen bricks by firing them (Zhang 1985b, 167). It was a long, continuous, and convoluted passage from the first kiln-baked clay vessels produced during the neolithic period some 6,000 years ago through the experimentations with different types of fired bricks. The firing of bricks reached a first peak during the Han dynasty, and then in the Ming period there was an extraordinarily wide use of fired brick in construction of all types. Both art and craft ebbed and flowed in their development, yet their evolution was one of continuous improvement. By the early Western Han period, when true bricks were being used in dwelling construction, the length, width, and thickness of bricks were standardized, with the length being twice the width and the thickness one-fourth the width (Wang 1982, 148). While archaeological excavations and extant monuments seen today give clear evidence of the improvements in brick manufacture, brick-laying techniques, and the building of exceptional structures such as pagodas, beamless halls, and barrel arches as well as underground tombs, they only hint at the use of fired bricks in house construction. Rather than attempting to speculate via chronicling the limited evidence that fired bricks were used in common dwellings in the past, this section will focus instead on practices and forms observable today that are likely similar to those of recent past centuries.

Although the making of fired bricks has a history of at least two millennia in China, only about 20 percent of all rural dwellings—17 percent in the northern wheat growing region and 23 percent in the southern rice region—surveyed in the early 1930s had brick walls. Kiln-fired bricks were more common in areas of greater prosperity, especially in the fertile valleys and lowlands of southern China rather than in the hills, and more than twice as likely to be found where the farmstead was large rather than small. In many areas, such as in the southwest and in the inner Asian frontier areas, they were indeed rare, representing only 4–5 percent of farm structures (Buck 1937, 443). Even in relatively prosperous Taiwan only slightly more than

Figure 3.89. *Zhuanyao*, or "brick kilns," vary from place to place, although they share many common characteristics. Most are dug into the ground, lined with stone blocks, covered with earth and old bricks, and entered either from the front or above. Near Guilin, Guangxi Zhuang Autonomous Region. [RGK photograph 1985.]

10 percent of sampled houses had kiln brick walls in 1952 (Raper 1953, 125). No similar survey reveals the percentage of fired bricks found in town and city dwellings, but it is reasonable to believe that the proportions were much greater than those in the countryside.

As China's house-building boom took off beginning in 1979, there was an unprecedented use of fired brick that allows us to observe traditional production and construction practices, many of which were discussed by Hommel in the 1920s. The initial forming of bricks to be fired is generally similar to that discussed earlier for adobe brick, but the full process demands higher levels of skill and technological know-how. Air drying, for example, must be carefully monitored over a period of days or even weeks and is dependent on ambient humidity levels. Once properly air dried, bricks must be placed in a kiln for firing. Although kilns vary in form from place to place, they all share common characteristics. Most are dug into the earth near where the bricks are formed and are faced with rough stone. Bricks to be fired are carried into the kiln through a ground-level opening or through an opening in the top (Figure 3.89). Once filled with bricks and fuel, the kiln is sealed with only a small draft hole left to regulate the fire. Kiln fuel varies from place to place and includes coal, charcoal, grain stalks, and branches of trees. The fire, which builds slowly, is normally maintained for at least twenty-four hours at a high temperature, after which the bricks are allowed to cool over a period of at least a week. As the release of steam from the top diminishes, this is clear evidence of moisture loss from the stacked bricks within the kiln. Although the color of bricks normally reflects the soil from which they are made, pouring water on them while they are cooling in the kiln produces gray bricks, which are preferred in some areas of northern China.

Bonds Used in Brickwork Walls. Brickwork, the arrangement of individual bricks across a wall's face that strengthens their interconnection by insuring that there are no coincident vertical joints, varies widely throughout China, as it does elsewhere in the world. Many Chinese brick bonds, however, are familiar to those living in Europe and North America, where local conditions and experience brought about a multiplicity of similar brick bonding styles. Load-bearing walls throughout China are normally built with care by masons who stagger the vertical mortared joints in order to strengthen the bond. On the other hand, bricks are sometimes carelessly laid to give form to non-load-bearing brick curtain walls. As elsewhere in the world, the tools of Chinese masons are simple. These include not only the common trowel and hammer but also a unique pointing device used to straighten joints that is cleaverlike. Hommel includes photographs of the common bricklaying tools of Chinese masons as well as a description of their uses in the early part of the century (1937, 278–293).

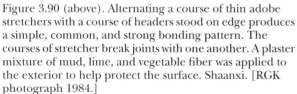

Figure 3.90 (above). Alternating a course of thin adobe stretchers with a course of headers stood on edge produces a simple, common, and strong bonding pattern. The courses of stretcher break joints with one another. A plaster mixture of mud, lime, and vegetable fiber was applied to the exterior to help protect the surface. Shaanxi. [RGK photograph 1984.]

Figure 3.91 (top right). The simple brickwork pattern of thin adobe brick described in Figure 3.90 is seen here on the gable end of a small dwelling. The wall is set on a fired brick foundation, and the roof is capped with fired clay tiles. Xi'an area, Shaanxi. [RGK photograph 1984.]

Figure 3.92 (bottom right). The adobe brick walls of this new dwelling appear to be the work of an amateur merely piling up brick segments with only minimal attention paid to breaking joints and maintaining levels. Some of the walls are load-bearing, as is indicated by the wooden elements laid between the courses of bricks. Southern Jiangxi. [RGK photograph 1993.]

There is substantial diversity of adobe and fired-brick bonding patterns [*qizhuanfa* 砌砖法 or *qizhuan-shi* 砌砖式] throughout China. The "bonding" of bricks involves arranging the stretchers (the long dimension), headers (the narrow dimension), and faces (the maximum areal dimension) in various ways. One of the simpler common bonding patterns involves thin adobe bricks with a course of horizontal stretchers alternating with a course of vertical headers (Figures 3.90 and 3.91). Described as having "no parallel in the Western world," this simple brickwork pattern is quite rigid and is used for foundation walls in common dwellings (Hommel 1937, 287). Other bonds appear to be nothing more than an amateur's piling up of brick pieces, as seen in the new adobe dwelling pictured in Figure 3.92, which is hardly the accomplished handiwork of a skilled bricklayer. Another common bonding pattern, as seen in Figure 3.93, is composed of rows of horizontal stretchers with staggered vertical joints. Also shown in Figure 3.93 is the brickwork bonding pattern of the low wall jutting out from the dwelling, known in the west as "English bond," with its alternating courses of headers and stretchers. Other brickwork bonding patterns are seen in dwellings throughout the book, although, unfortunately, some are either partially or completely hidden behind plastered walls. By varying the the thickness of the mortared joints, the size of the bricks, and contrasting the horizontal and vertical elements, bonding patterns become as much a functional building element as an inventive decorative one.

A particularly noteworthy brickwork pattern found throughout China is the box bond, which is used to create hollow-core exterior walls [*kongdou qiang* [空斗墙 or *douzi qiang* 斗子墙] throughout southern China (Figures 3.94, 3.95, and 3.96). Box bonds utilize fired bricks either of a single size or sometimes two different sizes. In both cases, the bricks are rather thin, often 24 by 12 by 6 centimeters. The base layer is begun either by laying two parallel courses of stretchers with a gap between them or by placing headers side by side in a row the length of the wall. Then the box bond pattern is created by alternating headers with stretchers laid on edge so that the full face of the brick is exposed on the outsides of the wall. The headers are set transverse to and

Figure 3.93. Two different brickwork bonds are seen here. Built of fired brick, the gable wall is composed of stretchers—courses with staggered tight joints. The low courtyard wall extending forward from the dwelling, however, is composed of an "English bond"—alternating courses of headers and stretchers. Huairou *xian*, Beijing. [RGK photograph 1987.]

through the rising wall while the stretchers are laid flush with the faces of the wall to form a series of boxes on the inside of the wall. In the most costly and substantial of box bonds, a "cap" [*gai* 盖, *ding* 丁, or *wo* 卧] to match the base is laid to enclose the "box" [*dou* 斗 or *shun* 顺]. More frequently, additional headers and stretchers on edge are raised above a *gai*, each layer breaking bond with the layer above and below, until finally a capping *gai* is added. *Sandou yigai* 三斗一盖 [three boxes, one cap] and *wudou yigai* 五斗一盖 [five boxes, one cap] are common in An-

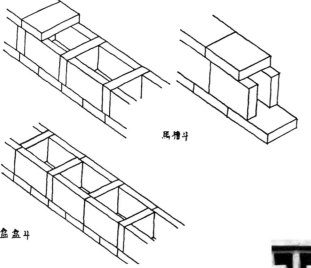

馬槽斗

高矮斗

盆盆斗

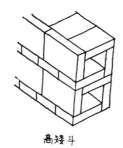

Figure 3.94. Hollow-core exterior walls, called *kongdou qiang* or *douzi qiang*, are found throughout southern China. The brickwork varies in the sizes of the thin bricks and how the thin bricks are bonded. All such walls, though, incorporate square or rectangular voids, or "boxes," similar to a traditional Chinese volumetric measure. This drawing by Liu Zhiping shows four different patterns of the box bond. [Source: Liu 1957, 377.]

Figure 3.95. As individual bricks in a *kongdou* wall become dislodged, they can be repaired relatively easily if replacement bricks are available. Here, the worker is pounding earth into some of the open cavities between the thin bricks in order to strengthen the wall. Bihu *zhen*, Lishui *xian*, Zhejiang. [RGK photograph 1987.]

Figure 3.96. Box bond patterns vary depending on the placement of headers and stretchers. Top left, Longnan *xian*, Jiangxi; top right, Nanjing *xian*, Fujian; bottom right, Xiaoshan *xian*, Zhejiang. [RGK photographs 1993, 1990, 1987.]

Figure 3.97. With increased resources, a village household has built a fired brick dwelling (bottom) that is essentially a duplicate of their adobe house (top). Guilin area, Guangxi Zhuang Autonomous Region. [RGK photographs 1984.]

raised *hangtu*, or tamped earth walls, instead. In recent centuries and even today, tamped earth and adobe bricks have been the materials used primarily by poorer households, while kiln-dried bricks are preferred by those who could afford them. As resources permitted, Chinese peasants have been known to replace portions of a tamped earth wall with adobe bricks and even later substitute fired brick for adobe piece-by-piece in their search for strength, durability, and resistance to water. This resourcefulness can be observed even today, as rural households stockpile fired bricks for future renovation projects. Even as building form remains the same, as seen in the two dwellings shown in Figure 3.97, an older adobe structure is replaced by a new brick house nearby. In some area, walls of mixed materials—*hangtu*, adobe brick, and fired brick—are believed to create a stronger wall than would be possible with any one material. In the central basin of Shaanxi province, for example, the first two-fifths to three-fifths of a wall continues to be built first using the *hangtu* method, followed by three or four courses of adobe bricks, then a layer of gray fired bricks, followed by another three or four courses of adobe bricks. A straw and mud plaster [*maicaoni* 麦草泥] is applied to conceal the contrasts in the materials (Zhang and Liu, 1983, 58). The relatively recent introduction of prestressed concrete is adding additional possibilities.

Stone

Except in the construction of foundations and podiums beneath buildings, stone—either as naturally formed rocks or shaped into slabs—is not used in China as a building material to the degree that matches its availability. Although stone and rock dwellings principally are seen only in relatively barren mountainous areas where soil suitable for tamp-

hui and Zhejiang provinces, though less substantial dwellings have seven or more *dou* in odd multiples. The air space within the walls offers only limited insulation from the summer heat. Because the walls are closed top and bottom, the heated air cannot be evacuated unless, by chance, poor construction or deterioration has opened a flue. Although the plastering of brick walls is common in order to complete the finish of a rough wall, higher quality brickwork is often left exposed to reveal the technical skill and artistry of the masons. (An extensive treatment of the history of Chinese masonry construction is found in Zhang 1985b, 166–213 and Zhang 1986b, 176–213.)

Employing either adobe brick or fired brick has always represented a tangible statement that a household had greater resources than a neighbor who

Figure 3.98 (top left). This lower wall is composed of rocks in various shapes and sizes that were collected from nearby stream beds. The upper wall is a *kongdou* hollow-core wall, once plastered but now visible because of rain wash. The ventilation window is made of bricks and represents the Chinese character for longevity. Furong *cun*, Yantou *xiang*, Yongjia *xian*, Zhejiang. [RGK photograph 1988.]

Figure 3.99 (top right). Between the stone boulder foundation and the red fired brick *kongdou* wall above are nearly thirty courses of stone fragments that are held together with layers of mortar. Changle *cun*, Zhuge *xiang*, Lanxi *shi*, Zhejiang. [RGK photograph 1987.]

Figure 3.100 (bottom right). The lower portions of this earthen wall are tamped and plastered, while the upper section is comprised principally of small courses of stones with some fired bricks among them. Guanxi *xiang*, Longnan *xian*, Jiangxi. [RGK photograph 1993.]

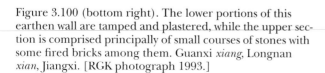

Figure 3.101. This multistory *weizi* fortress is framed in brick with a facing of stone and mortar infilling. On the interior is a wooden framework that serves to buttress the high walls. Shixing *xian*, Jiangxi. [RGK photograph 1993.]

Figure 3.102. Stone and thatched dwellings have always been common in fishing villages along the coasts of Taiwan, Shandong, Fujian, and Zhejiang. Fulong, Yilan *xian*, Taiwan. [RGK photograph 1963.]

ing or making bricks is limited because of a shallow depth to bedrock or the granular composition of the particles, some limited use can be observed in more prosperous areas and throughout China. Among the areas where houses are commonly made of stone are northern Hebei, western Shanxi, northeastern Shaanxi, western Liaodong, northern Guangxi, southwestern Guizhou, western Sichuan, western Yunnan, Tibet, Qinghai, and along the coastal areas of Taiwan, Fujian, Shandong, and Zhejiang. In any of these places, any stone structure represents a valid index of local geological conditions.

In Zhejiang most stone used for dwellings is used for the lower walls, mixing rough stones of various shapes and sizes that have been collected from nearby hill slopes or smooth stones that have been gathered from stream beds (Figure 3.98). Sometimes smaller stones are laid as courses and held by mortar, creating a mass of sufficient strength to support a *kongdou* brick wall (Figure 3.99). Stone is used widely in southern Jiangxi. As seen in Figure 3.100, the lower tamped wall supports an upper section of small parallel courses of stones set among some bricks. Some of the large multistory Hakka *weizi* fortresses, as seen in Figure 3.101, have facings of stone and mortar between substantial fired brick corner columns, which are usually battered. In the fishing villages of coastal China, simple cottages of stone and thatching have always been common (Figure 3.102). Near the Great Wall in northern Shanxi and Hebei, where building materials are extremely limited, small stones of various sizes are piled to form the sides and backs of single-sloped-roof dwellings (Figure 3.103). Once completed, the walls are covered with a lime-and-mud plaster to even the texture and to increase the imperviousness of the walls to water and air.

The Buyi/Bouyei in southwestern Guizhou are well known for their "rock architecture" [*shiyan jianzhu* 石岩建筑], stone foundations supporting wooden frameworks clad with walls of sedimentary limestone blocks, all capped with a flagstonelike roofing. Steps, water vats, stoves, watering troughs, grinders, seats, among many other utilitarian items, are made of stone and are seen throughout Buyi

Figure 3.103. Along the margins of the Great Wall in northern Shanxi and northern Hebei, where soils are thin and wood is lacking, simple single-sloped-roof structures made of small stones are common. To finish the surface and prevent the penetration of cold air and moisture, the stone is coated with a lime-and-mud plaster. Datong area, Shanxi. [RGK photograph 1985.]

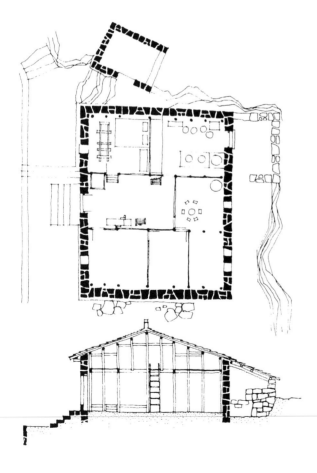

villages. Although some Buyi dwellings are built on level land, many more are built on the slopes of hills, with the upper portion occupied by the family and the lower part used for livestock (Figure 3.104). As slopelands are leveled for dwellings, rocks are exposed and then set aside to be used in making the heavy but non-load-bearing walls. Some walls are made of natural limestone boulders that vary in shape and size; others are dressed so that the walls appear to have been made of relatively uniform bricks. Towers of stone and stone stockades help to fortify some villages (Figure 3.105). Stones are often cut into triangular shapes and laid with the pointed ends facing inward and flat surfaces facing outward. In some areas, thin slabs of cut stone are sometimes fitted among the pillars and transverse tie beams of *chuandou*-type wooden frameworks. To form roofs, overlapping slabs of limestone, either of uniform or varying size are laid atop the rafters (Dai, Luo, and Wu 1989).

Figure 3.104. Among the Buyi who live on the Yunnan-Guizhou plateau, stone dwellings are built on level land as well as along the slopes of hills. Roofs are typically supported by a wooden *chuandou* frame with the massive stones forming non-load-bearing curtain walls. Zhenning *xian*, Guizhou. [Source: Dai, Luo, and Wu 1989, 3.]

Figure 3.105. Some Buyi villages and towns are dominated by stone blockhouse towers. Tianlong *zhen*, Zhenning *xian*, Guizhou. [Source: Dai, Luo, and Wu 1989, 50.]

North of the Zhangzhou area in southern Fujian, dwellings are constructed of massive hewn stone slabs or blocks [*tiaoshi* 条石] of granite cut from quarries. Instead of being raised and finished a course at a time, the granite slabs are stacked loosely, as seen in Figure 3.106 in order to "frame"

the building. Once all the slabs are in place, the blocks are finished with mortar, pointed, and "divided" by drawing dark lines (Figure 3.107). Even substantial portions of some of the so-called *tulou* [earthen dwellings] in Fujian are actually built of granite and stone boulders (Figures 3.108 and 3.109). While many utilize stone boulders for constructing heavy foundations and podiums and large stone blocks for fashioning gate frames, only one three-story circular fortress is completely made of stone. Shengpinglou 升平楼 in Hua'an *xian*, built in 1601, has battered circular walls formed from granite slabs, which decrease in depth from approximately 2.05 meters at the base to approximately 0.86 meters near the top (Figure 3.110). With some 120 commodious rooms, Shengpinglou has become virtually abandoned in recent years as households have moved into new dwellings (Huang 1994c, II, 141).

Cut slabs of hardened loessial soil and blocks of sandstone are used in some areas of Shanxi and Shaanxi to construct walls and arches of *guyao*-type structures. Those seen in Figures 3.111, 3.112, and 3.113 are on the hill slopes above the Huanghe River at Hukou in western Shanxi, an area devoid of any other building material. Far from the source of the stone, some dwellings in northern Zhejiang are built

Figure 3.106. Quarried granite slabs for walls as well as window and door frames are stacked loosely, then mortared. Linfang *cun*, Zhendong *xiang*, Fujian. [RGK photograph 1990.]

Figure 3.107. Once each of the granite slabs is in place and mortar is applied to seal and finish the joints, dark lines are drawn in order to regularize the pattern. Linfang *cun*, Zhendong *xiang*, Fujian. [RGK photograph 1990.]

Figure 3.108. As seen around the front gate, substantial portions of the lower walls of Jinjianglou are constructed of cut stone slabs to increase the wall's strength. The gate leads into a second concentric ring of the structure. Jinjiang *cun*, Shentu *xiang*, Zhangpu *xian*, Fujian. [Original photograph used with the permission of Li Yuxiang.]

Figure 3.109. The alternating courses of cut stone are clear in this view of the rear of Jinjianglou. Jinjiang *cun*, Shentu *xiang*, Zhangpu *xian*, Fujian. [Original photograph used with the permission of Li Yuxiang.]

Figure 3.110. Shengpinglou is the only three-story circular fortress that is made completely of stone. Built in 1601, the circular walls are formed of battered granite slabs, decreasing in depth from approximately 2.05 meters at the base to 0.86 meters near the top. Baoshan *cun*, Shajian *xiang*, Hua'an *xian*, Fujian. [Original photograph used with the permission of Li Yuxiang.]

Figure 3.113 (below). Interior view of the arched ceiling of a *guyao*. Hukou, Jixian, Shanxi. [RGK photograph 1996.]

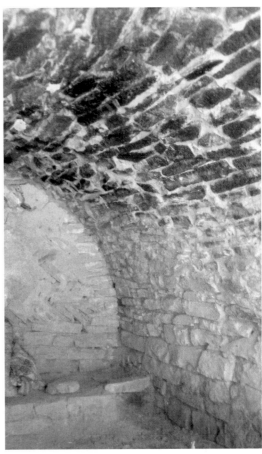

Figure 3.111 (above). On the western margins of Shanxi province that drain into the Huanghe River, there is a virtual absence of building materials except for sandstone and compacted loessial soil that can be cut into blocks. Cavelike structures constructed of rough stone blocks line terraces in Hukou, Jixian, Shanxi. [RGK photograph 1996.]

Figure 3.112 (left). Here, and elsewhere in the region, *guyao* structures are constructed of blocks of locally available stone that is held without mortar. Hukou, Jixi'an, Shanxi. [RGK photograph 1996.]

Figure 3.114. This symmetrical canalside townhouse, the home of the early twentieth-century woman revolutionary Xu Xiling, has a unique lower wall made of stone slabs with an upper wall made of *kongdou* cavity brickwork. Dongpu *zhen*, Shaoxing *shi*, Zhejiang. [RGK photograph 1987.]

Figure 3.115. The stone slabs of the lower wall are socketed into vertical stone columns. Dongpu *zhen*, Shaoxing *shi*, Zhejiang. [RGK photograph 1987.]

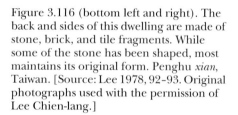

Figure 3.116 (bottom left and right). The back and sides of this dwelling are made of stone, brick, and tile fragments. While some of the stone has been shaped, most maintains its original form. Penghu *xian*, Taiwan. [Source: Lee 1978, 92–93. Original photographs used with the permission of Lee Chien-lang.]

Figure 3.117. This non-load-bearing wall has a base of stone with upper portions composed of stone, brick, and broken tile fragments. The two ventilation ports are formed of arcuate roof tiles arranged in geometrical forms. Zhenhai *qu*, Ningbo *shi*, Zhejiang. [RGK photograph 1987.]

of large stone slabs that are slotted into vertical columns along the lower third of the wall and *kongdou* cavity brickwork above (Figures 3.114 and 3.115).

Much of the character of stone walls comes from the shape, texture, and color of individual stone pieces. In some cases, patterns are quite regular, while in others they are rather random. Whether the quality of materials or level of craftsmanship are high or low, there is often a beauty to Chinese walls that arises from the attentive mixing of building forms (Figures 3.116 and 3.117). In raising a stone

structure, special attention is usually paid to the placement and quality of the stones in the corners as well as at the base, where stress is greatest. The durability of stone as well as its resistance to weathering and fire are some of its advantages, yet Chinese generally do not prefer stone dwellings if there is an alternative.

Timbers

In some areas of northwest, southwest, and northeast China where forests are extensive, load-bearing walls of roughly hewn logs are built and finished with a mud plaster. Where timbers are stacked to form walls that directly support the roof, a *jinggan* 井干, or "well frame," with a corrugated appearance is formed. Found especially in more remote upland areas, frontier log cabin-type dwellings have been built and used principally by ethnic minority groups on China's periphery. Simple log structures, which were probably houses, are depicted on bronze architectural models of the Han dynasty found in Jinning, Yunnan province. Depending on need and availability of materials, Kazak herders today still build seasonal log dwellings and outbuildings on the slopes of the Tianshan mountains in the Xinjiang Uygur Autonomous region to complement their tents (Figure 3.118). Each of the interlocked timber walls of these Kazak log houses is weathertight in spite of crude joint connections and varying diameters of logs used. Walls rise to a common height before a stack of logs of decreasing length are added to define a double-sloping roof. A shortcoming of stacked log structures is that their breadth and depth are rigidly controlled by the length of available timbers, with the result that most such dwellings are small and comprise only a single room.

Throughout the high, rugged, and dissected portions of southwest China, which are actually a spur of the Tibetan plateau, many of the minority nationality groups build at least some of their dwellings out of timbers [*muleng fang* 木楞房 or *muduo fang* 木垛房]. In a region that is sparsely settled and relatively remote, Yi, Nu, and Pumi especially have long utilized the extensive stands of coniferous and deciduous trees that are spread along the hill slopes. Even the

Figure 3.118. Rather crudely stacked *jinggan,* or "well frame" single-room log houses, are built by Kazak herders to supplement their mobile yurts. Northern slopes of Tianshan, Xinjiang Uygur Autonomous Region. [RGK photograph 1984.]

Bai, who are generally viewed as sinicized and live in well-developed courtyard-style dwellings in more prosperous areas, build *jinggan* dwellings in remote and rugged areas of Dali where their resources are limited. Although the use of full timbers consumes much more wood than the use of sawn boards or planks, log houses are relatively easy to construct using only simple knives and axlike tools applied to bountiful building materials found in heavily forested areas. Most log dwellings, such as the Yi dwelling shown in Figure 3.119, are mere rectangles of stacked logs without any fenestration in which the well-frame structure supports simple timber trusses that lift the roof. L- and U-shaped structures are also

Figure 3.119. The Yi, as with other southwestern nationality minority groups, such as the Nu, Pumi, Drung, Lisu, and some Naxi and Tibetans, build some of their dwellings out of logs. Usually without windows, Yi log dwellings are rectangular, U-shaped, and L-shaped and are often built on hillsides on level stone foundations. Xiaopenhe *cun,* Nanhua *xian,* Chuxiong Yi Nationality Autonomous District, Yunnan. [Original photograph used with the permission of Asakawa Shigeo 1992.]

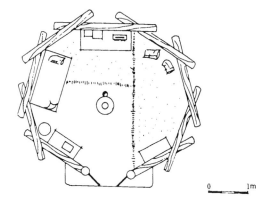

Figure 3.120. Some Mongols build yurtlike dwellings of stacked logs in the forests along the slopes of the Altai Mountains in northeastern Xinjiang. The interior layout maintains the plan of a Mongol *ger,* which is discussed in Chapter 6. [Source: Shi 1995, 283, 291.]

Figure 3.121. This reconstruction of a Hezhe log house is found in the Chinese Ethnic Culture Park in Beijing. Hezhe live in northern Heilongjiang along the riverine borders with Russia. [RGK photograph 1993.]

found extensively. The Pumi, a small ethnic group living in the northwestern mountainous portions of Yunnan province, build more complex log structures, sometimes with two stories, multiple rooms, and courtyards. Drung, Lisu, and Nu, as well as some Naxi and Tibetan villages in the forested uplands also include *jinggan*-style log dwellings.

Log dwellings throughout southwest China are generally built of only simply dressed tree trunks that are placed horizontally one on top of the other so that they overlap to form the corners of the structure. The unhewn logs normally project from the corners but are notched above and below in order to "lock" each of the levels in place in a relatively tight joint. Although there is normally some attempt to close the gaps between the logs with a crude infilling of slender pieces of wood, bark, and mud, no effort is made to seal the enclosing walls. Knives and axlike adzes are generally the only tools used in fashioning log dwellings.

Ten-sided log structures that mimic Mongol yurts are found in the Altai Mountains between Xinjiang and Inner Mongolia (Figure 3.120). Constructed of short logs with a diameter of 100 to 150 centimeters, these *jinggan*-style structures may reach as much as 3.75 meters in height. Notched where the logs overlap at the corners, the gaps between them are filled with mud. Sod clumps as well as a composition of soil and grasses are used to seal the roof, although an opening is left for ventilation and light (Yan

1995, 291–292). If the sophisticated log houses found in Beijing's Chinese Ethnic Culture Park are any indication, the Hezhe, who are China's smallest minority with a population of only about 2,000, are extraordinary builders. Actual log dwellings, however, have not been noted by researchers who have visited the Hezhe homeland in the forested valleys of the Heilongjiang, Songhua, and Wusuli Rivers in Heilongjiang, where they live by hunting and fishing (Figure 3.121).

Miliang Pingding: "Purlin and Rafter" Supporting Walls

Throughout Tibet and Xinjiang and adjacent areas of southwestern China, where four walls directly support a flat roof, one finds *miliang pingding* 密梁平顶, "purlin and rafter" structures (Figure 3.122). Built by various ethnic minorities, walls of *miliang pingding* dwellings may be of earth, stone, or logs. This structural type is one in which purlins [*lin* 檩, *lintiao* 檩条, or *chuanzi* 椽子], small-diameter logs approximately 3 meters in length, are laid from one endwall to the opposite endwall. When the interior space is too broad for a single purlin to span, intermediate columns are added to support some of the roof. Rafters are laid atop the purlins, followed by a layer of bamboo strips. On top of the bamboo strips, a mixture of mud and grass, approximately 20 cen-

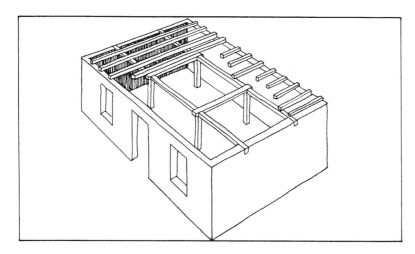

Figure 3.122 (left). The basic form of a *miliang pingding* [purlin and rafter] structure is a box with walls of earth, stone, or logs, upon which purlins are laid from one endwall to the opposite endwall. When the span is too broad, intermediate posts and beams are needed for additional support.

Figure 3.123 (below). Some Yi "purlin and rafter" *tuzhangfang* have a multi-story addition with a double-sloped roof whose upper structure depends on triangular trusses to lift the purlins. Such roofs are covered either with tile or thatch. Honghe Hani Yi Nationality Autonomous District, Yunnan. [Source: Yunnan sheng 1986, 173.]

timeters thick, is spread to seal the roof from water and offer protection from summer heat as well as winter cold. As a flat-roofed system in areas of limited rainfall, the level surface can be used to dry grain, fruits, and melons. Yi dwellings of this type found in western Yunnan province are called *tuzhangfang* 土掌房 [earthen palm houses] in Chinese. Such simple examples of *tuzhangfang* dwellings may be relatively simple (as will be seen later in Chapter 6); others have multiple stories and sometimes even have pitched roofs added. Adjacent to

the *miliang pingding* structure on the left in Figure 3.123, a truss lifts a pitched roof. This double-sloped roof may be covered with either tile or thatch, depending upon a household's resources. Architects have reported that *tuzhangfang* are sometimes even built in the interior regions of western China by Han, Dai, and Kazak ethnic groups. Wherever raw materials are limited, building conditions demand simplicity. Harsh climate makes this basic building form a suitable substitute for a traditional dwelling type (Yunnan sheng 1986, 160–174).

Roof Forms: More than Functional Protection

Although a roof may be an expressive feature of a dwelling and may be associated with powerful symbolism, it is principally a functional canopy sheltering the structure and interior living space from the elements. Climate has a preponderant influence on the various forms that Chinese roofs have taken. In areas of substantial rainfall, the major concern is quickly moving falling water to the eaves in order to minimize the infiltration of moisture into the building. Recognizing that water only moves downward and in one direction, pitched roofs—often with surfaces that operate to disperse water like the scales of fish or the feathers of birds—are most common. The shape and composition of a roof can also contribute to insulating the inside, shielding inhabitants from either heat or cold. From the neolithic period onward, craftsmen have developed a broad range of roof forms and materials appropriate for the various climatic regions spread across the vast country. Many Chinese roofs are simply utilitarian, providing crude waterproofing and water shedding, as earlier examples have suggested. Many more, however, exhibit a powerful elegance in terms of their curvature and covering, qualities that are more common in the residences of those with greater means than those who live in humble dwellings. Chinese have indeed always invested more effort in utilizing technique and expressing symbolism as they fashion roofs than is the case in the west, where the emphasis is usually on the facade instead (Tanaka 1995). The multiplicity of roof styles and profiles glimpsed in earlier illustrations will be categorized in the following sections.

Roof Styles and Profiles

Double-sloped roofs appeared as early as the seventeenth century B.C., as suggested by oracle bone pictographs (Deng 1980, 135). Over time, simple profiles became more complex. In addition to uncomplicated flat and shedlike roofs, it is possible to identify four major Chinese roof [*wuding* 屋顶]

types: *yingshanding*, *xuanshanding*, *sizhuding*, and *xieshanding*. Well developed some 2,000 years ago during the Han dynasty, these four basic types are differentiated by the relationship of the gables [*shanqiang* 山墙 mountain wall]—the triangular portion of a wall at the end of a pitched roof—and the eaves [*yanzi* 檐子]—the underpart of a sloping roof that overhangs a wall. These four types remain the principal profiles seen in Chinese dwellings today. Except for flat and shedlike roof profiles that are also encountered, these four usually result from the manipulation of the *tailiang* and *chuandou* wood framing systems, and to a degree the *ganlan* system, that are positioned beneath them. For the most part, Chinese roof profiles are symmetrical in both side and front elevations, the first emphasizing the gable end of a dwelling and the second the ridgeline. A mixture of roof styles is sometimes found in a single dwelling, indeed on a single roof. Although not properly a part of the roof, the high stepped walls known as *matouqiang* in southern China will be discussed in this section because of how they accentuate the associated roof profile.

The *yingshanding* 硬山顶 [firm mountain] roof profile is common throughout northern China in small rural dwellings and urban *siheyuan* quadrangle-type courtyard houses as well as in many areas of southern China, where it is mixed among other styles. This type is especially suited to areas of limited rainfall, where there is no critical need for shielding the gable end of a dwelling from weathering. The *yingshanding* roof profile comprises a gable that is flush with the end of the roof, with only some simple decorative brickwork to give the juncture any prominence, as seen in Figures 3.124 and 3.125. The eaves above the front and back facades of *yingshanding* dwellings are usually foreshortened to enable the low sun of winter to reach inside the dwellings. Sometimes the ridgeline at the peak is the focus of ornamentation. There is no record of *yingshanding* roof profiles prior to the Ming dynasty; their use appears to have increased with expanded availability of fired bricks. Many *shanqiang* of *yingshanding* dwellings are indeed load-bearing, directly carrying the purlins and the substantial weight of a tiled roof. Truncated *yingshanding* are found on the wing build-

Figure 3.124. Two parallel dwellings show the load-bearing nature of the gable wall [*shanqiang* or "mountain wall"] with the thick purlins resting directly on the wall. A small decorative detail accentuates the roof at this junction. Behind the two parallel dwellings is a structure that clearly has a *yingshanding* roof profile, with the upper triangular gable wall being flush with the end of the roof. This dwelling has the same roof details as the adjacent buildings. Huairou *xian*, Beijing. [RGK photograph 1987.]

ings of courtyard structures in Shaanxi. As seen in Figure 3.126, the peak of a single-sloped wing building is clearly flush with the gable and finished with tile copings. Some of the *weizi*, the imposing fortress-like structures of the Hakka in southern Jiangxi, also have *yingshanding* roof profiles atop their corner blockhouse towers (Figure 3.127). Roofs with flush gables are found on dwellings in the coastal areas of southern China where the lack of eaves overhang is seen as an advantage to counter strong winds that accompany the frequent passage of typhoons. However, it is a curiosity that *overhanging* gables are also common because their extending surfaces easily catch the winds and can be dislodged (Gao, Wang, and Chen 1987, 108).

Although not properly a *yingshanding* roof profile, since the gable rises significantly above the roof slope, the *matouqiang* 马头墙 [horses' head wall] is discussed here because it also does not have a roof overhang. Gable walls that rise in steps above the roofline to establish a striking functional and ornamental element are found from the Yangzi River southward, especially in Anhui, Jiangxi, Zhejiang, and southern Jiangsu provinces (Figures 3.128, 3.129, and 3.130). *Matouqiang* originated as fire walls [*fanghuoqiang* 防火墙 fire-shielding walls or *fenghuoqiang* 封火墙 fire-sealing walls] and came into wide use during the Ming period

Figure 3.125. All of the structures in the Qiao family manor are constructed of fine quality brick and tiles. The gable ends are all *yingshanding* type with a slightly raised ornamental brick and mortar coping. The two-story hall beyond has a straight ridgeline with a double-sloped roof. The wing building on right has a single-sloped roof that is slightly curved, while the structure to the front has a curved and unornamented ridge. Qiaojiabao village, Qixian, Shanxi. [RGK photograph 1996.]

Figure 3.126. Although the mud plaster wall cover and the adobe wall beneath can be eroded reasonably easily by rainwash if not protected by a gable overhang, many dwellings constructed of these materials have *yingshanding*-type gables. Found in the semiarid northwest, this truncated single-sloped roof is capped with a tile coping that provides only limited protection from periodic downpours. The petallike ventilation port is made of facing roof tiles. Lintong *xian*, Shaanxi. [RGK photograph 1985.]

Figure 3.127. The elevated gable atop a corner blockhouse tower of a Hakka *weizi* is clearly a *yingshanding* form. Constructed of fired brick, no part of the outer wall or even the stone podium beneath requires overhanging eaves for protection. Xinwei, Guanxin *xiang*, Longnan *xian*, Jiangxi. [RGK photograph 1993.]

Figure 3.128. *Matouqiang,* or "horses' head walls," rise in steps above the roofline. Originating as firewalls, they came into wide use during the Ming period as fired bricks became relatively inexpensive. They are found on dwellings as well as temples, clan halls, and other buildings. Dafu *xiang,* Shexian, Anhui. [RGK photograph 1987.]

Figure 3.129. The contrasting white walls and many angles of black-tiled *matouqiang* are a striking feature of dwellings in the villages and towns of the Jiangnan region. Zhejiang. [RGK photograph 1987.]

Figure 3.130. *Matouqiang* vary in detail and finish. Each of these is found in a different part of Zhejiang. Top, Zhenhai *qu*, Ningbo *shi;* middle, Lanxi *shi;* bottom, Lishui *xian.* [RGK photographs 1987 and 1988.]

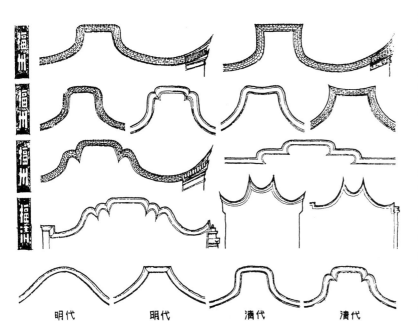

明代   明代   清代   清代

thus, the lack of eaves is of no environmental significance in terms of rainwash. Functioning much like
matouqiang are the sweeping, undulating endwalls in southeastern China.
Called *qiaoji* 翘脊 [upward turning
spine], these curving forms are found
in Fujian, Guangdong, Guangxi, and
Zhejiang (Figures 3.131, 3.132, 3.133,
and 3.134). Aesthetically pleasing and
difficult to construct, stepped *matouqiang* and soaring *qiaoji* are clearly distinctive features of Chinese domestic architecture.
Some smaller raised gables are unlikely to have originated as fire walls but may have had their origins in *yin-
yang* cosmology, as will be discussed later.

"Overhanging gables" [*xuanshanding* 悬山顶 or
tiaoshanding 挑山顶] have purlins that extend beyond the endwalls, thus enabling the double-sloped
roof to overhang the gables (Figure 3.135). This type
of roof profile offers some protection for the gable
walls, especially important if the walls are made of

as fired bricks became relatively inexpensive. Such
walls rise high above the roofline in order to retard the
spread of sweeping roof fires to adjacent dwellings,
temples, clan halls, and other buildings in towns and
compact villages. Often they formed party or common
walls between two structures in order to contain fires.
Usually symmetrical in their upper profile, they nonetheless vary significantly, depending to a large extent
on available space and resources. Sometimes they are
mere abbreviated forms, appearing as sweeping long
horns that are added to extend a
dwelling's flush gable forward.
More of them, however, rise dra-
matically and are accentuated with
dark tile copings that contrast
sharply with white walls, which are
typical throughout the regions
where they are found. *Matouqiang*
are normally composed of kiln-
dried bricks covered with plaster;

Figure 3.132. The sweeping curvature
of these matched endwalls "elevate"
this low building. Bandong *xiang*,
Minqing *xian*, Fujian. [Original photograph used with the permission of
Li Yuxiang.]

Figure 3.133. Constructed of *kongdou* brickwork, this elevated wall has a convex middle section and feather-like ends. Zhili *zhen*, Huzhou *shi*, Zhejiang. [RGK photograph 1988.]

Figure 3.134. Within a single village, the endwalls of buildings vary and give evidence of styles from all over the country. The low dwelling on the right has a *yingshanding* roof profile that is quite similar to those found in the north of China. On the right is a common *matouqiang* that would be suitable in the Anhui/Zhejiang area. To the rear is a curved endwall similar to those typicaly found in coastal southeastern China. Yangshuo, Guangxi Zhuang Autonomous Region. [RGK photograph 1984.]

Figure 3.135. "Overhanging gables" [*xuanshanding* or *tiaoshanding*] are formed when the roof purlins extend beyond the endwalls. The purlins supporting the roof on this dwelling are each held up by wooden pillars in a *chuandou* frame. The panels between the wooden members are made of woven bamboo covered with a white plaster. The depth of the eaves overhang on the end and at the back is suggested by the extent of shade cast on the structure. Langzhong area, Sichuan. [RGK photograph 1994.]

Figure 3.136. Complex hipped roofs [*sizhuding* or *sihuding*], with four sloping surfaces, are found on palaces and temples as well as some large and small residences. Songjiang *xian*, Jiangsu. [Source: Liu Dunzhen 1957, 82.]

adobe or bamboo. This type is usually accompanied by overhanging eaves on the front and back of the dwelling as well. Numerous examples exist throughout southern China, as will be seen in Chapter 5. Found throughout the country, it is peculiar that they are not common in some areas of substantial rainfall, such as in Taiwan and Fujian. The compact two-story *yikeyin* adobe or tamped earth dwellings found in central and southern Yunnan and used by Han, Tibetan, and Bai ethnic groups, however, typically have such protective "overhanging gables" roof profiles, which offer some protection to the outer walls and lead water into the interior skywell. The depth of eaves and gable overhang is usually determined by function, but sometimes the overhang is emphasized for aesthetic reasons. Archaeological evidence shows that "overhanging gables" were used during the Eastern Han period, but they did not enter the architectural mainstream until more than a half-century later in the Tang period.

Structurally rather complex hipped roofs [*sizhuding* 四注顶 or *sihuding* 四虎顶] and "combined gable and hipped gable roofs" [*xieshanding* 歇山顶] are most commonly seen today on extant Ming and Qing period palaces, temples, and large residences but are found on small dwellings as well. Involving intricate carpentry of radiating woodwork, they are found nonetheless on common dwellings and, perhaps surprisingly, even covering quite modest thatched dwellings, such as those of the Korean minority nationality. Hipped roofs have four sloping surfaces, with the hip

being the exterior angle where any two slopes come together. Four-sloped roofs first appeared during the Shang period according to *Kaogong ji* and representations on oracle bones (Zhang 1985b, 35). The sloping eaves of hipped roofs overhang the side walls just as they normally overhang the front and back. The *xieshanding* variant is generally known in the west as a gambrel roof. The shape comes from the foreshortening of the two hipped slopes on the ends of the roof, which forms gablets, small triangular shapes that fit beneath the peak. This alteration creates a combination of sloping elements to the profile, a challenge even to a skilled carpenter.

The architectural historian Liu Dunzhen tells us that the hipped roof had been used widely for dwellings prior to the Song dynasty, as can be seen in paintings of many periods, but subsequently in the Ming and Qing periods became restricted in its use because of the imposition of sumptuary regulations that limited hipped roofs to palace construction (1957, 30). Yet, in spite of such official restrictions, hipped roofs continued to be built throughout the imperial period on rural dwellings and other structures all over the country, except in areas near the capital, Beijing. With multiple ridgelines, the *sizhuding* profile is often quite graceful, as seen in Figure 3.136. In areas remote from imperial control and occupied by minority groups such as the Dai, Jingpo, De'ang, Blang, and Jinuo in Yunnan province, many simple dwellings have what appear to be rather complex roof profiles, such as the *xieshanding*, found atop their pile-supported dwellings of bamboo and thatch. Structurally, however, the technical means to create a *xieshanding* on a pile dwelling is not complicated, according to architects, since it involves only a relatively simple triangular truss linked to a half-gabled truss (Zhu 1992a, 102). Hipped roofs have always been a common feature of houses built by ethnic Koreans in northeastern China, and these are similar to those seen throughout the Korean peninsula.

No discussion of Chinese roof profiles would be complete without an examination of the varied embellishments along the ridges and eaves that significantly enhance the silhouette of the upper third of many Chinese structures. The Chinese differentiate a variety of roof "ridges" [*ji* 脊] besides the one nor-

Figure 3.137. Even on roofs of manor complexes, the roofline can be relatively sedate. The single roof ridge running forward is capped by a brick molding to seal the juncture between the two tiled roof slopes. Caojia Manor, Beiguang, Taigu, Shanxi. [RGK photograph 1996.]

mally recognized in western architecture that is formed at the upper juncture of a roof with two sloping planes [*wuji* 屋脊 or *zhengji* 正脊]. Laterally sloping ridgelines [*chuiji* 垂脊] include not only the ends of a double-sloped roof but also the hips of *sizhuding* and *xieshanding* roof profiles, called "propping ridges" [*cangji* 仓脊]. All of these ridges, as well as others on more complicated roofs, have become sites of profile enhancement on the roofs of buildings of many styles.

Seams along any of the junctures between different slopes demand particular attention, since it is there that seepage of water from outside and loss of heat from inside are most likely to occur. Identifiable V-shaped tiles used during the Shang and Western Zhou periods and cylindrical capping tiles in the Han dynasty were employed to overcome such problems. Yet, while attention to practical concerns relating to sealing vulnerable seams was a compelling reason for their development, the prominence of ornamentation on ridges and eaves overhangs suggests other purposeful explanations.

Throughout northern China, the most common addition to the roof ridges is a brick molding running the length of the ridge, sometimes with a slightly raised extension, even a projection, at each end (Figure 3.137). At its simplest, this molding is freely carved with line patterns, but sometimes the molding is but a base for substantial ornamentation.

Some Han funerary models show elevated ends of the main ridgeline, a suggestive sweeping upward that came to characterize many subsequent Chinese structures. Chinese architectural historians tell us that the purpose of raising the ends of the upper ridge was to further protect the part of the roof that would be the most likely to be lifted by the wind and expose the interior to wind and water damage. These ends gradually took the shape of very heavy, finial-like ornamentations or monuments known as *chiwei* 鸱尾 [owl's tail] or *zhengwen* 正吻 [animal's mouth], which were used as totems to guard against fire (Zhang 1985b, 188).

In southern Shaanxi, prefabricated and then fired roof ornaments are generically called "ridge mouths" [*jiwen* 脊吻], after the traditional "animal mouths," and are said to have the same magical power against fire. On traditional homes of wealthy merchants in the Guanzhong area of Shaanxi, *jiwen* and attendant ridge ornamentation is elaborate, involving carved animals, flowers, and birds and reminiscent of types found in southeastern China (Zhang and Liu 1993, 121–126). Rather complex compositions of arcuate or flat roof tiles, as seen in Figure 3.138, are found throughout north, northeastern, and southwestern China. These include ancient Chinese coin and other ornamental patterns that may have auspicious meanings.

In contrast to the reticent architecture of northern China, common houses, temples, shrines, and even graves display increasingly ostentatious embellishment the farther south one travels in China, reaching a peak in Fujian, Guangdong, and across the straits in Taiwan. Huang Hanmin classified the upward sweeping ridge ends in Fujian into five categories (Figure 3.139): "tail feather corner" style [*qiao-jiao* 翘角]; "martial ridge" style [*wuji* 武脊]; "civil ridge" style [*wenji* 文脊]; "pointed tip ridge" style [*jianji* 尖脊]; and "rounded ridge" style [*yuanji* 圆脊] (1984, 188–189). Although these appear similar, each is quite distinct and found only in specific regions of Fujian. The "tail feather corner" style rises precipitously from a flat ridgeline and is found in

Figure 3.138. Using stacked tubular or flat roof tiles, the ridgeline of these dwellings is both functional and ornamental. Left, Pingyao *shi*, Shanxi; right, Langzhong *shi*, Sichuan. [RGK photographs 1996, 1993, respectively.]

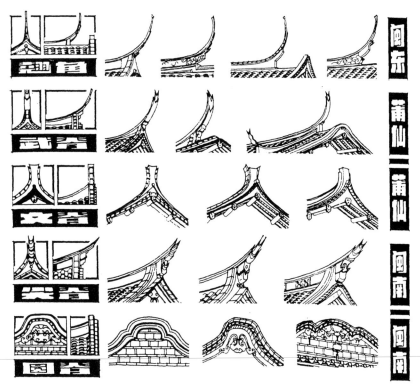

Figure 3.139 (left). The upward sweeping ridge ends seen in Fujian can be divided into five categories (from top to bottom): "tail feather corner" style in eastern Fujian; "martial ridge" style in the Puxian region; "civil ridge" style in the Puxian region; "pointed tip ridge" style in southern Fujian; and "rounded ridge" style in southern Fujian. [Source: Huang 1984, 188-189.]

Figure 3.140. Graceful "swallowtail" ridgelines can be seen throughout the island of Taiwan. Taibei basin, Taiwan. [RGK photograph 1965.]

east central Fujian. The "pointed tip ridge" style is found in southern Fujian and has a gently upward sweeping continuation of an already arcuate ridgeline but lacks the final verticality of the "tail feather corner" style. Between these two is the "martial ridge" style, rising precipitously but from an arcuate ridgeline. The "civil ridge" style is boxlike rather than pointed, while the "rounded ridge" style, found especially in southern Fujian, lacks any outward projection.

Some of these ridge forms are found across the straits in Taiwan, an island populated principally by migrants from Fujian and Guangdong. As outlined by Lee Chien-lang, three basic ridge style profiles are found in Taiwan: the so-called "swallowtail" style; the "horseback," or "saddle," style; and the "tile weigh-ing" style (1980, 263). All of these focus on the ends of the ridgeline above the gable. The "swallowtail" style [*yanweixing* 燕尾形], not surprisingly, is quite similar to the "pointed tip ridge" style identified by Huang Hanmin in Fujian. A majority of Taiwan's inhabitants migrated from the Minnan region of southern Fujian and clearly brought the style with them, even though the style was officially proscribed by sumptuary regulations on dwellings in Taiwan in the eighteenth and nineteenth centuries. Nonetheless, the *nouveau riche* on the Taiwan frontier often flouted regulations and erected magnificent mansions that included the graceful "swallowtail" roof profile just as such sweeping ridgelines were being added legally to temples all over the island. "Swallowtail" ridgelines traditionally were given shape with bricks cantilevered out from the ridge and supported by a metal rod, but today they are more likely to be molded from reinforced concrete (Figures 3.140 and 3.141).

Figure 3.141. The massive size of some "swallowtail" ridgelines can be seen from this illustration of work being done to reconstruct the roof atop the Antai Lin dwelling. Yuanshan, Taibei, Taiwan. [Source: Tseng 1988a, 51.]

"Horseback," or "saddle," style ridges [*mabeixing* 马背形, also called *majixing* 马脊形] maintain a low slung curved ridgeline like the "swallowtail" style but lack the "swallowtail's" upward sweep at the end of the roof ridge (Figure 3.142). Located below the wide ridge, truncated geometric shapes and various patterns, as seen in Figures 3.143 and 3.144, surmount the gable walls.

In recent years, some Chinese scholars have suggested that the decorative gable walls of *mabeixing* dwellings seen in Guangdong and Taiwan can be classified into five basic types that then can be related to "five phases" [*wuxing* 五行] cosmology (Lu, Ma, and Deng 1981, 34; Lu and Wei 1982, 155-156; Lin 1990, 98-99). A similar argument has been made for the variety of shapes found on *matouqiang* walls. Using this typology, an arcuate hump, the most commonly seen shape on the island, represents metal, and the remaining four shapes suggest water, wood, fire, and earth. Although using these divisions to differentiate types, Kao has found no evidence that masons and others building in Taiwan who create the five types are aware of a possible connection to *wuxing* cosmology (1989, 47 ff). Further, Kao's fieldwork shows that types that are in opposition and are mutually destructive [*xiangke* 相剋] and that never would have been chosen by someone conversant with the principles of *wuxing* are all too common on the island. This is especially true, Kao claims, of the common usage of "fire" shapes on a main structure and "water" shapes on abutting side structures. Kao has not been able to make connections either to directions linked to the "five phases" that are associated with the Eight Trigrams [*bagua* 八卦] or general notions of *fengshui* linked to "five phases" and topographic shapes (Kao 1989, 78). That one shape

Figure 3.142. "Horseback," or "saddle," style ridges [*mabeixing*] maintain a low slung curved ridgeline like the "swallowtail" style but lack the upward sweep at the ends of the roof ridges. Instead, each of the upper gables is an elevated geometric shape. Shilin *zhen*, Taibei, Taiwan. [RGK photograph 1965.]

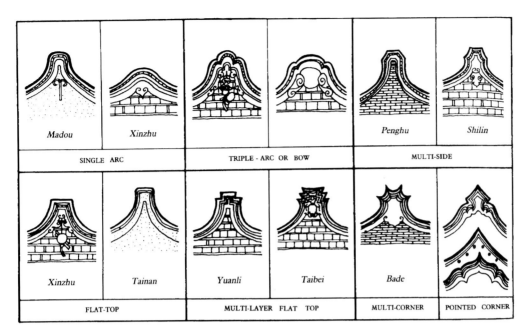

Figure 3.143. This chart illustrates the variety of truncated geometric shapes found on the upper gable walls in Taiwan. [Source: Lee 1980, 266.]

may balance another, however, is a possibility, as it may be necessary to determine the nature of "fire" and "water" in the shapes of surrounding mountains in order to arrive at a definitive answer to the role played by *mabeixing* shapes. Houses, indeed, were carefully sited, and their *wuxing* attributes must be considered beyond the structures themselves. Whether there is a clear symbolic reason for the differing shapes of *mabeixing* profiles, there is no doubt that the area above the gable on common Taiwan dwellings evidence an extraordinary richness that varies from place to place. Combined with the substantial ornamentation on gable walls, which clearly has symbolic meaning, it is indeed likely that the *mabei* shapes originated as emblems, although the reasons may have become less transparent over the years.

Gable-end profiles known as the "tile weighing" style [*wazhenxing* 瓦镇形] are found on Hakka dwellings especially in the Pingdong and Gaoxiong areas of southern Taiwan and in scattered parts of Taoyuan, Xinzhu, and Miaoli in northern Taiwan. The name itself is of recent origin, used first by Kao in 1975 to describe a rather plain three-dimensional weight set atop each of the vulnerable ends of a roof ridge (Figure 3.145). The meaning of the term goes beyond functionality to describe a guarding or protective purpose for the house. Often only a lozenge shape that straddles both slopes at the peak, *yazhen* sometimes appear in the shape of plum flower petals. When tied to other ornamentation that is clearly "protective" in the broadest sense, *yazhen* are a "security" device. More often, however, they are nothing more than functional ornamentation and are found on hipped roofs at critical junctions as well.

Midway between the northern and southern extremes of China is Zhejiang, where it is as rare to come across the baroque flamboyance of areas farther south as it is to encounter the sedate simplicity of northern rooflines. Most traditional Zhejiang dwellings have rather level and straight ridgelines, unadorned except for the side-to-side stacking of unglazed gray tiles as a coping along the ridge. Set into a lime plaster, this layered addition and cylindrical tiles laid end to end along the ridgeline add ornamentation, but they essentially are functional. If the ridgeline does not meet a raised gable, sometimes the ends of the ridge are elevated and extended in an upward sweeping movement to form a powerful silhouette that suggests the graceful tail of a bird or an arcuate hump, like those found farther south (Figure 3.146). Such profiles may

Figure 3.144. Examples of ornamented gable ends on dwellings in Taiwan. Top, Antai Lin dwelling, Taibei; middle and bottom, Xinxing *cun*, Zhanghua *xian*. [RGK photographs 1994.]

Figure 3.145. A "tile weighing" gable end style [*wazhenxing*] is found on Hakka dwellings in the Pingdong and Gaoxiong areas of southern Taiwan and in scattered parts of Taoyuan, Xinzhu, and Miaoli in northern Taiwan. Each of the forms is a three-dimensional weight set atop the vulnerable ends of the roof ridge. [Source: Kao 1989, 87.]

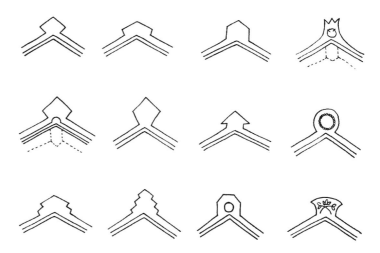

Figure 3.146. Roof ornamentation on dwellings in southern Zhejiang. Top left, Cangnan *xian*; top right, Ruian *xian*; bottom right, Wenzhou *shi*. [RGK photographs 1988.]

be solid or they may be perforated in order to lighten the appearance and "lift" the roofline. Unlike ornamentation in Fujian, Guangdong, and Taiwan, neither glazed tile nor ceramic shards are used to form roofline narratives made up of auspicious animals and birds.

Roofing Materials

Aside from utilizing geometric relationships, such as varying sloping patterns and altering angular connections, in order to counter nature, the composition of the roof covering itself has been a primary focus in enhancing protection of the interior. Early roofs were nothing more than saplings and branches laid on a slope, perhaps supplemented with a mud coating to shed rain and break the wind. As evidenced by texts such as the *Kaogong ji* [Records of trades], a Han period text based on earlier sources, and excavations such as at Fufeng in Shaanxi, roof tiles had been introduced by the eleventh century B.C. during the early Zhou period. The *Kaogong ji* even differentiates the necessary variations in roof pitch for different materials: 1:3 for thatched roofs and 1:4 for tiled roofs (Deng, 1980, 135). Chinese craftsmen over a long period of time developed a range of materials and compositions suitable as roof coverings under very different climatic conditions that have led to the pronounced regional variations that can be observed.

Plant Materials

The use of plants and mud as roof covering has had an enduring history in China, having undergone a long evolutionary path to the present. At the Banpo neolithic site in today's Shaanxi province, first straw and reeds were laid side by side; then rafters covered with a composition of straw and mud were added to serve as roofing. Roofs and walls of neolithic structures indeed were very similar in composition. Chinese scholars have hypothesized that the cooking fires used in such dwellings would have heated the clay in the roof and walls, slowly vitrifying them and rendering them watertight (Shan

1981b, 1-2). This may be a precursor discovery leading eventually to the use of fired roof tiles. In the Shang period, a further refinement was the use of reeds [*luwei* 芦苇] arranged along rafters and then covered with a 7-to-8-centimeter-thick coating of straw-reinforced mud, followed by an application of loess, fine sand, and lime—a kind of *sanhetu*, as discussed earlier. Identifiable V-shaped roof tiles were employed selectively along the ridge of some Zhou and Shang period dwellings, presumably to prevent water seepage at the most vulnerable part of the roof (Zhang 1985b, 35, 188). This convergent and concurrent use of plants, mud, and roof tiles continues to the present in many forms. There also have been simultaneously divergent paths in which the use of plants, mud, and roof tiles evolved separately, with one eventually dominating over the others. Before discussing the quite sophisticated development of mud composition roofs and baked roof tiles, a brief overview of the use of plants as roofing follows.

Besides being a common roofing material on dwellings of the poor, thatch [*maocao* 毛草] was traditionally used on the rural residences of some literati who sought inspiration from simple rural life. Containing natural chemicals that contribute to water-repellent and insulating properties, the composition of thatch varies from place to place. Throughout north and northeastern China, as shown in in Figures 3.147 and 3.148, thatching consists of wheat straw [*maijie* 麦秸], sorghum/*kaoliang* stalks [*gaoliang gan* 高粱秆], millet stalks [*xiaomigan* 小米秆], rice straw [*daocao* 稻草] and reeds [*luwei* 芦苇]. In the early part of the twentieth century, one observer in northeast China noted

the building of the thatched millet roofs and the use of kaoliang stems instead of timber. Rafters were set in the usual way and covered with a layer about 2 inches thick of the long kaoliang stems stripped of their leaves and tops. These were tied together and to the rafters with twine thus forming a kind of matting. A layer of thin clay mortar was then spread over the surface and well troweled until it began to show on the underside. Over this was applied a thatch of small millet stems bound in bundles 8 inches thick, cut square across the butts to 18

Figure 3.147. Thatched roofs are sometimes added to new brick dwellings in northeast China, a temporary solution until additional resources become available for a tile roof. Jinjiawan, Dongling *qu*, Shenyang, Liaoning. [Original photograph used with the permission of Elizabeth Leppman 1994.]

inches in length. They were dipped in water and laid in courses after the manner of shingles, but the butts of the stems were driven forward to a slope which obliterated the shoulder, making the courses invisible. In the better houses this thatching may be plastered with earth, mortar, or with an earth-lime mortar, which is less liable to wash in heavy rain. (King 1927, 143–144)

Thatched roofs of Korean minority nationality rural dwellings have always been especially thick, with as much as 30 to 50 centimeters of rice straw bundled above a 7-to-10-centimeter-thick layer of mud atop the rafters (Zhou 1992, 147).

In southern China, bundled rice straw [*daocao* 稻 草] and wild grasses [*yecao* 野 草] are sold in local markets by craftsmen who collect and bundle them so that they can easily be laid to make a new roof or to repair an old one (Figures 3.149 and 3.150). Buck's survey in the early 1930s showed that thatching covered a majority (55 percent) of common roofs in the large winter wheat–*kaoliang* region, which included parts of Hebei, Henan, Anhui, and northern Jiangsu. Thatch was extensively used even in the more prosperous Sichuan rice (44 percent) and Yangzi rice-wheat (41 percent) areas. Countrywide, however, thatched roofs accounted for only 28 percent of all roofing materials, exceeding only slightly those covered by packed mud and mud-lime (24 percent) and trailing far behind the 48 percent with tile roofs.

Thatch is a relatively light material that does not normally require a massive structural framework to support it. However, when thatching is poorly done, especially when insufficient attention is paid to needed slope and compaction, thatched roofs gain substantial weight when soaked during heavy summer rains, often causing them to collapse. Further, with the natural aging and decaying of supporting roof timbers, the eventual collapse of thatched roofs is inevitable unless there is periodic repair and replacement of rotting parts.

Figure 3.148. In preparation for laying a thatched roof on these stone mountain dwellings, a base of *kaoliang* stalks is being placed on the roof rafters. Taishan, Shandong. [RGK photograph 1985.]

Figure 3.149. A thin blanket of straw has been added atop a layer of oiled paper and plastic on this small tamped *sanhetu* dwelling. Hangzhou *shi*, Zhejiang. [RGK photograph 1985.]

Figure 3.150. Although the older portions of this long bamboo framed dwelling are covered with thatch, the newer section on the left has a tile roof. Tuku, Zhanghua *xian*, Taiwan. [Original photograph used with the permission of Lawrence Crissman.]

Mud Compositions

Traditionally there has been a widespread use of packed mud and mud-lime compositions in the drier areas of northern China, including northern Hebei, Shanxi, Shaanxi, the steppes of Inner Mongolia, Qinghai, Xinjiang, and in the northeastern provinces. No comprehensive study has been made of the folk practices for surfacing a mud roof.

Roofs of mud, generally termed *maijieni wuding* 麦秸泥屋顶, are multilayered compositions of vegetable and mineral matter that vary from place to place in northern and northeastern China. Roofs may be flat, slightly pitched, single-sloped, double-sloped, or even curved (Figures 3.151 and 3.152). In northern China, the presence of both semiaridity and extreme winter cold help govern the form of roofs. The most important function of a roof in northern China is to insulate the interior from the bitter cold outside yet keep whatever heat is generated on the inside from escaping. The wrapping effect of a thick mud roof tied to densely packed exterior back and side walls of earth or brick together increase thermal performance.

Although varying from place to place in details, such roofs traditionally began first with laying a roof board [*wangban* 望板], a reed mat [*luxi* 芦席], or both, over the rafters; in poorer dwellings this layer would be disregarded. Upon this surface, either reeds or sorghum stalks would be spread. In a bitterly cold area, such as Jilin province in the northeast where a substantial insulating thickness is critical, the layer reaches 10 centimeters, while in Henan and Hebei provinces it falls in the range of 5 to 6 centimeters. Two or three layers of a mud and straw composition are placed over the vegetable layer. The basic components are local earth and wheat straw, although in some areas around Beijing hemp was sometimes substituted for wheat straw. This composition was tamped down until smooth and then covered with one or two layers of a mixture of common white lime [*shihui* 石灰] and grey lime [*qinghui* 青灰].

As shown in Figure 3.153, Liu Dunzhen noted three slightly different methods. In Zhaoxian, Hebei province, three layers are added above reed matting. The first is a 10-centimeter-thick layer of mud. Then

Figure 3.151. Throughout the semiarid portions of northern China, flat composition roofs are found above walls in simple adobe structures as well as improved brick ones. Zhaoxian, Hebei. [RGK photograph 1984.]

Figure 3.152. Curved roofs in northeastern China are usually made of a composition of earth and vegetative matter. Here, as with flat roofs elsewhere, the roof serves the utilitarian function of a drying area at harvest time. Liaoning 1994. [Original photograph used with the permission of Elizabeth Leppman.]

Figure 3.153 (below). The layered composition of roofs in north and northeastern China. Left, Zhaoxian, Hebei, to the southwest of Beijing; middle, Jilin in the northeast; right, near Zhengzhou in Henan. In all three cases, rafters (1) are laid across the purlins. A layer of reed or *kaoliang* stalks (2) varying in thickness is added above as insulation; the thickest layer is approximately 10 centimeters on the Jilin roof. Atop this layer, mud mixed with wheat straw is added in successive layers (3, 4), each tamped with a wooden rammer. The outer roof surface (5) is finished with a mixture of lime, ashes, or mud according to local custom. [Source: Liu Dunzhen 1957, 28.]

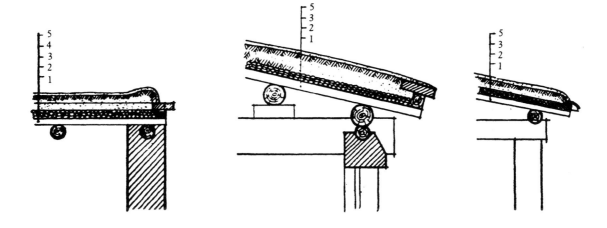

comes a mixture of mud, wheat stalks, and lime. Tamped down or put under pressure using rocks, this second layer is reduced from a thickness of 10 centimeters to 8 centimeters. The third and final layer is a composition of lime and mud in a ratio of 3 to 7. It too is put under pressure. Crushed coal cinders [*meizha* 煤渣] may be substituted for mud where they are readily available. Alkaline composition roofs have had a notable presence in the barren western hill areas of northeastern China stretching for several hundred kilometers. In western Jilin province, where the layer of wheat-straw mud on a roof has a depth of 20 centimeters, the top layer is usually a composition of alkaline soil. Clumps of alkalinized soil are collected in the spring as the gray-white alkaline rises to the surface after the frozen ground begins to melt. Dwellings throughout this region are maintained and strengthened with a fresh coat of pounded alkaline soil about 2 centimeters thick (Zhang 1985b, 125). In some cases where such soil is in short supply, alkaline water or saltwater may even be added to local mud to form the impervious composition (Liu 1957, 27–28).

The use of calcium oxide or lime—a white, lumpy caustic powder—is an old practice in China. Lime is produced through calcination, the roasting of limestone or shells to temperatures between 800 and 1000°C in order to bring about a reduction in moisture content and carbon dioxide and cause oxidation, but not enough to melt or fuse it. As depicted in the seventeenth-century *Tiangong kaiwu*, seen in Figure 3.154, it was recognized that "with calcining or heating, stones can be made to perform wondrous things" (Sung 1966, 201). Besides being used as a waterproofing adhesive in the layered composition roofs of northern China, lime also serves as the basic bonding component for plasters that harden after application to walls, floors, and ceilings. Lime can also be mixed with clay and water to form cement or added to sand, to form mortar.

Lime continues to be a widely used bonding substance throughout China. Wherever sedimentary rocks that contain more than 50 percent carbonate materials can be found, there are lime kilns, often side by side with kilns for firing bricks. Where significant amounts of calcified raw materials—even

Figure 3.154. When mixed with other materials, lime is important as a water repellent and sealant. In villages all over China, the calcination of limestone or shells of oysters is an old practice that is necessary in house construction. [Source: Sung 1966, 200.]

seashells—are available, large, semipermanent kilns are built of stone against the slope of a hill. Widely seen today are temporary kilns that continue traditional methods of calcination. Alternating thick layers of coal and roughly cut hunks of limestone within the brick-faced kiln, a hearth is formed with the appearance of an inverted cone with its apex removed. Burning is initiated from the bottom with coal dust or kindling and is allowed to continue for about a week until the high temperatures have reduced or crumbled the stone. After a dousing with water from the top, the kiln is allowed to smolder until it is time to remove the calcined limestone. Using shovels and hoes, the crumbly product is pulverized, then screened to eliminate cinders and other coarse materials. Transported to building sites, the *shihui* is further screened before mixing with clay, sand, water, and sometimes vegetable fiber for building purposes. The Chinese have acquired substantial experience in making and using *shihui* of many types, and this is reported to rural builders today in countless manuals, such as in Wei and Li (1986, 284-298).

Clay Tiles

The earliest reference to the use of roof tiles is found in Sima Qian's *Shiji*, placing them on houses during the Xia dynasty about 1561 B.C. Limited use of rooftiles along the ridgelines on compacted roof surfaces occurred later during the Shang dynasty. Roof tiles from the early Zhou period in Qishan, Shaanxi province, were quite primitive: molded dark gray tiles, decorated with rope patterns. Ingeniously held with a projecting fastening device, these tiles were probably only used on the vulnerable ridgeline and possibly along the eaves. Larger quantities of roof tiles have been found in many Zhou period Three Dynasties sites throughout central Shaanxi province. Both cylindrical and flat tiles were molded, cut, and then finished by hand, as relict fingerprints attest, before firing. Tiles increasingly came to serve decorative as well as fundamentally functional purposes. The making and laying of glazed tiles for temples, palaces, and halls during any period have always

represented advanced levels of technique, differing qualitatively from common tiles; however, these refined tile patterns will not be discussed here.

Advances in pottery-making appear to have influenced the development of both tile- and brick-making technology, with major advances made first during the Han dynasty and then later during the Ming dynasty. The resourcefulness of potters led to the production of tiles of many shapes and for many uses, unglazed and glazed, gray and colored. Over time, improvements in technique brought forth thinner yet less brittle tiles. How and by whom tiles were used throughout Chinese history is a complex story that cannot be fully understood. While Han dynasty funerary models portray a range of tile shapes used only on dwellings of wealthy nobles, excavations of sites during subsequent periods suggest that similar tiles found their way onto the roofs of common dwellings. As time went on, the presence of increasing numbers of tiles on the roofs of those with less means probably reflects a decrease in production costs.

Platelike tiles that were stacked on a roof probably came first, but it was technical innovations in the production of cylindrical shapes that led to the increasing use of roof tiles. The manner of laying roof tiles varies, as can be seen in Figure 3.155, involving manipulating concave and convex shapes. In preparation for tile laying, especially in northern China, a base layer of wood, twig, or reed matting is followed by a bedding layer of "sticky mud" or clay [*jiaoni* 胶泥], a bonding layer of lime, and finally the tiles

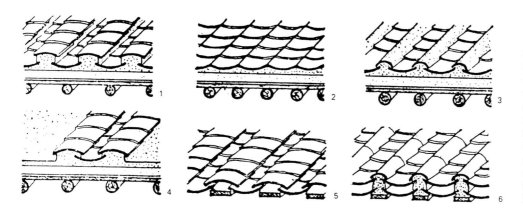

Figure 3.155. Tile-laying patterns vary across China. Among some of the common patterns are alternating concave and convex (1); adjacent concave (2); concave tiles with lime mortar capping (3); alternating tiles and mortar (4); southern overlapping and alternating concave and convex (5); southern double-tile for heat insulation (6). [Source: Deng 1980, 137.]

Figure 3.156 (top left). Before tiles are laid on a roof in northern China, a layer of wood, twig, or reed matting is put in place, followed by a bedding layer of mud and a bonding layer of lime. Taiyuan, Shanxi. [Original photograph used with the permission of Arthur J. Van Alstyne.]

Figure 3.157 (bottom left). Arranged in a series of concave channels, these tiles are being set into a mud base on top of a formed clay base. Beijing area. [RGK photograph 1985.]

Figure 3.158 (top right). In this roof reconstruction on a Qing dynasty dwelling, the workman has resurfaced the mud and lime base and is setting the tiles in an alternating convex and concave pattern. Wang family manor, Lingshi *xian*, Shanxi. [RGK photograph 1996.]

themselves (Figures 3.156, 3.157, and 3.158). During the Ming and Qing periods in northern China, waterproofing was enhanced with the use of *qinghui* 青灰, a green powder sometimes called "green lime." Mixed with hemp fibers and water to form a viscous paste, it was spread on the roof, compressed to remove excess water, and allowed to dry to an impervious layer. Clay "nails" of various shapes also have been employed to secure roof tiles, especially in areas of strong winds (Zhang 1985b, 185). The regularity of tiles laid in mud and lime is as much utilitarian as it is aesthetically pleasing (Figures 3.159 and 3.160).

Throughout southern China, it is often only the weight of the tiles themselves—rather than a bonding layer—that holds them in place. Since ventilation is more important than insulation in subtropical areas, this allows the house to breathe and to evacuate warm air that would otherwise build up in the interior. Rafters, either thin sticks or sawn timber, are placed between the purlins in order to form a frame-

work to hold the loose tiles (Figures 3.161 and 3.162). A single bay 3 meters wide and 3.5 meters deep comprises perhaps three thousand tiles, which demand a substantial load-bearing structure to support them (Ruitenbeek 1993, 75). Tiles laid lightly in this manner sometimes are shifted by the wind and gravity and must be rearranged periodically (Figures 3.163 and 3.164).

While tiles in general exceeded the ability of both thatch or mud-surfaced roofs to shed water, innovative changes in tile-laying and manufacture further helped to enhance their performance. An especially interesting and functional element of tile shape emerged after much experimentation: end tiles, eaves tiles [*wadang* 瓦当], placed at the ends of rows of roof tiles. Today eaves tiles are sometimes viewed as only decorative additions on historic buildings and common structures. They appear in many shapes— semicircular, circular, and somewhat triangular— and often with prominent molded or carved orna-

Figure 3.159. Scalelike in appearance and function, the tile surface sheds water rapidly. Huairou *xian*, Beijing. [RGK photograph 1987.]

Figure 3.160. Once set in mud and lime on a northern roof, arcuate tiles provide a corrugated surface for water to flow to the eaves. Beijing. [RGK photograph 1987.]

mentation on their exposed surface (Figures 3.165 and 3.166). Semicircular end tiles dominated until the Eastern Han period, when their use was superseded by round tile. Architectural historians have discovered that circular *wadang* drain water much faster along their circumference than do truncated semicircular end tiles, and they suggest that this difference, rather than aesthetic considerations, fostered the eclipse of semicircular shapes (Zhang 1985b, 186). Triangular dripping tiles similarly draw water rapidly

from a sloping roof and hasten its dropping to the ground below. That Chinese roofs are typically steeper near the ridgeline than they are at the eaves necessitated attention be paid to how to increase water flow along the eaves line.

Nearly half of all farm buildings throughout China in the early 1930s had tile roofs, according to Buck's survey (1937, 443). Regional differences, however, were quite striking. While more than two-thirds of dwellings in the rice region of the south had tile

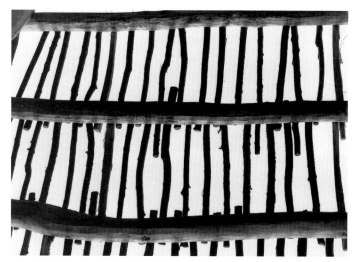

Figure 3.161 (top left). Placed on the slant between the purlins, thin stick rafters are widely used in the countryside to hold layers of tiles. Zhejiang. [RGK photograph 1987.]

Figure 3.162 (top right). Some rafters in higher quality dwellings are made of sawn timber, which provide a more uniform slope. Guilin, Guangxi Zhuang Autonomous Region. [RGK photograph 1985.]

Figure 3.163 (middle left). Laid loosely atop the rafters so that the upper portion of one tile overlaps another, the substantial number of fragile roof tiles provides a serviceable surface against rain, even though natural decay, wind, and gravity all conspire to loosen and rearrange them. Lanxi *shi*, Zhejiang. [RGK photograph 1987.]

Figure 3.164 (bottom left). Large and slightly bent tiles of uniform shape and size are set on the roof of this Hakka fortress. Gaobei *cun*, Guzhu *xiang*, Yongding *xian*, Fujian. [RGK photograph 1990.]

Figure 3.165. *Wadang*, eaves tiles, in Zhejiang are often highly decorated with calligraphic and symbolic motifs. [RGK photographs 1985.]

Figure 3.166. All of these triangular eaves tiles have curved bases and are separated by tubular tiles. The elevated tubes are capped at the ends by ornamented circular *wadang*. Top, Langzhong *shi*, Sichuan; middle, Qiao family manor, Qixian, Shanxi; bottom, Wang family manor, Lingshi *xian*, Shanxi. [RGK photographs 1994, 1996, 1996, respectively.]

Figure 3.167. Tile-making is carried out today just as was depicted in the seventeenth-century *Tiangong kaiwu*. A thin slab of clay is sliced with a wire bow from an oblong block of clay. The potter then shapes and smooths the surface of the slice along the side of a flexible cylindrical mold with his hands before setting the circular form on the ground to dry and split. [Source: Sung 1966, 133.]

rectangular block of kneaded clay, perhaps a meter high, is formed. It is from this block that the tile-maker's assistant, using a wire bow fashioned from wood or bamboo, slices a sheet of clay to the intended tile thickness. Since multiple tiles typically are produced from a single slice, its length and width will not only be dependent on the intended size of the tile but also on the size of the cylindrical mold. Lifted with the lower arms and hands, the slice is draped around a collapsible cylin-

roofs, only a quarter of farm houses in the northern wheat region did. At the extremes, 98 percent of dwellings found in the double-cropping rice region along China's southeastern coast, whereas only 11 percent of those in the inner Asian spring wheat region were covered with fired tiles. That small and medium-size farms were less likely than large farms to have tiled roofs on dwellings points clearly to the fact that available capital helped drive the use of this preferred roofing material.

The traditional methods of tile manufacturing discussed and photographed by Rudolf Hommel in the 1920s (1937, 270–274) parallel those depicted in the seventeenth-century *Tiangong kaiwu* (Figure 3.167), which can still be observed all over China today (Figures 3.168, 3.169, 3.170, 3.171, 3.172, 3.173, 3.174, and 3.175). First, suitable local clay taken from the fields or mud from river bottoms is worked with small amounts of water into a suitable consistency, either through the action of the bare feet of workmen or the treading of a large animal. Tile-making often occurs where raw materials are found rather than at a fixed production site, because it is easier to transport the simple tools and even build a kiln than it is to transport large amounts of soil. A

Figure 3.168. Blindfolded and led to walk in circles, this water buffalo is passing repeatedly over a mass of local river mud in order to work it into a suitable consistency for tile-making. Zhejiang. [RGK photograph 1987.]

Figure 3.169 (top left). Formed into a rectangular column of densely packed mud, a meter in height and length, the clay is smoothed and then cut into thin sheets using a wire bow. Zhejiang. [RGK photograph 1987.]

Figure 3.170 (bottom left). The thin sheet of clay is lifted with two hands and laid around a wooden mold, which itself is covered with a moistened cloth. Zhejiang. [RGK photograph 1987.]

Figure 3.171 (top right). Initially the sheet of clay on the wooden mold is smoothed with the hands. A shaping tool and vat of water, which will be used later, are shown in the foreground. Zhejiang. [RGK photograph 1987.]

Figure 3.172 (bottom right). Using a curved shaping tool, the tile-maker rotates the mold until the surface of the clay is even. Zhejiang. [RGK photograph 1987.]

Figure 3.173 (top left). Once shaped, the now tubular clay sheet is carried on the mold to a drying area. There the wooden mold is collapsed, separating it and the moistened cloth from the tubular clay shape. The clay shapes are stacked to air dry. Zhejiang. [RGK photograph 1987.]

Figure 3.174 (bottom left). Once the tubular clay shape is dry, it breaks easily with a twist of the wrist into four tile fragments. Zhejiang. [RGK photograph 1987.]

Figure 3.175 (top right). The roof tiles that are stacked in the foreground will be carried into the temporary kiln in the rear for firing. Zhejiang. [RGK photograph 1987.]

Figure 3.176. Slabs of split wood of various sizes and shapes are used to cover roofs by minority nationality groups throughout southwest China. This roof is a reconstructed split slab wood roof of a Hani dwelling in the Chinese Ethnic Cultural Park in Beijing. [RGK photograph 1993.

drical mold that tapers toward the top. Most cylinders seen today rotate like a potter's wheel, so the workman can remain at a fixed position; but it appears that the seventeenth-century frame was stationary and the workman moved about the cylinder. Made like a flexible shutter composed of multiple joints, the rotating tile-maker's mold typically has four raised vertical strips that leave indentations on the molded slab. It is these indentations that ultimately allow the workman to break the molded clay

sheet into four evenly shaped tiles. With only a couple turns of the mold, the tile-maker smooths the clay slab, first with his hand and then with a shaping tool held between the fingers and the palm, and then fuses the ends of the slab to form a truncated conical shape. A simple wire cutting tool is used to even the clay at the top of the mold. Then the mold with the tubular clay shape attached to its outside is carried to the drying yard. With a twist of the wrist, the two are disengaged as the wooden frame collapses. The tubular clay shapes are left to air dry either in the sun or in the shade, depending on the temperature and the day's humidity. After a day or so, the tubular shapes can be stacked to save space. Once sufficiently dry, each clay tube is then broken by hand along the inside indentations that were formed by the raised strips of the collapsible mold. Four concave segments, each forming an individual gutter-shaped tile, are ready for firing in a kiln, which normally turns them from light brown to gray.

Wood and Stone Shingles

In some of the mountainous areas of the northeast and southwest, shingles made of wood and stone traditionally have been used. Wood shingles [*mubanwa* 木板瓦] have a long history of use on log houses in Jilin province. They were traditionally cut from fallen logs into square shapes and laid, without bonding or other means of securing them, from the eaves to the ridge. Even though typically two-thirds of a shingle was overlapped and only one-third exposed, the wood shingles were prone to lifting during periods of heavy winds. A staggered stack of wood shingles would be placed the full length of the ridgeline, with extra height and weight added at each end of the ridge. Large shingles crafted from birch and pine bark were also used in Jilin province (Zhang 1985b, 110–111).

The roofs of log dwellings built by minority nationality groups throughout southwest China are often covered with slabs of split wood of various sizes and shapes (Figure 3.176). Instead of being secured with nails, the wooden slabs are held in place by stones or each other. Thin slabs of wood of various sizes and shapes are used to provide cover for the roofs of Yi log

Figure 3.177. Overlapping slate fragments of many shapes and sizes are used as roof covering on this Buyi rock dwelling. Guizhou. [Original photograph used with the permission of Joseph Chuo Wang.]

Figure 3.178. When available, large sheets of slate are used for roofing even new two-story dwellings. Northwestern Henan. [Original photograph used with the permission of Arthur J. Van Alstyne.]

houses and Hani dwellings. Thatching as well as split bamboo also are sometimes found on very simple log houses, while kiln-fired tile is a qualitative improvement on the dwellings of those who can afford it.

When locally available in the mountainous areas of China—such as among the Buyi in Guizhou—large slabs of overlapping slate fragments are used as roof covering (Figure 3.177). Because slate is not pliable, careful attention must be paid to finishing the seam at the roof ridge with a mud and lime composition. Even new two-story dwellings are sometimes roofed with slate sheets when they are available (Figure 3.178).

Part III
PLACES AND REGIONS

Map 4.1. Northern China, as a broad cultural region, includes the northeast, the region straddling the Great Wall, the Loess Plateau, and the North China Plain.

CHAPTER 4

Dwellings in Northern China

THE NORTHERN SETTLEMENT REGION is an area characterized by continental climate with long, severe winters and relatively short but hot summers, during which only modest precipitation falls. Strong dry winds during winter and dust storms in spring pummel much of the region for more than six months of the year. Dwellings throughout the region reflect these harsh climatic realities and give evidence of significant environmental adaptation. Sweeping as a broad arc from the remote areas of northeast China southward and then westward, as seen in Map 4.1, the region includes all of the North China Plain, the barren and semiarid areas adjacent to the Great Wall, and the unique loessial plateau in the middle reaches of the Huanghe (Yellow River). While there is no uniformity in the styles of northern houses, there are sufficient similarities in layout as well as building structure to justify focusing on one rather ordinary type and two types that are particularly distinctive: common rectangular dwellings, courtyard dwellings, and subterranean dwellings, respectively.

Single-Story Rectangular Farm Houses

Modest single-story rectangular dwellings [*danzuo pingfang* 单座平房] have always been more common throughout rural north China than either courtyard or subterranean dwellings. Usually found freestanding in dispersed settlements or clustered together in compact villages, as seen in Figures 4.1, 4.2, 4.3, and 4.4 and glimpsed earlier in Figures 2.8 and 2.11, *dan-*

zuo pingfang vary in style from place to place but are all rather unpretentious and spartan. *Danzuo pingfang* generally represent the penury and simplicity of traditional rural life, yet even large expensive brick dwellings being built today echo these simple forms (Figure 4.5). As economic conditions allow, it is always possible to improve and enlarge this linear nucleus of habitation. For generation after generation, however, most Chinese in the north no doubt have lived in simple single-story structures. Over the past twenty years, while there has been a qualitative improvement in the materials used to build *danzuo pingfang* as economic conditions have improved, there has also been the destruction of countless modest dwellings that had served peasants for centuries.

Northern *pingfang*—whether old and humble or new and pretentious—recall the quintessential elements of neolithic dwellings at Banpo: symmetry in frontal elevation, central entry, gabled endwalls, windowless side and back walls, double-sloped roof, and a southern exposure (Figure 4.6). Some architectural historians are now heralding a simple triple-*jian* structure in Gaoping *xian*, Shanxi, as the oldest surviving dwelling in China (Zhang Guangshan 1993). Reputedly built in the early Yuan dynasty (1279-1368), *Jizhai* 姬宅 has some structural features, such as *dougong* 斗拱, "eaves brackets," that were not common on later Ming and Qing dwellings (Figure 4.7). In combination with a front open to the sun, solid walls on three sides, and a depth that is almost always less than one-half the length, the elongated yet tight design of *pingfang* address the harshness of northern

Figure 4.1. Set amidst newer dwellings, this modest dwelling in northeast China is made of adobe brick with a mud plaster surface. The roof is thatched in a traditional manner. Jinjiawan, Dongling *qu*, Shenyang, Liaoning, 1994. [Original photograph used with the permission of Elizabeth Leppman.]

Figure 4.2. A cluster of dwellings made of stone in a nucleated village in northern Hebei province. Each *danzuo pingfang* dwelling faces south and has a walled courtyard at its front. Within the courtyard is a haystack, kitchen garden, and a latrine. [RGK photograph 1984.]

Figure 4.3. Flat-roofed *danzuo pingfang* dwellings are found in the semiarid areas of Ningxia Hui Autonomous Region. Simple wooden doors and ornate lattice windows are the only embellishment to these adobe dwellings. 1982. [Original photograph used with the permission of Arthur J. Van Alstyne.]

Figure 4.4. Photographed earlier in the century, humble thatched dwellings of this sort provided shelter and a home for countless Chinese peasant families in the past. A small courtyard is fashioned from upright grain stalks that are lashed together. The shading on the facade indicates that the dwelling faces south and only has a shallow eaves overhang. A small pen for animals is to the west side. North China plain. [Source: Unknown.]

Figure 4.5. This modern brick five-*jian danzuo pingfang* preserves all the elements of simpler structures even with a dramatic improvement in the quality of the materials and the width of each bay. Liuminying *cun*, Huairou *xian*, Beijing. [RGK photograph 1987.]

Figure 4.6. Quite similar to dwellings in Figure 4.4, this reconstruction of a neolithic rectangular dwelling at Banpo, Shaanxi, prefigured the later ubiquitous *pingfang* rural house style of north China. The dwelling has overhanging eaves, a southern exposure, and windowless side and back walls; however, it lacks a window on the southern wall. [Source: Xian Banpo bowuguan 1982.]

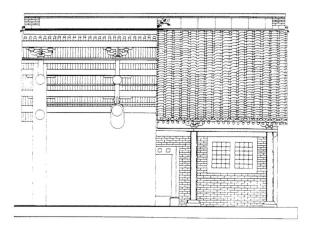

Figure 4.7. Reputedly the oldest surviving dwelling in China, this triple-*jian* structure is 10.65 meters wide and 7.75 meters deep. Architects have dated the dwelling from the early Yuan period because of the presence of *dougong* beneath the front eaves and its various building ratios. Zhongzhuang *cun*, Gaoping *xian*, Shanxi. [Source: Zhang Guangshan 1993, 30.]

winters reasonably well. The ridgepole supporting the roof of most northern dwellings is arranged in an east-west direction. Thus, the facade is normally oriented with the door and windows facing south, demonstrating a clear awareness of the ability to gain heat from winter sunshine. At the same time, the side and back walls are usually without windows or doors in order to provide a solid barrier against the intrusion of the predictably steady and cold northwest winds (Figure 4.8). Until recent decades, the walls of northern *pingfang* were generally constructed of readily and cheaply available tamped earth or adobe brick, built to a thickness that reduced the infiltration of cold air. Together with a thick roof that may be flat, concave, or pitched with a single- or double-slope, this dwelling type generally has provided substantial protection for enduring the bitter cold and powerful winds of northern winter and early spring.

In preparation for winter, sheets of paper traditionally were pasted on the inside of window frames and along cracks in the upper wall in order to lessen the seepage of cold air. With the natural deterioration of the paper over the course of the year, it was renewed annually, but only after the gaping holes welcomed the breezes of spring, summer, and fall. Because of the airtightness of these paper sheets, it was sometimes necessary during winter to poke a hole in the paper covering a window in order to vent poisonous gases. Then the vent hole was usually reinforced with a decorative papercut. Today, paper-covered windows are not common, and single-glazed glass predominates. Papercuts, a traditional folk art, were once affixed to the paper sheets covering the windows but now are pasted to the translucent glass surface instead. Ceilings and walls of northern dwellings, however, even today are often papered with thick white sheets that are stretched over a framework of *kaoliang* stalks or attached directly to the plaster. These white paper surfaces provide backgrounds for decorative embellishment. Recent scientific surveys have acknowledged the reasonable thermal comfort of traditional northern *pingfang* and have pointed to ways of improving it by increasing the insulation of the roof, reducing heat loss through the

Figure 4.8. Northern dwellings are almost always constructed so that the back and side walls are solid, providing an impenetrable barrier against predictably steady and cold northwest winds. Orientation to the cardinal directions places the back wall toward the north and the south wall positioned so that the interior of the dwelling obtains passive solar energy through substantial windows located along the south facade. The walls on this structure are load-bearing brick and stone, while the south facade is remarkably open. Northern Shanxi. [RGK photograph 1984.]

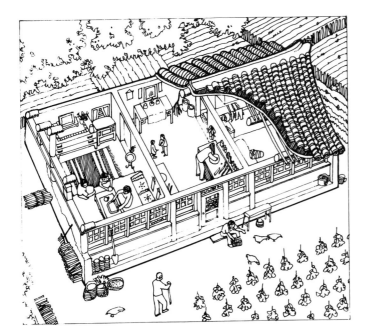

Figure 4.9. This cutaway drawing of a triple-*jian* northern farmhouse includes a central room with two adjacent bedrooms. Inside the central doorway are a pair of facing cooking stoves that provide heat during winter for each of the *kang* brick beds found in the abutting bedrooms. Located just inside the south-facing windows, each *kang* provides a bright working surface during the daytime and a warm bed at night. [Original artwork used with the permission of Bonnie Shemie.]

els for cooking do double duty in heating the bedrooms as well.

Once the bedding is removed and a low table placed on it, a *kang* serves as a dining and work area (Figure 4.11). Located just inside the south-facing windows of the facade, *kang* also act as passive solar collectors for the winter sun and thus become the warmest spot in a northern house. In summer, heat from the cooking stove is shunted along the periphery of the *kang* and exhausted directly outside through a chimney so as not to raise the temperature in the living space. Even in summer, however, *kang* remain the center of family life, as each provides a bright and surprisingly cool place for domestic chores such as sewing and food preparation. Eye-level ornamentation, such as papercuts and woodblock prints [*kangweihua* 炕围花], is usually pasted on the three walls surrounding the *kang*, serving as a repository of didactic axioms

windows and door openings on the front, and augmenting solar gain by employing various types of simple solar collectors (Wang Zhunqin 1991).

Known colloquially as *yiming liangan* 一明两暗 [one bright, two dark or one opened, two closed], northern rectangular dwellings commonly are sectioned into three rooms, a division facilitated by the building modules called "bays" [*jian*], a subject discussed in Chapter 2 (Figure 4.9). The central room into which the door of the dwelling opens generally serves as kitchen, common utility room, and corridor to adjacent interior bedrooms. Just inside the door of the central bay, as seen in Figure 4.10, is at least one, and often two, low brick stoves used for cooking. They also provide the heat for elevated bed platforms called *kang* 炕 or *huokang* 火炕 that are traditionally found in the adjacent *jian*. As a hypocaust heating system utilizing the hot air that passes from each of the cooking stoves through a warren of flues embedded in the brick of the heatable beds, each *kang* becomes in winter a significant heat-radiating surface and a comfortable bed once a quilt is unfolded on it. The whole heating unit is carefully sealed so that no smoke can penetrate the room. Whatever readily available grasses, straw, brush, and coal are used as fu-

Figure 4.10. One of a pair placed just inside the door of the central bay of many northern dwellings, this low stove is used for cooking and for providing heat to the *kang* in the adjacent room. Northern Hebei. [RGK photograph 1984.]

Figure 4.11 (left). Even in summer, when the bedding is removed, *kang* prove to be sunny spaces for relaxing and preparing food. On the low table is a tray of freshly made dumplings ready to be boiled. During winter, *kang* become warm heat-radiating surfaces because of the warren of flues embedded in the brick beneath. Unrolling quilted bedding makes it a comfortable place to sleep. Northern Hebei. [RGK photograph 1984.]

Figure 4.12 (right). In order to endure the bitterly cold winters of northeastern China, *kang* are sometimes built along the back and side walls as well as along the front wall. Sometimes they are U-shaped and linked to "heated walls" [*huoqiang*], which creates a range of heat-radiating surfaces. Special attention is paid to chimneys in northeastern dwellings because of the intensity and duration of heat in the stove during the coldest times of the year. Towering chimneys are usually located a short distance to both sides of a dwelling. Top, Jiaohalasuwu *cun*, Qi'qihaer, Heilongjiang; middle and bottom, Hulan *xian*, Heilongjiang. [Source: Zhou 1992, 142–144.]

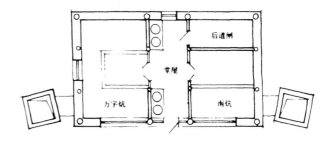

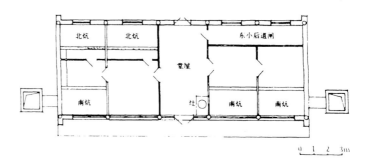

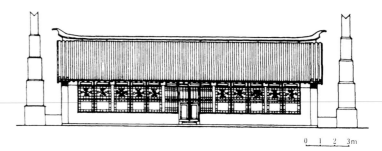

Figure 4.13. U-shaped *kang* are usually elevated above a floor surface and provide a ring of heat-radiating surfaces for daily life. In this new dwelling, the walls are papered and a large glass window allows winter sun into the dwelling. Northeast China [Source: Lu 1992, 31.]

and tales that are readily available for the socialization of children.

The *kang* found in the bitterly cold areas of northeastern China vary in location, size, and configuration from those seen elsewhere in north China. In Heilongjiang province, for example, *kang* are found along the back and side walls as well as along the front wall. As shown in Figures 4.12 and 4.13, they are sometimes U-shaped. When combined with "heated walls" [*huoqiang* 火墙], composed of flues running through earthen partitions, interior spaces are virtually surrounded by heat-radiating surfaces. Because of the intensity and duration of heat in the stove during the coldest times of the year, much attention is paid to chimneys in these northeastern dwellings. Usually set a short distance to both sides of the dwelling, each chimney towers high above the roofline. Whereas in north China paper traditionally was pasted inside of window frames, throughout northeastern China paper generally was glued to both the inside and the outside of the wooden frame. This was done to create a stronger barrier against the forces of winter, including withstanding greater wind pressures and preventing the accumulation of dust and snow on the window frame itself.

While the eastern room of northern *pingfang* is generally viewed as the superior room, serving as the bedroom for parents or grandparents, this is not the case in northern Liaoning province, where the western room is considered prime (Jiang 1994, 1). Because the room is seldom unoccupied, it is here that the household stores its valuable articles. The room on the western end of a *yiming liangan* dwelling usually serves as a bedroom for unmarried children or eventually that of a married son, his wife, and their children. Clothing and bedding are stored in stacked chests at the end of each *kang*, since this elevated area is likely to stay dry. Each room typically contains a bucket of wood, pottery, or enamel, so the family need not use the outside privy at night. In Heilongjiang province, where there are *kang* along several walls, different locations serve specific purposes. *Kang* along the southern wall are considered primary and are occupied by elders and the head of the household. *Kang* along the darker north wall are for servants and children. *Kang* along the west wall are for guests to sleep on (Zhou 1992, 141). Daily family activities, including eating, sleeping, and entertaining, take place atop the southern *kang*.

Although rectangular single-story dwellings of this type generally lack a formally marked yard or court-

Figure 4.14. Although *danzuo pingfang*, by definition, do not include a formal courtyard, they generally do have an "enclosure" at the front. Extending forward from the side walls, a perimeter "wall" is marked with piled stones or woven grain stalks to provide a place for a kitchen garden and storage. San Taizi *cun*, Laobian *xiang*, Yuhong *qu*, Shenyang, Liaoning, 1991. [Original photograph by Wu Xiujie.]

Figure 4.15. Facing due south, this recently constructed triple-*jian* dwelling preserves the essential features of a fully developed *danzuo pingfang*. Matching the dwelling in materials and color, the high wall encloses a substantial courtyard at its front. The gate, although on a side wall, is near the southeast corner. Northern Beijing. [RGK photograph 1987.]

yard, a common feature is a crudely delimited "enclosure" that extends forward from the side walls (Figure 4.14). Where space permits, low "walls" of piled stones or lashed grain stalks are placed along a perimeter in order to define an activity space for the household. In other cases, a fronting courtyard is defined by a high perimeter wall with access through a gate near the southeast corner (Figure 4.15). Within these fronting courtyards, one might find household possessions such as a wheelbarrow or cart, agricultural products waiting to be dried and stored, fuel needed for cooking, and even chickens and ducks ranging freely in search of food. It is rare to come across a defining perimeter on the sides or back of northern dwellings. An ordinary rectangular dwelling with a walled yard in front, however, is significantly less than an abridgment of the fully developed northern courtyard houses known as *siheyuan*, which will be discussed later.

The single-story dwellings of the Korean ethnic minority found in eastern Jilin, Liaoning, and Heilongjiang provinces in northeastern China are quite distinctive. Found among the fields, along roads, and in small clusters, Korean *pingfang* are quite different from contemporary Han dwellings. The horizontality of a Korean-style rural dwelling is often accentuated by a colonnaded facade shielding an elevated wooden platform [*qianlang langban* 前廊廊板] that is transitional space between outside and inside (Figures 4.16 and 4.17). Raised some 40 centimeters above the foundation stones, the *qianlang langban* is a functional space in which household members and visitors remove their shoes before entering and sitting directly on the *kang* inside. In summer, it serves as a kind of porch. Space within Korean-style rural houses in northeast China is divided by light wooden sliding screens that can be opened and closed according to need, a condition that is strikingly different from any found in Han Chinese dwellings. As with Han and other dwellings in areas of severe winters, openings on the back and side walls are not common. Instead of separate windows on the facade, as on Han dwellings, latticed door panels allow summertime ventilation in Korean-style dwellings.

As in the northern portions of Korea, roofs are often covered with mud and thick thatch, a condition well documented in the 1950s and 1960s in northeastern China (Zhang 1985a, 138–150). Korean-style dwellings also include *kang*, but they exceed in size those normally found in Han dwellings and are connected to much larger stoves. The external chimney, also larger, becomes a visual marker of Korean nationality dwellings. As in the Korean peninsula itself, underfloor heating systems called *ondol*, which are somewhat reminiscent of Roman hypocaust central-heating systems, are found in some Korean minority dwellings. Mud and stone are used to construct the

Figure 4.16. Appearing very much like dwellings in nearby areas of the Korean peninsula, this dwelling has an earthen/thatched roof with a colonnaded porch at the front. Along the side is a chimney made of wood and mud bricks that is set a meter or so from the dwelling. [Original drawing used with the permission of Wang Qi-jun. Source: Wang 1993, 71.]

Figure 4.17. A colonnaded and elevated wooden platform is raised forty centimeters above the foundation stones in Korean minority dwellings. Called a *qianlang langban*, it is transitional space between exterior and interior space, a functional surface on which household members and visitors remove their shoes before entering the dwelling. Reconstruction in the Chinese Ethnic Culture Park, Beijing. [RGK photograph 1996.]

ondol from the ground to floor level; then it is capped with slabs of stone approximately 5 centimeters thick, a layer of cement sealer, and oiled paper. Multiple flues are embedded under the floor and are fed by fires in the kitchen stove. Chimneys are placed just beyond an endwall and typically protrude well above the ridgeline of the dwelling in order to lessen the possibility of igniting the thatched roof. Each chimney is constructed with a brick base and a square vertical wooden "pipe." Some Korean dwellings in the Yanbian Autonomous Area of Jilin province echo Chinese dwellings before the Tang period, with their visually distinct and massive hipped tiled roofs. In-

stead of the simple intersections of four sloping surfaces, though, a vertical plane is inserted on both ends (Figure 4.18).

Courtyard Houses

A courtyard house is in many ways the classic model of a refined Chinese dwelling, the full flowering of domestic architecture, but such forms are much more than a dwelling unit attached to a walled courtyard. As discussed in Chapter 2, the archetypal northern courtyard dwelling is called a *siheyuan* 四合院, a structured

Figure 4.18. Line drawing of a well-to-do Korean nationality dwelling. The four slopes of the roof echo roofs of the Tang period. Longjing *xian*, Jilin. [Source: Zhang 1985, 150.]

residential quadrangle comprised of freestanding buildings arranged on four sides around a central courtyard. Constructed at different scales, *siheyuan* vary in complexity from the unpretentious and uncomplicated single courtyard compound of a small urban or rural family of modest means to the hierarchically structured courtyard complex of a wealthy merchant or imperial prince, whose multiple-unit *siheyuan* includes differentiated yet related space for a large extended family. The basic form of *siheyuan* is replicated at grander scales in temple and palace complexes. Variant forms of *siheyuan* are found widely throughout northern, northeastern, and northwestern China, reaching as far south as the northern banks of the Changjiang (Yangzi) River. Two related yet quite distinctive courtyard-type dwellings found to the south of the Changjiang will be discussed in the chapter on southern houses. With roots that reach deep

into China's building history, no indigenous dwelling type other than the *siheyuan* and its variants epitomizes so clearly the Chinese architectural principles of axiality, hierarchy, balance, and symmetry.

The three-thousand-year-old walled compound of the Western Zhou period excavated at Fengchu village, Shaanxi province, shown earlier in Figure 2.17, prefigured in a remarkably complete form the elements that are still seen today in *siheyuan*. Over the centuries, as fragmented historical and archaeological evidence suggests, *siheyuan* underwent modifications in plan and ornamentation even while retaining their fundamental form and basic elements. Extant *siheyuan* from the Ming and Qing dynasties exemplify the impact of different social, economic, and geographical factors on the *siheyuan* building form. Four basic northern *siheyuan* variations are generally recognized: Beijing *siheyuan*, Shanxi and Shaanxi *siheyuan*, northeastern *siheyuan*, and Hebei *siheyuan*. The Beijing *siheyuan* is acknowledged as the standard against which others are compared, as Table 4.1 indicates.

Whether historical or contemporary, each Beijing *siheyuan* is an oblong quadrangle encompassing at least one courtyard [*yuanluo* 院落, *yuanzi* 院子, or *tingyuan* 庭院] that is surrounded on four sides by individual halls. Covered corridors do not always complete a circuit around the courtyard connecting each of the halls (Figure 4.19). High outer walls of gray brick and clay roof tiles embrace each *siheyuan* compound, excluding the world beyond as they envelope and shield the dwelling. *Siheyuan* proclaim seclusion and separation when viewed from outside, but from the inside the feeling is one of both security and openness. Nelson Wu characterizes this as an "implicit paradox of a rigid boundary versus an open

Table 4.1
Comparison of Northern *Siheyuan* Styles

	Courtyard Shape	Roof Style	Height of Main Hall	Decoration	Location of Gate
Beijing	Approximately square	Double slope	Single story	Moderate	Southeast
Hebei	Rectangle	Flat	Single story	Moderate	Southeast or South
Shanxi and Shaanxi	Narrow rectangle	Single slope	Double story	Elegant	Southeast or South
Liaoning and Jilin	Large square	Double slope	Single story	Coarse	South

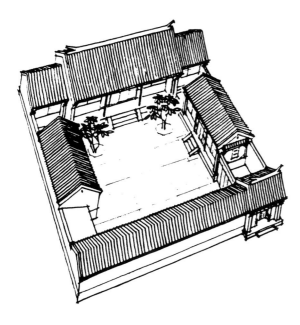

Figure 4.19. The basic elements of this simple *siheyuan* are carried over into more complex *siheyuan*: enclosure, single-story main hall and facing side halls, approximately square courtyard, moderate slopes on roof pitches, and a southeastern gate. [Source: Wang 1994, 144.]

The areas one first encounters inside a gate are usually the most public and active portions of the dwelling, including kitchens and space for servants and storage. The horizontal structure that encompasses them is known as a *daozuo* 倒座 ["inverted position" or "facing the rear"], since it sits in opposition to the main hall. A screen or spirit wall [*yingbi* 影壁 or *zhaobi* 照壁] either inside or outside the gate may further shield the interior from the gaze of passing strangers and serve as a focal point for ornamentation. The area around the entry is but the base of a hierarchical gradient that rises as one proceeds into the complex. If the quadrangle includes a forecourt separated from the main courtyard by a wall, the two are linked by a strikingly large and richly decorated inner gate [*chuihuamen* 垂花门 festooned gate], shown in Figure 4.20 and earlier in Figure 2.86.

The private inner quarters, including the main courtyard and linked structures, are beyond the festooned gate. Elevated on a podium on the north side of the inner courtyard [*neiyuan* 内院] and facing south is the principal building of the *siheyuan*, the *zhengfang* 正房. Viewed from the recessed court-

sky," where "the privacy . . . is a partial one; horizontally the yard is separated from the street by the wall or the surrounding buildings, but it shares both the sky and the elements of the weather with other houses and yards" (Wu 1963, 32).

To move from the external world into the residence, one passes first through a simple gate—the only entry into the compound—leading to a shallow space that masks the scale of the interior beyond. Traditionally whatever exterior decoration was seen at the gate represented the status of the occupant and was guided by sumptuary regulations. Depending on the rank and wealth of the household, the entryway might be of muted colors or might have columns and door panels painted bright red, as seen earlier in Figures 2.78 through 2.85. Carved steps, lintels, stone drums, and massive roofs over the doorway elevate many entries from being mere building entries.

Figure 4.20. Rising above the wall between two of the courtyards of this dwelling is a *chuihuamen*, an imposing "festooned gate" that is painted red and embellished with a tile roof and carved woodwork. Beijing. [RGK photograph 1984.]

Figure 4.21. Set four steps above the courtyard of this *siheyuan*, the three-bay-wide *zhengfang* has the main hall at its center. Here marked with carved doors and side panels, the elegant entry has been corrupted by a brick alcove addition on the right. Beijing. [RGK photograph 1977.]

Figure 4.22. The elevated three-jian *zhengfang* on the left (north) is connected with lower *xiangfang* by the covered walkway on the right (east). The high sun's rays of summer do not penetrate the overhang of the main structure, falling instead on the lower step, leaving the interior remarkably cool because of the reduced solar gain. Beijing. [RGK photograph 1984.]

yard, as seen in Figure 4.21, its interior location and raised position declare its seniority, providing space for family ceremonies, receptions, and bedrooms for parents or grandparents. *Zhengfang* are typically divided into three rooms, with a door leading only into the central reception room, the *tangwu* 堂屋, which then provides access to the adjacent side rooms [*taojian* 套间 or *erfang* 耳房] that serve as bedrooms. On the west and east sides of the courtyard are flanking "side halls" or "wing rooms" [*xiangfang* 厢房], detached structures separate from the *zhengfang* and *daozuo*. As seen in Figure 4.22, the flanking structures are linked by colonnaded corridors [*you-lang* 游廊]. Always diminished in scale and ornamen-

tation in comparison with the *zhengfang*, each *xiangfang* is divided into three rooms, which may serve as bedrooms for married sons or other children or as studies. Each of the four structures faces inward toward the courtyard, which has been described as being well shaped, with a configuration strikingly represented by the character 井. Representing about 40 percent of the total area of the complex, typical courtyards are paved with stone, planted with several flowering or fruit-bearing trees, and made green with potted plants. "Side halls" of northern *siheyuan* courtyard dwellings, unlike those to be discussed later in southern China, generally do not intrude upon any of the *zhengfang* unit, thus

Figure 4.23. This incipient Shaanxi-style dwelling is being built in stages. Viewed from the rear, it is clear that the side *xiangfang* were constructed first. The walled space remaining in the foreground serves now as a courtyard but will eventually be occupied by a horizontal main *zhengfang* structure that will link the *xiangfang*. Each *xiangfang* has a single-sloped roof draining inward to the narrow courtyard. A simple gate is located along the southeast section of the wall. Central Shaanxi. [RGK photograph 1991.]

Figure 4.24. The long, high blank wall comprises the back of one of a pair of *xiangfang* whose roofs slope inward to the interior courtyard. Entry is through a central gate in the southern wall and leads to a three-*jian*-wide *zhengfang*. Fenghuo *xiang*, Liquan *xian*, Shaanxi. [RGK photograph 1991.]

making possible an expansive and nearly square open area.

The courtyard houses in Shanxi and Shaanxi provinces are characterized by long, narrow courtyards and single-sloped roofs that drain only into the courtyard (Figures 4.23 and 4.24). Whether small or large in scale, the courtyards are three to four times longer from north to south than they are broad. While the basic elements of northern *siheyuan* can be discerned, regional characteristics are striking, especially in fully developed forms. As seen in the plans and perspective views of individual *siheyuan*, as seen earlier in Figures 2.22 through 2.24, courtyard dwellings usually include an entry gate at a southeast location as well as a spirit wall beyond the gate, a *chuihuamen* leading to the first courtyard, a middle gate, and a south-facing three- or five-bay main building. A sense of hierarchy is represented by the two series of interior steps as well as increasing height of rooflines as one progresses from front to back, from exterior to interior space (Figure 4.25).

The main three-bay structure of the narrow *siheyuan* shown in Figure 4.26 is constructed in a fashion that mimics cave dwellings common throughout central Shanxi. The lattice-framed windows are arcuate as are the walls and ceiling within. Steps lead to a high flat roof atop the main south-facing building that serves not only as a place from which a watchman can

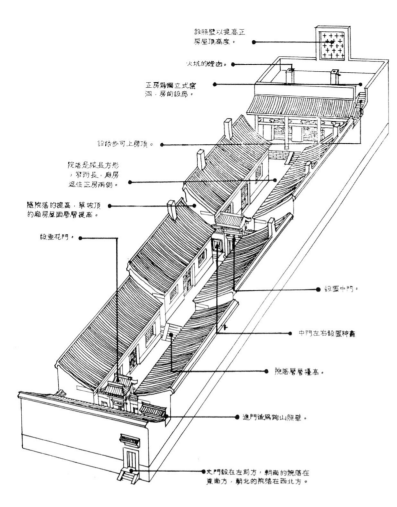

設明壁以提高正
房屋頂高度。

火坑的煙囪。

正房為獨立式窰
洞。房前設房。

設路步可上屋頂。

院落是狹長方形
，窄而長，廂房
延往正房兩側。

隨院落的提高，單坡頂
的廂房屋面層層提高。

設垂花門。

設置中門。

中門左右設置神龕

院落層層躍高。

進門後為跨山照壁。

大門設在左前方，朝南的院落在
東南方，朝北的院落在西北方。

Figure 4.25. Even with its long narrow court-yard and distinctive single-sloped roofs, this Shanxi *siheyuan* shares basic elements with Bei-jing *siheyuan*: an entry gate at a southeast loca-tion, a spirit wall inside the gate, a *chuihuamen* leading to the first courtyard, a middle gate, and a south-facing three-bay main building. Pingyao *shi*, Shanxi. [Original artwork used with the permission of Wang Qijun.]

survey the complex but also a place to relax during summer nights. The steps and flat parapeted roof maintain the sense of the sunken courtyard style cave dwellings dis-cussed below. Common dwellings tradi-tionally were built of adobe or tamped earth while the expansive complexes of the rich were of fired brick.

Throughout Shanxi, Shaanxi, and Henan provinces, there are extensive building complexes [*jianzhu qun* 建筑群] in which a multiplicity of *siheyuan* dwell-ings are combined with other architec-tural features, such as towers, gardens, and ancestral halls. Many of these com-plexes are walled and located within villages or towns in what today are consid-ered remote locations. Few provide obvi-ous evidence of the economic and social factors that contributed to their forma-

Figure 4.26. Although a longitu-dinal *siheyuan* of a prosperous merchant, the buildings con-structed alongside the narrow courtyard all mimic cave dwell-ings with their arcuate facades and interiors as well as wooden latticed doors and windows. The structure of the walls as well as the bountiful use of wooden tim-bers far exceed that of common residences, a subject discussed in Chapter 3. Pingyao *shi*, Shanxi. [RGK photograph 1996.]

tion. It is likely, though, that accumulated wealth from commerce and/or official position over several generations played key roles in bringing sufficient prosperity to a family or a location to make possible the building of such large residential complexes. The scant records that exist suggest that many of these families reached the zenith of their affluence in the two centuries between the middle of the eighteenth century and the early decades of the twentieth century. Although some of the residential complexes have deteriorated markedly over the past half-century because of neglect and natural forces, as well as deliberate destruction, others remain remarkably intact and beautiful, providing clues to past social and economic forces that are evident in no other way.

The emergence of fortified residential complexes appears to have been an architectural response to unsettled conditions that accompanied periodic dynastic decline in many areas of China. Rebellion, banditry, and general turmoil promoted the building of high walls around existing complexes in order to provide a level of enhanced security for the individual walled *siheyuan* courtyards contained within. In many cases, the larger village or town itself was walled so that there actually was a nested system of fortified units: village/town, residential complex, and individual dwelling units. Some village walls were rather temporary forms made of earth that survived only as long as there was a clear purpose for them. As stability replaced strife and they were no longer needed, the walls were sometimes razed, or eventually the forces of nature would obliterate them. In cases where the wealth of affluent clans made it possible, substantial fortifications of fired brick and stone— complete with parapets, towers, and sometimes moats—were built around their existing dwellings or a completely new walled complex would be carried out. Once completed, walled residential complexes of this sort were generally preserved as markers of a clan's strength and power. Throughout northern China, walled villages as well as some residential complexes found within them are called *baozi* 堡子 or *bao* 堡 [fortresses], toponyms that remain even in the absence of the fortifications themselves. The fortified complexes in southern and southwestern China that

will be examined in the next chapter suggest useful comparative elements.

Residential courtyard complexes in north China are usually designated as the *dayuan* 大院 or *zhuangyuan* 庄院 [manors or estates] of a single family or clan, such as "the Qiao family *dayuan*" or "the Kang family *zhuangyuan*." Some stand alone, while others comprise substantial portions of individual villages, towns, or cities. Widely regarded as an outstanding example of the latter is the grand complex of the Qiao clan in Qiaojiabao village, Qixian, Shanxi. Begun in 1756 by Qiao Guifa, the Qiao family manor [Qiao*jia dayuan* 乔家大院] came to occupy a total area of 8,725 square meters as a result of two major expansions, one in the middle of the nineteenth century and then again at the beginning of the twentieth century, just as the Qing dynasty was ending. The Qiao family thrived from trading activities centered at Xikou, today called Baotou, beyond the Great Wall in what is today Inner Mongolia. Specializing in the trade of pigments, flour, grain, and oils as well as running several pawnshops, the Qiao clan prospered, eventually expanding their business far beyond the borders of northern China. By the end of the nineteenth century, they operated coal mines, specialized shops, and an extensive banking network. Empress Cixi stopped here in summer 1900 as she fled with the young emperor to Xi'an in the wake of the arrival of an international expeditionary force in Beijing at the close of the Boxer Uprising. Changes in the national economy in the first decades of the twentieth century reduced the family's income and, according to popular beliefs, the profligacy of the fifth-generation descendants of the clan's founder led to bankruptcy of the clan. By the early 1930s, the family had divided its assets and the manor had begun to fall into disrepair, finally being abandoned after the Japanese invasion in 1937. After 1949, the complex was taken over by local authorities, who used it as an army barracks as well as for other governmental functions. Substantial destruction occurred during the Cultural Revolution. In 1985, the manor's fortunes—if not those of the clan—turned again as the complex was designated a museum and substantial funds apportioned for its repair. The grandeur of the Qiao family's *dayuan* is

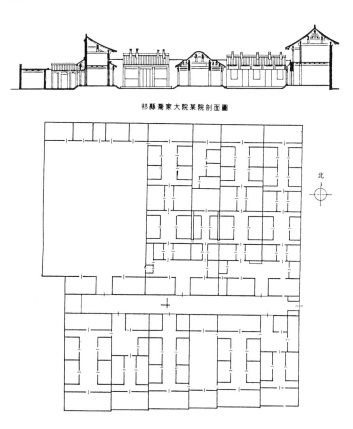

祁縣喬家大院某院剖面圖

北

Figure 4.27. At the top is a section view from north to south (right to left) of one of the upper *siheyuan* courtyard complexes in the Qiaojia manor. With six major courtyard compounds (three to the north and three to the south of the east/west lane) and some twenty smaller courtyards and side yards aligned north/south, Qiaojia *dayuan* includes 313 main and flanking rooms with gates. Begun in 1756, the complex continued to expand until the beginning of the twentieth century. The large open area in the upper left was destroyed during the Cultural Revolution. [Source: Yan, Yang, and Zhang 1994, 115–116.]

apparent to viewers of Zhang Yimou's 1991 film *Raise the Red Lantern.* Zhang's story is one of deceit, treachery, and sexual favors in a wealthy Chinese clan at the beginning of the twentieth century, all occurring within the confines of a grand feudal mansion. His tale, however, is not that of the Qiao family whose rise and fall is itself worthy of being told.

In order to meet the needs of a large and growing extended household, the Qiao family manor complex eventually came to comprise six major courtyard compounds with some twenty smaller courtyards and side yards. Some say that the layout of the courtyards, rooms, and lanes auspiciously resembles the character 喜 for "joy." In the adjacent buildings surrounding the courtyards, there were 313 rooms built for a total floor space of 3,870 square meters (Figure 4.27). A number of renovations around 1921 introduced western-style ornamentation and modern features, such as bathrooms, electricity, and etched window glass but did not

change the traditional character of the residential structure. As the manor complex took form, grey brick outer walls were built to connect the even higher back walls of courtyards. Capped with parapets, these 10-meter-high walls without windows presented a formidable and secure enclosure for the Qiao family (Figures 4.28 and 4.29). Because the manor is approached via narrow village alleys and never viewed from afar across the fields, its overall scale appears even more imposing as one encounters its main gate because of the height of the adjacent brick walls. Atop some of the flat roofs, several tall towers were built to rise high above the walls so that patrolling night watchmen could survey the inside and outside of the complex from passageways and steps that circuited the complex. Just inside the front gate, an east-west running lane paved with stone leads to the ancestral hall at the end and provides access to the six major courtyards of the complex, three larger ones on its north side and three smaller ones on its south side (Figures 4.30 and 4.31). Each set of steps and gates is staggered so that no two are directly opposite each other. Near each of these entries are stepping stones to assist riders on horseback as they mount and dismount.

Beyond each of these six entry gates on the lane is a series of courtyards and structures, each differing somewhat from the others, even as they are all typical of Shanxi domestic architecture. On the north side of the lane, only two of three sets of courtyards remain. One was completely destroyed during the Cultural Revolution and has been replaced with a

Figure 4.28. The high outer walls of thin grey brick encircling the complex are formed by the abutting structures, and are capped here and there with parapets. The exterior walls lack windows, and entry to the complex is through a single gateway along the eastern wall. Qiaojia *dayuan*, Qixian, Shanxi. [RGK photograph 1996.]

Figure 4.30 (below). From inside the main gate, an east to west lane separates the three courtyards on its north from the three on the south. To the right are gates to the first two northern courtyards; the third entry and its courtyard were destroyed during the Cultural Revolution. Qiaojia *dayuan*, Qixian, Shanxi. [Original photograph used with the permission of Li Yuxiang.]

Figure 4.29. At this southeastern corner of the encircling wall of the Qiaojia manor, a vertical stone with the words "The stone of Mount Tai dares to resist" serves as a protective amulet. Qiaojia *dayuan*, Qixian, Shanxi. [RGK photograph 1996.]

Figure 4.31. This ornamented *pailou*-type gate is similar to the others that lead from the east-west lane to a courtyard complex. Qiaojia *dayuan*, Qixian, Shanxi. [RGK photograph 1996.]

garden (Figure 4.32). Of the two remaining courtyard complexes on the north side, each has an east to west entry courtyard as well as several narrow rectangular inner courtyards that run north to south. The oldest courtyard is called *laoyuan* 老院 [the old courtyard] and was built in the mid-eighteenth century by Qiao Guifa.

Once past an entry courtyard that runs east to west, there are two narrow inner rectangular courtyards that run north to south and are linked by a hall (Figure 4.33). Midway between these two longitudinal courtyards is a single-story *guoting* 过厅, or "transitional hall," with a rolled roof that leads to a dramatic courtyard framed by side buildings with somewhat curved roofs (Figures 4.34 and 4.35). On the north side of the second courtyard and entered through an elaborate gate is a two-story *zhengfang*. Called here an "open building" or "bright building" [*minglou* 明楼], it faces south and has a sweeping double-sloped roofline (Figures 4.36 and 4.37). Although five bays wide, the *minglou* has no internal partitions so that it can be used as a single room. Its second story cannot be accessed directly from an inside stairway but can only be entered from an adjacent rooftop. Unlike elsewhere in north China, the Qiao family used its *zhengfang* exclusively for ceremonial purposes, such as making offerings and welcoming guests. Long, five-bay-wide *xiangfang* structures run north to south

Figure 4.32. The northwesternmost courtyard complex was destroyed during the Cultural Revolution and is now a garden. This view from the garden, looking toward the two-story main hall, shows the high back and sloping ridgeline of one of the side halls and the gabled roofline of the single-story "transitional hall." Qiaojia *dayuan*, Qixian, Shanxi. [RGK photograph 1996.]

Figure 4.33. View of a narrow north to south courtyard looking back toward the entry gate. Within each courtyard the single-sloped roofs are all pitched to drain toward the courtyard. Qiaojia *dayuan*, Qixian, Shanxi. [RGK photograph 1996.]

Figure 4.35 (below). Looking inside a building through the carved lattice windows toward the narrow courtyard and the "transitional hall" beyond. Qiaojia *dayuan*, Qixian, Shanxi. [RGK photograph 1996.]

Figure 4.34 (above). View from the northernmost rooftop of the complex back across a narrow courtyard to the *guoting*, or "transitional hall," that leads inward from another narrow courtyard. All roof slopes drain toward the stone-lined courtyards. Qiaojia *dayuan*, Qixian, Shanxi. [Original photo used with the permission of Li Yuxiang.]

Figure 4.36. View from inside a courtyard looking north toward the south-facing two-story main hall, or *zhengting*. Single-story wing buildings impinge upon the space in front of the two bays of the main structure. Qiaojia *dayuan*, Qixian, Shanxi. [RGK photograph 1996.]

alongside the narrow inner courtyard and contrast with three-bay-wide *xiangfang* in the outer rectangular courtyard. Although perpendicular to the *minglou*, they are not physically joined together. Both side structures have single-sloped roofs pitched at a forty-five degree angle that rise higher on the outer wall in order to dampen the impact of winter winds and also lead rainwater into the courtyard. These *xiangfang* were used by the household for daily activities, such as eating and sleeping. Inclined toward the interior and with a prominent eaves overhang, the lower roofline of these side halls creates a human scale for the otherwise constricted courtyards and surrounding high walls, providing at the same time a sense of openness that belies the narrow shape and diminished size of the courtyards. Internal passageways with open portals provide corridors around the complex for women and others who need not enter the main courtyards and gates (Figure 4.38).

The use of elevated and curtained beds instead of

Figure 4.37. Ornately decorated entryway to the two-story main hall. Qiaojia *dayuan*, Qixian, Shanxi. [RGK photograph 1996.]

Figure 4.39. An elaborate heating system in the Qiaojia manor necessitates a large number of high chimneys, some of which are elaborately ornamented with architectural and propitious motifs. Qiaojia *dayuan*, Qixian, Shanxi. [RGK photograph 1996.]

Figure 4.38. Subsidiary lanes, with open portals placed along them, allow some connection among the courtyard units without accessing the courtyards directly. Qiaojia *dayuan*, Qixian, Shanxi. [RGK photograph 1996.]

heated *kang* by the Qiao family is at variance with general northern practice of providing winter warmth from the radiated heat of *kang*, upon which members of the family would spend much of the cold winter. Much of the Qiao family complex, however, was

heated by an expansive system that used an extravagant consumption of fuel to keep whole rooms warm, clearly expressing the wealth of the household. This was accomplished by linking large stoves to chimneys via a warren of flues [*nuange* 暖阁] that ran under the brick floors and through some walls in order to supply radiant heat from many directions. As a result, more than 140 chimneys, some of which are elaborately ornamented, populate the upper walls and roofs (Figure 4.39). Except for the embellished exterior entryway that faces a wall with 100 variations of the Chinese character for longevity carved on it,

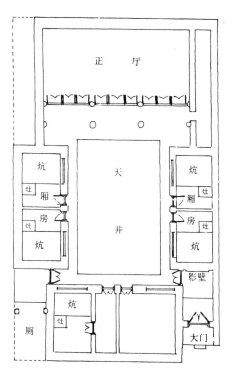

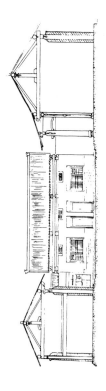

Figure 4.40. Plan and side elevation of the oldest dwelling in Dingcun, located in the northeast part of the village. Said to date from 1593, it preserves characteristics of Beijing-style residences: entrygate on southeastern wall (1); *yingbi*, or spirit wall (2); three-*jian*-wide colonnaded main hall (3); a pair of three-*jian*-wide flanking *xiangfang* (4) and facing *daocuo* (5), courtyard (6), toilet (7), and *kang* (8). The *xiangfang* are partitioned into two rooms—each with a *kang* running from front to back and an adjacent stove—rather than into three *jian* allowed by the structure itself. Dingcun, Xiangfen *xian*, Shanxi [Source: Tao 1992, 55.]

brick, wood, and stone carving were limited to inside locations for the experience of only family members.

Central and southern Shanxi possess other clusters of magnificent dwellings and prominent manor complexes of merchant families that date from the Ming and Qing dynasties. While neither the history of these families nor the role of kinship ties in the economic life of northern China have been studied in great detail, the scale of many dwelling complexes suggests areas of fruitful historical research. Many dwellings and manor complexes are at some distance from the major cities of the province, standing alone or comprising substantial portions of what appear to be isolated and backward villages and small towns. Many Shanxi residences are being proclaimed today as distinctive based upon their age, the renown of the forebears who built them, the extent and integrity of their architectural structures, and the nature of surviving wood, brick, and stone ornamentation.

Most authorities agree that the oldest set of Ming and Qing residences in Shanxi are those of the Ding family in Dingcun 丁村, Xiangfen *xian*. Of forty designated structures, perhaps ten have halls and courtyards that were built in the sixteenth and seventeenth centuries during the Ming dynasty. Two complete dwellings are said to date to the Wanli period (1573-1620). The earliest *siheyuan*, dated to 1593, is located in the northeast part of the village and preserves characteristics of Beijing-style residences: entrygate on southeastern wall, three-*jian*-wide colonnaded main hall, three-*jian*-wide flanking *xiangfang* and facing *daocuo*, *zhaobi*, and *kang*, although the courtyards are rectangular (Figures 4.40 and 4.41). An interesting aspect of the *xiangfang* is that they are partitioned into two rooms—each with a *kang* running from front to back and an adjacent stove—even though they were built as three-*jian*-wide structures. The second oldest *siheyuan*, dating from 1612, was built with two courtyards and associated structures; today only fragments remain. Some dwellings are older but have undergone such modification that they no longer represent Ming styles (Figure 4.42). For the most part, Ming dwellings are characterized by relatively

Figure 4.41. View from the courtyard of the three-*jian* main hall, or *zhengfang*, of the Ming dynasty dwelling shown in Figure 4.40. Dingcun, Xiangfen *xian*, Shanxi. [Original photograph used with the permission of Li Yuxiang.]

simple *siheyuan* quadrangles that conform to sumptuary regulations of the times. While some of the Qing period dwellings are uncomplicated, others involve receding two-*jin* and interconnected courtyards with substantial attention to hierarchy and the separation of outer and inner realms (Figures 4.43 and 4.44). Local historians attribute the survival of fine examples of Ming and Qing dwellings not only to the remoteness of Dingcun from this past century's tumult but also to family inheritance practices that demanded shared ownership. When two brothers divided their father's real estate, one would take an "upper" share and the other a "lower." This horizontal division worked against any one individual's desire to demolish and rebuild without the consent of the other (Pan 1995, 29–30). In 1985, six contiguous dwellings built between 1723 and 1986 were desig-

Figure 4.42. Entry to this dwelling is through a side door on the southeast wall. To the right of the entry is the back wall of the eastern *xiangfang*, or wing room, and the endwall of the main hall. The structure is dated to 1528 and has undergone extensive changes over the years. Dingcun, Xiangfen *xian*, Shanxi. [RGK photograph 1996.]

Figure 4.43. View from the main hall of a Qing period U-shaped *san-heyuan*. Matched *xiangfang* are here also divided into two rooms even though the columns reveal a three-*jian* structure. The eaves overhang leads rainwater to the impluvium and drains. The low outer wall connecting the *xiangfang* is dominated by a gate in the middle. Dingcun, Xiangfen *xian*, Shanxi. [RGK photograph 1996.]

Figure 4.44. Ornamented gate at the entry of a Qing dynasty dwelling in the southern section of the village. Dingcun, Xiangfen *xian*, Shanxi. [RGK photograph 1996.]

nated as the Dingcun Folkways Museum [*Dingcun minsu bowuguan* 丁村民俗博物馆], reputedly the first such specialized museum in China to focus its exhibits on Han folk practices within architecturally significant historical structures.

The Cao family manor [Cao*jia dayuan* 曹家大院] at Beiguang, Taigu, has a rigid symmetrical plan with each of the structures increasing in height from front to rear (Figure 4.45). When viewed from the towers along the northernmost wall, as seen in Figure 4.46, the narrow courtyards, flanking *xiangfang*, and transitional halls proceed in a descending rhythm toward the front. Until recently the complex was occupied by a large number of families and had fallen into disrepair. It has now been emptied, cleaned, and is undergoing extensive renovation (Figure 4.47). Several pavilions sit atop the tall building blocks along the north side of Cao manor, providing prospects for enjoying the scenery and the breeze as well as vantage points for family watchmen (Figure 4.48).

The Qu family manor [Qu*jia dayuan* 渠家大院] in Qixian city has recently been opened as the Shanxi Museum of Merchant Culture [*Jin shang wenhua bowuguan* 晋商文化博物馆] to recognize the role of the Qu family in banking. Covering a total area of 5,300 square meters, the complex includes eight large courtyards, nineteen smaller ones, and nearly 240 "rooms." The building area represents approximately 3,200 square meters and includes a five-*jin* sequence of courtyards. Some of the structures are said to have been built during the latter

Figure 4.45 (top left). Oriented from north to south, the Cao family manor has an austere symmetrical plan with each of the east-west running structures increasing in height from front to rear. The back of each of the perimeter buildings forms a wall around the complex. Beiguang, Taigu, Shanxi. [RGK photograph 1996.]

Figure 4.46 (top right). Looking to the south from a three-story rear towerlike building, narrow courtyards are defined by flanking *xiangfang* and connected to each other through transitional halls. Beiguang, Taigu, Shanxi. [RGK photograph 1996.]

Figure 4.47 (bottom right). View through a transitional hall from one narrow courtyard to another. The complex has only recently been emptied of its residents and is undergoing extensive renovation. Beiguang, Taigu, Shanxi. [RGK photograph 1996.]

Figure 4.48 (bottom left). One of several pavilions that are perched atop the tall building blocks along the north side of Cao manor. With rooflines more akin to palaces than the dwellings below, the pavilions create prospects for enjoying the scenery and catching the breeze. Beiguang, Taigu, Shanxi. [RGK photograph 1996.]

Figure 4.49. Heavily ornamented interior entry between courtyards in Qujia manor, Qixian. [RGK photograph 1996.]

half of the eighteenth century. Throughout the complex there is lavish ornamentation in carved wood, brick, and stone (Figure 4.49).

While it is improper to speak of fully developed manor complexes as vernacular housing, since they represent the dwellings of elites, they nonetheless represent an evolutionary house form related to simpler prototypes that at an even grander scale are echoed in the plans of China's magnificent imperial palaces. Among all Chinese housing, the courtyard house has been the most enduring and widespread form. Varying in shape, scale, and proportion, courtyard houses are found throughout the country and often have distinctive regional names that disguise the fact that they are essentially mutations of the classic northern *siheyuan*. The courtyard form was adapted by Han settlers to meet varying climatic conditions in different parts of the country they occupied, ranging from the cold and dry north to the hot and wet south, and it was adopted by non-Han minority populations on China's periphery to meet their diverse social circumstances.

Subterranean Dwellings

Some forty million Chinese live below ground in subterranean dwellings or cavelike structures [*yaodong* 窑洞 or simply *yao* 窑] that are dug into the ochre-colored loessial uplands that stretch through the provinces of Henan and Shanxi in northern China to Shaanxi and Gansu in northwestern China. Smaller numbers of this significant dwelling form are found in the adjacent areas of Hebei, Qinghai, Inner Mongolia, and Ningxia and as far away as Xinjiang. In some settlements of northern Shaanxi province, more than half of all villagers live below ground, and in some areas this exceeds 80 percent. Throughout much of rural Shaanxi, Shanxi, and neighboring Henan, at least 20 percent live in *yaodong* of many types. Numerically, however, the largest concentration of *yaodong* are found in a core region stretching from Qingyang in eastern Ningxia; Qianling, Huangling, Yan'an, and Mizhi in Shaanxi; Taiyuan, Linfen, and Pinglu in Shanxi, to Gongxian to the west of Zhengzhou in Henan province. *Yaodong* are only found north of the Qinling range and to the west of the North China Plain.

The term "*yao*" means "kiln," suggesting the beehivelike structures used throughout China's countryside to fire bricks and tiles. "*Dong*" represents the recessed cavities or holes in the earth that most people would simply call "caves." Indeed, the architectural historians Liang Sicheng in the 1930s and Liu Dunzhen in the 1950s wrote of this building type as "cave dwellings" [*xueju* 穴居]. Chinese usage of the term "*yaodong*" [kilnlike caves] also extends to structures of stone, brick, or tamped earth built at grade level that mimic underground forms in appearance and basic character.

China's loessial uplands encompass the largest such dissected plateau in the world. Lying within a semiarid and arid climatic zone, with precipitation varying between 250 and 500 millimeters per year and falling mainly in summer torrents, the region is also one of strong continental temperature extremes. Summer temperatures often exceed 35°C, while winter temperatures drop below 0°C. Loessial soil, or simply loess, known in Chinese as "yellow earth" [*huangtu* 黄土], is essentially finely textured silt that has been transported by strong and steady seasonal northwestern winds from the Gobi Desert and Mongolian uplands into the topographically rugged middle reaches of the Huanghe River. Over several millennia, this region has been continuously blanketed with layers of windblown silt that has been compacted to depths between 50 and 200 meters, although some areas appear to have depths of 300 meters. Loess possesses physical and chemical properties that have made it an optimal building medium in an environment with only limited possibilities. While the soil is rather dense, it is also quite soft, generally uniform in composition, and free of stones, so it can be cut into easily with simple tools. A cement-like crust some 20 centimeters thick forms on excavated surfaces as the surface soil dries out. Nonetheless, since loess is easily eroded by summer rains, it is carried in enormous quantities into the dendritic river system via gully wash. The intensity of this erosion has bequeathed the soil's Chinese name "yellow earth" [*huangtu*] to northern China's principal river, the Huanghe or Yellow River, because of the color of its turbid and sediment-loaded flow.

Once covered with grasses and dense forests and a productive cradle of Chinese agrarian civilization, virtually all of the loessial uplands has been dry and denuded for at least two millennia. Extensive deforestation resulted from accelerating firewood collection, charcoal-making, land reclamation, and brick-making (Fang and Xie 1994). As the availability of timber declined and without the economic wherewithal to bring in building materials from outside the region, Chinese peasants for centuries came to dig into the soil to make their underground abodes just as prehistoric peoples with much less technology had done earlier.

Subterranean dwellings seen today, however, are hardly primitive caves. They have evolved in structure and plan to represent a significant dwelling type that is perhaps better called "earth-sheltered housing." Remarkably cool in summer and warm in winter because of the conservation of heat by the thick and solid earth "roof" and surrounding "walls," subterranean dwellings have proved to be a remarkably suitable adaptation in a region of pronounced seasonal temperature extremes. The use of the term "cave" in the following discussion is not employed in a disparaging way but is used simply to express the product of hollowing out space inside the earth. The "structure" of subterranean dwellings differs from that of other Chinese dwellings in that there is no apparent three-dimensional external form that is derived from commonly known building principles. Rather, subterranean "structures" acquire a singular identity from their internal form instead of their external design. Internal volumetric space, in effect, precedes structure, although there clearly is a complementary relationship between these building elements. Space is actually created without consuming the materials needed to fashion it. Even the excavated soils can be used for purposes such as leveling the site or for building tamped earthen walls around a courtyard.

The selection of a suitable site is the most important decision made by those contemplating construction of *yaodong* housing. Besides attention to the seasonal passage of the sun and the impact of other natural elements on the dwelling site, particular concern has always been paid to unique topographic conditions, surface and underground drainage, and the specific chemical and structural nature of the local soil. These factors all contribute to specific local decisions made concerning the dimensional ratios of height, width, and depth as well as the nature of the structural arch and enclosing facade. Although one can note an extraordinary range of earth-sheltered dwellings throughout the loessial region that express these differences, three general patterns dominate: cliffside *yaodong*, sunken court-

Figure 4.50. Connected by paths, each of the separate *kaoshan yaodong* dwellings in this village is tucked into an appropriate cliff face. Lishi *xian*, Shanxi, 1982. [Original photograph used with the permission of Arthur J. Van Alstyne.]

Figure 4.51. Slumping has brought about the collapse of several levels of *kaoshan yaodong* along this irregular slope. Several unused *yaodong* are visible as is an abandoned *siheyuan* complex, perhaps an old temple, that has *yaodong* associated with it. [Original photograph used with the permission of Kentaro Yamato.]

yard *yaodong*, and surface *yaodong*. Sometimes underground or partially underground elements are combined with structures built above ground in order to form an integrated dwelling complex. Although the significant variations in the plans, sections, and details of subterranean dwellings found throughout the loessial region have been well documented by Chinese specialists, it is not yet possible to determine conclusively the specific role of environmental and social factors in their formation. An accessible summary of this diversity, based on published and unpublished Chinese sources as well as his own extensive field observations, is provided by Gideon Golany (1992, 66–108).

Cliffside subterranean dwellings [*kaoya shi yaodong* 靠崖式窑洞 or *kaoshan shi yaodong* 靠山式窑洞] are dug horizontally into the slopes of deeply dissected hills or into the flanks of elongated ravines, especially in the Guanzhong and northern portions of Shaanxi and in central and southern Shanxi province. Following the irregularity of the topography, jagged lines of cliffside dwellings usually are found cut into south faces of slopes so that each dwelling will benefit from the light and heat brought by the passage of the win-

Figure 4.52. Shaved to shear verticality, this cliff face was tunneled to create thirteen *yaodong* of varying heights, widths, and depths. The excavated earth was used to form a level terrace and tamped to form a low wall around a courtyard. To inhibit deterioration, a brick and stone facade and an overhanging cap were added. Lishi *xian*, Shanxi, 1982. [Original photograph used with the permission of Arthur J. Van Alstyne.]

ter sun, a seasonal condition favored as well in the construction of surface dwellings elsewhere in northern China (Figures 4.50, 4.51, and 4.52). If a slope face is high and stable, it is possible to place a number of stepped or terraced levels of cliffside structures staggered one above the other. Inattention to the limitations of local soils and drainage, however, can lead to early abandonment even when a design might appear appropriate (Figures 4.53 and 4.54). Even where soils and drainage are acceptable, the owner of a *yaodong* must remain vigilant to counteract any deterioration of the soil from slumping due to gravity or erosion by rain. When a *yaodong* is not maintained properly, its natural structural qualities weaken and the excavation crumbles. A deteriorated *yaodong* must be abandoned, since its original structural integrity cannot be reclaimed.

Throughout most of the relatively barren areas of Shanxi and Shaanxi, population has always been widely dispersed and the economic circumstances of individual households has historically been very poor. As a result, relatively small and uncomplicated *yaodong* have generally been built in a scattered fashion—singly or in groups, facing different directions or in tiers—to take advantage of favorable microclimates and accessibility to limited water sources. *Yaodong* are sometimes dug into opposing faces of

narrow and irregular ravines and gullies in northern Shaanxi and in western Henan. In such cases, sunlight and ventilation are optimal in one area but deficient in another. Cliffside *yaodong* are found opening directly to unbounded level areas that lie before them or are enclosed by walls of various heights in order to create courtyardlike residential forms. Sometimes they are joined to freestanding aboveground structures. Villages that are made up of cliffside *yaodong* are often loosely structured in order to take advantage of the positive characteristics of terrain and microclimates.

The configuration of a loessial cave generally results from pragmatic decisions. Builders first concern themselves with the calcareous content of the soil because there is greater coherency of the loess and a possibility of spanning distances to a maximum of 5 meters where the lime content is high (Hou 1982, 72). In some areas where sandstone cliff faces are exposed, villagers tunnel directly into the stone to form *yaodong*. In any of these cases, peasants have always chosen high and dry locations that are not too far from a water source because damp soil is least desirable for constructing a secure cave. Construction itself varies.

Rudimentary cliffside *yaodong* are often quite individualistic in their overall plans and profiles, as seen

Figure 4.53. If a slope face is high, it is possible to create multilevel terraces for a skyscraperlike set of *yaodong*. Expressing the passion for self-reliance at the time, a *yaodong* school was built in the 1970s along seven terraces above Fenghuo brigade, Liquan *xian*, Shaanxi. Unfortunately, misunderstandings concerning the soil types and associated drainage problems led to the virtual abandonment of the school in the 1980s, when a new building was constructed for students. [RGK photograph 1977.]

in Figure 4.55, varying generally from province to province. As will be apparent in many of the later illustrations, subterranean dwellings often have an elliptical shape to the facade, although semicircular, parabolic, flat, and even pointed configurations also are widely seen. Side walls are vertical for perhaps 2 meters before arching upward to form a ceiling. Geometrically exact but crude caves are sometimes built simply as "sheds" to store straw and tools (Figure 4.56). Excavated walls of *yaodong* that are to be inhabited are normally coated with a plaster of loess or loess and lime to slow the drying and flaking of the interior. Papering the walls with newspapers, colorful posters, and photographs is a relatively recent innovation that at once brightens the living area and also protects the walls from absorbing condensed moisture. Usually the floor of subterranean dwellings is simply earth that has been compacted to a bricklike hardness. While supplementary support of the interior walls/roof is uncommon, the facade normally is strengthened with adobe, fired bricks, or tamped earth in order to support door and window frames that are hewn or hand-planed.

A yet-to-be-excavated entry in fact is usually framed in wood and braced with brick before excavation begins (Figure 4.57). If a stone arch is to frame the facade, a stonemason builds it into the slope using

Figure 4.54. Collapsed and abandoned *yaodong* at Fenghuo. [RGK photograph 1991.]

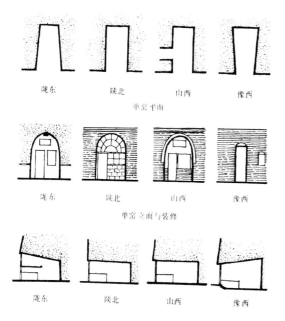

Figure 4.55 (above). The general plan, facade, and profile of individual *yaodong* vary from west to east. Each column (from left to right) represents a different province: eastern Gansu, northern Shaanxi, Shanxi, and western Henan. [Source: Hou, Ren, Zhou, and Li 1989, 41.]

Figure 4.56 (right). Some *yao* are dug simply to serve as storage sheds without any facade. Xifengzhen, Gansu. [Original photograph used with the permission of Jay Manzo 1991.]

Figure 4.57. After setting up a wooden framework to give shape to the rounded arch facade and stabilizing the slope with a brick facing, the workers use simple tools to excavate the *yaodong*. Earth dug from the slope is spread on the terrace in front of the dwellings. Lishi *xian*, Shanxi, 1982. [Original photograph used with the permission of Arthur J. Van Alstyne.]

chiseled out earth as its initial support. Once the keystone is set, digging can start. Sometimes a false arch is sculpted above the actual opening to suggest greater height. To reduce surface erosion and direct the flow of water away from a dwelling, a tile overhang or parapet may be added to the facade. Some openings are wide at the entry and become narrower as depth increases, while others have a constricted entry with an opening that flares in the interior. Broad openings certainly facilitate the entry of both light and air, but the trade-off is a substantial loss of heat during the winter. Where protection from cold winds is the most critical factor that must be addressed, a narrow entry will sometimes be created even at the expense of diminishing natural lighting and ventilation to less than optimal levels. While the ceiling height of most cliffside dwellings is uniform, some are higher in front and lower in the rear, creating a so-called *laba xing* 喇叭型, or "trumpet-shaped," profile. In general, however, the width and height of Chinese *yaodong* are essentially in the ratio of 1:1, while the depth of the vaulted unit is usually twice either of these dimensions. Small earth-sheltered dwellings generally do not exceed a depth of 10 meters into a hillside, although some larger ones may reach 20 meters.

Excavation is normally rather slow not only because farmers do the work themselves but also because prolonging the pace provides time for the soil to dry out slowly, a condition necessary to maintain its stability. The best time for excavation is when the soil is moderately moist but not wet, perhaps several weeks after a rain. Sometimes periodic interruptions in the digging are necessary when soil moisture is substantial, as in late summer. Only common farm tools, such as mattocks, crude shovels, and baskets, are used. Burrowing normally begins from above, at the location of the arched ceiling, and proceeds down to floor level. As soil is removed, it is usually spread to form a level terrace at the entry of the caves. Alternatively, some of the soil can be formed into adobe bricks or pounded into a frame in order to build a wall. The removal and placement of significant volumes of soil sometimes necessitates excavating the floor of caves a meter or so above existing grade level so that depositing the excavated earth outside will create a raised terrace that will facilitate drainage away from the dwelling, mitigating any possibility of flooding. A cave of approximately 19 *chi* (about 6 meters) deep, 10 *chi* (about 3 meters) high, and 9 *chi* (about 3 meters) wide takes roughly forty days to excavate (Myrdal 1965, 45). While an additional period of three months or more is then necessary for the cave to cure or dry out completely before occupancy, local conditions may prolong excavation into a multiyear construction process. With proper maintenance, subterranean dwellings dug into earth can be used for several generations, but when neglected they typically begin to break down through settling and eventually collapse. In northwestern Shaanxi, according to American geologists earlier in the century who explored the loessial region for nearly a year, "many acres were found pitted with loess sinks and openings . . . indicating the former existence of underground villages of far greater extent than anything encountered at the present" (Fuller and Clapp 1924, 223).

According to other observations in the early 1920s by Fuller and Clapp in portions of central and western Shaanxi province, Chinese villagers sometimes created "cliff dwellings" by utilizing weathered reentrant horizontal crevices along ridge faces or penetrating thick loess in order to dig "rock dwellings" into the sandstone beyond. Described as similar to the cliff dwelling shelters of Native Americans, natural rock crevice dwellings occupied the weathered softer layers of sandstone shelves that lay between more resistant strata. Although rather irregular in height, they nonetheless were usually fitted with doors, windows, and chimneys. Descriptions of rock dwellings by Fuller and Clapp were varied: "widely distributed and of considerable numbers," "cannot be considered common," and "comparatively few are occupied at the present time." There were indications that many that were visited may have been "originally cut as temples and were appropriated and recut into dwellings after ceasing to be used for religious purposes." Often on two levels, they were linked by inside stairways cut into the rock and had flat ceilings (Fuller and Clapp 1924, 215, 224-225). That cliff dwellings of these types have not been described by Chinese researchers in recent decades suggests that they were a housing type born of extreme poverty and in a time of great disorder.

Figure 4.58. Rock dwellings were cut into the granite slopes of Donggou ravine perhaps as early as the Tang dynasty. Most are about 1.8 meters high with a floor area of about 4 square meters. Some include stone *kang* and associated stoves. Baihaituo Mountain, Yanqing *xian*, to the west of Beijing, 1996. [Original photograph used with the permission of Yang Liming.]

Although there is no way to know precisely the conditions under which individual cliff and rock dwelling complexes appeared, there has been recent documentation of a village of 117 rock dwellings at the foot of Baihaituo Mountain in Yanqing county to the west of Beijing. Each of the rock dwellings was cut into the precipitous granite walls of Donggou ravine to a height of approximately 1.8 meters and a floor area of about 4 square meters (Figures 4.58 and 4.59). Stone conduits lead rainwater along the slope. In many of the dwellings there are stone *kang*, stoves, and stands. Separate storage rooms are attached to many. Each of the several levels is connected by stone steps that are cut into the face of the cliff. Although there is no clear evidence of when the rock dwelling village was completed, some researchers believe that it is the product of a non-Han group during the Tang dynasty, who historical records indicate migrated into the area; others suspect that the village might have been constructed to temporarily garrison frontier troops ("Ancient Rock" 1996, 28).

Cave dwellings and above-ground structures throughout the village of Zhaojiahe, Chengcheng *xian*, Shaanxi, are all built within surrounding mud walls that reach 2 to 3 meters in height. Examining the daily uses of space and the meaning of space within the *yuanzi* courtyards of village *yaodong*, Liu Xin has demonstrated how these spaces and struc-

Figure 4.59. Narrow stone steps were cut into the cliff face in order to connect the various residential levels. Baihaituo Mountain, Yanqing *xian*, to the west of Beijing, 1996. [Original photograph used with the permission of Yang Liming.]

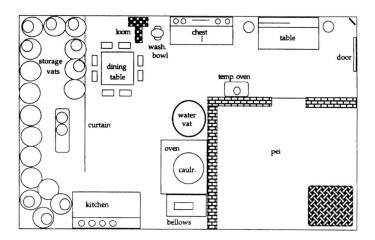

Figure 4.60. This plan of a *yaodong* shows the division of space into three realms, one focusing on the bed—labled *pei*, the local name for *kang*—near the door, another on the table, and the third behind the curtain in the rear where grain and other essentials are stored. Although the bed is close to the entry and the table deeper into the dwelling, the bed is viewed as "hidden," while the table is "open." Zhaojiahe *cun*, Chengcheng *xian*, Shaanxi. [Original drawing used with the permission of Liu Xin.]

tures help mediate social relations and constitute economic realities in rural Shaanxi (1996, 1998). The presence of separate toilets and kitchens clearly marks that a courtyard is shared by relatives, and the placement of structures plainly reveals relationships among those who live together. According to Liu, nothing expresses the "cultural logic" of *yaodong yuanzi* better than their importance as storehouses: "everything not only *needs* but also *should* and *is always prepared* to be saved. Storage is not a function of the *yuanzi;* rather, the *yuanzi* exists in order to accomplish the function of storage" (Liu 1996, 9). This logic continues into individual *yaodong*, where interior space is divided into three realms, one focusing on the bed, another on the table, and the third the storage area behind a curtain at the rear (Figure 4.60). Even though the bed is closest to the outer wall, it is viewed as "hidden" because it cannot be seen directly by anyone standing at the door. The dining table, on the other hand, is placed two-thirds of the way into the underground room, deep into its recesses, yet is visible from the outside because it is aligned with the doorway itself. During the day, the bed is occupied only by women as they prepare meals, and the men gather only at the tables. Only at night does a man join his wife and often their children on the bed. Valuable grain and steamed bread are kept behind the curtained rear third of each *yaodong*. Food storage, eating, and food preparation represent a spatial hierarchy from back to front, and the *yaodong* itself represents a relatively self-sufficient en-

clave in which a farmer "boasted" that "if there were natural disasters and no further agricultural production, he and his family would still be able to survive for at least another two years within their *yao*" (Liu 1996, 13).

Earth-sheltered housing is often found in relatively large groupings composed of individual *yaodong* chambers that are linked to form a dwelling with many rooms. The exterior and interior of a typical cliffside residence for seven people in three separate but interconnected units is located some 60 kilometers northwest of Xi'an in Qianxian, Shaanxi province (Figures 4.61, 4.62, and 4.63). A path leads from the road to a prominent gate, shown earlier in Figure 2.80, in the southeastern corner of a 3-meter-high tamped earth wall that encloses a large courtyard in the front of the cave complex, just as is the case with the traditional Beijing courtyard houses. In the courtyard there is a kitchen garden, a flower garden, a summer stove, a pigpen, and a small storage building. This earth-sheltered complex includes two bedrooms located in adjacent but unconnected chambers and a separate deep cave for cooking and storage. The bedrooms are furnished with a traditional *kang* as well as a frame bed. The room with the *kang* maintains a traditional location just inside the south-facing window, as is common in northern aboveground houses, but the room with the frame bed observes the principal known as *qiantang houshi* 前堂后室 [main room in front, bedroom in back]. In this rectangular multipurpose room, no partition separates the different spaces for each use.

Figure 4.61 (top left). "Rooms" of this *kaoshan yaodong* dwelling open out to a courtyard ringed with a 3-meter-high tamped earth wall. The wooden door, window, and transom frames have been fitted into an adobe brick wall to form the parabolic facade. The ornamentation on the windows and doors are papercuts of the Chinese character *shuangxi*, for "double happiness," used to designate the dwelling of newlyweds. Qianxian, Shaanxi. [RGK photograph 1984.]

Figure 4.62 (top right). View from inside one of two bedrooms shows a *kang* just inside a small window facing south. The other bedroom has a frame bed. The vaulted ceiling is papered with posters and newspapers, including an announcement of the 1982 census. Several pieces of wooden furniture and piled bedding are shown. Qianxian, Shaanxi. [RGK photograph 1984.]

Figure 4.63 (bottom left). A separate parabolic cave serves the household as a kitchen and storage room. The low adobe brick stove on the left is connected via flues to the *kang* in the adjacent bedroom but is poorly vented, as the accumulated soot shows. Dry storage for fuel is found in the rear. Crocks for water and baskets provide storage for foodstuffs. Qianxian, Shaanxi. [RGK photograph 1984.]

Figure 4.64. Pockmarked landscapes of *aoting yaodong* present a unique village form. Taken in winter, this view from an airplane looks at the recessed cubes from the north, revealing the substantial shadows that penetrate the sunken courtyards and shade many of the caves. If viewed from the south, however, the facade of the main rooms dug into the northern wall would be seen to enjoy sunlight. Henan. [Source: Graf zu Castell 1938, 86.]

Sunken courtyard-style subterranean dwellings [*xiachen shi yaodong* 下沉式窑洞, *aoting yaodong* 凹庭窑洞, or *dixia tianjingyuan yaodong* 地下天井院窑洞] are found principally in western Henan, southern Shanxi, nearby portions of Shaanxi north of the Wei River, and in eastern Gansu. These areas encompass the expanses of mesalike loessial plateau that have undergone very little dissection, and it is here that peasants traditionally excavated large pits of varying sizes to depths of at least 6 meters below grade. When viewed from the air, as shown in Figure 4.64, the bleak landscape appears pockmarked, a condition accentuated by the shadows of the winter sun. Square sunken courtyard shapes are most common, often reaching 81 square meters in size (Figure 4.65). The area of rectangular and L-shaped courtyards often does not exceed 54 square meters (Figure 4.66). Among the regional names used to describe this subterranean form are

"below grade courtyard" [*diyin yuan* 地阴院] or "pit courtyard" [*dikeng yuan* 地坑院] in Shanxi, "skywell courtyard" [*tianjing yuan* 天井院] in Henan, and "cave courtyard" [*dongzi yuan* 洞子院] in Gansu.

The section and perspective views seen in Figures 4.67 and 4.68 reveal that each pit forms a recessed courtyard whose four vertical side walls provide separate flat surfaces into which one, two, or three *yaodong* are dug. Entry from grade level is via a ramp or stairs sliced into the soil. Either is usually cut into the soil

Figure 4.65. A relatively square *aoting yaodong* creates a box of light, an atriumlike room in which a household can carry out much of its daily household work. It is here that a family often eats and entertains friends throughout three seasons of the year. It is only during the coldest days of winter that the household retreats to the warmth of the interior enclosed spaces. Qianxian, Shaanxi. [RGK photograph 1984.]

Figure 4.66 (left). Rectangular in shape, this sunken courtyard-style dwelling is surrounded by stabilized walls. The lower portions of the walls are faced with brick, the upper portions plastered, and at the top they are capped with a tile coping. A *zhaobi*, or spirit wall, is visible at the bottom of the photograph. The crown of the tree peeks above the ground and provides some shade from intense summer heat. Gongxian, Henan, 1991. [Original photograph used with the permission of Jay Manzo.]

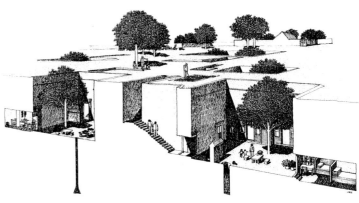

Figure 4.67 (top right). This perspective view shows the recessed courtyard with its four sidewalls into which one, two, or three *yaodong* are dug. Sloped entries lead to the ground above. While a tree is often planted within a courtyard, vegetation is kept far away from the pit on the surface because of the potential damage from roots. Henan. [Original line drawing used with the permission of the family of the late Paul Sun.]

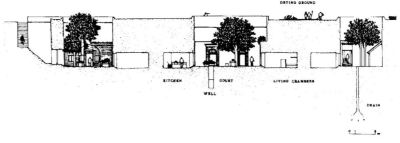

Figure 4.68 (right). Across the top is a section view through several *aoting yaodong*. The courtyard floor is often as much as 8 meters below grade, with the height of an arched living space reaching at least 3 meters. Henan. [Original line drawing used with the permission of the family of the late Paul Sun.]

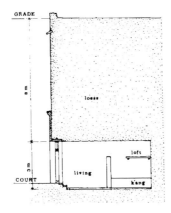

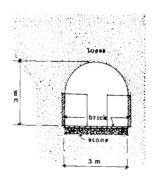

along the southern or southwest side of a sunken courtyard, locations least favorable for occupancy. Inclined passageways from above either run along a straight line or, as seen in Figures 4.69 and 4.70, include a 90° angle in order to lessen the gradient of the slope. The gradient must be reasonable not only for walking but also for moving equipment and crops in and out. The incline itself is sometimes enclosed with an arching roof, which forms a dark tunnel as in Figure 4.71, or it is left open like a trench. The actual entry may be an enclosed gate at ground level that leads to the ramp and another gate at the courtyard, or a gate may be constructed only at the below-ground level of the recessed courtyard (Figure 4.72). It is common to find the gate framed in fired bricks or stone and fitted with wooden panels that can be secured at night. In some cases, as seen in Figure 4.73, a *zhaobi*, or spirit wall, may be placed in the below-ground courtyard immediately inside the gate at the end of the sloping ramp.

With the *aoting yaodong* complex oriented in relation to the cardinal directions, chambers are normally dug into all four walls. These walls are left natural or they are finished with a lime plaster and capped with brick and tile to protect them from deterioration (Figures 4.74, 4.75, and 4.76). Since only one sunken wall surface can provide a southern exposure, the *yaodong* dug here usually becomes the location of the main chambers of the dwelling, with bed and sitting rooms for parents and grandparents. Only during the early summer when sun angles are highest, however, does direct sunlight reach into this face. In winter, when the sun is low above the horizon and the daylight period short, the depth of the courtyard effectively shades all of the excavated space except for the upper portion of the south-facing wall, a decided disadvantage. Living space for other family members is dug as needed into the east and west side walls. Southern chambers with a north-facing wall are normally used only for

Figure 4.69 (top). Sliced into the loessial soil, this L-shaped entry ramp descends from grade level to a gate that leads into the courtyard. Flat stones are placed along the edges to retard erosion. Houwang *cun*, Pinglu *xian*, Shanxi. [RGK photograph 1996.]

Figure 4.70 (bottom). Looking back up an L-shaped accessway, the shallow brick steps on the left are for walking while the ramp on the right is to facilitate the use of a wheelbarrow or bicycle. Houwang *cun*, Pinglu *xian*, Shanxi. [RGK photograph 1996.]

Figure 4.71 (top left). Some ramps lead quickly to a tunnel that continues to a gate deep in the ground at the entry to the courtyard beneath. With limited storage space below, bulky piles of straw are stacked outside on the "roof" of the *yaodong*. Houwang *cun*, Pinglu *xian*, Shanxi. [RGK photograph 1996.]

Figure 4.72 (top right). At the base of the L-shaped ramp is an entry portico. Constructed of fired brick and capped with a tile roof, it contains a two-panel wooden door, which can be secured. At the New Year, couplets are pasted here on the door. Houwang *cun*, Pinglu *xian*, Shanxi. [RGK photograph 1996.]

Figure 4.73 (bottom right). Just inside the gate in the below-ground courtyard, as one might find in a street-level *siheyuan*, a *zhaobi*, or spirit wall, is placed. Houwang *cun*, Pinglu *xian*, Shanxi. [RGK photograph 1996.]

Figure 4.74 (top left). To protect the flat wall surfaces from deteriorating from rainwash or gravity displacement, they are sometimes capped with brick and tile and finished with a lime plaster. Houwang *cun*, Pinglu *xian*, Shanxi. [RGK photograph 1996.]

Figure 4.76 (bottom right). An arch of brick or stone is often used today in order to help stabilize the weakened wall where excavation has given shape to a room. Along the plane where two arches join, a pier adds further support. A path of brick rings the courtyard, and several shortcuts paved with brick cross it. Houwang *cun*, Pinglu *xian*, Shanxi. [RGK photograph 1996.]

Figure 4.75 (above). This close-up of the intersection of a protected and unprotected corner of the courtyard of Figure 4.76 shows the dramatic disintegration of the surface of the pit wall. The wall and the rooms within will eventually subside if they are not properly maintained. Houwang *cun*, Pinglu *xian*, Shanxi. [RGK photograph 1996.]

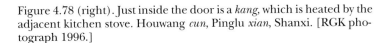

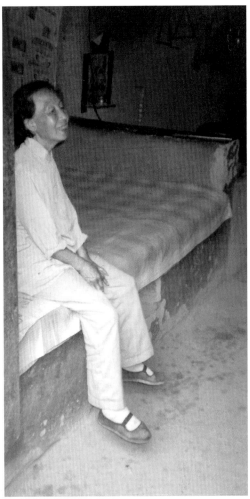

Figure 4.77 (above). Only minimal light enters any of the excavated rooms through the open door, window, or transom, and even less light enters during winter when openings are often shuttered. A single light-bulb hangs from the ceiling, upon which newspapers are glued as wall-paper. The walls of this room have been excavated laterally beyond the bounds of the facade. Houwang *cun*, Pinglu *xian*, Shanxi. [RGK photograph 1996.]

Figure 4.78 (right). Just inside the door is a *kang*, which is heated by the adjacent kitchen stove. Houwang *cun*, Pinglu *xian*, Shanxi. [RGK photograph 1996.]

storage, as a privy, or to stable animals. It is along this north-facing wall that the entry ramp or stairs usually reaches the courtyard. Most excavated rooms have multiple uses, but none of them is brightly lit (Figure 4.77). In some cases, a narrow back room reaches deeper into the earth beyond the chamber adjacent to the sunken courtyard. Except for the arcuate ceilings, the interior of each chamber resembles those seen elsewhere in northern China. Large *kang*, which serve as beds and sitting areas, are common features of *yaodong* throughout northern China (Figure 4.78). Usually located along an outer wall and connected to at least two walls, *kang* are built-in close to their associated stoves. Shallow alcoves and lateral indentations for storage, as seen in Figure 4.79, are often found along the sides of the receding chambers. Newspapers and posters are affixed to the walls for decoration and to reduce flaking.

The sunken courtyard becomes a "walled" compound for the flanking excavated rooms, a significant outdoor living space open to the sky that is reminiscent of traditional northern courtyard houses. Depending on available resources, the floor of the courtyard and the parabolic arches on the exterior walls of each chamber may be faced with fired brick. While the limited amounts of rain or snow that falls in these semiarid areas is not a major problem, blowing dust and dirt are of major concern. As a result, low parapets of stone, brick, or tile are frequently laid along the upper edge of the excavated

Figure 4.79. Shallow spaces and shelves are frequently dug into the walls of individual chambers. Some are used to store small objects, such as tools and bottles, while others serve as niches for tutelary deities, such as the Kitchen God. Houwang *cun*, Pinglu *xian*, Shanxi. [RGK photograph 1996.]

Figure 4.80. Only 10 centimeters high, this low parapet minimizes the amount of surface dust that can blow down into the courtyard. Faced with brick and constructed with a sloping band of "roof tiles" to keep rainwash from the walls, this upper wall treatment provides major protection. Houwang *cun*, Pinglu *xian*, Shanxi. [RGK photograph 1996.]

opening of better dwellings to impede the cascading of earth into the courtyard (Figure 4.80). Within the courtyard, one might find a tree or two, a trellis to support some vegetable vines, a shallow well, a dry-well-type drain, and almost always a covered cistern in which to store water. Cooking during summer— when there is no need to warm the *kang* or introduce heat into the cool interior—often takes place outside on portable clay braziers when the weather cooperates (Figure 4.81). In winter, however, stoves con-

nected to *kang* are kept burning using wood and plant stalks to maintain warmth inside.

While a village of sunken courtyard-style dwellings leaves a landscape of large indentations that are generally quite orderly, much of the nearby level land above is actually tilled and planted with hearty crops, although it is not common for planting to take place immediately above subterranean rooms. Special attention is paid to keeping vegetation away from the upper edge of a sunken courtyard in order to reduce

Figure 4.81. This animal-like clay brazier stands on four legs and has a gaping mouth in which to insert fuel. A pot or wok can be placed above it for cooking *alfresco*. Houwang *cun*, Pinglu *xian*, Shanxi. [RGK photograph 1996.]

the penetration of roots that might draw moisture from deep in the ground and lead to a deterioration of the stability of the perpendicular walls. The surface areas between the sunken courtyards of a village nonetheless provide abundant expanses to meet seasonal agricultural needs, such as threshing grain and storing hay.

Subterranean dwellings represent a positive adaptation to environmental conditions by creatively utilizing an abundantly available resource—the soil—ingeniously exploiting terrain that normally would not be suitable for housing construction, and effectively capitalizing on the thermal qualities of the earth. In a region in which wood and brush for cooking fuel are themselves strikingly scarce, the reduction in need for wooden building materials is fortunate. Further, when the outside temperature during July and August is above 36°C in the Xi'an area, the temperature 4 to 6 meters below ground in subterranean dwellings is a relatively comfortable 14°C to 15.5°C. During January and February, when above ground temperatures drop to their lowest, interior temperatures below ground are still between 14.5°C and 16.5°C, depending on the location in the dwelling (Hou, Ren, Zhou, and Li 1989, 248-249). Interior diurnal temperature ranges likewise are quite stable, a condition that is best appreciated late at night when outside temperatures typically plummet. These numbers are espe-

cially striking when compared with those inside surface dwellings. According to the observations of Western explorers, "their warmth, after a day in the saddle in wintry weather, was far from unwelcome and greatly to be preferred to the benumbing cold of the *yamens* of the magistrates and other buildings" (Fuller and Clapp 1924, 224). In saving energy and land, both in short supply in the loessial region, earth-sheltered dwellings provide a haven from hostile environmental conditions. Powerful earthquakes, however, have brought periodic devastation to those living in subterranean dwellings in the loessial uplands. It has been estimated that as many as a million people died in collapsing *yaodong* and other dwellings in the loessial region in 1921. In the eyes of many, *yaodong* are equated with poverty and limited resources. It is not surprising, then, that as farmers have more cash income, more and more are abandoning their caves—sometimes even filling the indentations and leveling the earth—and building above-ground dwellings (Figure 4.82). This effort to make progress, however, is made difficult by the fact that the new houses are neither as warm in winter nor as cool in summer. They are, however, better ventilated than nearby subterranean dwellings. Major efforts are being made by Chinese architects to address the shortcomings of *yaodong*: limited interior light, inadequate ventilation, and high humidity levels.

Figure 4.82. Throughout the loessial uplands, new above-ground dwellings are being built as Chinese farmers earn more money. In some cases, the new house replaces the subterranean one, but often the new house is used only in the summer. Houwang *cun*, Pinglu *xian*, Shanxi. [RGK photograph 1996.]

Some *yaodong* are semisubterranean, with only a portion of the dwelling actually embedded within the earth. In these cases, stone, adobe, or fired brick is used to construct a building that fronts the excavated chambers, becoming in effect an extension of the interior underground space. How such structures are added depends principally on the slope of the hillside, resulting in all or part of each of three sides and the roof being cut into the earth. Whatever structural infilling is then necessary is completed by enclosing exterior space with brick or stone. In some cases, only minor volumes are underground. Taken to the extreme, a dwelling may appear to be a series of linked caves but is actually a structure built completely above ground in imitation of subterranean forms.

Cavelike structures that are free-standing rather than partially or completely excavated below ground can be seen throughout the loessial region. Found in areas where there are cliffside and sunken courtyard *yaodong* similar to those described earlier, above-ground *yaodong* are built in unexpected locations as well. While they are most common in poorer rural portions of Shanxi, Henan, Shaanxi, and Inner Mongolia where vertical slopes are scarce and where loes-

sial soil is thin, they are also found in urban areas where their overall style reveals that they are occupied by wealthy people.

Above-ground cavelike dwellings, called *guyao* 锢窑 [aligned *yao*], are usually rectangular in shape and comprise at least three adjacent arcuate units (Figures 4.83 and 4.84). They imitate subterranean dwellings not only in the appearance of their facades but also in their overall dimensions and in the use of vaulted arches that carry the weight of substantial amounts of earth. Chinese architects refer to this unique building form as "earth-sheltered architecture" [*yantu jianzhu* 掩土建筑 or *futu jianzhu* 覆土建筑] in order to capture the significance of the thick layer of insulating earth used to cap these dwellings. The surrounding walls of *guyao* appear to differ little from common load-bearing walls that support roofs seen throughout China. However, although the outer walls of *guyao* enclose interior space, they do not directly support roof timbers and a roof surface. Instead, the side walls serve as piers that help contain the lateral thrust of the interior arches and that support the substantial volume of earth that is piled in the voids above the vaulted structures. These massive amounts of earth there-

Figure 4.83. In some of the poorer areas of the loessial region, free-standing dwellings that mimic *yaodong* are constructed with side-by-side interconnected rooftops. [Original photograph used with the permission of Kentaro Yamata.]

Figure 4.84. *Guyao* [aligned *yao*] are usually rectangular in shape, arranged in a three-jian alignment, and have wooden facades quite similar to the *yaodong* found in the same region. A parapeted roof and a courtyard provide working spaces for the household. Jingsheng *cun*, Lingshi *xian*, Shanxi. [RGK photograph 1996.]

fore provide an extraordinary level of insulation to the roof and sidewalls (Figures 4.85).

Although common building technologies and local materials are used to construct *guyao*, special attention is paid to the preparation of the foundation, which must support not only the heavy walls but ultimately the substantial earth-laden roof. At the structure's perimeter, the soil base is rammed at least three times, with new soil added to the foundation trench as it becomes compacted and lowered through tamping. Stones or fired bricks are usually laid as the base of the foundation. The thick load-bearing side walls of *guyao* are massive, ranging between 1.5 and 1.7 meters in width. Interior load-bearing partition walls are approximately one-third as thick as the endwalls and typically only reach about 1.5 meters above grade level before arching. Vaults are established using either stone, fired brick, or adobe as voussoirs arranged in semicircular or pointed sections. A braced wooden centering framework is employed during construction in order to shape each of the geometrical barrel vaults. Front and back walls are built higher than the vaults in order to form a caisson to contain the soil overburden. Construction of *guyao* is quite slow, since the foundations and barrel vaults themselves take shape over

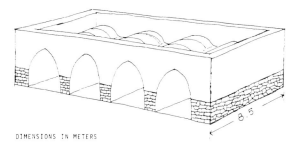

DIMENSIONS IN METERS

Figure 4.85. The outer shell of a *guyao* has walls like a thick box, which are necessary to contain the substantial volumes of soil added for insulation. [Source: Golany 1992, 84.]

several years to allow time for settling and correcting any deformations. Well before the substantial weight of earth is added above the barrel vaults, several layers of limestone and ashes are applied as waterproofing. What some see as abandoned stone or brick *guyao* throughout the loessial region are actually unfinished works in progress, which underscore the contemporary popularity of this building form. Once the external structure is completed, a facade with a brick base is constructed to support wooden doors and lattice patterned windows that are covered with translucent paper. Doors are usually placed on one side of the facade in order to accommodate a *kang* inside.

Large numbers of exquisite cavelike dwellings and even crude *guyao* are found in the cities and towns of Shanxi and Shaanxi provinces. Some are the deliberate choice for upper-class families. Rarely, however, are the urban dwellings independent ob-

long cavelike structures, as is common in rural areas. Instead, as in Pingyao, Shanxi, they are usually composed of three or four building units that frame a courtyard (Figure 4.86). Such courtyard complexes appear from the outside like any northern formal *siheyuan*-type courtyard residence with their windowless high walls and a single dramatic entryway (see, for example, Figure 2.84). Once the gate is entered, however, the ambience and intimacy of a rural village of subterranean cavelike dwellings is felt, even as one is aware of being in a well-structured courtyard with high-quality workmanship. Just as with other Shanxi and Shaanxi courtyard-style dwellings discussed earlier, the open areas between flanking structures are narrow rectangles that are longer than they are broad (Figure 4.87). As in rural areas throughout northern China, no windows or doors are found along three of the thick exterior walls of these structures, but the south-facing wall of the main building and the courtyard-facing walls of the flanking structures have windows and doors with full lattice panels. The *zhengfang*, or main building, is either three or five *jian* wide, with each *jian* appearing like a vaulted cavelike unit (the facade of one was shown in Figure 4.26). Entry is normally through the central *jian* into a common room that leads to bedrooms on each side—a *yiming liangan* configuration. The central *jian* as well as the view back of the arcuate ceiling and papered lattice are strikingly cavelike

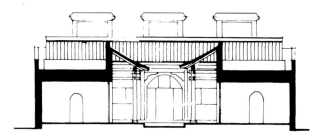

Figure 4.86. In some areas of central and southern Shanxi and Shaanxi, cavelike structures are the building style of choice for even wealthy urban dwellers. From outside they appear to be courtyard dwellings, with high walls and a single entry. But inside one observes the arches of *yaodong*. This urban dwelling has five arched units in its *zhengfang*. Pingyao *xian*, Shanxi. [Source: Yan, Yang, Zhang 1994, 122.]

Figure 4.87. Once inside, the appearance is of a prosperous rural village of subterranean cavelike dwellings that has been embellished with substantial wooden ornamentation. The flanking structures are usually built so that they frame a courtyard in the form of a *siheyuan.* Chengguan *zhen,* Pingyao, Shanxi. [Original photograph used with the permission of Li Yuxiang.]

(Figures 4.88 and 4.89). Each of the adjacent bedrooms typically has a *kang,* as would also be true in village *yaodong* and in other types of northern dwellings (Figure 4.90). On the roof of such dwellings, however, one is likely to find impressively ornamented chimneys (Figure 4.91). Flanking wing structures do not always mimic cave dwellings but instead are often high single-sloped roof buildings with complicated lattice designs. Structurally, urban *guyao* are essentially the same as those built in rural areas, although typically there are qualitative differences in the materials used and in the degree of ornamentation. The extensive use of fired brick for paving and walls is a clear indication of wealth. Stairs often lead from the courtyard to a paved roof terrace that is ringed with a brick parapet. Unlike rural *guyao,* urban *guyao* are generally more elaborate in the treatment of their exteriors, with extensive wooden overhangs supported by carved wooden columns and brackets as well as substantial carving of wooden balustrades and corbels.

Whether in villages or cities, above-ground cavelike *guyao* preserve the positive attributes of *yaodong* while eliminating some of their negative points. In terms of their thermal performance, the substantial earth, stone, and brick walls on three sides and on the roof as well as the earth foundation provide excellent insulation from severe cold in winter and heat in summer. At the same time, they retain heat generated within the *guyao* during the winter. Thus, interior ambient temperatures differ very little throughout the day or from season to season. The pronounced humidity and safety problems associated with earthquakes in underground dwellings are lessened in structures above the ground. Air circulation is typically better within dwellings adjacent to courtyards above ground than in dwellings below the ground. Arcuate caves are so fundamentally a part of the concept of "dwelling" that even new multistory brick structures are built to echo more humble origins (Figure 4.92).

Complexes of below-ground and above-ground dwelling units at many scales and with mixed building styles are found throughout the region. In most cases, they reveal incomplete plans or plans in progress that take form as a household's needs and

Figure 4.88. Exterior view of the arcuate latticed facade of the central *jian* of a five-bay-wide *zhengfang*. Chengguan *zhen*, Pingyao, Shanxi. [RGK photograph 1996.]

Figure 4.89. When viewed from inside the dwelling during the day, the paper-covered lattice frames are very striking. Chengguan *zhen*, Pingyao, Shanxi. [RGK photograph 1996.]

Figure 4.90. In each of the bedrooms that adjoin the central *jian* there is a *kang* and associated stove. The *kang* are located just below the south-facing window. Chengguan *zhen*, Pingyao, Shanxi. [RGK photograph 1996.]

Figure 4.91 (right). Atop the flat roof are ornamented fired clay chimneys connected to the *kang* in the rooms below. This shows the gaping mouth of a dragon. Chengguan *zhen*, Pingyao, Shanxi. [RGK photograph 1996.]

Figure 4.92 (bottom). These newly built two-story brick residential blocks resemble *kaoshan yaodong* found in the vicinity. The "smashing of the Gang of Four" upon the death of Chairman Mao in the fall of 1976 is marked by the slogan on the wall. Fenghuo, Liquan *xian*, Shaanxi. [RGK photograph 1977.]

financial means change. The relatively small complex shown in Figures 4.93 and 4.94 includes a two-story cliffside *yaodong* and a single-story outbuilding arranged within a walled courtyard. The lower story of the *yaodong* forms the traditional plan with its three-unit composition. With two flanking niches for images and incense, the central unit dominates with a high cornice above its entryway. Adjacent *yaodong* also include brick *kang* for the use of other members of the household. Stairs lead to a long terrace nearly 3 meters wide and to two caves used for storage. On the west side of the courtyard is a standard northern-style rectangular building with a double-sloped roof. The absence of *kang* suggests that the two rooms may be used during the summer only. As is standard throughout northern China, the entry gate is located in a southeastern position.

As discussed in the earlier section on courtyard dwellings, large-scale "manors" or "estates" [*dayuan* 大院 or *zhuangyuan* 庄园] are found throughout Shanxi, Henan, and Shaanxi provinces. Some of these include cliffside *yaodong*, above-ground *guyao*,

Figure 4.93 (above). A relatively small complex of mixed building styles, including a two-story cliffside *yaodong* and a single-story outbuilding, are arranged within a walled courtyard. Stairs lead to a long terrace and to two caves used for storage. A common northern-style rectangular structure with a double-sloped roof serves as a wing building. The entry gate is located in a southeastern position. Gongxian, Henan. [Source: Liu Dunzhen 1957, 130.]

Figure 4.94 (right). Plans of the lower (left) and upper (right) spaces of the dwelling pictured in Figure 4.93 show the location of the entry (1); latrine (2); courtyard (3); guest rooms (4); altars (5); stove (6); *yaodong* (7); alcove (8); terrace (9); and balustrade (10). Gongxian, Henan. [Source: Liu 1957, 129.]

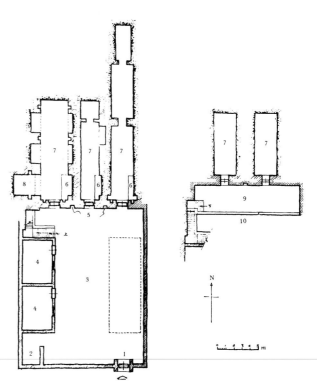

Figure 4.95. Perspective view of the Jiang family manor showing the three terraces and the intermixing of above-ground and below-ground dwelling units. Mizhi *xian*, Shaanxi. [Source: Hou, Ren, Zhou, and Li 1989, 204-205.]

and other building elements and plans common throughout northern China. The Jiang family manor in Mizhi *xian*, Shaanxi, the Wang family manor in Lingshi *xian*, Shanxi, and the Kangbaiwan manor in Gongxian, Henan, are three examples of extensive courtyard complexes that include substantial numbers of subterranean dwellings.

Jiang*jia zhuangyuan* 姜家庄园, the Jiang family manor, was completed in 1886. Built on three terraces and divided into upper, middle, and lower compounds, the overall complex is ringed by a crenelated wall (Figure 4.95). *Yaodong* were excavated along the slope in the upper compound and are reached by stairs from the middle level and below. Facing *guyao* dominate the middle compound with a broad courtyard between them that is entered via a portico from the compound below. The lower courtyard is framed by a pair of facing *xiangfang*. On the north side of the lower courtyard is a broad set of stairs leading up to and passing between two large *guyao*. On the south side of the lower courtyard is a set of fringing structures that are separated by stairs and a gate.

During the late Qing period, the Wangs were one of the four most powerful families in southern Shanxi. Over time, the Wangs built rooms and courtyards said to exceed 45,000 square meters, and, according to a boastful broadsheet passed out to Chinese tourists, "five times that found in the Qiao family manor." The Wang family manor [Wang*jia dayuan* 王家大院] extends across the base of a gentle loessial terrace in Jingsheng village some 12 kilometers from the small county seat of Lingshi. The complex is divided into eastern and western "fortress courtyards" [*baoyuan* 堡院] with courtyards of various sizes and shapes aligned along several north-south axes. Each of the fortresses has its own main gate. Thirteen *yaodong* with four attached courtyards are found along the rear of the "eastern courtyard" (Figure 4.96). Each is divided into units of three, comprising a *zhengfang* to the rear and a pair of flanking *xiangfang* built as *guyao* to look like subterranean dwellings. The larger "western courtyard" complex was designed with one north-south lane that is crossed by four east-west lanes forming the Chinese character 王, the name of the family. Set within this alignment are twenty-seven symmetrical courtyard units of various sizes, many of which are heavily ornamented with carved wood, brick, and

Figure 4.96 (top left). Said to be five times the area of the Qiao family manor, the Wang family manor is divided into eastern and western "fortress courtyards." This rear portion of the western courtyard includes *yaodong* and flanking *xiangfang.* A *zhaobi*, or spirit wall, with the character *"fu"* for good fortune is placed just inside the gate. Jiangsheng *cun*, Lingshi *xian*, Shanxi. [RGK photograph 1996.]

Figure 4.97 (middle left). Courtyards of various sizes and shapes are aligned along several north-south axes and are heavily ornamented with carved wood, brick, and stone. Jiangsheng *cun*, Lingshi *xian*, Shanxi. [RGK photograph 1996.]

Figure 4.98 (top right). Stairs leading to the upper story reveal the abundant use of carved wood ornamentation. Jiangsheng *cun*, Lingshi *xian*, Shanxi. [RGK photograph 1996.]

Figure 4.99 (bottom left). Extensive renovation of the Wang family manor is being carried out with the expectation that it will become an important stop on the itineraries of Chinese and foreign tourists visiting Shanxi. Jiangsheng *cun*, Lingshi *xian*, Shanxi. [RGK photograph 1996.]

Figure 4.100. Kangbai-
wan manor is the largest
walled complex of cliff-
side *yaodong*, above-
ground structures, and
courtyards in northern
China. Set against a hill
slope and built on sev-
eral terraces, the com-
plex took shape between
the late Ming and the
late Qing dynasties. In
addition to 73 *guyao*, 150
single-story and multi-
story above-ground
structures, and 20 *yao-
dong*, there are court-
yards and terraces.
Kangdian *cun*, Gong-
xian, Henan. [Source:
Hou, Ren, Zhou, and Li
1989, 208.]

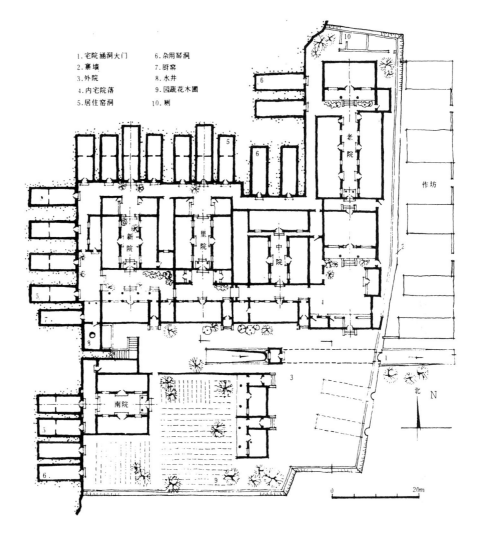

stone (Figures 4.97 and 4.98). As with other manor complexes, the Wang family manor is undergoing extensive renovation in hopes that the arrival of tourists will help bring prosperity to this remote area of the province (Figure 4.99). Throughout Shanxi there is optimism that its historical commercial importance will return because of the acumen of its business people, the opening of a modern expressway between Taiyuan and Beijing that has cut travel time in half to six hours, and the designation of world-class monuments, such as the walls surrounding Pingyao, the art-historically significant Datong grottos, and the temples of Wutai Mountain. Even in remote areas of western Shanxi, such as in Fenxi

xian, efforts are being made to bring forth the commercial glory of its powerful historical families. Here, it is the remnants of the late Ming and early Qing Shi family manor [Shi*jiagou* 师家沟 Shi family gulch] that provides the evidence of past eminence and future promise.

The largest walled complex of cliffside *yaodong*, above-ground structures, and courtyards in northern China is Kangbaiwan manor 康百万庄园, found just to the south of the Huanghe River in Kangdian *cun* village, Gongxian, Henan province (Figures 4.100 and 4.101). Built on several terraces, this manor complex was begun during the late Ming period, continued to take shape well into the nineteenth

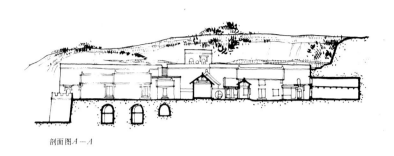

剖面图 A—A

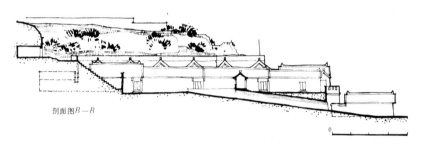

剖面图 B—B

Figure 4.101. Used with plan shown in Figure 4.100, the top section view A-A runs from the north to the center of Kangbaiwan, while B-B runs from the left to the right through the secret passageway. A crenelated protecting wall can be seen on the left of section A-A. Kangdian *cun*, Gongxian, Henan. [Source: Hou, Ren, Zhou, and Li 1989, 209.]

century during the Qing dynasty, and finally covered some 64,300 square meters. In addition to 73 *guyao*, 150 single-story and multi-story above-ground structures, and 20 *yaodong* dug into the loessial ridge at its back, there are courtyards spread across the sloping terrace. The elements of its overall plan, especially the preservation of conventional units even as local innovations were made, were discussed earlier in the section on courtyard dwellings. A crenelated protecting wall with underground passageways was built around it in 1821. It is said that the Empress Dowager Ci Xi visited here on her way back to Beijing from Xi'an in 1901 after the conclusion of the Boxer Uprising (Hou et al. 1989, 203–210; Liu and Han 1995, 114-119).

Whether actually dug into the ground or modeled above ground using stone, brick, earth, or even concrete, subterranean-type dwellings that are found throughout the loessial region remain a dominant and strikingly unique housing form. The builders of such structures have long recognized both environmental constraints and opportunities, developing what Hong-key Yoon has called "geomentality," a successful ecological adaptation (1990, 101).

CHAPTER 5

Dwellings in Southern China

SOUTHERN CHINA ACTUALLY BEGINS along the south-facing slopes of the Qinling range and the banks of the eastward flowing Huaihe River, along a physiographic line that is as much a cultural as a physical edge. The Qinling/Huaihe demarcation separates the drainage basins of the Huanghe and Changjiang Rivers and has been a significant marker of China's cultural divisions. Encompassing more than half the area within the Great Wall, southern China extends from relatively temperate areas with distinct four-season climates southward into the subtropical and tropical portions of the country where winters are absent. The region includes within it the extensive drainage basin of the Changjiang (Yangzi River), with broad and varied flood plains in its middle and lower reaches; the rugged hill lands of Hubei, Hunan, Jiangxi, southern Anhui, and southwestern Zhejiang, whose streams feed the Changjiang; the fragmented coastal provinces that sweep southward from southern Zhejiang, Fujian, and Guangdong toward the Guangxi Zhuang Autonomous Region; the island provinces of Taiwan and Hainan; and the physiographically complex basins and dissected plateaus of Sichuan, Guizhou, and Yunnan (Map 5.1). Abundant rainfall and mild temperatures together nourish diversity in the natural vegetation growing throughout most of the region. As a result, the types of raw materials employed in housing construction far exceed those used elsewhere in the country. Not only are many more kinds of timber and soil available but bamboo is so widely distributed and found in such variety that it became quite early a reasonable substi-

tute for wooden pillars and, when woven, was used for walling.

Throughout much of southern China, fragmented topography and isolated drainage basins kept people apart throughout much of Chinese history. As a result, there has arisen a complicated and well-documented mosaic of territorially defined material culture traditions that vary to a much greater degree than is seen in northern China. This striking diversity is especially evident along the southern border areas, where there are some forty different ethnic minority groups. The conspicuous differentiation of material culture is even observable among the Han in southern China. Although one can acknowledge that migration has played a key role in the distribution and formation of Chinese dwelling types, it is not possible at this juncture to write authoritatively about routes of diffusion, patterns of formation and reformation, and cultural regions. Even scholars of Chinese dialects who are certain of the role that migration has played in the dialect geography of China have made little progress in this regard except for sketching the numerous migrations at various scales and speculating about their impact (Li Rong et al. 1988).

Prior to the Yuan dynasty, the three major migrations were from north to south, bringing with them an eventual shift in the "center of gravity" of China's population. After the Yuan, the principal migrations were from east to west, with the notable exception of the movement of population into the northeast region of China (Manchuria) in the early twentieth century. These great interregional migrations took

Map 5.1. Southern China, as a complex cultural region, includes the middle and lower Yangzi River valley, the south Yangzi hill areas, the southeast coast, and the southwest portions of the country.

place as some areas became saturated or as people suffered from natural and man-made misfortune (Zhou 1991). State-sponsored military and civilian migration and the episodic mass movement of people in response to famine together display an extraordinary level of geographic mobility that must certainly have revealed itself in patterns of material culture. During the Qing period alone, the scope of interregional migration expanded to the degree that some 25 million Chinese moved from the North China and Middle Yangzi macroregions into the peripheral frontier areas of the Northeast, Southwest, and the Upper Yangzi. These population movements have been described as "the largest long-distance land migrations in premodern history" with a profound "impact . . . on China's demographic and linguistic" map (Lee and Wong 1991, 54–55). They occurred during a period in which China's population itself tripled from 150 to 500 million and its land mass doubled to 10 million square kilometers.

In only a few instances in the following discussion will an effort be made to relate a building form to migration history and resulting cultural change. It is hoped that future researchers will bring issues of diffusion from hearth areas into the scope of their work and use Chinese material culture—including dwellings—to help trace the spread of material culture along routes of movement. Ethnic and subethnic consciousness, conflict with indigenous peoples, unsettled social order, lineage strength and weakness, male/female migrant ratios, distance from imperial authority and ability to discount sumptuary regulations, the nature of local building materials, among a host of other factors, all contributed to the varying forms one encounters throughout the country. Yet as seen throughout this book, the strength of precedent—the maintenance of well-developed forms and technologies—brought with it a striking level of universality of Chinese material culture over time and space even as it seemingly tolerated pronounced local and regional variations.

It is generally believed that Chinese pioneers brought the basic northern rectangular shape and courtyard models to the south and then adapted them to local conditions. Yet, evidence of southern neolithic forms differing from those known in the north—as presented in Chapter 3 about Hemudu—show that separate regional building traditions evolved side by side before merging with and eventually being dominated by northern Han norms. The substantial variations that are observable from one area to another in the south reflect more than dissimilarities in climate, topography, and economy, however. They also exhibit the extent to which migrating Han pioneers adopted local building forms and practices and the degree of receptivity by indigenous groups to Han Chinese norms. The confluence of building patterns apparent today illustrates well the acculturation process over the centuries.

Building conventions found in southern China often echo northern patterns but at the same time stand out with distinctive vernacular architectural forms. In examining representative housing forms found in southern China, this chapter will discuss a range of single-story and multistory dwelling types found in inland Sichuan province and coastal Guangdong and elaborate on four distinctive regional housing types: the enclosed multistory dwellings of Anhui, Jiangxi, and Zhejiang; the unique fortresses of the Hakka, a Han subgroup, found in Fujian, Guangdong, and Jiangxi; urban residences in the Jiangnan region; and the uncommon dwellings of non-Han ethnic minority groups in Yunnan and Guangxi provinces. While vernacular forms can be locally identified and mapped as regional types, it is rare for them—with some obvious exceptions that will be discussed—not to be found elsewhere in the country, often side by side with other types. This lack of exclusivity means that one frequently finds exotic buildings mixed among what appear to be relatively homogeneous patterns. Some other examples of southern dwellings were presented in Chapter 3 in the discussion of building principles.

Single-Story and Multistory Dwellings

Modest single-story dwellings are seen widely throughout southern China just as they are in northern China. However, unlike the relatively simple rectangular single-story dwellings of the north, southern dwellings are generally more varied in shape and complex in building structure. Multistory dwellings, on the other hand, are rare in rural and urban northern China, but two- and sometimes three-story dwellings are common throughout southern China. Besides environmental factors and economic conditions related to small-scale farming, social conditions also contributed to the emergence of more heterogeneous house forms in southern China. In order to accommodate to varied conditions in the uplands and lowlands, peasants built isolated farmsteads and small dispersed villages that not only take advantage of sunny slopes, local microclimates, limited arable land, and available water but also reflect social conditions. While large extended families and clans are often associated with Chinese society, small families living in modest houses have probably always been more common. Even with small households, however, there usually is some change over time. As a family fluctuates in composition and size and as its resources wax and wane during a life cycle, their simple farmhouses also usually undergo at least a modest additive transformation.

Dwellings throughout southern China often employ ingenious interior sunken spaces called *tianjing* 天井, so-called "heavenly wells" that are open to the sky above. As discussed in Chapter 2, *tianjing* are small enough that they are not generally regarded as courtyards, at least in the sense that the term is generally used in northern China. *Tianjing* of many sizes respond well to the hot and humid conditions characteristic of much of southern China. While the single central courtyard of a northern *siheyuan* may exceed 40 percent of a dwelling's total area, *tianjing* rarely exceed 20 percent, even when they are a dominant forecourt called a *tingyuan* 庭院 . Many southern dwellings include multiple *tianjing*, with none larger than the size of a single room and many no larger than a mere light shaft or well. Shaded transitional arcades formed by broad eaves overhangs and open rooms complete the spatial structures of many southern dwellings. Variations from province to province and even within provinces are substantial whether the dwellings are single-story [*danzuo pingfang* 单座平房] or multistory [*danzuo loufang* 单座楼房]. Further elaboration of *tianjing* will follow in the section on dwellings in Anhui, Jiangxi, and Zhejiang.

Dwellings of Inland Sichuan

With an area roughly the size of Texas and comprising nearly 10 percent of China's population, greater than that of any European country, it is not surprising that there are great variations in settlements and housing throughout Sichuan province, including the newly established Chongqing Municipality. These differences arose from the actions of indigenous people under local conditions across a vast area in the remote past that were subsequently modified over time as Sichuan's population grew because of substantial migration from other regions of the country. Han settlers today dominate the rich subtropical Red Basin at Sichuan's core, while they are interspersed among many minority groups in the surrounding rugged mountains that isolate Sichuan from the rest of China. While excavated artifacts from prehistoric archaeological sites throughout the province disclose building patterns still seen today in Sichuan's rural housing stock, it is likely that many indigenous housing types simply vanished as the Han secured their hold in the southwestern frontier. The presence of distinct house forms in Sichuan that are characteristic of other regions of the country naturally underscores the fact that the forebears of most of the province's population originated elsewhere. As people migrated, they brought with them cultural patterns that had taken shape at other places under quite different conditions.

Archaeological evidence from Sanxingdui 三星堆, probably the site of the capital of the ancient Shu kingdom, reveals rectangular dwellings with interior space divided into outer and inner rooms that are sited facing predominantly southeast and southwest. Even when orientation deviates from these general norms, such as an excavated dwelling with a door opened toward the north instead of southeast or southwest but with a covered portico, it appears that a conscious attempt was made to balance building design and structure with actual local environmental conditions (Zhuang 1994, 3). As seen in Figure 5.1 at the Shang dynasty site Shierqiao 十二桥, excavated in 1986, an embryonic form of piled dwelling, known as *ganlan* 干栏, has living space elevated on a platform above the ground, with an open space below in

Figure 5.1. An early prototype for piled dwellings has been excavated at Shierqiao near Chengdu, a Shang dynasty site excavated in 1986. Later called *ganlan*, this dwelling type has living space on the platform above the ground in order to mitigate high humidity, protect against flooding, and provide a degree of safety from animals and snakes. [Source: Zhuang 1994, 19.]

Chinese settlement generally did not directly displace indigenous peoples, Han immigrants were "intrusive . . . intent on refashioning the frontier into a typically Han world" (von Glahn 1987, 3). In western Sichuan through the Qin and Han periods, there were extraordinary improvements in housing structure and form as well as a general transformation of life as refugees and garrisoned soldiers brought with them designs from more advanced and cosmopolitan areas and modified them to meet the requirements of a frontier they were bent on domesticating.

Evidence of this early cultural infusion is detailed order to mitigate high humidity and protect the dwelling from flooding. In structure and general appearance, these ancient piled dwellings are similar to modest contemporary structures built beside many fields where farmers have created outposts to watch their crops during the harvest season (Figure 5.2). Unfortunately, the relationship of these discoveries in Sichuan to those elsewhere in China is not clear, since it is not yet possible to understand fully the nature of cultural interaction between cultures throughout China (Li 1985, 205–206).

Cultural contact with the northern heartlands substantially increased because of migration into the southwest after China was unified by the Qin in the third century B.C., continuing during the Han dynasty that followed and persisting at high levels through the Song period a thousand years later. As Han Chinese pioneers spread throughout the region, they encountered tribes living in hillside villages fortified with palisades of trees or logs, graphically suggested by the character *tun* 囤, which the Chinese used to describe the small settlements ringed with a wall of some sort. Even though early

Figure 5.2. Although piled dwellings are no longer common in Sichuan, one can see similar structures built by farmers on the edges of their fields. Used during harvest time, they are occupied much of the day and night as observation sites from which to watch their crops. Zhuangyuan *cun*, near Langzhong, Sichuan. [RGK photograph 1994.]

Figure 5.3. Unearthed near Chengdu in 1975, this Han period (A.D. 25–220) tile reveals three-dimensional details of a large walled compound with several subdivisions, a standard three-bay structure placed along an axis, and a dominating tower. Built atop a podium, the triple-bay *zhengting* is framed in wood, roofed with tile, and looks onto a major courtyard linked to other courtyards via gates. Sharing some similarities with Han buildings in the north, it nonetheless was open and had a prominent eaves overhang, both conditions responding well to Sichuan's subtropical climate. Men and women are shown sitting or kneeling on the floor, as was the custom in China at the time. The tile displays domestic animals and an outfitted kitchen. [Source: Lim 1987, 31. Illustration used with the permission of The Chinese Culture Center of San Francisco.]

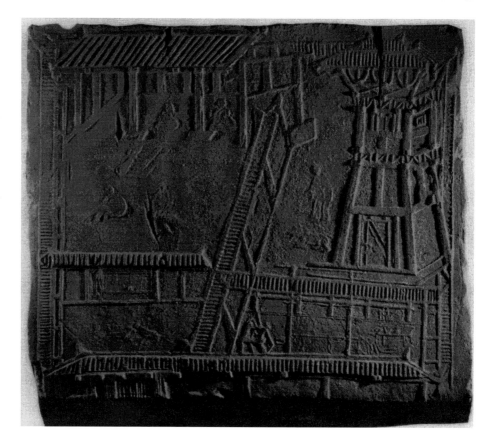

by engravings on Han dynasty bricks excavated in recent decades in the Chengdu area. By the Later Han period (A.D. 25–220), as can be seen in Figure 5.3, well-developed walls, courtyards, and buildings similar to those found elsewhere in China at the time were being built in Sichuan. Shown on this tile is a series of walled compounds and a standard three-bay structure placed along an axis where it faces a major courtyard linked to two other smaller courtyards via gates. Built on a podium, framed in wood, and covered with roof tile, the main structure is a *zhengting-tang* 正厅堂, a principal hall with proportions appropriate to a low-level official. While evidently similar to northern buildings with its post-and-beam *tailiang* structure—observable on the gable end—this rectangular dwelling was open and had a prominent eaves overhang supported by corbel brackets, both conditions responding to the need for ventilation and protection from rain in Sichuan's subtropical climate. As in earlier times and elsewhere in China dur-

ing the Han period, men and women continued to sit or kneel on the floor.

This engraved pictorial tile also shows a subsidiary area with a well, kitchen, place for drying clothes, and a prominent multistory tower separated from the main living area on the left by a wall and gate capped with eaves tiles. The overhanging hipped roof of the commanding timber-frame tower contrasts markedly with the gable roof of the low dwelling, together hinting at the likely richness of architectural forms at an early time even in this remote area. The closed middle portion of the tower was probably used for the secure storage of valuables, including the protection of the household's grain stocks from dampness. While the lower level conceivably contained a bed for a guard as well as stairs to the upper levels, the upper story itself was for observation purposes (Zhuang 1994, 4–5).

Square watchtowers [*diaolou* 碉楼], built of tamped earth, brick, and stone with a wooden super-

Figure 5.4. Dramatic *diaolou*, or watchtowers, are still found in some villages and towns in the rugged mountainous areas of eastern and southern Sichuan near the borders of Yunnan and Guizhou. Fubao *zhen*, southern Sichuan. [Source: Ji and Zhuang 1994, 86.]

structure and prominent roof rising between 10 and 20 meters, once were commonly associated with times of strife in rural Sichuan. Indeed, throughout China during the Han period, similar high towers [*qiao* 谯 or *qiaolou* 谯楼] may have been quite common, as records prescribed that they be built every 10 *li* for surveillance purposes. Literary and archaeological evidence further confirms the extensive building of multistory timber-frame *lou* in many areas of the country (Tanaka 1995). Within Sichuan's frontier settlements, *diaolou* were a necessary precaution in order to guard vulnerable dwellings and provide a place of refuge for household members. Some can still be observed in eastern and southern Sichuan in Han villages near the borders of Yunnan and Guizhou and in the minority areas of the upland west (Figure 5.4). Over time, the building of watchtowers increased during periods of turmoil and decreased when there was order, just as was the case with the ebb and flow of ramparts and fortresses of many types elsewhere in the country (Ji 1994, 4). While most watchtowers once served primarily defensive needs, some of the thousand or so relics that remain today in remote regions were probably built as pavilions for the entertainment of guests or for solitude rather than for defense.

Tomb models of the Han period also show structures built on piles above the ground in a manner suggestive of indigenous building forms suitable in the subtropics. A pottery model of an elevated granary, shown in Figure 5.5, combines the symmetrical components and decorative elements of northern buildings with a lifted substructure and a porch. Trip-hammers and pestles, everyday tools for hulling rice, that are placed beneath the granary portray the functional utility of the open, yet protected, space beneath. A three-dimensional red sandstone sculpture of a two-story dwelling, unearthed in Lushan *xian* on the western edge of the Red Basin in 1953, also references both local and Han architectural components (Figure 5.6). Carved from a single block, it is rather crude and solid, presenting mixed messages concerning cultural interaction. The supporting columns are heavy and quite different from those normally associated with indigenous mountainside buildings. Large open windows and the absence of a prominent eaves overhang appear inappropriate for the climate in Sichuan. The division of social space is represented well via the female shielded by a half-opened door in the upper story and the use of open space beneath by a male for entertaining guests. The link between the ladder and the central entry is not clear.

Early building forms were altered and refined in succeeding centuries as they were joined by other styles brought by migrating populations from other regions, especially from the middle reaches of the Changjiang River during the Ming and Qing periods. Peculiarly, some Sichuan dwellings seen today continue to resemble northern dwellings in that they do not have a roof overhang suitable for the subtropics (Figures 5.7 and 5.8). Perhaps these forms originated with northern migrants and continued to be built by

Figure 5.5 (top left). Excavated in the Chengdu area, this is a pottery funerary model of a relatively simple granary. Similarly, the storage area would have been lifted off the ground on piles to reduce moisture and provide protection against rodents that might spoil the stored grain. The shaded area created below would have provided work space for men to use trip-hammers and pestles to hull the grain. [Source: Lim 1987, 91. Illustration used with the permission of The Chinese Culture Center of San Francisco.]

Figure 5.6 (top right). This three-dimensional sculpture of a two-story dwelling was carved from a single block of red sandstone. Supporting columns are heavy and unlike those found in indigenous *ganlan* structures. Large open windows and the absence of a prominent eaves overhang seem to be inappropriate for subtropical Sichuan. A female is shown shielded by a half-open door, while a man is entertaining guests below. [Source: Lim 1987, 108. Illustration used with the permission of The Chinese Culture Center of San Francisco.]

Figure 5.7 (middle right). Without an eaves overhang wide enough to shade the dwelling and shed rainwater away from the foundation and walls, this rectangular dwelling in the eastern part of the province has many similarities to northern prototypes, including being built directly on the ground. Its depth and width, its loose tile roof, and its siting near a windbreak grove of bamboo, however, reveal some attention to subtropical conditions. Near Chongqing, Sichuan. [RGK photograph 1983.]

Figure 5.8 (bottom right). Also with a limited eaves overhang and built directly on the earth, this L-shaped rural dwelling in northern Sichuan shares many characteristics with the dwelling shown in Figure 5.7. Near Langzhong, Sichuan. [RGK photograph 1995.]

Figure 5.9. A dweller-built house of piled stone, adobe brick, and thatch, this modest dwelling is found atop a hill. The old owner maintains his own kitchen garden at the front door. Zhuangyuan *cun*, near Langzhong, Sichuan.

Figure 5.10. Although structurally more complex with its mortise and tenon pillars and beams, this modest three-bay dwelling includes a low wall of tamped earth, above which is woven split bamboo walling. Eaves brackets are extended to the slender peripheral pillars in order to make a portico. The doors are made of woven bamboo. Zhuangyuan *cun*, near Langzhong, Sichuan. [RGK photograph 1995.]

their descendants without paying full attention to all the modifications that might have been beneficial in the subtropics. The limited fenestration, on the other hand, suggests an attempt to keep sunlight from directly heating the interior, a condition that would have been facilitated in the north by a facade of windows. The width and depth of the dwelling, moreover, are both somewhat broader and deeper than northern dwellings. With a bamboo windbreak to its back and rice paddies to its front, the farmstead itself typifies rural life in Sichuan's *yuanzi*.

Far more numerous throughout Sichuan are single-story dwellings of various sizes, shapes, and materials that have a deep eaves overhang in order to protect the walls from rainwash and to shade the interior from strong rays of the sun. The shape and floor plan of rural dwellings evidence a high degree of flexibility in accommodating to irregular terrain in an effort to maximize microclimates. Rectangular, L-shaped, and U-shaped structures that are simple in plan and economical in materials are all common, examples of which were illustrated in Chapter 3. *Sanheyuan* and *siheyuan* courtyard styles that are organizationally and structurally complex as well as larger dwellings with multiple courtyards are also widely

seen. Many structures, however, are proportionally reduced in scale when compared to those found elsewhere in China. Even where resources are limited and where only readily accessible building materials such as earth, bamboo, and thatch are employed, a humble dwelling includes elements found repeated in larger and more complex structures.

In mountain and peripheral areas of Sichuan's basins, one still sees simple rectangular adobe dwellings with thatched roofs—often with an attached shed—that were clearly built by the farmers themselves (Figure 5.9). Modest truncated rectangular houses often include a portico *in antis* that is shaded by a thatched roof with a 45-degree pitch. In eastern Sichuan, as shown in Figure 5.10, three bays are defined by a mortise and tenon pillar-and-beam frame composed of roughly hewn slender timbers. Each of the pillars directly holds a transverse roof purlin that altogether support the weight of rafters and thatching. To define living space, two of the three bays are wrapped with a 1.5-meter-high tamped earth wall capped with panels

Figure 5.11. This is a three-bay rectangular dwelling of a moderately prosperous farmer as evidenced by the fired brick and tile construction. The roof is steeply pitched and includes a sufficient overhang from which to suspend crops for drying prior to storage. Foothills of Mt. Emei, western Sichuan. [RGK photograph 1981.]

of split bamboo lath interlaced at a 90-degree angle. The right bay is used for cooking and storage. Other, more substantial fired brick rectangular dwellings typically have steeply pitched roofs and a sufficient overhang from which to hang crops to dry (Figure 5.11). They often include an attached utility shed or kitchen. The construction of such a large farmhouse was illustrated earlier in Figures 3.30 through 3.34.

L-shaped structures with a colonnaded facade appear in limitless varieties of the basic form. The short wing building, whether of wattle and daub with a thatch roof, adobe, or fired brick and tile, often serves as a summer kitchen. Figure 5.12 shows a close-up of the wing of a simple L-shaped farmhouse. Constructed of a wooden skeletal frame with a thinly thatched roof, the walls are formed of wattle and a mud plaster. Here the wing serves as a kitchen, evidenced by the accumulation of soot at the open area under the gable and near a vent in the upper wall. Figure 5.13 shows a common L-shaped dwelling built of both sun- and kiln-dried brick in the Chengdu area of western Sichuan. The dwelling shown in Figure 5.14 follows the same plan yet is built with higher-quality building materials. Qualitative improvements in traditional materials, such as an ample wooden framework to support a tiled roof, and a greater proportional scale in terms of height, width, and depth results in similar but even larger structures.

Windows in Sichuan dwellings are often small and placed high on the wall where they can catch air and ventilate the interior without bringing in direct sunlight. Although usually made of a lattice pattern, they

are not commonly covered with paper. Doors are usually left open to facilitate ventilation. Steeply pitched thatch and tile roofs serve well to shed the rainfall that generally exceeds 1,000 millimeters annually in most areas of the province. Since bamboo and timber are abundant, relatively thin-frame skeletal structures, often utilizing mortise and tenon *chuandou* frames, are common. Walls of interwoven split bamboo lath covered with a whitewashed mud daub are also common

Figure 5.12. This attached wing of an unpretentious L-shaped farmhouse is constructed of a wooden skeletal frame with walls of wattle and a mud plaster. Serving as a kitchen apart from the living area of the house, the room is often filled with smoke that escapes through various openings in the endwall. Zhuangyuan *cun*, near Langzhong, Sichuan. [RGK photograph 1995.]

Figure 5.13. This L-shaped variant of a basic Sichuan dwelling has a steeply pitched roof that overhangs the walls and is constructed of a mixture of adobe and fired brick. Western Sichuan. [RGK photograph 1983.]

Figure 5.14. Following the common L-shaped plan, this fired brick and tile dwelling is clearly built of better materials and with a higher level of craftsmanship than the other dwellings described earlier. Zhuangyuan *cun*, near Langzhong, Sichuan. [RGK photograph 1995.]

throughout the province as are tamped earth and adobe brick curtain walls.

Actual courtyard-style dwellings that are reminiscent of *sanheyuan* and *siheyuan* structures found elsewhere in China are called *sanhetou* 三合头 and *sihetou* 四合头 in Sichuan. The open U-shaped courtyard dwelling of Deng Xiaoping's boyhood, shown in Figure 2.39, is a *sanhetou*. With striking black wooden framework and brightly whitewashed infilling panels, this style of dwellings is clearly identified with Sichuan. The intervening wall panels are usually much

more regular in shape and size in Sichuan than are similar forms seen in Jiangxi and Zhejiang provinces. This regularity is seen clearly in a late Qing dwelling in the Nanchong area, some 150 kilometers north of Chongqing, that is the birthplace of Luo Ruiqing, Chairman Mao's onetime security chief. As seen in Figure 5.15, in the corner of the courtyard held by the *zhengting* and a truncated wing, there is an extensive use of unpainted wooden panels that have been allowed to weather. It is only under the eaves that one sees whitewashed panels. Although the wing is short

Figure 5.17. Appearing to float amongst the paddy fields, this *yuanzi* and its *siheyuan* incorporate a large courtyard as their nucleus. Chengdu region, Sichuan. [Source: Graf zu Castell 1938, 155.]

Figure 5.15 (top left). Reportedly built during the Guangxu period (1875–1908) of the late Qing dynasty, this is the birthplace of General Luo Ruiqing, Chairman Mao's onetime security chief. Luo lived here from his birth in 1906 until 1926. Viewed from the front, the courtyard is broad and narrow and embraced by U-shaped structures. Today the courtyard has been tidied up and planted with vegetation, but traditionally this was a busy place for farm work. Unpainted and weathered wooden panels form the lower sections of the front walls, while under the eaves are found whitewashed panels. Shuangnushi *cun*, Wufeng *xiang*, Nanchong, Sichuan. [RGK photograph 1995.]

Figure 5.16 (top right). Viewed from the side, the intersection of the *zhengting* and the wing involves complex carpentry. Exposed dark timbers contrast with encased whitewashed panels of similar size to create a half-timbered effect reminiscent of parts of England and Germany. Shuangnushi *cun*, Wufeng *xiang*, Nanchong, Sichuan. [RGK photograph 1995.]

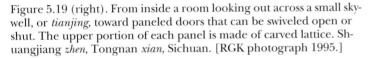

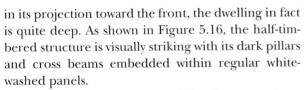

Figure 5.18 (above). View across the rooftops of Qing dynasty *siheyuan*. Most are narrow structures that recede back from the street with repeating divisions of halls and narrow *tianjing*. Several dwellings are two-story half-timbered structures reminiscent of houses found in the countryside. Langzhong *shi*, Sichuan. [RGK photograph 1995.]

Figure 5.19 (right). From inside a room looking out across a small skywell, or *tianjing*, toward paneled doors that can be swiveled open or shut. The upper portion of each panel is made of carved lattice. Shuangjiang *zhen*, Tongnan *xian*, Sichuan. [RGK photograph 1995.]

in its projection toward the front, the dwelling in fact is quite deep. As shown in Figure 5.16, the half-timbered structure is visually striking with its dark pillars and cross beams embedded within regular whitewashed panels.

Unlike houses that have a defined courtyard, no wall separates any of the dwellings discussed earlier from the abutting fields, which come almost to the front door. As seen in most of the illustrations, the position of each dwelling in the landscape is defined by a thicket of bamboo. The presence of a *siheyuan* in a rural area is clear evidence of a level of well-being far beyond that of villagers who live in either a rectangular, L-shaped, or U-shaped dwelling. Sichuan *sanheyuan* and *siheyuan*, as shown in Figure 5.17, are

typically either found alone or scattered together with a few other similar dwellings in tiny hamlets marked by a thicket of bamboo and eucalyptus trees, which provide a windbreak and a degree of privacy. Although small housing clusters of this type are called *yuanzi* 院子, which translate as "courtyards," each is actually a diminutive hamlet. Marked clearly by the dark green edges of protective vegetation, *yuanzi* seem to float amidst the paddy fields.

In towns and cities throughout Sichuan, multiple-*jin siheyuan* dating from the Qing dynasty are found in great numbers. As with other *siheyuan* of merchants and officials in southern China, Sichuan *siheyuan* typically are deeper than they are wide, with alternating halls and various sizes of *tianjing*. In

Figure 5.20. Exquisitely carved door and window panels are common in the better dwellings in the province. Arranged around the expanse of a *tianjing*, the lower panels are carved in bas-relief, while the upper portions are perforated to facilitate ventilation. Langzhong *shi*, Sichuan. [RGK photograph 1995.]

many cities, such as that shown in the view across the rooftops of Langzhong in northern Sichuan in Figure 5.18, there are large numbers of Qing dynasty structures. Often there are two-story half-timbered structures reminiscent of houses found in the countryside mixed among the single-story *siheyuan*. As with *tianjing* elsewhere in southern China, and as discussed in Chapter 2, the skywells help to ventilate the interior and bring rainwater inside (Figure 5.19). The connection between interior space—the rooms—and exterior space—the *tianjing*—is mediated by paneled doors arranged around the expanse of each skywell that can be swiveled open or kept closed (Figure 5.20). Usually elegantly ornamented with both geometrical and didactic forms, the lower panels are often carved in bas-relief, while the upper portions are perforated in order to maximize ventilation (Figure 5.21).

Figure 5.21. Decorative lattice patterns range from the geometrically simple to those that include inlaid motifs. Langzhong *shi*, Sichuan. [RGK photograph 1995.]

Dwellings of Coastal Guangdong

Until 1988 when Hainan island was administratively separated from it, Guangdong was China's southernmost province. With a long and fragmented coastline that faces the warm ocean and bisected by the Tropic of Cancer, which passes just to the north of the city of Guangzhou, the province is divided into two nearly equal parts. The southern half, including virtually all of the rugged coastal areas, is essentially tropical, while the areas to the interior north are subtropical, primarily because of higher elevations and fragmented landscapes that moderate temperatures. Central and eastern Guangdong are dominated by the delta of the Zhujiang River, often called the Pearl River Delta, that is actually composed of crisscrossed deltaic outlets of many small rivers. Because of Hong Kong's location near the mouth of this river system and the fact that the New Territories of Hong Kong were until 1898 a part of Guangdong province, some examples from Hong Kong are included in this section on Guangdong. Hong Kong today is a Special Administrative Region of China after Britain relinquished its sovereignty over the Crown Colony in 1997.

With fertile soils as well as abundant heat and water, the region is intensively farmed and has a long history of dense agricultural and urban settlement. As in other areas of southern China, vernacular builders pay attention to mitigating high temperatures, abundant precipitation, and intense humidity as they create housing forms. Because the noon sun is nearly directly overhead for several months each year, *tianjing* throughout this area are correspondingly diminished in size in order to reduce the intrusive blazing heat of the high tropical sun. Diffused natural light rather than the intense glare of direct sunlight is preferred for illuminating the interior of dwellings. The overall

compact shape of individual dwellings, which are usually clustered together, further minimizes the exterior surface areas that are exposed to the sun. The result is a thermally efficient building mass suitable to the subtropics in which shade from nearby dwellings contributes significantly to mutual cooling. In Guangdong, as well as in portions of Hainan, Taiwan, and Fujian, particular attention has also been paid to guarding against the destructive impact of strong winds, especially those associated with typhoons, which invade the southeast coastal areas over a seven-month period each year. Addressing similar environmental problems in these areas has led to a variety of different housing types.

Although historically considered remote from the hearth areas of Chinese civilization, southern China nonetheless shares some dwelling patterns with areas much farther north. Archaeological evidence over the past forty years has revealed not only substantial neolithic settlements but, significantly, important finds of the Qin and Han periods that provide direct and indirect evidence of early housing forms. Both the Qin and Han periods were characterized by extensive territorial expansion involving military conquest and colonization. The migration of farmers and soldiers brought Chinese architectural forms

Figure 5.22. View of the rear of an L-shaped "carpenter's square type" Eastern Han period dwelling. It is composed of two segments—a two-story rectangular structure attached to a short single-story one—joined at right angles and embracing a small walled yard. Dayuangang, Guangdong. [Source: Guangzhou 1983, 231.]

from the north, and the forms themselves evolved as they came into contact with well-established indigenous southern patterns.

Tombs of the Han period (206 B.C.–A.D. 220) reveal clearly the multiplicity of housing forms that developed during these years of imperial expansion. Among the funerary objects, or *mingqi*, which represent the worldly possessions of the deceased, pottery models of dwellings are especially numerous at many excavated sites in Guangdong and Guangxi and to a lesser extent in Hubei, Hunan, and southern Hehan (Lewis 1999, 34–35). By virtue of their presence in elaborate tombs, however, such models represent what may be country houses rather than the modest huts that most peasants must have occupied (Boyd 1962, 87). Although some of the models are single story, most are two stories, with the ground floor and courtyard used for animals and the upper story serving as living quarters. The two levels were connected by ladderlike stairs. Structurally many of them represent the use of timber framing with an infilling of tamped earth. Most include overhanging gable roofs covered with tiles. Rooflines generally lack pronounced curvature, although there often is a tendency for an upward sweep of the ridge line at each end. Some also clearly show open latticework panels of wood or brick.

Four representative dwelling patterns have been identified among the remarkably realistic pottery models: "railing type" [*zhajushi* 栅居式], "carpenter's square type" [*quchishi* 曲尺式], "three-sided type" [*sanheshi* 三合式], and "tower type" [*lougeshi* 楼阁式]. Each typically incorporates a small "courtyard," a precursor of *tianjing* but with walls so low that the space cannot be called a "skywell." The "railing type" has been described as similar to the pile dwellings—with space beneath for animals and space above for humans—still found in areas inhabited by minority nationalities in southwestern China. Chinese archaeologists believe that the "railing type" is an early type that was later displaced by the others.

The "carpenter's square type" is L-shaped with two segments—a two-story rectangular structure and a short single-story structure—joined at right angles and embracing a small walled yard at the back (Figure 5.22). A pitched roof with a ridge raised at the ends dominates the two-story structure.

The "three-sided type," or *sanheyuan*, is symmetrical in plan, with two flanking structures and a yard between them, and forms a U shape, as seen in Figure 5.23. The facade shows a two-story, three-*jian* structure that is marked with trellislike lattice forms that extend nearly to the ground—quite unlike those seen today, which are placed above an apron wall. Francis Wood has speculated that these "apron walls were lower in the Han because people sat on mats on the floor; focus of interior design may well have affected the external proportions" (1996, 686–687). In this model, two wings are connected by a low wall and embrace a courtyard in the rear. One of the single-story structures is a stable, while the other is a toilet for the household.

"Tower types" are more complex than the "three-sided type," with a plan involving two back-to-back,

Figure 5.23. View from the rear of a *sanheyuan*, or "three-sided type." It is symmetrical in plan with two flanking structures on each side and a yard between them to form an Ω shape. A stable is found in one of the wings and a latrine in the other. Mayinggang, Guangdong. [Source: Guangzhou 1983, 73.]

Figure 5.24. Pottery *mingqi* of a fortress, or *chengbao*, was uncovered in excavations in Guangdong and is reminiscent of forms still seen in neighboring Jiangxi. [Source: Guangzhou 1983, 93.]

"three-sided" components that form an H shape. The rectangular horizontal structure is typically higher than the flanking wings, sometimes reaching as high as five stories with multiple roof levels. Enclosed yards are normally located in the back of these structures, a pattern quite different from that normally seen in dwellings today. Aside from prominent entryways, each dwelling typically also had an Ω-shaped hole for the use of domestic animals as they freely moved in and out of a dwelling.

In addition to individual dwellings, pottery models of fortresses [*chengbao* 城堡] also have been uncovered (Figure 5.24). Usually square in shape and symmetrical in plan, Han *chengbao* typically have cantilevered corner towers that rise above high surrounding walls and are reminiscent of structures still seen in southern Jiangxi province (Guangzhou 1958; Guangzhou 1981; Guangzhou 1983).

There is a certain disjunction between the details of these Han dynasty houses and dwellings of the late imperial period that can still be seen today as well as questions about the relationships between pottery and "real" architecture (Lewis 1999, 114-121). However, as seen earlier in Chapter 2, the common use of compact plans, enclosure, and small open interior ar-

eas clearly has continued to be flexibly adapted in various environmental and social conditions. Compact plans with small open interior spaces are usually square, allowing not only for the building of individual residential units that meet the needs of small households but also for the efficient formation of densely packed clusters of multiple residences that are found widely in the region.

Siting, thermal insulation, shading by blocking the penetration of the sun's rays, and maximizing ventilation—all of which are functionally interrelated—are the principal means employed in Guangdong and other southern areas to deal with intense solar energy resulting from elevated sun angles, long periods of daylight, high temperatures, heavy precipitation, and sultry humidities. Pronounced summers and relatively warm winters are addressed through the manipulation of gross as well as detailed architectural features. The placement of doors, windows, and skywells are usually carefully considered because these are openings into which the direct or indirect rays of the sun can penetrate the interior, allowing heat to accumulate to potentially unbearable levels.

A southeastward orientation for dwellings, openings, and channels inside buildings to facilitate air flow makes good use of the remarkably steady wind patterns characteristic of coastal China, especially during the summer. Field observations in southern villages give clear evidence that prevailing winds and general microclimatic conditions are usually well understood by villagers. Even the casual observer can see that siting patterns of dwellings vary from one area to another in a regular way. In one survey of hundreds of traditional dwellings in Nanhai *xian*, Guangdong province, for example, not a single dwelling was oriented due south; all were oriented toward the southeast, generally between forty and forty-five degrees from true south, in order to take advantage of prevailing wind currents (Lin and Li 1992, 61).

High relative humidities of at least 80 percent are common year-round throughout southern and much of central China. Relative humidity is highest during the period of so-called "plum rains" [*meiyu* 梅雨], which bring each year a month or so of overcast skies and intermittent drizzle and showers during late May and June. While gentle rains are favorable for transplanting rice, they fill the air with so much water vapor that condensation forms easily within the dark and cool recesses of many southern dwellings, on floors, walls, and other surfaces. Arriving when the plum crop ripens, plum rains are also called "mold rains" [*meiyu* 霉雨], using a Chinese homonym, because of the propensity of household items to mildew from little sunlight and high humidity.

Even though heat buildup can be moderated by ventilation, it is clearly best to reduce its intrusion in the first place. The mutual shading of compact structures in tight formations, each with limited openings in their walls, is a first line of defense in many towns and villages. Interior rooms in larger structures throughout Guangdong typically are relatively narrow and deep. The addition of a recessed portico and eaves that overhang *tianjing* from each of the tightly packed interior buildings further block solar gain in the interior. The use of leafy plants and trellised vines wherever possible within interior open spaces also sometimes contributes to an amelioration of microclimates by shading and by measurably reducing ambient temperatures via the evaporation of water from the plants.

In Guangdong, as in other areas of southern China, exterior walls are usually thick in order to afford some insulation from the heat outside. Many such walls—even those of modest dwellings—are frequently coated with a white lime plaster, which reflects energy. If any windows are present in the encircling walls, they are typically placed high not only to provide a degree of security but also to reduce ground radiation and draw in some ambient air. Although the dark tiles on the roofs offer a pleasing visual contrast to the white walls, they are highly absorptive of solar radiation. Even so, the thinness of the tiles inhibits heat buildup, and if the tiles are laid loosely, as they often are, warm air can escape from the high rooms through the permeable roof. Roof surfaces sometimes include a double layer of tiles in order to insulate the interior from the higher temperatures outside. These strategies are combined with interior plans that are remarkably open even while quite fragmented, with the result that air courses through the passageways.

A particularly striking urban dwelling in Foshan *shi*, a city southwest of Guangzhou, reveals well the attentiveness to subtropical environmental conditions (Figures 5.25, 5.26, and 5.27). Built in 1843 by two families, the *Donghuali* 东华里 residential complex incorporates three parallel and symmetrical units that are at once linked together and separated by two narrow lanes that run nearly 150 meters between the units. Each residential unit incorporates a compact series of three halls and three *tianjing*. There is a rhythmic increase in the height of the halls from the front to the back of each unit. The side halls are all narrow and front on a small *tianjing*. The dramatic curvature of the upper gable walls not only ornaments the structures but helps to shade them as the sun passes across the sky during each day. Thick white walls help reflect radiant energy. Limiting the numbers of windows prevents ambient heat outside from reaching the interior, yet the placement of doors, as can be seen in the plans and elevations, helps ventilate the interior by drawing moving air into the dwelling that will flush out heat and help reduce the accumulation of moisture that might condense in the cool interior (Foshan shi 1994, 260).

The research of Lu Yuanding and Wei Yanjun on ventilation in southern China has revealed the design

Figure 5.25. Viewed from across the rooftops, *Donghuali* comprises three parallel sets of symmetrical halls that are separated from each other by two narrow lanes that run approximately 150 meters between them. [Source: Foshan *shi* 1994, 261.]

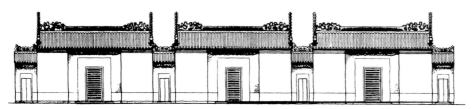

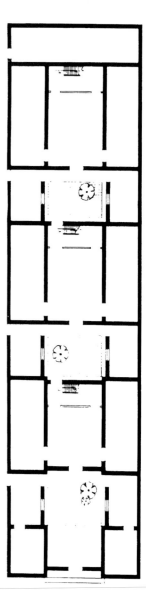

Figure 5.26. Top, an elevation of one set of halls shows three triple-*jian*-wide units, each with a central door and each separated from the others by an alley door. When the doors are open, air can rush through the complex. Right, the plan shows a narrow series of three two-story halls, each separated from another by a *tianjing*. Side entries lead into *tianjing*. [Source: Foshan *shi* 1994, 260–261.]

Figure 5.27 (below). The dramatic curve of the upper gables of each hall is decorative and helps to shade the structure as the sun passes across the sky during each day. Each of the hall/*tianjing* units and associated *xiangfang* is a compact cluster of spaces. [Original photograph used with the permission of Andrew Li.]

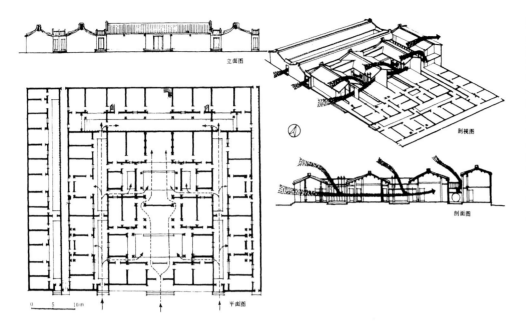

立面图

俯视图

剖视图

剖面图

平面图

0 5 10 m

Figure 5.28. Air is channeled through large southern dwelling complexes via a system of *tianjing* and corridors. Utilizing the steady wind currents characteristic of the region, the air is drawn into one of five north-south passageways that run nearly the length of this complex. Chaozhou, Guangdong. [Source: Lu and Wei 1982, 151.]

for enhancing "breathing" within larger residential complexes by channeling air and evacuating it from systems of *tianjing*. As can be seen in the section and plan of a modularized dwelling in Chaozhou in Figure 5.28, *tianjing* of many sizes and shapes are symmetrically positioned within the complex. Air currents that blow steadily from the south in this region can enter one of five north-south passageways that run nearly the length of the complex. In addition, air can enter from above into the east-west running *tianjing*. The interrelationship of the *tianjing* and interior corridors produces a "ventilation system" [*tongfeng xitong* 通风系统] in which areas are differentially heated and cooled. The resulting convectional currents enhance the pumping of air through the complex, ventilating the interior and helping remove humidity before it condenses (Lu and Wei 1982, 150–151). A similar system of inducing air flow and then venting it via the disposition of open spaces, open corridors, and open-sided structures has been described for dwellings in the Quanzhou area of Fujian (Dai 1991, 171).

The careful alignment of open doors in relatively simple dwellings in tropical Hainan, as seen in Figure 5.29, facilitates the thorough ventilation of the residential area, cooling while it helps reduce humidity

by moving the moist air. In towns of coastal Guangdong and in rural Hong Kong, where there is a need to keep doors open for ventilation, ingenious wooden cagelike doors called *tanglong* 躺笼 [also called *muzha men* 木栅门] slide into stout granite sockets in order to provide security even as they welcome the breeze (Figure 5.30). *Tanglong*, with their strong wooden cross bars, are usually accompanied by a substantial inner wooden panel that can be used to seal the entry, and sometimes a waist-high folding panel is used for partial closure (Figure 5.31).

Ventilation not only removes heat but plays a significant role in reducing humidity levels by flushing out moist air before it can condense on interior surfaces. The selection of building sites that optimize the capturing of steady winds characteristic of the southeast coast is critical in this regard, as is the creation of channels that lead prevailing winds directly and indirectly through even a complex building. This effect is accomplished not only by placing openings in strategic locations but by taking advantage of differential pressure within the building that is due to even slight differences in temperature and that has a pumping effect. In larger structures, rooftop transom windows [*qichuang* 气窗] supplement the multiple levels of air flow that continuously converge and

Figure 5.30. In order to enhance ventilation and to provide security in the dwellings of rural Hong Kong and in the towns and villages of nearby coastal Guangdong, ingenious "gates" called *tanglong* are formed from horizontal wooden bars that slide as a unit into granite sockets hewn into the door frame. Coastal Guangdong. [RGK photograph 1993.]

Figure 5.29. Front doorways throughout this village are aligned due south in recognition of the prevailing sea breezes. Rear doors are placed opposite the front doors in order to facilitate the passage of air for cooling and the removal of humidity. Longlin *cun*, Qiongshan *xian*, Hainan. [Original photograph used with the permission of Catherine Enderton.]

diverge within a dwelling (Figure 5.32). Other details, such as ventilation ports that are placed high on gable walls and lattice windows on rooms adjacent to *tianjing*, further contribute to moderating tropical and subtropical conditions within dwellings.

Especially along the coastal lowlands, the threatening impact of high winds and pounding rain associated with summer and early fall typhoons, which carry with them abrasive sand and corrosive salt, has led to the building of only single-story structures. This is because low structures are less likely to block the passage of intense tropical storms with their potentially destructive fury. When viewed in terms of their plan, some of these dwellings echo northern *siheyuan* rather than the compact *tianjing*-type houses characteristic of the south. In the Shantou and Chaoan (formerly Chaozhou) area of eastern Guangdong province, as seen for example in Figure 5.33, many characteristics of a classical *siheyuan* are present even though the dwelling shown is clearly a southern one with its attention to ventilation and shading. Although the central courtyard has an area greater than that generally found in southern dwellings, it is

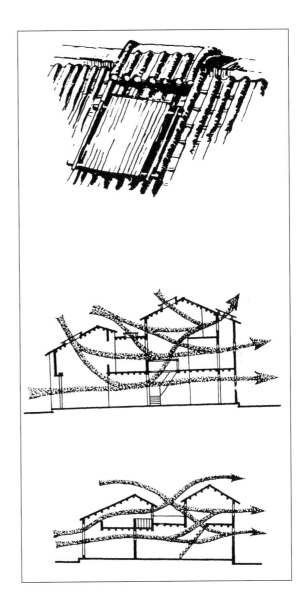

Figure 5.31 (top left). Interior view of a *tanglong* and two open hardwood door panels. A waist-high folding panel may also be used to afford some privacy yet allow air and light to enter. Different combinations of these three door components can be used, depending on what level of ventilation and privacy are required. Donghuali, Foshan *shi*, Guangdong. [Original photograph used with the permission of Andrew Li.]

Figure 5.32 (top right). In multistory dwellings in central Guangdong, *qichuang*, or rooftop transom windows (top), help draw air into the tight interiors. The complexity of the ventilation in the large dwelling in central Guangdong (middle) differs only in degree from that in the smaller dwelling found in Shantou, along the northeast coast of the province (bottom). [Source: Lu and Wei 1990, 253.]

Figure 5.33 (bottom right). Built low to counter heavy coastal winds, this *siheyuan* is called a "four metal points" or *sidianjin*-style dwelling because each of the gable walls has the sloped-shape profile of the Chinese character for "metal." The courtyard, called a *tianjing* in Guangdong, is much larger than those generally found in Guangdong. The plan for this dwelling was shown earlier in Figure 2.66. [Source: Lu and Wei 1990, 325.]

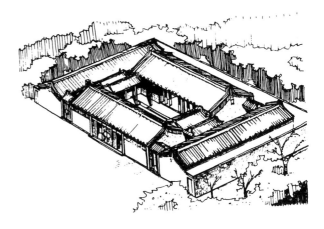

Figure 5.34. Some of the multistory villas called *lu* were built on open lands in the countryside by wealthy Chinese who returned to their native villages in retirement. The interior floor plan of most *lu* usually retain traditional Chinese layouts, although the fenestration is more similar to western patterns. [Source: Lu and Wei 1990, 132.]

still called a *tianjing* rather than a *yuanzi*. The arrangement of the surrounding buildings on four sides clearly marks it as a *siheyuan*-type dwelling. Symmetry, axiality, and clear hierarchy are prominently seen in elevation, plan, and function of the dwelling. Yet, because the rectangular *tianjing* is longer from east to west than from north to south, there are only limited opportunities for the intense rays of the sun to penetrate rooms; in fact, the elongated *tianjing* is shaded during much of the day. In addition to the central elongated courtyard and four smaller "courts" in the corners, there is an encircling walled alley that "opens" the structure so that even strong winds pass through the dwelling without being obstructed. The *tianjing* also comprises a substantial number of sheltered arcades with wide roof overhangs and four rooms that are open to the central

courtyard. Along coastal Guangdong, this type of *siheyuan* is called "four metal points" [*sidianjin* 四点金] because each of the gable walls has a slope profile similar to the Chinese character for "metal." Combining *sidianjin* modular units with other similar or different plans allows the construction of larger dwellings for extended families (Lu and Wei 1990, 62–75, 324–325).

The nineteenth- and twentieth-century history of Guangdong reveals the province as one of the most open areas of China, not only as the homeland province of a majority of Chinese migrants in a worldwide diaspora but also as a focal region for dynamic trade and significant economic development. As a result, there is perhaps a greater number of dwellings in rural Guangdong that echo or imitate foreign styles than elsewhere in China. While some such foreign-style dwellings, as well as churches, banks, and schools, were built by westerners following designs that they were familiar with at home in Europe or America, many more were built by "overseas Chinese," individuals who lived abroad as sojourners either for long or short periods before returning to their home villages and towns in China to pass their final days. There are many examples of small and large villas called *lu* 庐 built by wealthy returnees on open lands in the countryside. Generally two or three stories high, many were clearly inspired by foreign architecture, although, as seen in Figure 5.34, some also incorporate Chinese elements. The interior floor plan of most *lu* often retained traditional Chinese layouts although fenestration on all levels and sides was plentiful (Wei 1991, 125–126).

Much more dramatic than *lu*, however, are the imposing, fortresslike, multistory towers that are found in large concentrations in the rural areas of Kaiping, Taishan, Xinhui, and Enping that comprise the so-called *qiaoxiang* 侨乡, or "native places of overseas Chinese," in central Guangdong (Figures 5.35 and 5.36). Generally termed *diaolou* 碉楼, or "watchtowers," they are modern versions of what was described earlier in Sichuan as having a history that reaches to the Han period. In Sichuan, early *diaolou* were built for the purpose of surveillance as well as for refuge during periods of disorder. Although historical records in Guangdong suggest similar struc-

Figure 5.35. Most of the watchtowers, or *diaolou,* seen today in rural Guangdong were built in the 1920s and 1930s, a time during which there was substantial fear of robbers and thieves. This reinforced concrete tower, built on a 4-by-4-meter base, is approximately 12 meters high. Xiqi *cun,* Taishan *xian,* Guangdong 1989. [Original photograph used with the permission of Jonathan Hammond.]

Figure 5.36. Although the lower three stories of this *diaolou* lack distinction, the upper stories include turrets, a cupola, finials, and a colonnaded arcade. Kaiping *xian,* Guangdong. [Source: Unknown.]

tures were built there in the past, few remain today. One outstanding example is Yinglonglou 迎龙楼, a 300-year-old three-story watchtower in Kaiping *xian.* With limited fenestration, a secure entry, and four corner towers, records show it as the tallest structure in the villages at that time. It was used by villagers for safety during times of turmoil as well as during major floods.

The *diaolou* seen today in the "overseas Chinese" villages of Guangdong, however, were principally built during the 1920s and 1930s, an unsettled time in China often called the "warlord period." Falling between the end of the imperial dynasty in 1911 and the belated consolidation of the country under the Nationalist government in 1927, this period was one of widespread banditry. Fear of robbers and thieves

prompted many methods for ensuring security, such as building fortified towers along the perimeter of villages in order to secure the protection of all of its residents whenever needed. Much of the time, *diaolou* were not occupied, even though stocks of grain and water were usually stored within and guarded by a watchman. During times of strife and sometimes even at night during periods of relative calm, households would leave their village dwellings and secure themselves inside the *diaolou* with their valuable possessions. In some villages, new dwellings were actually attached to watchtowers in order to incorporate space needed for daily living into the tower. In enhancing both functionality and security in this way, the upper

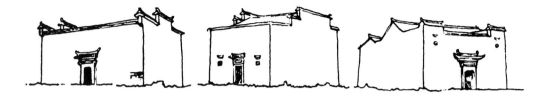

Figure 5.37. Appearing as austere boxes with only limited exterior ornamentation and fenestration, Ming dynasty dwellings are well documented in the Huizhou region of Anhui. Left, Shexian, Tuolin *xiang;* middle, Shexian, Xixinan *xiang;* right, Xiuning *xian,* Jiandong *xiang.* [Source: Zhang et al., 1957, 16.]

floors could be used for storage of valuables, with other tower rooms used for sleeping.

More than 1,400 multistory *diaolou* still remain in Kaiping *xian* (Lu and Wei 1990, 135). Most *diaolou* are square or rectangular and are rather similar to each other in terms of the massing of the multistory structure. Built tightly of bricks with only small and narrow openings, all of which could be well secured from the inside, the structural body is essentially a solid and secure column. The uppermost story or two, however, often was elaborately designed with cantilevered platforms, cupolas, turrets, finials, openwork, arches of many shapes, and arcades, and many different types of ornamentations. Chinese architects have referenced many of these designs as attempts to imitate European models, calling them Italianate, Middle Eastern, Islamic, Renaissance, Roman, and English in style (Lu and Wei 1990, 135–144; Wei 1991, 126–129).

Enclosed Single-Story and Multistory *Tianjing* Dwellings

Throughout southern China, while there are residences that preserve the general front elevations of northern courtyard-style dwellings, more of them appear from the outside like tall squat boxes enclosed by white plastered walls, strikingly contrasting the general horizontality of Chinese structures. In plan view, even though some are quite compact and others more expansive, most include spatial elements that echo northern courtyard-style *siheyuan:* orientation to the cardinal directions, side-to-side symmetry, axiality, halls adjacent to courtyards, and an explicit hierarchical organization of space. As discussed in Chapter 2, they are like *siheyuan* in that they are inward-facing and closed off to the outside world by walls and with only limited fenestration. Unlike northern courtyard houses, however, they are generally densely packed structures that lack the spacious and open feeling of *siheyuan*. All include so-called "skywells" [*tianjing* 天井], the abbreviated rectangular cavities of many sizes that are employed widely in southern China. As functional space, even as they become rather large, *tianjing* are so distinctive that no one would mistake them for a *yuanzi*, the term normally used to describe a courtyard.

Dwellings of Anhui, Jiangxi, and Zhejiang

Many multistory *tianjing* dwellings in Anhui, Jiangxi, and Zhejiang provinces date from the Ming dynasty (1368–1644) and are among the oldest occupied houses in China (Figure 5.37). The best surviving examples are Huizhou dwellings, the residences of prosperous merchants and pawnbrokers who had made their fortunes in urban centers all over China. They built their residences in their home districts in the upper reaches of the Xin'anjiang River in a region known generally as Wannan 皖南, or "southern Anhui." While early wealth in the region was based on the local production of tea and high-quality paper and ink used by calligraphers, Huizhou people by the Ming period were amassing wealth by sending their sons out from villages to China's major cities in order to pursue commerce. Through skill and acumen, Huizhou salt, fish, tea, and lumber merchants came to play a disproportionately large role in the national economy than their numbers might suggest. Hui-

Figure 5.38. Although it is not possible to date this modest dwelling, it is clearly built in the triple-*jian* Ming style with its plain facade, tile roof copings, central doorway, high windows, and *zhao,* canopies over the door and windows. Maoping *cun*, Luci *xiang*, Tonglu *xian*, Zhejiang. [RGK photograph 1987.]

Figure 5.39. Built along the road connecting Tunxi in Anhui and Hangzhou in Zhejiang, this two-story old dwelling is similar in width to the one in Figure 5.38. However, the much more elaborate entryway and the receding rooflines tell us it is a grander dwelling of an earlier period. Ningyuantang, Zhanqi *cun*, Shexian, Anhui. [RGK photograph 1987.]

zhou merchants tended to maintain their families in the Wannan region, even though they worked elsewhere, generally returning home themselves to retire. Throughout their productive years, they invested substantial assets in building magnificent residences, clan halls, and other minor structures with a pronounced cosmopolitan flavor that reflected not only their wealth but also the strength and vitality of their families.

Although concentrated principally in the historically important area of southeastern Anhui prov-ince, similar Huizhou-style dwellings are found in neighboring western Zhejiang and northern Jiangxi (Zhang et al. 1957; Wu 1980; Cheng and Hu 1980; Boyd 1962, 92-103; Shan 1984, 1992; Knapp 1989b, 38-51). In external appearance, most appear quite modest, even austere, because of the general absence of ornamentation. Built compactly of brick, Huizhou residences generally range between three and five bays in width and have a depth that at least equals their width, although some are arranged in clustered units of three-bay dwellings (Figures 5.38,

Figure 5.40. This canal-side neighborhood of Qing period compact dwellings is found to the east of Jingdezhen, Jiangxi. The ground-level window openings are a recent addition. Likeng *cun*, Wuyuan *xian*, Jiangxi. [Original photograph used with the permission of Li Yuxiang.]

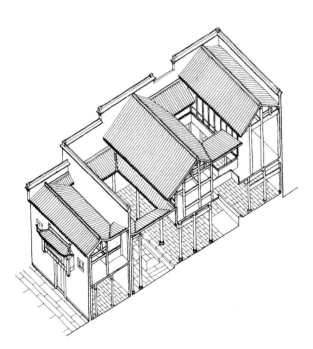

Figure 5.42. Similar three-bay structures are arranged in a clustered unit that incorporates a broad low wall with a plain gate that defines a courtyard fronting lavishly ornamented entrances. Zhanqi *cun*, Shexian, Anhui. [RGK photograph 1987.]

Figure 5.41. Built during the transition period from the Ming to Qing dynasty, this three-bay-wide residence recedes three parallel *jin* deep and has two *tianjing* openings. Each level increases in height as one moves from front to back. Ningyuantang, Zhanqi *cun*, Shexian, Anhui. [Source: Dongnan daxue 1996, 56.]

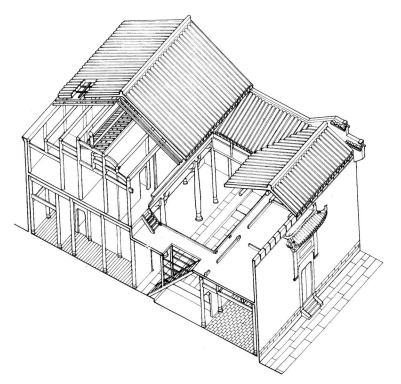

Figure 5.43 (top). Five bays wide, this was the residence of Wang Yongsheng, the governor of Shexian during the Wanli period (1573-1620) of the Ming dynasty. Elegant wood and bamboo carvings are noticeable throughout the dwelling. [Source: Dongnan daxue 1996, 36.]

Figure 5.44 (bottom). Heavily weathered, this towering compact dwelling is claimed to date from the Yuan dynasty (1279-1368). Chengkan *cun*, Shexian, Anhui, 1994. [Original photograph used with the permission of Luo Laiping.]

5.39, 5.40, 5.41, 5.42, and 5.43). During the Qing dynasty (1644-1912) and into the twentieth century, rural and urban dwellings of this type continued to be built. Several villages in Anhui proclaim that they are museums of period architecture from China's imperial past because of the large number of surviving buildings contained within them. Xidi village 西递村 claims 120 structures dating to the Qing period, while rival Chengkan village 呈坎村 boasts more than 200 from the Qing and more than 30 from the Ming period. Figure 5.44 shows a towering block in Chengkan village that is claimed to date from the Yuan period (1279-1368).

Just as with northern *siheyuan*, little attempt was made to display wealth and status to the outside world except by inference through the scale of the dwelling and perhaps by the adornment of the entryway (Figure 5.45). While entry is normally through a double-leaf gate at the center of a symmetrical facade, some dwellings have southeast gates that are reminiscent of those of northern *siheyuan*. Principally decorative and at a scale that sometimes seems to overwhelm, carved brick, stone, and wood "canopies" or "hoods" [*menzhao* 门罩] are seen above entryways (Figures 5.46 and 5.47). "Canopies," because of their placement high above the gate and because they barely project from the wall, offer only limited protection from pouring rain during storms, although they do deflect cascading rainwater that washes down the high walls from the wooden gates below. In some cases, the horizontal lines of *menzhao* were elaborated with prominent vertical elements to create a *menlou* [门楼], a multilevel trabeated flat arch "structure" in raised relief that mimics in many ways a freestanding *pailou* [牌楼], or ceremonial gateway. Windows were uncommon in the outside walls of these tight dwellings, but if included they were small, placed only in the upper story, and capped with a decorative horizontal "canopy." White walls were accentuated with black tile copings arranged either

Figure 5.46 (top). The contrast of the white walls and black tile copings is amplified by the *menzhao* over an upper window and the large gate structure in the center. The lower windows and doors are probably recent additions. Hongcun, Yixian, Anhui. [RGK photograph 1987.]

Figure 5.45 (above). The wealth and status of the head of a household can be inferred from the entryway, which may range from a simple *menzhao* or "canopy" covering (top) to a more complex *menlou*, a multilevel flat arch "structure" (bottom). [Source: Zhang et al., 1957, 18.]

Figure 5.47 (left). This recessed entryway leads to the large two-story Wang Dinggui residence, which was built near the end of the Qing dynasty. Hongcun, Yixian, Anhui. [Source: Shan 1992, 125.]

along a straight line or tiered in a steplike gable wall. Slightly upturned at each end, these black copings are decorative and divert rainwater away from the foundation.

Sumptuary regulations presumably governed the external appearance of dwellings, leading to at least a superficial simplicity and lack of ostentation that actually masked to outsiders the grandeur often found within Huizhou residences. Elaborately carved wood, brick, and stone panels, balustrades, roof members, brackets, pillars, and doors that together expressed wealth and a well-developed aesthetic were customary within these residences. Few areas of China exceed Huizhou in the abundance and intricacy of ornamental carving and the richness of the themes depicted. The carving of wooden structural members, such as beams and decorative panels and other elements associated with overhanging verandas and inner eaves, was widely employed throughout the Ming and Qing periods in Anhui, Jiangxi, and Zhejiang. Exquisite wooden openwork and raised relief designs were facilitated by the availability of high-quality timber brought to the Huizhou area from southwestern China for sale to the wealthy (Ma and Song 1988). Engraved brick carving in this region can be traced to craftsmen who molded patterned bricks here as early as the Han dynasty. Brick carving evolved in succeeding centuries to become, by the Ming period, a separate craft known as "design chiseling" [*zaohua* 凿花], which rivaled wood carving in the complexity of technique and the elegance of detail. Improvements in brickmaking technology created plastic forms that were as durable as stone, but stone carving predates both wood and brick (Song and Ma 1990). In Huizhou, as elsewhere in China, stone was employed in locations, such as column bases, where heavy loads had to be carried. Even here, well below eye level, expressive carving was carried out. Large perforated windows separating areas within a dwelling also were the focus of ornamented sculpturing in stone, as were elaborate balustrades placed along steps (Chen, Ma, and Song 1988).

The main reception hall and bedrooms of a Huizhou dwelling were situated on the upper story, with the ground level reserved for servants, visitors, and secondary household functions, such as cooking and personal hygiene. At least one room of the cool and dry upper story was reserved for storing grain. Each hall was clearly differentiated from the others in hierarchically explicit language: *tingtang* 厅堂 [reception hall], *zhengting* 正厅 [main hall], *zutang* 族堂 [ancestral hall], *menting* 门厅 [gate hall], *houting* 后厅 [back hall], *ceting* 侧厅 [side hall], and *guoting* 过厅 [passage hall]. Generally the ceiling of the ground floor area was lower than that of the upper story, indicating proportions reminiscent of pile dwellings found farther south. At least one steep staircase located behind one of the larger halls typically linked the two levels.

Even with a distinctive multistory compact shape resulting from the limitations of terrain and overcrowding and high perimeter walls reflecting a preference for privacy and security, nothing distinguishes Huizhou dwellings more than their *tianjing* 天井. Exposed to the heavens above, sunken below grade level, and delimited by four intersecting frames, each clearly suggests in plan and elevation the verticality of a 井, a Chinese "well." *Tianjing* are often narrow, only 1 or 2 meters across, although some may reach 50 square meters in size and thus approximate true courtyards. The varying sizes and locations of *tianjing*, reflecting adaptations to particular sites and the demands of different households, create dwelling floor plans that are O-, inverted U-, H-, or figure 8-shaped, as discussed earlier in Chapter 2. *Tianjing* are "empty spaces" that serve more than the important functional purposes of drawing light, air, and rainwater into what appears from the outside to be a dense and solid structure. Cary Y. Liu suggests that *tianjing* also have "a ritualistic aspect that energizes the 'emptiness'" in that each is actually an axis that "fixes the human abode between the heavens above and the earth below" (1994, 28, 34). He postulates that the term "*tianjing*" is probably abridged from *tianhua zaojing* 天花藻井, the term used for a coffered ceiling that, following Stein (1990, 147–162), was a ritual "window to the heavens" with powerful cosmological significance.

One of the best documented Huizhou dwellings is that of Wu Xizhi, a prosperous merchant, in Xixi-

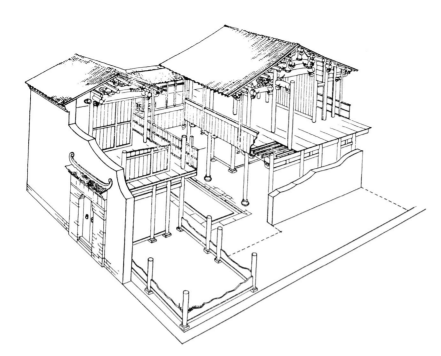

Figure 5.48 (top). The perspective drawing of a prosperous merchant's dwelling shows the relationship between the *tianjing* near the center series of front rooms, subsidiary side halls, and a main reception hall along the back side. Xixinan *xiang*, Anhui. [Source: Zhang et al. 1957, 55.]

Figure 5.49 (bottom left). The shallow impluvium at the base of the *tianjing* makes it possible for rainwater to be collected and drained away from interior spaces. [Original photograph used with permission of Shin Hada.]

Figure 5.50 (bottom right). Upper-story galleries with hinged lattice windows and a colonnaded arcade on the first floor open the interior to the passage of air and light into the various rooms via the elongated *tianjing*. Shuttered lattice windows on the second story also open onto the *tianjing*. [Original photograph used with permission of Shin Hada.]

Figure 5.51. Built within the last century, this streamside dwelling appears to have lost its fronting wall and some of its earlier grandeur. Yixian, Anhui. [RGK photograph 1987.]

Figure 5.52. Common in many of the villages of southwestern Zhejiang, multistory structures take many shapes and sizes. Each, however, is marked by white walls with limited fenestration and a black line of coping along the roofline. With the sun high in the sky, long shadows are cast by the thin "canopies" above the doors and windows, effectively blocking the sun from reaching directly inside. Changle *cun*, Zhuge *xiang*, Lanxi *shi*, Zhejiang. [RGK photograph 1987.]

nan xiang, Anhui (Figure 5.48). As can be seen from the plan and perspective drawing, the *tianjing* is placed near the center of the residence and is bounded by a series of front rooms, subsidiary side halls, and a main reception hall, or *tang*, along the back. At its base, the *tianjing* includes a shallow impluvium in which rainwater is collected and drained away from interior spaces (Figure 5.49). Upper-story galleries with hinged lattice windows and a colonnaded arcade on the first floor open the interior to the passage of air and light into the various rooms, few of which have exterior windows (Figure 5.50). As elsewhere in the Huizhou area, the upper story was used as the family's living quarters while lower rooms beneath provided space for servants and

guests. Beyond the staircases that link the two levels, a pair of smaller utility *tianjing* and ponded water are seen along the side of the residence. Only one courtyard and associated structure remains of this once grand dwelling, the bulk of which was destroyed over the past forty years.

Although surviving Ming and Qing residences of this type are not found in Jiangxi and Zhejiang in the concentrations characteristic of the Huizhou area of Anhui, enclosed two-story *tianjing*-style dwellings are seen in significant numbers in the small towns and villages throughout the region. Most lack the simple grandeur of Ming structure but maintain some of the basic characteristics of their antecedents (Figures 5.51 and 5.52).

Urban Residences in the Lower Changjiang Region

Forming the core of the prosperous Jiangnan region, the densely populated, intensively farmed, and highly commercialized floodplains of the lower Changjiang River continue along the adjacent indented bays and coast to form a zone of canals, streams, ponds, shallow lakes, and paddy fields that the Chinese refer to as "water country" [*shui xiang* 水乡] and "rice and fish country" [*yumizhi xiang* 鱼米之乡]. Between the two metropolises of Nanjing and Shanghai, distinctive urban residential forms have taken shape: high-density, low-rise dwellings in the small and medium-size water towns, such as Suzhou, Zhouzhuang, Kunshan, Shaoxing, Huzhou, and Jiaxing and row dwellings that are a mixture of Chinese and foreign influences in the great entrepôt Shanghai. Village settlements throughout the region echo the more fully developed residential patterns found

in the market towns to which they are linked by the crisscrossing of watercourses (Knapp 1989, 13-17).

Many water towns are laid out in a gridded pattern with principal canals running east to west so that dwellings face north and south. Figure 5.53 shows three common water town settlement patterns with characteristic canals, arcades, lanes, and bridges. Among the most common configurations are:

Canal	Dwelling	Road	Dwelling	Canal
	Dwelling	Road	Canal	
	Dwelling	Road	Canal	Dwelling
	Dwelling	Road	Canal	Shed
Dwelling	Arcade	Canal	Arcade	Dwelling
	Dwelling	Canal	Dwelling	
	Dwelling	Road	Dwelling	

Many structures include a shop on the lower level, with the dwelling above or behind. Some face a canal in the front and a lane in the back, while others have the reverse pattern. When taken together, open

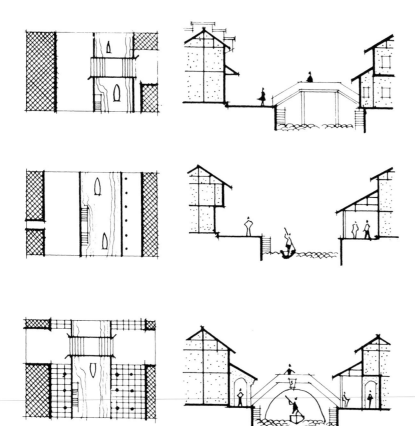

Figure 5.53. Structures abut canals in varied patterns in the towns and villages of northern Zhejiang and southern Jiangsu. The top figure shows a lane on only one side of the canal with a bridge linking the dwellings on the other side; the middle figure shows an uncovered lane on one side with an overhanging arcade on the other; and the bottom figure exhibits a pattern with arcades of different depths on each side of the canal. [Original drawing used with the permission of Shen Dongqi.]

Figure 5.54. Presenting a mixture of shaded arcades and open areas, this canalside scene provides space for the activities of daily life, including washing and drying clothes. Dongpu *zhen*, Shaoxing *shi*, Zhejiang. [RGK photograph 1987.]

fronts and backs underscore that movement both by water and by foot is essential in the daily life of residents. Arcades or covered walkways [*zoulang* 走廊 or *buxinglang* 步行廊] are common features of many villages and towns in northern Zhejiang and southern Jiangsu, where they offer protection from the intense summer sun and frequent downpours. As part of a residence, overhanging arcades provide sheltered overflow space for daily activities, such as eating meals and watching children play, and a convenient location for drying clothes that are washed in the waters of the canal (Figure 5.54). Arcades take many forms, including providing the necessary structural support for overhanging rooms above. In the absence of an arcade, sailcloth canopies provide similar shaded spaces in many cases.

Many water town structures serve both as a place of residence and of small-scale commerce, including shophouses that carry goods for sale to meet the daily needs of nearby households, workshops for processing raw materials or fabricating small items, and small establishments, such as teahouses, wine shops, and restaurants. Rooms above serve principally for sleeping and are usually divided only by partitions that do not reach the ceiling. Most of a family's daily life is played out in public in the spaces below and in front of the structure, where work and living commingle. In this way, entrepreneurs are able to keep an eye on their goods day and night, and all family members can participate in the business. Craftsmen are able to make their wares while being available to customers who come to buy them. (For a discussion of shophouses elsewhere in China, see Ho 1994.)

Compact, rectangular, timber-framed waterfront dwellings in Suzhou are among some of the most beautiful yet simple in China. As with other larger southern residences, they usually have contrasting white walls with grey tile roofs that are highlighted with dark brown or red woodwork on their canalside and streetside facades. Even though as narrow as 4 meters in width and between 4 and 6.5 meters in height, some structures incorporate an open shaft or skywell [*tianjing*], often large enough to view as a minor courtyard.

The narrow tree-shaded and stone- or cobble-

Figure 5.55. The small lane on the right is but a back alley compared with the broader canal, which declares its primacy as main access route to the dwelling via stone steps. A narrow corridor connects the lane with the waterway, steps, and dockage. [Original drawing used with the permission of Liu Mengchou.]

paved lanes of Suzhou present only simple wood- or stone-framed gateways in the masonry walls (Figures 5.55 and 5.56). Inside, however, there is often a small secluded courtyard, sometimes with a well, that is surrounded by a one- or two-story structure (Figures 5.57 and 5.58). The canal side of the dwelling, however, is usually more visually complex, with windows, woodwork, and steps, which declares the primacy of water in the daily life of Suzhou's residents. The steps leading from canal level up to the dwelling provide mooring for the shallow draft vessels that ply the canal and limited space for domestic chores. Some of these structures have commercial spaces on the lower level as well with shop fronts accessible from either the land, water, or both ends. The simplicity of most Suzhou dwellings contrasts with the grand and elegant private gardens that epitomize life of the literati in imperial China (Figure 5.59). Only a handful of classical urban gardens remain in Suzhou, private settings that, while artistically created in the manner of landscape paintings, served as the backdrop for a good life (Joseph Chuo Wang 1998).

Civic and domestic architecture with a European flavor is bountiful in China's coastal and riverine cities, many of which were once treaty ports and, in the case of Hong Kong and Macao, colonies. European, Japanese, and North American expatriates throughout the nineteenth and early twentieth centuries frequently re-created villas, apartment houses, hotels, churches, and a wide variety of commercial buildings after styles common in their home countries.

Just as traditional *siheyuan* are residential markers of Beijing's *hutong* [lanes], the innovative *longtang* of cosmopolitan Shanghai represent a unique hybrid

Figure 5.56. From the narrow lane, the view into a small courtyard is through a stone- or wood-framed doorway. Suzhou. [Original photograph used with the permission of Joseph Chuo Wang.]

Figure 5.57 (top left). Inside the gate of many Suzhou dwellings, there is a small secluded courtyard, which may contain a well and private workspace for the family. [Original photograph used with the permission of Joseph Chuo Wang.]

Figure 5.58 (top right). Protruding awnings, cluttered steps, and overhanging vegetation present a variegated composition along this narrow canal in Suzhou. [Original photograph used with the permission of Joseph Chuo Wang.]

Figure 5.59 (bottom). Hidden behind plain masonry walls like ordinary Suzhou houses is a private garden and its associated residence, a "picture-in-three-dimensions" with its rockeries, ponds, plants, prospects, and living spaces. Shizilin Garden, Suzhou. [Source: Unknown.]

258

PLACES AND REGIONS

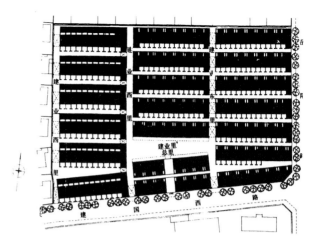

Figure 5.61. The overall plan of a *lilong* neighborhood of 254 units reveals rows of common buildings opening off narrow sublanes. White spaces within each of the black units show the placement of *tianjing* of various sizes. Jianyeli, Shanghai. [Source: Shen 1993, 85.]

Figure 5.60 (above). Viewed from above, *longtang* are somewhat barrackslike in that they are arranged in densely packed row-by-row clusters. They combine aspects of western townhouses with the requirements of Chinese life. [RGK photograph 1985.]

Figure 5.62 (right). Built in the 1930s, each two-story *longtang* in the eastern part of Jianyeli includes a 9-square-meter uncovered court just inside the entry gate and a narrow *tianjing* barely 1 meter wide in the rear. [Source: Shen 1993, 85.]

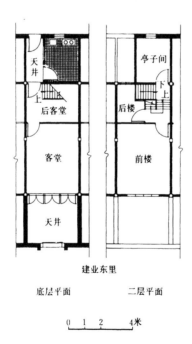

house type identified with the "neighborhood lanes" [*lilong* 里弄]. "*Longtang*" 弄堂 is the term used by Shanghainese to describe the narrow rectangular multistory dwellings found in the densely packed neighborhoods that emerged to accommodate Chinese who moved into the foreign concession areas. Later, *longtang* proliferated throughout metropolitan Shanghai, varying in quality and scale from district to district to meet the needs of those with different incomes. Spurred by a burgeoning real estate market, *longtang* began to be built in great numbers in the 1870s and continued to be constructed into the 1940s with variations in structure, ornamentation, and style that reflected the changing times. While sharing common components, *longtang* nonetheless took many forms even while providing similar living spaces (Figures 5.60 and 5.61).

Characteristically narrow, linear, and compact, most *longtang* are two or three stories high; often there is a subsidiary portion that is only a single story. Usually only a bay or two wide and arranged as row houses along narrow lanes, each *longtang* plan includes a small court, or *tianjing*, immediately inside the gate (Figure 5.62). While there are similarities with prototypical *siheyuan* and *sanheyuan* found elsewhere in China, the spatial proportions of *longtang* are tighter and more compact, and *longtang* generally make more efficient use of space.

Lilong neighborhoods are arranged in a hierarchy involving streets, lanes, sublanes, and individual *longtang* that provide a layering of public space, semipublic space, semiprivate space, and private space (Luo and Wu 1997, 78–79). Gates and walls modulate activities and define relationships. Unlike Beijing *hutong,* where the visual effect is essentially horizontal with only decorated gates breaking the line, the variety of gable forms and tall ornamented gates found within Shanghai's *lilong* forces the eye to look upward.

The entrance to an individual *longtang* dwelling is through a *shikumen* 石库门, a prominent stone gate that usually appears to have been influenced by western architectural styles. The framing pillars, and especially the lintels and pediments above, reveal affinities with western classic orders and frequently include carved or molded adornment in European styles. Above the gateway, the presence of bold numbers declaring the year of construction is clearly a western convention, while the presence of carved characters naming the *lilong* reveals its Chineseness. The compact and flexible layout of *longtang* reveals a striking adaptation to changing urban life-styles in treaty port Shanghai. Dense population and high land costs militated against horizontally expansive dwellings, yet the internal/external and private/public relationships within *lilong* facilitated neighborhood formation. The sense of community nurtured under these circumstances is sentimentally recalled as Shanghai today is being transformed by blocks of apartment towers populated by anonymous residents who lack affinities with those who live nearby as neighbors.

Fujian, Guangdong, and Jiangxi Fortresses

Large multistory complexes found in Fujian, Guangdong, and Jiangxi provinces are truly unique and imposing architectural forms. Most were built by a Han Chinese ethnic subgroup known as Hakka and also called "Kejia" in modern standard Chinese, the so-called "guest families" 客家, from a term applied by local Chinese settlers to newcomers and subsequently adopted by the in-migrants to describe themselves. Between the fourth and nineteenth centuries, perhaps five great waves of migration brought Hakka from the central plains of northern China southward, first to the Gan River valley in Jiangxi and then successively into the rugged contiguous portions within a small triangle framed by southwestern Fujian, northern Guangdong, and southern Jiangxi. Throughout all of their migrations and eventual settlement among other Han Chinese, Hakka maintained their separateness and identity as a subethnic group. Hakka dwellings provided residence for far more than the multiple generations of an extended family that one might find even in a large and complex courtyard-style dwelling elsewhere in China. Using space that was organized vertically as well as horizontally, Hakka residential complexes provide structural and architectural confirmation of the importance of patrilineal clan organization within single-surname communities. Although "fortresses" are generally identified only with the Hakka, it is clear that the Hokkien or southern Fujianese who speak the Minnan dialect and live in the Zhangzhou region to the east of areas of Hakka concentrations also built and continue to live in structures quite similar to those described as "Hakka" (Huang 1994, 1:35). Most of the discussion that follows focuses on Hakka fortresses, although not to the exclusion of those built by others.

Sometimes unwelcomed to the point of hostility by other Han settlers who had preceded them in marginal and rugged hill lands, Hakka pioneers generally created settlements that expressed not only a need for protection against communal violence but also the requirements of their cooperative clan system. As a result, Hakka built stronghold structures of impressive size, strength, and structural complexity in these areas, even though in other areas where security was not a concern they built more open, less fortified dwellings. Migrational offshoots also moved into distant Sichuan, rugged Guangxi and Hunan, and across the straits to the island of Taiwan, but it was only at the junction linking Fujian, Guangdong, and Jiangxi in nearly fifty *xian,* or counties, that Hakka built true fortresses. Here, at least seven Fu-

Figure 5.63 (top). Older square and circular Hakka fortresses are mixed among more recent rectangular structures within this valley. Nanjing *xian*, Fujian. [RGK photograph 1990.]

Figure 5.64 (bottom). A modest yet imposing rectangular structure with a complex roof structure. Gaobei *cun*, Guzhu *xiang*, Yongding *xian*, Fujian. [RGK photograph 1990.]

large-scale Hakka and Hokkien *tulou* seen today, however, were built of a composite material known as *sanhetu* 三合土 rather than just earth, as was discussed in Chapter 3. Some *tulou* were actually constructed completely of cut granite or had substantial walls of fired brick. Thus to call them "earthen dwellings" is clearly a misnomer. Still, the term "earthen dwellings," or "*tulou*," continues to be widely employed in describing these structures. In doing so, however, one must be careful to qualify the term as a broadly descriptive label for a building type rather than as a narrow term defining a specific building material. While most Chinese authors continue to use the term "*tulou*," Pan An has suggested abandoning it and replacing it with the broader term "ensemble architecture" [*juju jianzhu* 聚居建筑] in order to recognize the extent and complexity of most of the structures and the fact that most are not made of "earth" (Pan 1995, 91-94).

jian *xian*, ten Jiangxi *xian*, and sixteen Guangdong *xian* are considered "pure" Hakka areas, while more than seventy other *xian* have significant Hakka enclaves mixed with other Han groups (Lin and Lin 1992, 6-16).

While Hakka dwellings include relatively modest rectangular and L-shaped single-story structures housing only one household, the most imposing ones are large-scale fortresses [*zhai* 寨], often simply called *tulou* 土楼, which are multistory, varied in style, and spacious enough to provide residence for more than a hundred people (Figures 5.63 and 5.64). The term "*tulou*" translates as "earthen dwelling," and many authors write as if such structures have always been constructed of fresh earth [*shengtu* 生土], as indeed is the common building practice in many areas of northern and southern China. Most

While walls can be seen as axiomatic components of Chinese construction—whether around cities, dwellings, or temples—the commanding nature of the walls of Hakka residential complexes clearly sets them apart. Even compared with portions of the Great Wall, which ranges between 7.8 and 14 meters high, the 10-to-20-meter-high citadel-like walls are indeed impressive. These fortress emsembles are striking not only because of their scale and shapes but also because of their spatial composition, which is distinctive even though it echoes the layout of Chinese residences elsewhere. Although the massive round structures known as *yuanlou* 圆楼 found principally in southwestern Fujian are the best known Hakka fortresses, no less significant are the imposing *weizi* 围子 of southern Jiangxi and the often magnificent *wufenglou* 五凤楼

Figure 5.65. Half-moon shaped Hakka complexes have been discovered in several townships of Chaoan *xian* in southeastern Fujian along the border with Guangdong province. Concentric arcs range up to five in number and ring an ancestral hall at the core. Daping *cun*, Xiuzhuan *xiang*, Chaoan *xian*, Fujian. [Original drawing used with the permission of Huang Hanmin.]

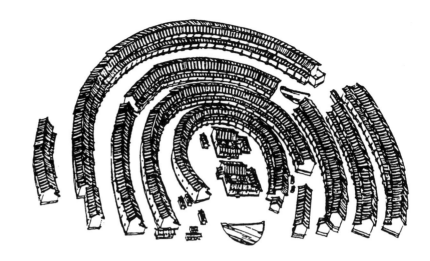

[five-phoenix mansions] of eastern Guangdong and southwestern Fujian, each of which will be described in this section. Besides various sizes of round and square-shaped residential ensembles, which are well known, Hakka and others built structures as rectangles, ovals, semicircles, pentagons, octagons, horseshoes, and even half-moon shapes (Figure 5.65). In addition, idiosyncratic configurations similar to Chinese characters such as 同 and 富, which proclaim in their form a desire for "unity" and "wealth," are also found. Some shapes are so large that one or two smaller concentric forms are nested within the high surrounding outer walls. *Yuanlou* and *weizi* are veritable impregnable walled castles, while *wufenglou* are somewhat more exposed and the half-moon shaped settlements lack any fortifications at all. Unlike castles in Europe and Japan, Hakka fortresses are rarely located at high and commanding positions. Round and square-shaped Hakka structures are found both in Fujian and neighboring Guangdong provinces. In southern Jiangxi, square-shaped *weizi* are common, but round shapes are extremely rare. Octagonal and semicircular shapes are found in five Fujian *xian*, occasionally in eastern Guangdong, but rarely anywhere else.

There appear to be historical and geographical reasons for the distribution of different Hakka housing forms. The time of migration, the nature of initial occupancy, and the relationship with neighbors all appear to have played roles in the emergence of specific Hakka *tulou* types. In the oldest settled Hakka areas, such as in Jiaying, Meizhou in Guangdong, the Gannan area of Jiangxi, and in Ninghua and Shanghang of Fujian, five-phoenix and horseshoe styles appear to have always been quite common. This is perhaps because the domination of the Hakka never was seriously threatened in these areas, and thus there was less need for impregnable fortresses. Here, early Hakka arrivals built rather open dwellings in a style that evoked the manor dwellings of officials, the so-called *daifuzhai* 大夫宅, in areas of northern China from which the Hakka migrated.

Imposing round or square bastions were generally built along the borders of Hakka-dominated areas and where Hakka lived among others, yet not all of them were built in response to the potential of strife. Turmoil certainly was often a factor, such as during the early third of this century when many substantial walled enclaves were built all over rural China in response to widespread banditry and general lawlessness, but there were other considerations as well. Evidence of this can be gleaned from data collected in a comprehensive survey of 700 so-called *tulou* carried out in Nanjing *xian*. Table 5.1 shows the historical dominance of square over round shapes. Examples of each were built quite early: the remains of four square structures can be traced to the thirteenth century, while three round ones originated in the fourteenth century. An earlier extant round fortification on a hilltop in Gaobei Village in neighboring Yongding *xian* has been dated to 1279 (Zhang 1994, 844). The earliest of four *tulou* structures still standing from the Ming dynasty in Zhangpu *xian* is Yidelou 一德楼. Built in 1558, it has a three-story round exterior wall but a

Table 5.1
Variations in Shape of Residential Ensembles over Time

Period	Round	Square	Semicircular	Rectangular
1200–1299		4		
1300–1399	3	3		
1400–1499	10	4		
1500–1599	11	30	1	
1600–1699	9	52		
1700–1799	8	67		1
1800–1899	6	52	5	2
1900–1939	35	75	1	
1940–1959	57	68	1	
1960–1969	85	59	1	
1970–1979	12	15		
1980–1989	3	18		
Total	239	447	9	3

Source: Lin and Lin 1992, 18.

large square structure within its circular courtyard. Based on surviving structures constructed before the twentieth century, square structures far exceed round ones, 212 to 47, and semicircular and rectangular shapes are but minor forms.

Fully a third of all such residential ensembles still standing in Nanjing *xian* in the 1990s were built before 1900, but it is a startling fact that 427, nearly two-thirds, were built after 1900. Over the past ninety years, almost as many large round ones (192) have been built as square ones (235). This relatively recent building history suggests that reasons other than defense played roles in their construction, even given the periodic turmoil of modern times. The accelerated building of structures using traditional materials and forms after the founding of the People's Republic of China, especially, was a response to population pressures and economic conditions rather than turmoil. In the 1960s, more round structures were built than square ones, but in recent decades square and rectangular shapes have dominated while the number of related households living together has decreased as more families establish single-family houses in Fujian's villages.

Even as recently as 1987, according to the 1988 survey, a round *tulou* was built in Meilin *xiang* of Nanjing *xian* to accommodate eight households with a total of fifty-three members (Huang 1994c, 1:160).

Some researchers see the actual antecedents of Hakka round dwellings in the smaller circular fortifications that were traditionally built of stone in the uplands of the Zhangzhou region of Fujian, where Hakka *yuanlou* were later built in large numbers. The remains of at least a hundred such round stone mountain strongholds [*yuanxing shanzhai* 圓形山寨] from the Han and later periods still dot the hilltops of southern Fujian, and written records of the Han, Tang, Song, and Yuan dynasties record their presence and utility in the pacification of the region (Zeng 1992, 70–71). In a comprehensive study that recognizes this history of circular mountain fortifications made of stone, Huang Hanmin, a pioneer in the study of Fujian's vernacular architecture, postulates an evolutionary sequence to explain the eventual emergence of large round fortresslike structures in the region (Figure 5.66). While his progression points to an increasing need over time to build

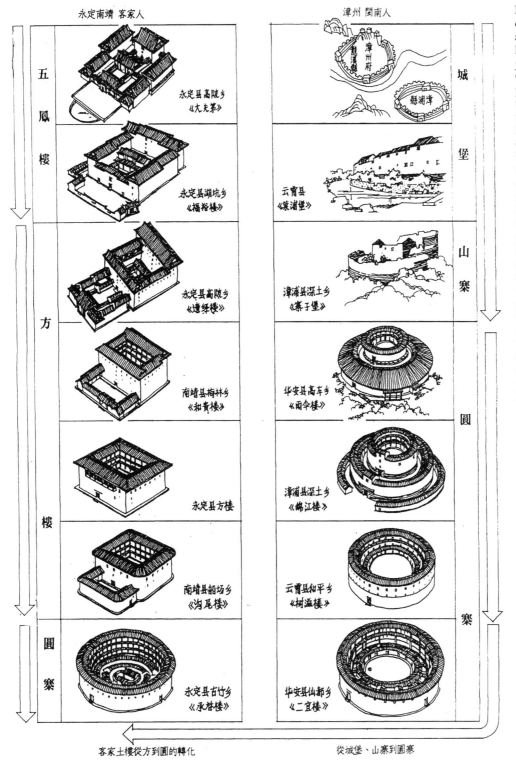

Figure 5.66. This chart hypothesizes a simultaneous evolution of round *yuanlou* structures. On the right is a progression related to Minnan people, the indigenous inhabitants of southern Fujian, beginning with their early walled enclaves, mountain strongholds, and later various round dwelling complexes. Shown on the top left is the earliest Hakka ensemble form—a *wufenglou,* or "five-phoenix mansion" with origins in the north—that over time took a round form. [Original drawing used with the permission of Huang Hanmin.]

large, secure, and relatively simple structures for extended clans, it also indicates practical considerations relating to construction techniques and structure that builders confronted and adopted. While the early rectangular Hakka buildings, known as *wufenglou*, were walled enclosures modeled after northern structures, their overall form did not provide sufficient security to protect the Hakka from periodic turmoil they encountered in some areas of the southern frontier. Relatively low walls, abundant fenestration, and extensive wooden roof frameworks that were vulnerable to fire were modified by Hakka builders over time. Increasingly, Hakka built more solid and tighter structures that were square in shape and had higher and thicker walls, limited exterior openings, and less complex roof systems.

Subsequently, according to Huang, there was a transformative progression from square fortresses to round ones as the four corners of square *tulou* were beveled and smoothened into an arc, such as can be seen in Manweilou 满尾楼 in Xikeng Village in Nanjing *xian*. This form is somewhat reminiscent of some traditional Chinese walled cities that also had curved corner walls. Once builders experimented with curvature, it took little time for circular structures to emerge from curved framing systems. Further, pragmatic considerations that went beyond defense and construction techniques must have contributed to the decisions to build round buildings.

In terms of maximizing enclosed space, a circular wall was able to wrap more interior space than a square wall of the same length by a factor of approximately 0.273, according to Chinese calculations. Further, not only were scarce building materials saved by constructing circular exterior walls as compared to straight ones but wooden members needed to construct interior living quarters could be standardized in dimension, thus reducing the level of carpentry skills needed to complete the project. In addition, the difficult joinery necessary to link the intersecting planes atop a square structure could be overcome through the modularization of components when a circular roof was constructed. Experience also made it clear, some observers suggest, that round shapes were more resistant than other shapes to earthquake damage and were able to deflect the strong winds of

typhoons. An additional consideration favoring a round shape was that it permitted an equitable and egalitarian division of residential space, spatial affirmation of an aspect of Hakka life that differs from the hierarchical associations so often seen in Chinese architecture (Huang 1994, 1:107–110).

Yuanlou: *Fujian Round Dwellings*

Perhaps a thousand unique *yuanlou* 圆楼 [round buildings], also called *yuanzhai tulou* 圆寨土楼, are located in the rugged valleys of southwestern Fujian, centering on Yongding, Nanjing, Pinghe, Hua'an, Zhangpu, and Chaoan *xian* as well as in Dapu and Raoping *xian* of adjacent eastern Guangdong province (Zeng 1992, 76). Mixed in among square, rectangular, and elliptical shapes, circular *tulou* appear in plan view as if they are landed UFOs (Figure 5.67). *Yuanlou* range widely in size. Five standing *yuanlou* exceed 70 meters in diameter, a breadth just a little short of the length of an American football field, and there are several less than 20 meters in diameter. Perhaps the largest of these structures is Zaitianlou 在田楼, an octagonal complex in remote Zhaoan *xian* along the border with Guangdong province (Figure 5.68). With a reported diameter of 90.6 meters from east to west, 86.6 meters from north to south, walls 2.4 meters thick, and an inverted U-shaped interior structure, it is a formidable structure . Reported diameters of *yuanlou* vary from source to source, and it is not always clear whether the diameter is reported from outer wall to outer wall, but among the largest are the following:

Longjianlou	龙见楼	Jiufeng *cun*, Pinghe *xian*	80-m diameter
Jueninglou	厥宁楼	Luxi *cun*, Pinghe *xian*	76-m diameter
Shunyulou	顺裕楼	Shiqiao *cun*, Nanjing *xian*	75.1-m diameter
Eryilou	二宜楼	Dadi *cun*, Hua'an *xian*	71.2-m diameter
Chengqilou	承启楼	Gaobei *cun*, Yongding *xian*	62.6-m diameter

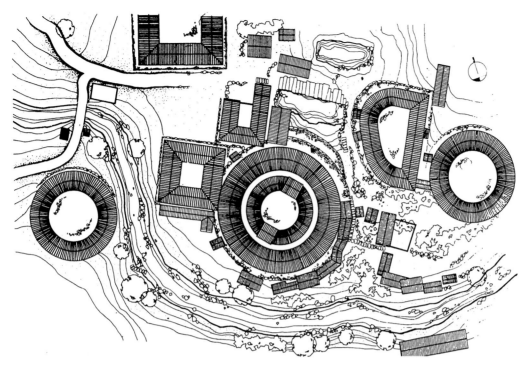

Figure 5.67. Appearing like landed UFOs and other geometrical forms, this village plan depicts various shapes of Hakka ensembles. Hukeng *xiang*, Yongding *xian*, Fujian. [Source: Yongding 1990, 37.]

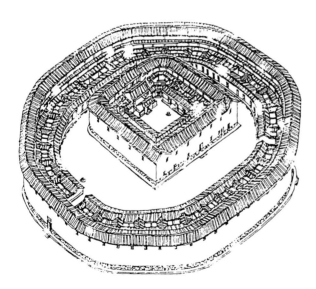

Figure 5.68. Somewhat octagonal in shape, Zaitianlou has a diameter of 90.6 meters from east to west and 86.6 meters from north to south. Within its 2.4-meter-thick walls, there is an inverted U-shaped interior structure with a main hall. Dapian *cun*, Guanpo *xiang*, Chaoan *xian*, Fujian. [Source: Huang 1994c, 15. Original drawing used with the permission of Huang Hanmin.]

Among the smallest *yuanlou* is Rushenglou 如升楼, built more than a hundred years ago in Hongkeng *cun*, Hukeng *xiang*, Yongding *xian*. It has an external diameter of 17.4 meters and an internal diameter across the circular courtyard of only 5.2 meters. The compact shape and size of Rushenglou [Like a *sheng* building], as seen in Figure 5.69, are said to evoke the Chinese canisterlike volumetric dry measure for grain, which is called *sheng* 升. While *yuanlou* vary from two to five stories in height, over two-thirds are three stories. Some *yuanlou* include several concentric rings of ancillary structures that generally do not exceed two stories.

Chengqilou 承启楼, with a circumference of 229.34 meters, a diameter of 62.6 meters, a height of 12.4 meters, and lower walls 1.9 meters thick, is among the largest round dwelling complexes still standing. Considered by many to be the most imposing and distinctive of Fujian's circular *tulou*, Chengqilou was chosen in 1986 to grace a Chinese postage stamp in a collection on folk architecture (Figure 5.70). Built over a three-year period beginning in 1709 in Gaobei *cun*, Guzhu *xiang*, in the rugged east-

Figure 5.69. Perhaps the smallest *yuanlou* is Rushenglou [Like a *sheng* building], said to appear like the Chinese volumetric dry measure for grain called *sheng*. Hongkeng *cun*, Hukeng *xiang*, Yongding *xian*, Fujian. [RGK photograph 1990.]

ern portion of Yongding *xian*, Chengqilou was structured to accommodate four branches of the fifteenth generation of the Jiang family in equal portions of the structure. The *yuanlou* comprises three full concentric rings and an inner semicircle that embraces an ancestral hall and a half-moon-shaped central courtyard (Figures 5.71 and 5.72). Although only 57 households with over 300 members now live in Chengqilou, records suggest that when the clan was most prosperous as many as 80 households with more than 600 members occupied the 370 rooms it holds. Over the years, many household members moved away, leaving their rooms locked up and the wood of their "apartments" to weather (Huang 1994b, 2:85, 90). Viewed from across the busy interior, each of the four levels is divided into household units. Kitchens are found on the bottom floor with bedrooms and storage space on the floors above.

Figure 5.70. Of the seven denominations in the set of vernacular architecture stamps, the one representing the Fujian *yuanlou* Chengqilou was valued at 1 *yuan*. [RGK collection.]

The encircling corridors are used for storage as well as for hanging laundry to dry (Figure 5.73).

The high walls of these residential ensembles, as discussed in Chapter 3, are generally built on elevated stone bases that vary in height but generally are at least a meter thick (Figure 5.74). Although the term "*tulou*" implies that walls are made of "earth," as mentioned earlier, most walls actually are constructed of a composite mixture of earth, sand, and lime called *sanhetu*. The *sanhetu* composite is tamped into a movable wooden framework that functions as a mold to shape the walls of the encircling enclosure as it rises one level at a time. Walls are typically battered and have only a limited number of openings. Most *tulou* have only a single entrance, although some have subsidiary gates approximately 90 degrees from the main gate. Except for the gateways and small ventilation ports used to evacuate smoke from kitchen stoves inside, openings are normally not cut into the wall at ground level. Whether and where windows appear on upper levels, and what the nature of the wall itself will be, depends to a great degree on the need for security when the *yuanlou* is built.

The fortified nature of Zhenchenglou 振成楼 [Inspiring Success Building], one of a hundred *tulou* of various sizes in Hongkeng village, Hukeng *xiang*,

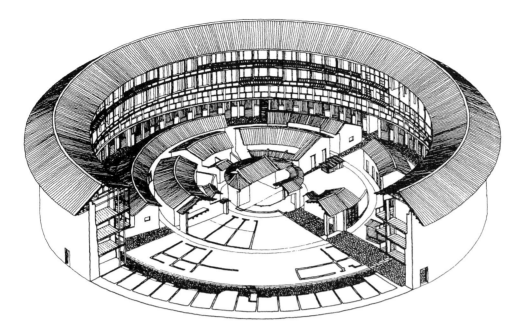

Figure 5.71. Three concentric rings and an inner semicircle comprise the basic plan of Chengqilou. The battered walls and the associated wooden framework on the inside support a heavy tile roof. Gaobei *cun*, Guzhu *xiang*, Yongding *xian*, Fujian. [Source: Mogi, Inaji, and Katayama 1991, 195.]

Figure 5.72. The inner semicircle embraces an ancestral hall and a half-moon-shaped central courtyard. Gaobei *cun*, Guzhu *xiang*, Yongding *xian*, Fujian. [Source: Mogi, Inaji, and Katayama 1991, 190.]

Figure 5.73. Vertically structured dwelling units rise along the outer wall of Chengqilou. Some of the households maintain two adjacent stacks of rooms. Each of the kitchen doors on the ground floor is marked with couplets placed there during the New Year. Bedrooms and storage areas are found on the floors above. At each level, encircling corridors are used for storage and space for hanging laundry and baskets. Gaobei *cun*, Guzhu *xiang*, Yongding *xian*, Fujian. [RGK photograph 1990.]

Figure 5.74. The close placement of residential ensembles is evident in this view between Chengqilou on the left and a square structure on the right. The varying heights of the stone plinths upon which the structures are built are visible, as are the unplastered walls. Stone steps and a path lead to other units. The drip line of the eaves leads water into a recessed drain. Gaobei *cun*, Guzhu *xiang*, Yongding *xian*, Fujian. [RGK photograph 1990.]

Yongding *xian*, can be seen in Figure 5.75. It is a four-story structure with windows only on two levels of the upper wall. The windows are embrasured—the walls framing the sides are angled so that the opening inside is wider than the opening outside—in order to afford increased security and make surveillance from inside safer. The structure was built in 1912, an unsettled period of transition as the Qing imperial dynasty ended and the Republic of China was coming into existence. The path to the fortress does not lead directly to the gateway but instead approaches at an angle from the side before turning sharply onto an elevated platform surrounding the structure. This condition relates to *fengshui*, attentiveness to siting, but also has

defensive significance as well. As with other fortresses, the massive stone entry portal leads into a gate hall [*menwu* 门屋], an area that is normally occupied throughout the day by women, children, and old men. Here they "guard" passage into their complex as they perform work such as husking rice and preparing food to be cooked. Beyond the *menwu* is usually an open circular courtyard, but Zhenchenglou has a secondary ring of structures surrounding a central courtyard in addition to the symmetrical outer apartment units. The division of space within the outer walls of Zhenchenglou is quite similar to that of other *yuanlou*—apportioned equally with most rooms of similar size—with individual entries into each "apartment"

(Figure 5.76). A closer examination here reveals a carefully crafted auspicious configuration that, while not unique, is significant. Zhenchenglou was artfully planned to express the Eight Trigrams, or *Bagua*, a cryptic divinatory text believed to have great symbolic power in Chinese culture and that is used in properly siting a dwelling. While there are several *tulou* that are actually octagonal in shape with eight straight intersecting walls, Zhenchenglou is round on the outside with its interior living space divided into eight clearly differentiated units to invoke the Eight Trigrams. Each of these eight units is separated from the others by a tamped earth wall, and each is subdivided into three or six "bays," or *jian*, the common Chinese building units that are fronted by four linear courtyards that face the animal sheds. While the outer walls that ring Zhenchenglou are of an earthen composition, the structural space within is all built of wood. Wooden floor joists are secured deep into the *sanhetu* walls, and a wooden framework of interlocked pieces is assembled to support much of the weight of a heavy tiled roof.

The lower outer wall of Eryilou 二宜楼, an 18-meter-high, four-story *yuanlou* in Dadi *cun*, Hua'an *xian* built in 1770, is constructed of cut stone nearly 2.5 meters thick. There is no fenestration below the fourth story, and the solid gate, framed with granite blocks, is made of wood more than 10 centimeters thick, encased with an iron skin, and reinforced with iron rods (Figure 5.77). Like Zhenchenglou, there is clearly a symmetrical and concentric organization of interior space around a core "inner courtyard" [*neiyuan* 内院] that is bounded by a low inner ring of structures punctuated by sixteen elongated skywells or *tianjing* (Figure 5.78). Unlike Zhenchenglou, which has an elevated stage for the performance of opera on its northern side that leads to a *zutang* 族堂 [ancestral hall] via two covered corridors, the defined location for venerating ancestors within Eryilou are found in individual *zutang* in rooms located on the uppermost level.

Unlike bays in rectangular Chinese dwellings that have right angle corners, each bay in a *yuanlou* like Eryilou is essentially trapezoidal in shape, narrower at

Figure 5.75. Except for a single entry portal that is framed by a white border with the name of the complex inscribed above it, the lower two stories of Zhenchenglou have no fenestration. Openings are only placed along the third and fourth levels. Hongkeng *cun*, Hukeng *xiang*, Yongding *xian*, Fujian. [RGK photographs 1990.]

Figure 5.76 (top left). Each of the ground-level units along the outer wall is entered through an individual doorway. The units are apportioned equally and are similar in size. Zhenchenglou, Hongkeng *cun*, Hukeng *xiang*, Yongding *xian*, Fujian. [RGK photograph 1990.]

Figure 5.77 (top right). Formed of cut stone, the lower outer wall of four-story Eryilou reaches 18 meters and is interrupted at ground level by only a single solid gateway framed with granite blocks. Dadi *cun*, Xiandu *xiang*, Hua'an *xian*, Fujian. [Original photograph used with the permission of Li Yuxiang.]

Figure 5.78 (bottom right). The symmetrical and concentric plan of Eryilou includes a four-story outer structure, a low inner ring, and a core "inner courtyard," or *neiyuan*. [Source: Huang 1994c, II, 18. Original drawing used with the permission of Huang Hanmin.]

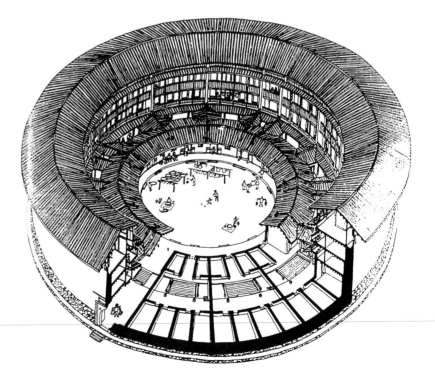

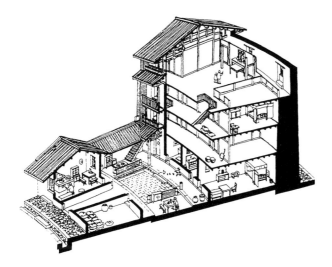

Figure 5.79. Each household lives within an "apartment," two or three bays wide, that rises through four stories in the outer ring and includes a single story inner ring separated from each other by a *tianjing*. Kitchens are found in the lower inner ring, bedrooms on the lower floors of the outer ring, and the ancestral hall on the top floor of the outer ring. [Source: Huang 1994c, II, 19. Original drawing used with the permission of Huang Hanmin.]

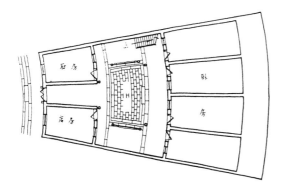

the interior and broader toward the outer wall. Pillars and beams are regular in shape, making possible modular construction using standardized building units. Overhanging arcades [*huilang* 回廊 or *zoumalang* 走马廊] ring each level of the circular structure, providing access and creating partially covered "gray" space for work. Each household lives within an "apartment," two or three bays wide and rising through the upper stories, as seen in Figure 5.79. Kitchens are all located at ground level in the inner ring and face elongated open areas located in front of the animal pens. The kitchen includes large water containers, a stove that is vented to the outside by several openings, storage space for fuel, and cupboards. Throughout much of the year, food preparation takes place outside the kitchen in the open area or under the veranda. Summertime cooking is also carried on outside using temporary stoves, and water is drawn from a common well (Figure 5.80). An adjacent bay is fitted with a square table and four benches to be used for meals. Family members, however, often do not eat at the table but gather instead outside the kitchen door to chat with neighbors, and it is here also that other household chores, such as washing clothes and sewing, are carried out.

Sets of steep stairs lead to verandas that ring the upper three levels. Grain and other bulky foods are stored on the second floor because the area is dry and not too distant from the kitchen. Laundry is frequently hung along the overhanging veranda of the second floor.

Figure 5.80. At the center of some *tulou* is a common well for the use of all of the residents. Hekeng *cun*, Shuyang *xiang*, Nanjing *xian*, Fujian. [RGK photograph 1990.]

Bedrooms are located on the lower floors, although in other *yuanlou* such as Zhenchenglou bedrooms are found on the upper floors. Vacant space on any of these levels is used to store valuables owned by the family, including large wooden coffins that Chinese purchase to afford peace of mind to elderly family members. Because windows are located only on the upper two levels, it is here that the rooms are most comfortable, both naturally airy and lighted.

Within Eryilou's inner courtyard, there are two wells for the use of all residents. They are located midway between the inner structure and the outer structure on the east and west side. The courtyard is paved with substantial stone slabs, a qualitative improvement over the round stones or firmly tamped earth found in less prosperous structures. As is true in most such structures, the shared space is usually tidy, since it represents community space that is used for drying grain and laundry. Ample space is available for children as well as chickens and ducks to wander. The courtyards of some *tulou* today are cluttered with privies, pigsties, outdoor kitchens, and heaps of building materials, perhaps a mirror of times past when life within could be rather self-sufficient during periods of banditry and turmoil. However, since 1949, a time of relative security, it has been common to move pigsties and latrines outside the *tulou* in order to improve sanitation. Today one is also likely to see valuable firewood as well as less precious items stacked along the outer wall, where the overhanging eaves protect them from the weather.

Wufenglou: *Five-Phoenix Dwellings*

Five-phoenix dwellings, known as *weiwu* 围屋 or *weilongwu* 围垄屋 in eastern Guangdong and *dawu* 大屋 or *dalou* 大楼 in western Fujian, are among the most prevalent Hakka dwelling types. Varying greatly in size, five-phoenix complexes outnumber round and square *tulou* four to one, according to one estimate (Lin and Lin 1992, 79). There are complex associations to the phoenix and the number five that contributed to their widespread use. By juxtaposing rhetorical images and linking them to physical structures, builders and residents recall classical imagery that expresses Confucian behavioral ideals. Seen as

an auspicious creature, the phoenix [*feng* 凤] appears early on the roofs of Han buildings to symbolize "the virtues of local scholars who were filial, loyal, and 'ready to serve'" {Powers 1991, 239}. By analogical reasoning, the image of five phoenixes is associated with the stability of the five directions and the harmonization of the five colors. The body parts of each phoenix further symbolize the five virtues of a ruler: the head, virtue itself; the back, benevolence; its bosom, trust; its feet, correctness; and its tail, martial valor.

Perhaps the best known *wufenglou* complex is Daifuzhai 大夫宅, first described by Liu Dunzhen in 1957 on the basis of a report done earlier by Zhang Buqian, Zhu Wuquan, and Hu Zhanlie (Figure 5.81). Located just off a main road in Datongjiao village, Gaobei township, Yongding *xian* in southwestern Fujian, it was constructed between 1828 and 1834 along the break of a north-facing hill. From a distance below its entry, Daifuzhai appears somewhat like a palace with its succession of halls and impressive mixture of gable and hipped-roof styles. Entry is through a multitiered gateway to a lower hall [*xiatang* 下堂], then a courtyard followed by a middle hall [*zhongtang* 中堂] that opens to an inner courtyard and finally the upperhall [*shangtang* 上堂 or *houtang* 后堂]. The successive passage from outer space to inner space as one transits the halls and courtyards along Dafuzhai's central axis is at the same time a movement from below to above. Together, they represent a spatial scripting of hierarchical relationships that is magnified by the fact that the upper hall is an impressive four stories tall. Some researchers have speculated that this style evokes buildings that once must have been built in the Zhongyuan or Central Plains of northern China, but Liu Dunzhen was unwilling to accept this without archaeological evidence and referenced this style of dwelling to complexes seen in the Shaoxing area of Zhejiang province (1957, 47-48). While later archaeological discoveries of Shang and Western Zhou sites in the north clearly identify precursor forms for hierarchically and symmetrically arranged halls and courtyards, it is not yet possible to link them to large dwelling complexes subsequently lived in by the ancestors of Hakka before they migrated to the south.

Liu Dunzhen categorized the *wufenglou* of Fujian with other large composite structures found in central and northern China that combine elements of the traditional *siheyuan* and *siheyuan* courtyard styles: bilateral symmetry, axiality, hierarchy, and enclosure. Yet, as *wufenglou* became more intricate and complex structures, there is a clear divergence from northern norms. The presence of upper, middle, and lower halls, the change in elevation from high in back to low in front, and the placement of a large pond or field at the front entrance are all distinguishing elements of *wufenglou* (Figure 5.82). Three halls placed horizontally along the main axis with two connecting structures, collectively called *santang erheng* 三堂二横, represent a common five-phoenix compound form, although some *wufenglou* include as many as nine halls and four connecting structures.

Daifuzhai, like many other five-phoenix complexes, incorporates both arcuate rear and front areas whose shape has geomantic properties. The protecting curved and elevated configuration along the upper perimeter behind some Daifuzhai is made up of a stone wall that rises with a series of terraces. At the front of the complex is a large rectangular area—a utilitarian threshing floor [*hechang* 禾场 or *heping* 禾坪]—that is fronted by a half-moon-shaped

pond [*chitang* 池塘], a water source for washing clothes and for use when there is a fire emergency. Throughout Guangdong province, the encircling back wall is usually elevated and has a definite armchair or omegalike shape [Ω], described as horseshoe-shaped by Chinese authors. Termed a *weilong* [围垒 encircling ridge or sometimes 围龙 encircling dragon] because of the elevated protecting wall and mountain slope behind, the form has powerful *fengshui* significance, especially when combined with the half-moon-shaped pond that is usually found at the front. Magnificent *weilong* are found in Meixian, an area of concentrated Hakka settlement with many unique dwelling forms (Figure 5.83). With their arcuate backs, they sometimes appear like enormous armchairs, securely set on a hillslope in order to protect their residents from danger and catch the breezes to provide them with comfort within their enclosures.

In central Fujian, there is a distinctive type of architectural complex that has elevated carpentry to very high levels, even though the basic form is composed of earth and stone. Termed *tubao* 土堡 [earthen citadels], these residential complexes are dominated by piled roofs, multiple layers replicated *en echelon*, above a sweeping U-shaped form created from neatly laid stone block walls that rise almost to

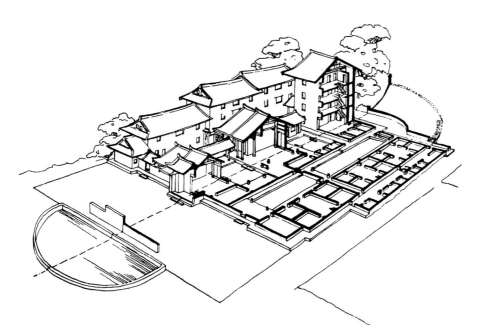

Figure 5.81. Imposing *wufenglou* have a plan that expresses axiality, bilateral symmetry, and hierarchy similarly to the northern *siheyuan*, although there is some divergence from northern norms with upper, middle, and lower halls and a change in elevation from front to back. A large crescent-shaped *fengshui* pond or *mingtang* appears at the front. Daifuzhai Datongjiao *cun*, Gaobei township, Yongding *xian*, Fujian. [Source: Liu Dunzhen 1957, 123.]

Figure 5.82 (top). Viewed from a distance, this *wufenglou* maintains an austere regularity in its form and ornamentation. Daifuzhai, Hongkeng *cun*, Hukeng *xiang*, Yongding *xian*, Fujian. [Original photograph used with the permission of Li Yuxiang.]

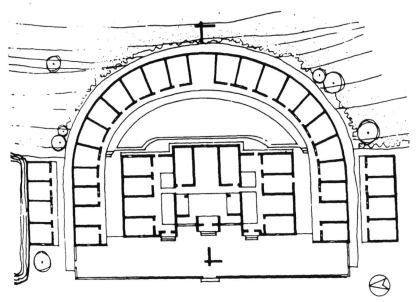

Figure 5.83 (right). Geometrically regular *weilong* usually rise to the rear and are situated within the embrace of a protecting hillslope in order to satisfy requirements of *fengshui*. Dapu *xian*, Guangdong. [Source: Lu and Wei 1990, 91.]

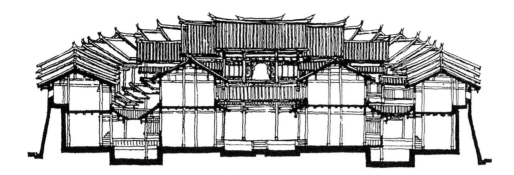

Figure 5.84. Piled high and replicated at many levels, the complex roof of this earthen citadel-like *wufenglou* represents extraordinary levels of carpentry needed to lift it. Yangtou *cun*, Huainan *xiang*, Yong'an *shi*, Fujian. [Source: Gao, Wang, Chen 1987, 212.]

the eaves (Figures 5.84 and 5.85). One of the best examples is Anzhenbao 安贞堡, located in Yangtou *cun*, Huainan *xiang*, Yongan *shi*, and built between 1885 and 1900. Within this citadel, there are 320 rooms, 18 halls, 5 wells, and 12 kitchens, providing sufficient space to accommodate nearly a thousand related people. Built to provide secure defense, the 4-meter-thick stone walls are capped by firmly tamped earth upper walls into which are cut 96 small openings for surveillance and 198 gun ports, and overseen by several watchtowers. The symmetrical interior structures are built adjacent to the outer stone walls and face a cluster of central halls, with the ancestral hall at a higher rear position. As seen in Figure 5.86,

there is such an abundant use of hardwoods, fashioned by carpenters as structural and ornamental members, that the elegant interior belies the formidable masonry of the exterior (Huang 1994c, 30–31).

Weizi: *Jiangxi Fortresses*

As strong and substantial as are the many fortress and citadel-like complexes found in Fujian and Guangdong provinces, none exceeds the veritable forts or strongholds found in Jiangxi province. Although generally called *weizi* 围子 or *weiwu* 围屋, denoting a walled settlement, they are also often called *diaobao* 碉堡 and *diaobaolou* 碉堡楼, terms used in Chinese

Figure 5.85. Stone block walls march up the hillslope to protect the Anzhenbao citadel. Between the eaves above and the stone below, tamped earth walls provide a medium to hold gun and observation ports. Yangtou *cun*, Huainan *xiang*, Yong'an *shi*, Fujian. [Original photograph used with the permission of Li Yuxiang.]

Figure 5.86 (above). The interior rooms, halls, and corridors are crafted of hardwoods. With 320 rooms, 18 halls, 5 wells, and 12 kitchens, there is space in the citadel for nearly a thousand family members. Yangtou *cun*, Huainan *xiang*, Yong'an *shi*, Fujian. [Original photograph used with the permission of Li Yuxiang.]

Figure 5.87 (middle). Funerary objects discovered in Han dynasty tombs in Guangdong and adjacent areas reveal early forms of walled enclosures with corner towers. [Source: Guangzhou 1981, n.p.]

Figure 5.88 (bottom). Small in size and simple in internal order, this imposing *weizi* is 16 meters wide, exclusive of its four commanding corner towers. Xinyou *cun*, Longnan *xian*, Jiangxi. [RGK photograph 1993.]

Figure 5.89 (top). View along the front wall of Xinwei, looking toward one of the two larger corner towers. With three-story high massive walls and scattered upper wall loopholes, it is a well fortified castlelike village. [RGK photograph 1993.]

Figure 5.90 (bottom). This block-shaped corner tower is matched by another and rises two stories above the surrounding walls. Guanxi *xiang*, Longnan *xian*, Jiangxi. [RGK photograph 1993.]

to describe fortifications or fortresses. Enclosed by walls that at first glance appear to be similar to those around other Hakka complexes elsewhere in southern China, *weizi* nonetheless are genuine strongholds with reinforced brick and stone walls, high corner towers, and even small apertures from which to shoot. Hundreds of *weizi* are concentrated in southern Jiangxi, particularly in Longnan, Quannan, and

Dingnan *xian*. Longnan *xian* claims 216 within its boundary alone. Some villages have two or three *weizi*, while others have as many as eight, all placed relatively close to each other. Mixed among the fortresses, one can see individual dwellings that have emerged during times of peace. Virtually all *weizi* are occupied by residents with a single surname, united by consanguinity and functioning as a corporate entity with substantial wealth and power.

Some *weizi* appear remarkably similar to funerary models, *mingqi* 明器, that have been unearthed from Eastern Han tombs over the past two decades (Figures 5.87 and 5.88). However, because such *mingqi* were discovered in Guangdong province to the south of Jiangxi and from a period that predates the migration of Hakka into southern China, these funerary models must not be considered as early Hakka structures. It is more than a curiosity that the *weizi*-like *mingqi* that have been discovered have been unearthed far from the northern Han Chinese Zhongyuan hearthlands where popular lore tells us they originated, but archaeological evidence has yet to uncover examples. Thus, discussion of the origin and diffusion of proto-Chinese architectural forms is complicated by limited and incomplete evidence. Still, even in the absence of archaeological discoveries in the north and a fragmented series of dates that do not permit linkages over time and space in the south, the remarkable correspondence between Jiangxi *weizi* built in recent centuries and Han tomb *mingqi* buried two thousand years ago in Guangdong province clearly confirms both the ancient existence of Hakka and their role in preserving this unique and imposing architectural form.

Several Jiangxi *weizi* date from the seventeenth century, constructed during the turmoil between the end of the Ming and the establishment of the Qing dynasty as Hakka returned to the region from Guangdong and Fujian (Wan 1995, 69). There is evidence that "old" Hakka and "returned" Hakka engaged in *xiedou* 械斗, or communal conflict, that led to escalated levels of *weizi* construction (Zhang Sijie 1993, 2–3). The largest extant *weizi* is a nearly square shape wrapped by perimeter walls measuring 83 by 93 meters and encompassing 8,000 square meters of interior space (Figures 5.89 and 5.90). With four corner

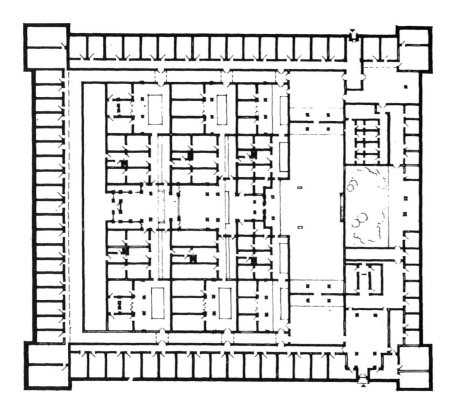

Figure 5.91. Nearly square in shape, and with a main entry and a subsidiary gate opposite it, Xinwei is wrapped by perimeter walls measuring 83 by 93 meters and encompasses 8,000 square meters of interior space. Along the outer walls, rooms are uniform and somewhat cell-like. The layout of the interior core, including a tightly packed symmetrical set of two-story dwellings and an ancestral hall that are aligned hierarchically along three parallel lines, is similar to that found in a triple *jin* northern courtyard dwelling. Guanxi *xiang*, Longnan *xian*, Jiangxi. [Source: Huang, Shao, and Li 1990, 45(1).]

towers, three massive stories, two small entries, and scattered upper wall loopholes, this *weizi*, called Xinwei 新围, "new fortress," is a well fortified castlelike village. In addition to relatively uniform cell-like rooms ringing the inside of the wall, the interior core encompasses a tightly packed symmetrical set of two-story dwellings and an ancestral hall that are aligned hierarchically along three parallel lines (Figure 5.91). This layout is somewhat similar to that found in a triple *jin* northern courtyard dwelling, with numerous gates of many shapes and sizes as well as a centrally located ancestral hall (Figures 5.92, 5.93, and 5.94). Fourteen slender *tianjing*, or skywells, bring air and light into the residential complexes within. Partition walls and gates fragment the interior space, and a mazelike series of narrow lanes serves to link structures, yet the stratified and hierarchical ordering of space must have been apparent to all living within. Together with a well, a garden, and an ancestral hall, Xinwei was a self-contained community (Huang, Shao, Li 1995, 135).

Yanyiwei 燕翼围 [Swallow Wing Fortress] is a lofty and imposing structure built between 1649 and 1654 in Yang village, some 60 kilometers from the Longnan county seat (Figure 5.95). The tight brick outer wall, which exceeds 12 meters in height, including a 2.5-meter-high cut stone base, encloses 1,443 square meters (Figures 5.96 and 5.97). Openings in the wall are few and rather scattered on the upper levels. Many are deep embrasures with only a slit on the outside wall but wide enough on the inside for a person to maneuver with a rifle or other means of defense (Figure 5.98). It is the protruding blockhouses [*paolou* 炮楼] for cannon that have given the name "swallow wing" to the fortress. A unique feature of this *weizi* are two holes through a projection from the wall high above the ground. It is believed that they were designed to serve during siege as a means to dump waste materials in order to protect hygiene within. Unlike many other *weizi*, Yanyiwei had an expansive open courtyard with a single well on the eastern

Figure 5.92 (left). Interior structures are made of high-quality fired bricks with an abundant use of wooden columns and beams as well as clay tiles, all of which echo building norms elsewhere in China. [RGK photograph 1993.]

Figure 5.94 (left). Interior space within Xinwei is somewhat fragmented by partition walls, while gates of many shapes and sizes separate and connect, leading from hall to hall as well as from small courtyard to courtyard. Guanxi *xiang*, Longnan *xian*, Jiangxi. [RGK photograph 1993.]

Figure 5.93 (bottom). Some gates and structures within the interior are rather simple, formed of adobe bricks. [RGK photograph 1993.]

Figure 5.95 (top left). Yanyiwei [Swallow Wing Fortress] today rises among many smaller dwellings that abut it, but it likely once stood alone among the fields. Yangcun, Longnan *xian*, Jiangxi. [RGK photograph 1993.]

Figure 5.96 (middle left). Close-up of the upper wall, focusing on the protruding blockhouses called *paolou*. Yangcun, Longnan *xian*, Jiangxi. [RGK photograph 1993.]

Figure 5.97 (bottom right). Viewed from below, the walls rise more than 12 meters from a 2.5-meter-high cut stone base. Narrow openings in the wall are few and rather scattered on the upper levels. Yangcun, Longnan *xian*, Jiangxi. [RGK photograph 1993.]

Figure 5.98 (bottom left). The narrow slits seen along the outside wall broaden on the inside so that a person looking out has a broad field of vision and is able to securely maneuver a rifle across this line of sight. Yangcun, Longnan *xian*, Jiangxi. [RGK photograph 1993.]

Figure 5.99 (left). Four levels, each with a balconied corridor, are built into the encircling walls. They all once looked out onto an expansive open courtyard that included a single well to serve all of the residents. Today this courtyard is crowded with single-story buildings constructed with crude materials that contrast with the quality of the encircling structures. Yangcun, Longnan *xian*, Jiangxi. [RGK photograph 1993.]

Figure 5.100 (below). A cantilevered overhang capped with tile, like that on the massive roof, covers a wooden veranda that rings the third story. The veranda itself shields the area below from rain. Yangcun, Longnan *xian*, Jiangxi. [RGK photograph 1993.]

side. Today, however, one sees single-story structures crowding it. The ancestral hall is positioned along the wall directly opposite the gate on the western side. As can be seen in Figure 5.99, there are four stories within the *weizi*, three used for residential purposes and the fourth used for storage. A cantilevered overhang capped with tile, like that on the massive roof, covers a wooden veranda that rings the third story. The veranda itself shields the area below from rain (Figure 5.100).

Jiangxi *weizi* successfully combine strength with utility, protection from outside danger with encouragement of an open and structured community within. Fortified *weizi* continued to be built throughout the nineteenth and early decades of the twentieth century in response to unrest in China's countryside. Besides maintaining security, Jiangxi *weizi* provided a reasonable and cost-effective means to house collateral relatives in an apartmentlike structure. Some *weizi* seen today were built as recently as the 1960s, even under conditions of stability where defense was not a necessity. In recent years, as family structure has changed, some fortresses have been enlarged and modified for factories as rural China has become increasingly commercialized (Figures 5.101 and 5.102).

Figure 5.101. Some old rural *weizi* have been enlarged and modified in recent years for factories as China has become increasingly commercialized. Fenestration of the two abutting structures tell a story of contrasting needs, light and openness for today as opposed to security and enclosure in the past. Southern Jiangxi. [RGK photograph 1993.]

Figure 5.102. No longer needed for surveillance or for shooting rifles, this gun port has been reconfigured as an exhaust for a small stove. Southern Jiangxi. [RGK photograph 1993.]

Wai: *Defensive Architecture of Hong Kong*

With the lease of the New Territories in 1898 for a period of ninety-nine years, the British colony of Hong Kong came to include a variety of enclosed and unenclosed rural settlement dwelling complexes. Although nearly 100 Hong Kong place names used today include the character *"wei"*—pronounced *wai* in Cantonese—which refers to a fortresslike structure, only twenty-six residential complexes still retain their full walls. A few others have deteriorating wall fragments, reminders of a past when security was guaranteed only if there was a defensive wall. And some dwellings with *"wai"* in their name show no evidence of ever having been walled. Extant walled structures in the New Territories take two basic forms, either as a collection of row houses that are surrounded by a high wall or as smaller inward-facing residential compounds in which the high back walls of rooms constitute the external enclosure (Lung 1995, 67ff). Piracy, regional conflict, and the presence of bandits and rebels, especially in the sixteenth through the seventeenth centuries, all contributed to the building of fortified dwelling complexes, but this building tradition continued even into the turbulent decades of the early twentieth century.

Figure 5.103. Although less formidable than the fortresslike structures discussed earlier, Kat Hing Wai/Jiqingwei proved nonetheless secure through several centuries of disorder. The surrounding walls reach 5.5 meters with 8-meter-high corner towers. As seen in this view, many of the common dwellings within have been replaced by multistory modern structures. Kam Tin/Jintian, New Territories, Hong Kong. [Source: *Rural* 1979, 33.]

The best known of Hong Kong's defensive architectural complexes is Kat Hing Wai/Jiqingwei 吉庆围 in Kam Tim/Jintian, a dramatic and symmetrical structure that took form between 1662 and 1721. With roughly square dimensions of 84 by 88 meters, brick perimeter walls reaching 5.5 meters in height, 8-meter-high square watch towers, and a 6-meter-wide moat, Kat Hing Wai was a secure citadel for members of the Tang clan who had occupied the area since the Northern Song period in the tenth century (Figure 5.103). Although oriented west to east rather than north to south, the plan is sited to conform to auspicious *fengshui* considerations, including hillslopes to the rear and embayed water to the front across the fields.

Within the walls, Kat Hing Wai is a honeycomb-like assemblage of individual dwelling units of uniform size and form (Figure 5.104). A 3-meter-wide lane runs from the front gatehouse to a shrine at the rear. On each side of the lane are six sets of ten rowhouses. Eight of the rows are comprised of identical units with matching depth and breadth. Three of the other rows are foreshortened, and the last is intermediate in size to the others. Most units are similar to those discussed earlier in the section on Guangdong, comprising a front room and a rear room that are separated by a *tianjing*, or sky-well. Each of the rear rooms includes a cockloft accessible via a ladder. Only the *tianjing* and doorway allow air and light into each dwelling unit. Each of the units faces slightly south of west.

Among the remaining inward-facing residential compounds is Sam Tung Uk/Sandongwu 三栋屋 [Three-ridgepole Dwelling], a traditional rural structure that has been swallowed up within the urban development of once quiescent Tsuen Wan/Quanwan. Compounds of this type, built without freestanding outer walls, were once found throughout the rural New Territories. Built in 1786 by the Chen clan whose ancestors had originated in Fujian, the complex came to take a rectangular shape, including a core comprising three rows of halls, a pair of flanking side halls, and a long rear structure (Figure 5.105). Backwalls and endwalls of the encircling buildings are without windows and provide security for occupants within this inward-facing complex. Sam Tung Uk was saved from destruction, restored in 1987, and is now open to the public as a folk museum, the largest museum in Hong Kong occupying a rejuvenated historical building.

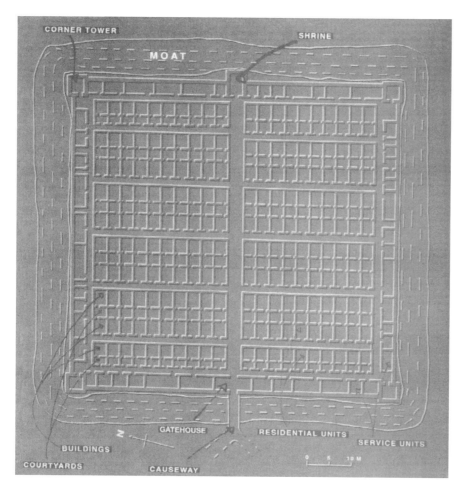

CORNER TOWER · SHRINE · MOAT · GATEHOUSE · RESIDENTIAL UNITS · SERVICE UNITS · BUILDINGS · COURTYARDS · CAUSEWAY · N · 0 5 10 M

Figure 5.104. Formal in plan, Kat Hing Wai is a honeycomblike assemblage of individual dwelling units of uniform size and form. Bifurcating the plan is a 3-meter-wide lane running from the front gatehouse to a shrine at the rear. Six rows of ten dwelling units are arranged on each side of the lane. Eight of the rows are comprised of identical units with matching depth and breadth. Three of the other rows are foreshortened, and the last is intermediate in size to the others. Kam Tin/Jintian, New Territories, Hong Kong. [Source: Lung 1995, 65.]

Figure 5.105. Built among the fields in 1786, Sam Tung Uk/ Sandongwu today sits amidst the elevated roads and high-rise buildings of urban Hong Kong. Built without freestanding walls, the back wall and endwalls of the inward-facing structures provided security. After extensive restoration, Sam Tung Uk was opened in 1987 as a folk museum. [Original aerial photograph used with the permission of the Antiquities and Monuments Office, Hong Kong.]

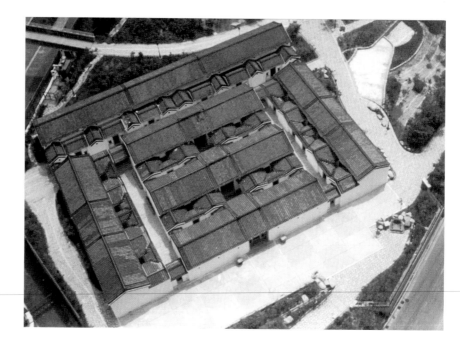

Ethnic Minority Houses in the Southwest

Forty-six of the fifty-six ethnic groups within China live in the southwest, a complex geographic region that sweeps in an arc from the lofty Tibetan plateau eastward to include the basins and dissected uplands of Sichuan, Yunnan, and Guizhou provinces as well as western Hunan and northern Guangxi. Throughout the region, pockets of ethnic minorities are loosely scattered among clustered territories of others, with one group inhabiting the higher remote ridges, another living on the lower slopes, and still others populating the basin and valley bottoms. As discussed earlier, Han migration into Sichuan and other portions of the region brought Chinese settlers to a spacious and fractured frontier area dominated by disparate indigenous groups. The cultural norms brought by Chinese pioneers, however, were far from uniform, varying in myriad aspects of the "little traditions" of the migrants' localities of origin. The complexity of cultural interactions at different times and in different places over the centuries resulted in dissimilar processes of assimilation and acculturation. Fluctuating migration flows and changing trade relationships impacted cycles of both conflict and relative harmony. The distinctions between the various minority groups in China are usually more blurred than clear because of substantial acculturation as well as actual physical assimilation. The southward infiltration of all groups and the complex cultural borrowing among them have long been acknowledged but are not yet well understood (Lebar, Hickey, and Musgrave 1964). Over the past fifty years, "with astonishing rapidity, peoples in the southwest who had once been quite different from China's majority Han population have largely abandoned their ways of life and beliefs. . . . Yet at the same time, ironically, Chinese government policy dissuades most of them from completely abandoning their ethnic status" (Unger 1997, 67). This tension is observable in the mutations of traditional domestic architectural forms. It is not always clear which combination of primary and secondary "form-generating forces," as they are termed by Rapoport, guide the creation of and changes in housing types (1969, 83). Nonetheless, it is clear that the abandonment of traditional house styles that some view as "backward," but which are actually well-ventilated because of the nature of structure and materials, in favor of Han-style "modern" brick and tile dwellings is indeed unfortunate.

Ganlan: *Stilt Dwellings of the Southwest*

Distinctive stilt or pile-supported houses, called *ganlan lou* 干栏楼 [stiltlike structures] and sometimes *diaojiao lou* 吊脚楼 [scaffoldlike structures] because of their underlying framework, have a well-documented history of construction by ethnic minority groups throughout southwestern China. Many such groups subsequently adopted and modified structural types brought into the region by Han migrants even while other members of the same nationality continued to build dwellings built above the ground on piles. *Ganlan* dwellings vary widely in size and are found in upland areas as well as in fertile river valleys. While some are structurally quite simple, others are more intricate and involve the use of sophisticated framing systems similar to those employed by Han populations elsewhere in southern China.

Among the most developed *ganlan* dwellings are the so-called "bamboo-storied dwellings" [*zhulou* 竹楼] of the Dai nationality, found in Xishuangbanna of southern Yunnan, whose form and plan have been strongly influenced by environmental factors. Although today rarely completely built of bamboo, they are generally referred to as "stilt bamboo houses" even when they are constructed of wooden poles and sided with wooden walling and glass windows (Figures 5.106 and 5.107). Dai villages are generally found in lowlands amidst bamboo groves and near stream channels. Dai myths chronicle the "discovery" of *ganlan*-style dwellings from two very different origins, both of which involved floods. One progression brought the Dai from early cave dwellings though simple flat- and shed-roofed shelters, while the other accounts an evolution from tree houses. It is said that Dai dwellings raised on stilts with multiple roof pitches are reminiscent of the outstretched legs, neck, wings, and tail of a golden phoenix. A copper model of a pile dwelling from the Warring States/Western Han period (475 B.C.–A.D. 24) has been excavated from tombs at Shizaishan, Jingning in Yunnan (Zhu 1992a, 76–80).

Figure 5.106. This view across a nucleated village reveals common shapes and sizes of Dai *zhulou.* Manhuang *cun*, Menghai *xian*, Xishuangbanna Dai Autonomous Prefecture, Yunnan. [Original photograph used with the permission of Zhu Liangwen.]

Figure 5.107. *Zhulou* were originally built of bamboo but are now usually constructed of sturdy wooden poles, as seen in this close-up. The floor is elevated above the ground, while space beneath is left unwalled. High roofs and porous walls of the enclosed portion allow air to circulate. Ganlanba *cun*, Jinghong *xian*, Xishuangbanna Dai Autonomous Prefecture, Yunnan. [Original photograph used with the permission of Zhu Liangwen.]

Zhu Liangwen has outlined certain fundamental differences between Han and Dai that can be seen in contrasting architectural elements (1992a, 84–85):

> Han dwellings generally look inward towards a courtyard, are hierarchically arranged along an axis, and are likely to grow to meet family needs.

> Dai dwellings on the other hand, are open to the surrounding environment, lack solid walls, and are built with little attention to either hierarchy or axiality in their plans. Married children are not expected to live with their parents but to set up separate dwellings.

Interior, exterior, and intermediate shaded spaces all offer areas for work and leisure (Figure 5.108). The underpart of a Dai dwelling, as seen in Figure 5.109, is typically about 2 meters high and is shaded from the sun by the relatively porous structure above and the overhanging roofline. As a result, this open space traditionally was the coolest portion of the dwelling during the daytime. Here women could work at their loom or pound rice with a mortar and pestle and children could play. This area was also used for storing farm implements and fuel, such as charcoal and fire-

wood, and for penning domestic animals, such as pigs, dogs, chickens, and ducks, and stabling cattle at night. Although Zhu describes the barnyard smells that infiltrate the dwelling above as "the scent of security" for a household, he acknowledges that in recent decades, as knowledge of hygiene has been popularized, animals are usually penned some distance from the dwelling. Although traditionally a removable ladder led from the ground to the elevated veranda of Dai dwellings, today a single exterior stairway serves the same purpose. Open on three sides and usually found on the eastern end of a dwelling, the veranda becomes an important space for work and relaxation once the sun has shifted into the western sky in the afternoon (Figure 5.110). Besides the covered veranda, Dai dwellings normally include an adjacent but somewhat lower open porch with a balustrade on its outer edges. Early in the day and before sleep, it is a location where family members wash so that water runs down without being tracked into the interior. Here also family members can work when there is need for better light than can be ob-

Figure 5.108. This cutaway view of a common Dai dwelling reveals the shaded ground level, stairway, covered veranda, living area with a hearth, and sleeping spaces, and an open balcony. [Source: Yunnan sheng 1986, 216.]

Figure 5.109. With the floor raised above the ground, the ground level is shaded from the sun and is a cool place for women to work at their looms and children to play during the daytime as well as a place for penning animals and storing farm implements. As more attention is paid to hygiene today, animals are generally kept out of this area and are stabled away from the dwelling. Manzhailahan *cun*, Mengla *xian*, Xishuangbanna Dai Autonomous Prefecture, Yunnan. [Original photograph used with the permission of Zhu Liangwen.]

Figure 5.110. Located between an open balcony and the inner rooms is a covered veranda. Open on three sides and protected by a deep eaves overhang, the veranda is well shaded yet open to catch the breeze. As in the interior, people sit directly on the wooden floor. Manduanzhai, Jinghong *xian*, Xishuangbanna Dai Autonomous Prefecture. [Original photograph used with the permission of Zhu Liangwen.]

Figure 5.111. The Jinuo are a small minority nationality numbering less than 20,000 and living among the Dai in Jinghong *xian* in Xishuangbanna in southern Yunnan, where they engage in the cultivation of Pu-er tea. Their relatively simple *ganlan*-style dwellings, elevated above the ground, include many of the features for Dai and Jingpo dwellings. [Source: Yunnan sheng 1993, 41.]

Figure 5.112. The Tujia live in the rugged and heavily forested mountains of western Hubei and Hunan, an area of relatively mild temperatures but heavy rains. Considered descendants of the early Ba people, they have interacted with Han in-migrants since the early twelfth century. As a result, they have become assimilated and live in housing that cannot be clearly distinguished from those of the Han. A fine example of Tujia *ganlan* building that includes tiled and upsweeping rooflines as well as sophisticated carpentry is this dwelling in Zijiazhai, Yongxun *xian*, Xixiang Tujia-Miao Autonomous Prefecture, Hunan. [Original photograph used with the permission of Li Yuxiang.]

tained beneath the structure. Interior space within Dai dwellings is generally dimly lit, since windows were not traditionally part of the exterior walls. A large living room with a raised ceiling reaching to the roof rafters allows for combining function of eating, sleeping, and entertaining. A fire pit or hearth is typically found in this large room and is kept lit year-round. Family members traditionally sleep together on mats arranged in a row in an adjacent interior room, separated from the living room only by curtains. Dai dwellings range in size. Relatively modest structures that are square in plan are supported by thirty to forty stilt-columns and have a floor area of 70 to 80 square meters, while larger and more complex dwellings may be as large as 200 square meters with up to eighty vertical columns supporting multitiered roofs (Zhu 1992a, 95–96).

Elevated *ganlan*-style dwellings are also built by the relatively small ethnic minority groups such as the Jingpo, Blang, Pumi, Drung, De'ang, Jinuo, Lisu, Nu, and Hani who live along the upland hillslopes of Yunnan, the Buyi, Dong, and Shui in rugged Guizhou and the Tujia in western Hunan. Layout and form in these areas vary as local builders are able to flexibly accommodate differences in local relief and available materials (Figures 5.111 and 5.112). Although stilt houses are seen in some Yao, Miao, and Zhuang villages, the fact that these more populous nationalities are widely distributed throughout southwestern China and have been heavily influenced by Han culture has led to a great variety of housing styles. Most *ganlan* houses of minority groups have thatched roofs and non-load-bearing adobe, bamboo lattice, or mud plastered walls placed between the stiltlike columns.

Figure 5.113. Jingpo, who number around 100,000, live among the Dai, De'ang, Lisu, Achang, as well as the Han in *ganlan* dwellings among forests and bamboo groves in the Dehong Dai-Jingpo Autonomous Prefecture of Yunnan. Dwellings are usually oblong in shape, with an enclosed upper story, an open underpart, and a covered veranda. Roofs are thatched. [Original drawing used with the permission of Wang Qijun.]

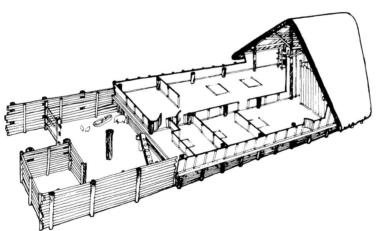

Figure 5.114. This cutaway view of a rectangular Jingpo structure shows a raised residential area partitioned by split bamboo screens into rooms, many of which have fire pits around which family members sleep. The semienclosed ground level is used for storage and to stable animals. Sometimes, as in this drawing, pens are added to the end of the dwelling if the terrain allows. [Source: Yunnan sheng 1986, 333.]

Representative of *ganlan* dwellings built by these smaller ethnic minority groups, Jingpo dwellings, as seen in Figures 5.113 and 5.114, are rectangular structures with a raised residential area partitioned into rooms with a semienclosed underpart used for storage and to stable animals. The wooden framework itself lifts the structure, providing support for the roof and making possible the placement of woven walls of readily available materials of vegetable origin. Thatched roofs, secured with vines, typically cover small and modest Jingpo *ganlan* dwellings. Access to living space is by way of stairs that lead to an extended platform, a kind of balcony at the entrance along the narrow end of the dwelling. Broad and high, this open platform, called a *menlang* 门廊 [entry arcade] in Chinese, is used as a gathering place for family and friends as well as a work space for domestic chores such as weaving.

Figure 5.115. The Zhuang, the most numerous of China's national minorities, are for the most part fully assimilated and live in dwellings quite similar to those of the Han. In the mountainous areas of northern Guangxi, however, large Zhuang *ganlan* dwellings are found in significant numbers. The flexibility of scaffoldlike wooden structural frameworks makes it possible to build large houses and bear the weight of tiled roofs. Zhuang dwellings are usually entered on one of the long sides, like those of the Han, rather than through the gable end as is common in other minority nationality dwellings. Pinganzhai, Longsheng Multi-nationality Autonomous *xian*. [Source: Li 1990, 19.]

Built 60 to 100 centimeters above the ground, the elevated rectangular living space is divided into outer and inner sections. Adjacent to the entry arcade, the outer section is a large room used to receive guests and provide visitors, when necessary, sleeping space. The interior includes bedrooms and a kitchen for family use. Fire pits, some of which are quite complicated in structure, are found not only in the kitchen but also in some of the bedrooms. Although there are similarities among various *ganlan*-type dwellings of the minority nationalities in southwestern China, distinctive elements in form, plan, and structure have been identified and recorded for each (Yunnan sheng 1986; Wang and Chen 1993).

Large *ganlan*-style dwellings have also been built by the Zhuang and Dong in remote mountainous areas of northern Guangxi and in adjacent areas of Hunan and Guizhou provinces. Although the Zhuang are identified as China's largest ethnic minority group and once spoke a Dai language, they have generally been acculturated to such a degree that they are often indistinguishable from local Han villagers and live in similar houses. Zhuang *ganlan* structures are rectangular in shape like Dai and Jingpo dwellings found in Yunnan and are flexibly built along hill slopes according to local topographic conditions (Figure 5.115). However, unlike many ethnic minority houses in the southwest that are entered through the gable end, Zhuang dwellings are entered, like Han houses, along the long side that faces south. Here a long narrow open veranda, not much wider than the stairs, runs the length of the dwelling. Thirty timber columns, some of which exceed 5 meters in height, are set into a rubble stone base and support not only a raised floor 1.8 meters above the ground but also a heavy tile roof that has been stabilized with mortise and tenon crossbeams. The ground level not only provides storage area but is also outfitted with pens to contain horses, cattle, and pigs. The upper living area includes a large main hall that is ringed by bedrooms and a kitchen (Guangxi minzu 1991, 19).

While Dong *ganlan* dwellings are similar to those of other groups, none exceed them in the purposefulness and sophistication of their carpentry, especially in view of the fact that most of their villages are found along streams in narrow mountain valleys (Figure 5.116). Although Dong streamside villages nestle below lushly forested hill slopes, Dong nonetheless plant and harvest much of the timber used in their dwellings and public structures. Fir saplings traditionally were planted whenever a child was born and were harvested when the child reached the age of eighteen and was ready to be married. Calling fir trees "eighteen-year trees" created a connection between the maturity of the tree and the child. Fir saplings today mature in only eight to ten years because of improved cultivation practices, but Dong farmers still refer to the timber they use as "eighteen-year trees" (Ma 1989, 354). Complicated carpentry that involves not only stilts at multiple levels but also mortise and tenon crossbeams characterize Dong structures of all types. Along the streamside edges of Dong villages, dwellings often overhang the water with suspended verandas and are supported by columns set on stone blocks that rest in the shallows (Zhu 1996, 4). Besides employing sophisticated *chuandou* carpentry in the building of *ganlan* dwellings, the Dong also built throughout northern Guangxi and southeastern Guizhou provinces unique and elaborate multitiered timber drum towers [*gulou* 鼓楼] and long covered bridges, called "wind and rain bridges" [*fengyuqiao* 风雨桥], with pagodalike timber additions atop them. The Chengyang "wind and rain bridge" in northern Guangxi is 77 meters long and 3.75 meters wide. Built between 1912 and 1924, the covered bridge includes a series of five multitiered pavilions that each reach a height of 11.5 meters (Li 1990, 239 ff.).

Whether one is describing rudimentary Jingpo, delicate Dai, or complicated and towering Dong *ganlan* dwellings, each elevated structure gives evidence of appropriate and successful adaptation to natural

Figure 5.116. Complicated and sophisticated carpentry characterizes the *ganlan* dwellings of the Dong nationality who live in the rugged areas straddling the borders of Guangxi, Guizhou, and Hunan. Along the edges of streams, dwellings often overhang the water and are supported by columns set on stone blocks that rest in the shallows. Along hill slopes, as shown here, substantial fir poles and beams give firm support to two- to three-story dwellings. Sanjiang Dong Autonomous *xian*, Guangxi Zhuang Autonomous Region. [Source: Li 1990, 421.]

conditions. The high temperatures and humidity of China's subtropical zone provide a climate relatively free of environmental stress. Besides affording enhanced air circulation and reducing the amount of the sun's direct radiation, which help to cool and temper humidities, the raising of living space above the ground offers some protection from the encroachment of insects, snakes, and animals as well as water that cascades through villages during major downpours. Minority dwellings throughout southwestern China, including the relatively crude abodes of the Lahu that are reminiscent of neolithic buildings in structure and spatial organization, exhibit effective and pragmatic accommodations to local natural conditions using only simple technologies. The weathered textures of natural materials used in minority dwellings as well as the distinctive silhouettes that arise from endless variations in roof profiles

Figure 5.117. In the remote areas of northern Yunnan, Naxi still build single-story house compounds arranged in a village cluster for ten to thirty families. The main structure in each compound includes space for receiving guests, sleeping, cooking, and storage. A raised triangular hearth provides interior space for eating, entertaining, and sleeping. Directly opposite from and parallel to the residential unit is an area that serves as a stable. In this photograph, Han-style red paper couplets have been hung alongside the entry in anticipation of the New Year, while two pine trees are the focus of a Naxi sacrifice to ancestors ritual. Lijiang *xian*, Mingyin *xiang*, Yunnan. [Original photograph used with the permission of Charles McKhann.]

and building elevations contribute to village landscapes with an apparent organic unity.

Han-Influenced Minority Dwellings

Many of the buildings of ethnic minority groups in Yunnan, Guizhou, and Guangxi provinces have been strongly influenced by Han architectural norms. Over the centuries, some minority nationality groups, such as the Yi, Bai, and Naxi in Yunnan, the Miao in Guizhou, and the Zhuang in Guangxi, were heavily influenced by the dominant Han culture and became substantially assimilated. Although the overall plan and structure of Bai, Yi, Naxi, Miao, and Zhuang dwellings usually mimic those of their Han Chinese neighbors, characteristic ornamentation and the presence of Buddhist shrines and offerings set them apart. Furthermore, the celebration of festivals and life cycle rituals carried out within the homes of these minority groups serve to distinguish their separate ethnic identities even when the house form itself appears alien. Today, Chinese architects write of the pronounced ethnic character of Bai, Yi, Hani, and Naxi dwellings even as they elaborate on the influence of Han Chinese building forms and technologies (Yunnan sheng 1986, 11, 21, 89). Little is usually written of the simpler precursor building types in less developed and remote areas that continue to be lived in by members of nationality groups.

The Bai, for example, who have developed a distinctive architectural style that resembles ageless Han forms, also build *ganlan* pile dwellings and log structures in the rugged hills of the Dali region (Dali Baizu 1994, 86–95).

The Bai, among the most populous minorities in western Yunnan today, once dominated the tributary Nanzhao kingdom between 937 and 1253 A.D., but were conquered by the Mongols in the thirteenth century after which their interactions with Han increased substantially. Although noting many of the distinguishing elements of Bai culture, western field researchers, such as Francis L. K. Hsu and C. P. Fitzgerald, earlier in this century documented the extent of their assimilation as sedentary agriculturalists and townspeople. Describing Bai courtyard-style dwellings in the town of Dali, Fitzgerald stated that "if there was ever an indigenous type of house unlike the Chinese kind, it has entirely disappeared" (1941, 47). Yet, Fitzgerald reports details such as "end walls with black and white arabesque patterns" and "small pointed windows let into the end and back walls" that are distinctly Bai.

The Naxi, only a fifth the size of the Bai population, occupy the rugged Lijiang region at elevations above 2,400 meters, just to the north of Bai concentrations in northern Yunnan. Since at least the thirteenth century, the Naxi have engaged in agriculture and interacted with Han settlers. By the Ming period,

Figure 5.118. Built around a walled courtyard entered through a gate, this Naxi single-story house has walls of tamped earth and a roof of wooden shingles. The overhanging gables allow air to circulate into the complex. Haibei *cun*, Naxi Lijiang Autonomous *xian*, Yunnan. [Source: Liu 1990, 275.]

the Naxi were building *siheyuan*-type dwellings with accentuated upturned ridgelines the origins of which are traced to Han immigrants from the north (Yunnan sheng 1986, 85). Traditional rectangular timber houses are still being built by Naxi, sometimes described here as Mosuo, who live in the relatively remote villages of the Yongning area of northern Yunnan. The single-story wooden-framed house with a roof of wooden shingles, as seen in Figure 5.117, contains space for receiving guests, sleeping, cooking, and storage. This structure, however, does not stand alone but is part of a compound that includes a stable and courtyard. In examining Naxi conceptions of domestic space, McKhann describes a radial model with a center and a periphery as well as an axial model that is characterized by hierarchy (1989, 159-162). These notions of space are not incompatible with those associated with Chinese courtyard houses, and thus, as contact with Han settlers became more intense and as resources permitted, it appears reasonable that Naxi house forms evolved to include Han designs. Chinese ethnologists believe that this change from a Naxi indigenous house form to a Han-style courtyard resulted from a "transformation from matrilineal to patrilineal descent as a natural process of social evolution," but other observers see it as "resulting from a policy of forced sinicization" in the past (McKhann 1995, 55).

Although relatively simple single- and double-story rectangular dwellings continue to be built by the Bai and Naxi, two distinctive courtyard types that replicate Chinese courtyard-style dwellings found elsewhere in the country have been well documented. Termed *sanfang yizhaobi* 三坊一照壁 [three subdivisions and one screen wall] and *sihe wutianjing* 四合五天井 [quadrangle with five skywells], these plans are similar to what is called in north China *san-*

heyuan, a three-sided building form, and *siheyuan*, a quadrangle building. Dwellings in the Yongning area of northern Yunnan, a region populated by people whom Chinese ethnographers have classified as Naxi but who identify themselves as Mosuo, live in dwellings that reflect a matriarchal social organization quite different from the classical patriarchical organization of Chinese courtyard houses (Figure 5.118). Here, a kitchen—rather than a northern hall or a courtyard—is the focal area of the dwelling (Dries-Daffner 1992, 14-15).

Bai *sanfang yizhaobi* dwellings, just as with Naxi forms, are U-shaped *sanheyuan*-type complexes that include a main hall with adjacent supplementary rooms, a perpendicular pair of facing wings, and a screen wall and entry that complete the enclosure of a courtyard (Figure 5.119). Like Han courtyard structures, the encircling halls are also usually three *jian* in width, but Bai and Naxi halls are normally two stories. Overhanging roofs provide an encircling arcade similar to those found in Han structures elsewhere in southern China. These broad overhangs create an important transitional space, midway between indoors and outdoors, that is especially suitable to subtropical areas and is found in virtually all dwelling

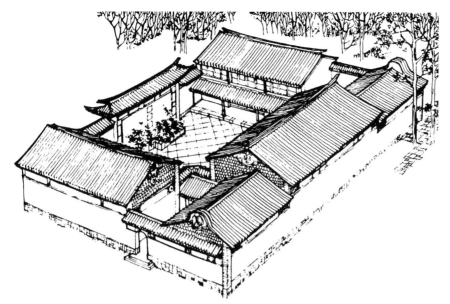

Figure 5.119. Called *sanfang yizhaobi* [three subdivisions and one screen wall], the plan of this Bai dwelling is a *sanheyuan*, a three-sided building form that evokes Han notions of spatial organization with its inward-facing structures and enclosing wall. Enclosure is accomplished by linking a main hall, a flanking pair of perpendicular wings, and a screen wall. Unlike Han courtyard structures, the encircling halls of both Bai and Naxi dwellings are normally two stories. [Source: Yunnan Sheng 1986, 21.]

types in Yunnan (Zhu 1992b, 123). Besides the central courtyard, such dwellings also typically include two small corner skywells called *loujiao tianjing* 漏角天井 [corner funnel skywell] or *loujiao wu* 漏角屋 [corner funnel room]. With access to the outside through a side gate, the "corner funnel skywell" of the Bai house is adjacent to the kitchen and pigpen. Both Bai and Naxi dwellings follow the Han pattern of an entry in the southeastern corner of the front wall. The *zhaobi*, or screen wall, completes the enclosure of the courtyard. As a focus for ornamentation, the *zhaobi* and entryway are more elaborate in detail and scale in Bai than Naxi dwellings. Some Naxi dwellings with multiple courtyards clearly preserve elements similar to those found in the large Hakka *wufenglou* of Fujian, which have been attributed to the Central Plains of northern China. Heightened by differences in elevation along the slope, this dwelling type clearly expresses the hierarchy, axiality, and symmetry of not only Han vernacular dwellings

all over the country but also China's grand building traditions.

Chinese architects have labeled compact dwellings in the Kunming area of Yunnan as "seal-" or "chop-" type [*yikeyin* 一颗印] dwellings because they are normally square and squat like a common Chinese seal (see introduction of this type in Chapter 2). Usually only a single *tianjing* is found in seal-style dwellings in Yunnan, with the *tianjing* located immediately inside the entryway (Figure 5.120). While exterior walls are high and have only limited fenes-

Figure 5.120. While basically a U-shaped *sanheyuan*, Yunnan *yikeyin* are distinctive in plan and overall form. Built tightly around the *tianjing*, the side rooms support a double-sloped roof, short and gentle to the outside and steeper and longer to the *tianjing*. Kunming, Yunnan. [Original photograph used with the permission of Zhu Liangwen.]

tration like those found in Anhui, Jiangxi, and Zhejiang, the plan and structure of the side halls and their roofs are quite distinct. Instead of a simple coping atop the exterior walls, each side wall supports a structure with a short, gentle roof sloping to the outside and a steeper and longer roof sloping to the central *tianjing*. As with other indigenous housing styles, *yikeyin* hold within them the complete needs of a household. Not only are there defined areas for daily living but there is substantial space provided for stabling animals and storing goods. The tightness of the structure means that the animals, especially at night, are kept close to the sleeping quarters of the household in a traditional *yikeyin*. The stable is adjacent to the main hall in the back third of the main structure. While preserving the compact shape, high walls, and interior *tianjing*, many similar houses are constructed of adobe bricks or tamped earth, clearly building materials of the poor (Li Xingfa 1992, 176-177).

CHAPTER 6
Dwellings in Western China

Encompassing more than a third of the country, China's "Far West" is a vast landlocked region that has historically been viewed as China's periphery. As China's Inner Asian frontier, it is geographically as much west as it is north in terms of the cardinal directions. The realm is one of substantial physical contrasts, stretching from the lofty Tibetan plateau northward to encompass the dry basins and snowy mountains of Xinjiang, Qinghai, and Gansu and including the sweeping grassland expanses of the Mongolian plateau to the east. As the region has been through much of history, it remains today an outlying peripheral area of relatively sparse populations quite remote from the centers of political and economic power in eastern China. Physically dissimilar to the Han-dominated areas to the east, much of the region is uninhabitable because of low temperatures, scant precipitation, rugged terrain, and unsuitable soils. On the high and cold Tibet-Qinghai plateau and within the extensive arid and semiarid areas of Xinjiang and Inner Mongolia, limited rural settlement has traditionally been based more on transitory herding than on sedentary agriculture, yet in well watered and protected valleys small-scale farming has been important.

Major concentrations of non-Han minority nationality groups populate this vast realm, creating in many cases an intermixed mosaic of settlement forms. Tibetan, Uygur, Kazak, Kirgiz, Uzbek, Tajik, Tatar, Mongol, and Russian minority nationality groups, whose numbers range from 7 million to less than 5,000 within China, share ethnic affinities with populations beyond China's borders. Hui, Dongxiang, Tu, Yi, Salar, Bonan, Moinba, Lhoba, Qiang, Nu, Drung, Yugar, Xibe, Oroqen, Ewenki, and Daur usually live amidst larger ethnic minority groups and the dominant Han, frequently sharing with their neighbors many aspects of material culture, including the form of their dwellings. Four of China's five autonomous regions—politically at the same level as provinces—are found in interior China: Tibet (Xizang), Xinjiang, Inner Mongolia, and Ningxia. This affords a degree of political and cultural autonomy to the Tibetan, Uygur, Mongol, and Hui ethnic groups that are found in large concentrations within them. Where there are compact communities of an individual minority nationality, political subdivisions similar to *xian*, or counties, give recognition to their presence. Han Chinese dominate in most cities in interior China and in rural areas where settlements have been established to reclaim barren lands (Gaubatz 1996).

As a geographic realm, western China reaches beyond the political boundaries of the autonomous regions to include topographically, climatically, and culturally similar areas that interpenetrate and overlap the bordering provinces of northern China and southern China discussed in the preceding two chapters (Map 6.1). These include adjacent upland areas of northwestern Yunnan and western Sichuan provinces in southern China as well as much of Gansu and portions of Shaanxi provinces in northern China. The upland plateau fringe areas of western Sichuan known as Xikang were once part of historical Tibet but in the 1950s were separated from

Map 6.1. Western China, as a vast and complicated cultural region, includes the uplands of western Sichuan and Yunnan, the Qinghai-Tibetan plateau, Xinjiang, Gansu, and the Mongolian plateau.

Figure 6.1. Tibetan herders traditionally have used large portable tents that are somewhat loaflike in shape. With a middle core framed by two end sections, the interior space is created by a pair of poles and exterior braces made of notched tree limbs that are connected to the poles by taut rope. An opening at the top that lets in light and ventilates smoke is covered with a flap made of yak hair or skin. [Source: Ren 1934, 45.]

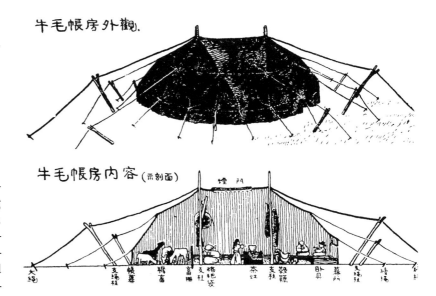

it, creating three vast upland autonomous districts for Tibetan/Zang and Yi minority populations in western Sichuan. Composed of parallel north to south trending mountains between which are found canyons carved by Asia's major rivers, the Huanghe (Yellow), Changjiang (Yangzi), Mekong, Salween, and Irrawaddy, this region offers very little level land and generally has an inhospitable climate. The easternmost portions of the Mongolian plateau similarly were administratively separated from Inner Mongolia in 1969 and added to Liaoning, Jilin, and Heilongjiang provinces in northeastern China in order that this border zone with the Soviet Union could be placed under a unified military command. In 1979, these areas were reamalgamated and the ethnic minority subdivisions returned to the Inner Mongolian Autonomous Region. The profusion of ecological and economic adaptations of numerous and distinctive cultural groups throughout China's western region are clearly reflected in the varying dwelling types and settlement forms found there.

Dwellings on the Tibetan Plateau and Its Margins

While most of China's 4.5 million Tibetans live in Xizang, the Tibetan Autonomous Region, many also live in the uplands of neighboring Sichuan and Yunnan in southwest China as well as Qinghai and Gansu provinces in northwestern China. These adjacent areas may be considered part of greater Tibet even though they are not today administered by the autonomous

region. Generally practicing animal husbandry and agriculture across an area that exceeds 2 million square kilometers, Tibetans sparsely inhabit not only the cold and dry plateau regions that lie more than 4,000 meters above sea level but also warmer river valley bottoms along Tibet's southern margins. In their struggle with relatively harsh environments of many types that vary across the world's largest and highest plateau, Tibetans have created a variety of reasonably comfortable dwellings that utilize readily available materials. Tibetan herders seasonally live in tents made of yak skin and other materials, while most Tibetans live in compact dwellings made of stone that vary in quality and height according to economic and local environmental conditions. Strong winds, cold winter temperatures, short warm summers, limited rainfall, thin soils, irregular topography, and sparse vegetation all conspire to make life difficult for those who live on the high and vast Tibetan plateau. Whether for tents or structures, building sites are generally along southern slopes that are open to the warmth of the sun yet buffer the bitter prevailing winds that come from the north.

While small Tibetan tents typically are square, larger ones are oblong and somewhat loaflike in shape (Figure 6.1). Comprised of two sections with a middle area between them, the enclosing covering is supported by a pair of poles that pierce the interior and

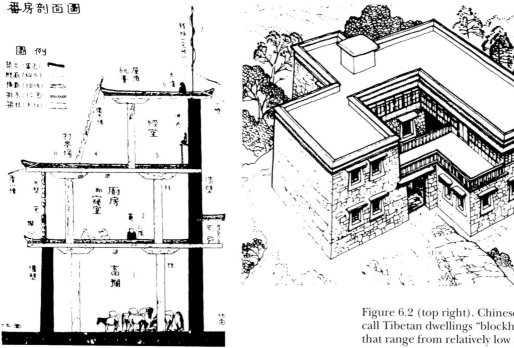

Figure 6.2 (top right). Chinese architects usually call Tibetan dwellings "blockhouses" or *diaofang*, that range from relatively low and modest one- or two-story stone structures, some of which have a small courtyard, to towers of stone. [Source: Liu 1990, 221.]

Figure 6.3 (top left). Among the early representations of Tibetan dwellings was this drawing of a tall blockhouse in the lofty Xikang region of what is today western Sichuan. The ground floor includes stables (1) for horses, cattle, and sheep. The kitchen (2) and living quarters are located on the floor directly above the ground-level stables. An overhanging toilet (3) juts off the back of the kitchen level. Notched wooden logs (4), shown here connecting the third level with the roof, connect each of the lower levels as well. On the narrower third level is a small chapel (5), and above it on an open platform are an incense burner (6) and a prayer banner (7). This drawing compresses some of the space, so that the threshing area (8) on the third level appears relatively small. [Source: Ren 1934.]

Figure 6.4 (bottom left). The facade of a compact Tibetan dwelling. Lacking fenestration, the structure appears like a blockhouse with its stone walls. Xikang, Western Sichuan. [Original photograph used with the permission of Olivier Laude.]

Figure 6.5. Within Lhasa, urban dwellings are usually only a single story, as this view across the rooftops shows. Lhasa, Tibet. [RGK photograph 1981.]

Figure 6.6. Urban dwellings in Tibet often have larger windows than those found in more remote rural areas. Lhasa, Tibet. [RGK photograph 1981.]

are lifted by exterior braces made of notched tree limbs. The poles, braces, and the roof covering itself are strengthened by anchoring them to the ground with a score of taut cords. In the upper central section between the poles there is an opening that lets in light and ventilates smoke; it can be covered with a flap made of yak hair or skin. Entered from one end, space immediately inside on the left is for women while that on the right is for men. Near the center and beneath the opening in the cover is a cooking stove traditionally made of mud. Beyond is storage space and an area to stable young animals. A prayer flag often flies from the pole farthest from the door.

Traditional Tibetan houses are normally multistory, appearing like tall pill boxes in that they are taller than they are broad in order to conserve heat and materials. Chinese authors usually refer to Tibetan dwellings as "blockhouses" [*diaofang* 碉房] because of their fortified appearance as well as frequent towering forms (Figures 6.2, 6.3, and 6.4). Most are square in shape and at least two stories and often three or four stories tall—some even reach seven stories—including a top level that encompasses a functional flat roof and several rooms. They are compact and tightly built with fenestration limited only to those directions optimal for direct sunlight. Urban dwellings within the Lhasa region, however, are usually only one story, while near Shigatse they are two stories (Figures 6.5 and 6.6). Set atop each dwelling is an open area, protected from the wind by screens

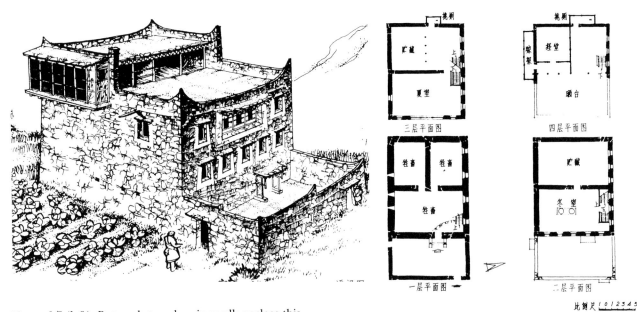

Figure 6.7 (left). Battered stone bearing walls enclose this tightly built four-story blockhouse with its enclosed courtyard and principal fenestration to the front. The structure is 10 meters wide and 23 meters deep. E'eryazhai, Maerkang *xian*, Abei Zangzu Qiangzu Autonomous Prefecture, Sichuan. [Source: Ye 1992, 42.]

Figure 6.8 (right). These four drawings show the floor plans for the dwelling in Figure 6.7. The bottom left drawing reveals small air chinks in the stone wall for ventilating the three stable areas in the ground level beyond the courtyard. Steps lead from the stables to the first level (bottom right drawing) with its stove for winter use, large battered windows for ventilation and light, and a storage area to the rear. The third level (top left) includes summer living space, storage area, and a projecting and overhanging toilet on the back wall. Above these three levels is an open terrace (top right) for threshing that is attached to a covered chapel. An overhanging covered structure called a "drying rack" completes the plan. E'eryazhai, Maerkang *xian*, Abei Zangzu Qiangzu Autonomous Prefecture, Sichuan. [Source: Ye 1992, 42.]

or rooms, that can be occupied in order to receive the warmth of the sun, thus the name "flat roofed stone towers" [*pingding diaofang* 平顶碉房].

The vertical division of functional space is clearly shown in Figures 6.7 and 6.8 of a four-story dwelling in E'eryazhai village, Maerkang *xian*, in the autonomous prefecture for Zang and Qiang minority groups in western Sichuan. A single entry leads from the outside into a small courtyard surrounded by a low wall that is used by both animals and humans. In the low ground level of the dwelling, horses, cattle, and sheep are stabled where they not only afford security but also provide the warmth of their bodies to the heating of the structure and its residents above. It is rare for windows to open to the outside from the animal pens, although sometimes the walls are chinked for ventilation and the penetration of some light. In recent years, however, significant progress has been made in moving stables from beneath the dwellings to the outside. Adjacent rooms at this lower level are used to store tools as well as animal excrement used for fuel once it has been dried outside. Passage from the stable and storage areas to the living area above as well as to higher floors in common dwellings traditionally was by a "ladder" that was nothing more than a tree trunk into which notches had been cut. The use of stairs was limited to large houses in the past, but they are quite common today.

While the ground level ranges from 2.5 to 2.8 meters in height, the main living level above is somewhat lower, generally about 2.3 meters high. A winter room is at the front of the dwelling on the second level, and a summer room is at the same location on the third level. The winter room is bounded and insulated by a storage area for grain and fuel on the

Figure 6.9. Formed into patties, yak dung and other waste material is mixed with straw before being stuck to the sun-facing walls of dwellings. Here they dry before being stored for use as fuel for cooking. Lhasa area, Tibet. [RGK photograph 1981.]

western side with windowless thick blind walls, the warm stable beneath, and five windows on the south and three on the east side, which face the sun over the course of a day and help to keep the room relatively warm during the season of coldest weather. This room is clearly a kitchen, with a cooking stove or hearth [*huotang* 火塘] that is kept lit year-round, but it also serves as bedroom and activity room for family members who take advantage of the heat generated there. The kitchen is ventilated through an opening in the ceiling that draws smoke into the room above. Western visitors to Tibet's villages throughout the nineteenth and early twentieth centuries often mentioned the absence of functioning chimneys and the "ordeal by smoke" as one sat in or moved about Tibetan dwellings. Stein summarizes the observations of travelers about such inadequacies as well as floor-by-floor variations in Tibetan houses in different parts of the plateau (1990, 159–162).

Directly above the winter quarters is an equally large room that serves as the summer living area, with windows on three sides to enhance ventilation. An adjacent storage area includes an "overhanging toilet" [*tiaoce* 挑厕 in Chinese], an enclosed wooden closet with staggered holes cut in its base as squat toilets. Without windows, this cantilevered "outhouse" area generally receives an updraft of air through the

holes in the floor. Human waste drops two stories to the ground below on the backside of the dwelling, a phenomenon described as "convenient and sanitary" (Ye 1992, 171). Here it dries or freezes depending on the season and can be collected easily. Human waste as well as animal dung are important sources of fuel for cooking throughout Tibet. Yak dung and other waste material are mixed with straw and formed into patties that are stuck to the sun-facing walls of dwellings where they dry before being stored for use as fuel for cooking (Figure 6.9).

Stairs sometimes lead to a fourth floor, where a major portion is actually a flat roof terrace marked with a low parapet. This terrace is used for drying grain and vegetables, while behind is a room and wall, which effectively block the strong prevailing winds (Figure 6.10). The room is a kind of chapel, where Buddhist religious articles and pictures of the Dalai Lama or Panchen Lama are kept, a room described by Chinese authors as a Lama's bedroom [*Lama woshi* 喇嘛卧室] or "scriptures room" [*jingtang* 经堂]. Richly decorated with religious paintings, deities, and scriptures, many such rooms today also have "battery-operated prayer wheels permanently revolving" (Mackerras 1995, 114). Tibetan houses throughout the countryside generally have prayer flags and colorful threads attached to juniper twigs flapping above them as well.

Figure 6.10. Whether a rural dwelling or an urban one, as is shown here, the roof is the site for a shrine. Often these spaces are quite colorful with flying prayer flags and colorful threads attached to juniper twigs. Lhasa, Tibet. [RGK photograph 1981.]

Facing the direction of the prevailing northwest winds, a protruding covered structure called a "drying rack" [*liangjia* 晾架] is often built. A secondary "overhanging toilet" is also sometimes cantilevered on the back side of the top floor, somewhat offset above the one below. Where there are three floors to a Tibetan dwelling, this is seen as "the hierarchical stacking of the three levels of the world," with the upper level reserved for Gods and dignitaries, the second level for family members and various deities, and the bottom level for animals (Durocher 1990, 55).

The walls of most Tibetan dwellings are load-bearing and made of irregular fieldstone [*pianshi* 片石],

rubble [*maoshi* 毛石], or crushed stone [*suishi* 碎石] that can be readily collected from the nearby hill slopes. Interior walls also are often of stone, but the walls around courtyards are often of adobe brick (Figure 6.11). "Stone is never quarried, due to a religious belief that the powerful deities that reside in stone would be displeased and bring bad luck to the family building the house" (Durocher 1990, 76). Settlers usually collect stones that have been abraded by wind and water rather than using soils as is done in many areas of China because in most areas of the Tibetan plateau, earth layers are quite thin and thus insufficient for making tamped walls. Where silty soil is available, however, thick tamped earth walls are sometimes raised above a meter-high base of stone (Figure 6.12). When limited amounts of clay soil are used in construction, it is necessary to improve the deficient quality of the soil by mixing it with chopped barley stems to increase its plasticity. After combining soil and barley chaff, the mixture must sit for approximately a week in order to let the vegetable matter partially decompose before bricks can be formed in molds.

Shallow soils as well as harsh climatic conditions due to low precipitation and temperatures conspire to limit tree growth that would produce long and straight timbers in abundant numbers for general use in building. Wooden timbers, however, are needed in most dwellings as joists, which are laid atop walls to support floors or a flat roof. In anticipation of needing some timber for future construction, Tibetan households traditionally cultivated a small number of trees, such as poplars, willows, and junipers, by starting them as seedlings in pots and then transplanting them to well-watered locations along riverbanks. The straight trunks of these poplars make them suitable for needed pillars and beams, while the irregularity of willow wood allows its use for door and window frames. The branches of any of these are used to fashion flooring and roofing.

Over the centuries, Tibetans have proved quite successful in constructing houses of limited materials that are surprisingly resistant to the periodic earthquakes that shake this tectonically active region. In addition to characteristic compact shape, other means are employed to stabilize multistory dwellings. Deep stone footings support mortared stone walls that are battered

Figure 6.11 (top). Although stone blocks are normally not quarried, irregular fieldstone and rubble are trimmed into reasonably regular bricklike shapes in order to fashion a wall. Adobe bricks are used in the construction of the courtyard wall. Lhasa area, Tibet. [RGK photograph 1981.]

Figure 6.12 (bottom). Although soils are thin across much of the Tibetan plateau and are not widely used as a building medium, in some areas earth is tamped between forming boards in order to raise a wall. Tamped earth walls are usually set on a meter-high foundation of piled stone. Naqu *xian*, Tibet. [Source: Chen Lusheng 1995, 72.]

on the outside—wider at the base and inclined as they rise—but vertical on the inside to form a trapezoidal section. In addition, each ringing course of stone is laid so that it is higher at the corners and depressed near the center of the wall. Stones are generally left in their natural state, assembled dry with the gaps between them filled with various sizes of pebbles and earth. Entasis in the vertical dimension and slack in the horizontal dimension are combined with linkages to the interior load-bearing walls of long narrow rooms that together act to stabilize the structure. With exterior walls inclined inward 3 to 5 degrees, some taller dwellings appear as if they are truncated pyramids. Roughly hewn logs perhaps 4 to 6 meters long are spaced every 60 to 70 centimeters as joists to support floors made of a composition of branches, grasses, and mud. Much care is expended in sealing the roof by varying the coarseness of the soil and mixing it with cut grasses used to make mud mixtures that are then successively layered, tamped with the feet, and dried. In some areas of western Sichuan occupied by Tibetans, it is reported that cattle urine is blended into the mixture (Ye 1992, 136–137). A terrazzolike finish results when the surface is burnished with a butter mixture (Yang 1993, 192). Because of limited rainfall, composition roofs are quite serviceable, especially when constructed with a slight slope to drain rainwater. Some Tibetan roofs are made of slate slabs where slate is available.

Similar solid blockhouse-type structures of stone or adobe are built by the Qiang, who number nearly 110,000 and live in the upper reaches of the Minjiang River in western Sichuan in an area that was once part of Tibet. Until recent times they practiced slash and burn practices on the steep hill slopes. Dwellings are often two or three stories in height—stepped into the hillside—with animals stabled on the ground level

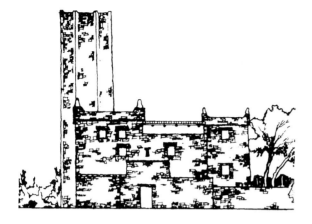

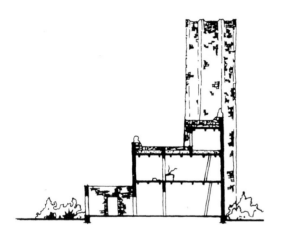

(Figure 6.13). Living space and storage is found on the upper stories, and the flat roof is used for drying grain and laundry as well as for relaxation. One or more larger stone dwellings in a mountain hamlet settlement are accompanied by tall towers that vary somewhat in terms of utility. Some are purely defensive, used only during periods of danger, while others are occupied on a regular basis. Quadrilateral, hexagonal, and octagonal tower shapes have been reported, with heights ranging from four to fourteen stories (Cao 1992, 72ff).

On the extreme eastern margins of the Tibetan plateau in southwestern Sichuan and northwestern Yunnan are the rugged and cold Liangshan Mountains. Here, as well as in the uplands of neighboring northwestern Guizhou and nearby areas of northeastern Yunnan, Guizhou, and Guangxi, are found the Yi, the fourth largest minority group in China. Generally called "Lolo" in the past, a term the Yi saw as insulting, the Yi are a nationality group with a startling degree of cultural diversity and social stratification (Harrell 1995, 63ff). In the Liangshan Yi Autonomous Prefecture of southern Sichuan and the Chuxiong Yi Autonomous Prefecture and other areas of west central Yunnan, Yi traditionally have built distinctive "earthen palm houses" as well as log houses, structures that vary according to the social status of the occupants. "Earthen palm houses" [*tuzhangfang* 土掌房] generally appear like compact palm prints made of earth, placed low on a hill slope as a defense against strong winds and heavy snow (Figure 6.14). Although square

Figure 6.13. Like Tibetans, the Qiang build multistory blockhouses of stone and sometimes adobe on the steep hill slopes of western Sichuan. Dwellings are usually stepped into the hillside, with animals stabled on the ground level and living space above. In some Qiang villages, tall stone towers are used as a refuge during times of strife. Maowen Qiang Autonomous Prefecture, Sichuan. [Source: Cao 1992, 73–74.]

Figure 6.14. "Earthen palm houses," or *tuzhangfang*, are compact and low dwellings made of earth. Built low on a hill slope, they are not impacted by either strong winds or heavy snow. [Source: Yunnan sheng 1986, 168.]

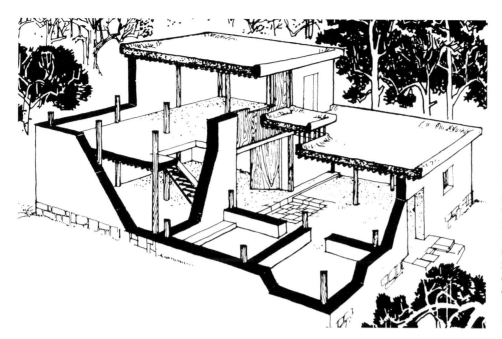

Figure 6.15. In this cutaway view of an adobe-walled Yi dwelling without a courtyard, the upper structure covers but half of the larger lower structure. The remaining portions of the flat room are used as a level area on which to dry grain, and the adjacent high and dry enclosed area is used to store it. The lower story includes a kitchen and storage area toward the front, with a main room and bedrooms in the rear. Although a pigsty is sometimes built into this front section, more typically animals are stabled outside the dwelling. [Source: Yunnan sheng 1986, 162.]

or rectangular *tuzhangfang* with a utilitarian flat roof are also built by Han, Dai, Naxi, and Hani settlers who live among the Yi and Tibetans in this region, Yi dwellings are usually somewhat larger and sometimes combined single- and double-story structures (Figures 6.15 and 6.16).

A newly formed Yi family traditionally lived separately from the husband's parents, contributing to a multiplication of smaller dwellings. While most Yi dwellings include simply a large room, others are built with small courtyards and second stories. Unlike two-story houses in Tibet, the ground level of a Yi dwelling is residential space, and the animals are kept outside in adjacent pens. A large upper-level room is typically used to store grain that has been dried on the flat roof. Exterior walls are always of adobe bricks or

tamped earth rather than stone rubble. According to observations made in 1943, traditional Yi dwellings were dark and dank: "Upon entering the room, one immediately feels suffocated in the nose and mouth by widespread clouds of smoke from the fire in the hearth, . . . the center of all family activities. . . . In the center of the house stands the stove, on the right are the grindstone and animal pen, and on the left the sleeping quarters and grain storage." (Lin 1944 59-

Figure 6.16. Flat-roofed *tuzhangfang,* described by Charles McKhann as "pueblo-style," are built by the Naxi in Muli *xian,* Sichuan. [Original photograph used with the permission of Charles McKhann.]

Figure 6.17. In northern Yunnan, Yi construct simple log dwellings that sometimes take an L- or U-shaped plan. The walls are roughly dressed and usually without windows. The roof cover is made of wood slabs and brush. Da'erdishulohe *cun*, Ninglang Yi Nationality Autonomous *xian*, Yunnan. [Original photograph used with the permission of Asakawa Shigeo.]

60). In recent years, greater attention has been paid to making the roof watertight by increasing its thickness with at least six layers of various materials and in opening windows in the wall for ventilation (Yunnan sheng 1986, 162, 168). The thick earthen walls and roof provide substantial insulation from the cold or heat.

Yi log dwellings [*muleng fang* 木楞房 or *muduo fang* 木垛房], especially common in northern Yunnan, are usually simple rectangular structures with only minimal dressing of the timbers, which are simply notched and piled (Asakawa 1996). Attached structures sometimes create L- or U-shaped plans. Whatever the shape, the walls are generally without windows (Figure 6.17). Interior space is often divided into two rooms with at least one loft for sleeping. The simple roof structure is supported by the dead weight of the timbers. Slabs of wood of various sizes and shapes are used to provide cover for the roofs of Yi log houses. They are rarely secured with nails but are held in place by stones. Thatching is sometimes used as well. Similar log houses are built by the Nu, Lisu, and Pumi minority groups who live among the Yi in the rugged forested areas of Yunnan (Wang and Chen 1993, 86–91, 157ff). *Yikeyin*, as discussed in Chapter 5, also were adopted by Yi in Yunnan who found such structures an appropriate housing form.

Dwellings of Qinghai

Qinghai, a province as well as a physiographic extension of the Tibetan plateau, is a vast, sparsely populated region that is transitional to the warmer and drier areas to its north. Han settlers dominate in the towns and villages of the east near Xining, but elsewhere Tibetan, Hui, Tu, Salar, and Mongol settlers are distributed in concentrations generally apart from each other. Dwellings of Tibetans, Hui, and Mongols in Qinghai generally differ little from those elsewhere in China where the groups are found in much greater numbers. The 200,000 Tu and 90,000 Salar, on the other hand, are not found in significant numbers beyond the borders of Qinghai.

The Tu are concentrated in areas to the east of Qinghai Lake and south of the Qilian range in areas in which they are still a minority. Their language is related to the Mongol language, and although they are identified as a distinct nationality group, they are sometimes thought to be descendants of Mongolians who occupied eastern Qinghai during the Yuan dynasty (Ma 1989, 114). Once principally herders of sheep and goats, Tu probably lived in yurtlike tents, but since at least the Ming dynasty Tu have been farmers and merchants living in dwellings similar to Han and other settlers in the semiarid northwest.

Perhaps originating in the Samarkand area of Cen-

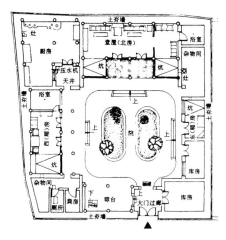

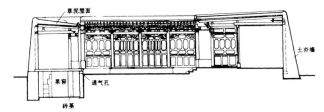

Figure 6.18. Living in villages along the banks of the Huanghe River in southeastern Qinghai, the Salar build low tamped earth walled structures that surround a courtyard. Entry is through a single gate into a courtyard approximately 40 centimeters below a surrounding raised foundation on which bedrooms and other halls are built against the outer walls. The 4.5-meter-tall tamped earth wall surrounding the dwelling is battered, approximately 1 meter thick at the base and tapering to perhaps 40 centimeters at the top. The roof is a composition of earth and vegetative matter. [Source: Liang 1995, 179.]

tral Asia, the Salar live today principally in Xunhua county of southeastern Qinghai along the banks of the Huanghe River. Sharing a Turkic language and the Islamic religion with Uygurs and Uzbeks, Salar today are mainly farmers practicing irrigated agriculture. Salar live in square walled structures, called in Chinese *zhuangkuo* 庄廓 and also *zhuangke* 庄窠, that have similarities with common Tibetan, Uygur, and

even Han courtyard-style dwellings. Salar dwellings are usually larger and more refined than the courtyard dwellings of others. Occupying a total area of at least 333 square meters, each *zhuangkuo* is surrounded by a high tamped earth wall perhaps 4.5 to 5 meters high made from the readily available loam associated with the upper reaches of the Huanghe River.

Enclosed on four sides by the tapered earthen wall and with entry through a single gate in the southeast side, the focus of each *zhuangkuo* is a central courtyard approximately 40 centimeters below a surrounding raised foundation on which connecting structures are built against the windowless outer wall. As is Han practice, a screen wall inside the gate makes it possible for the gate to be open yet the courtyard inside not visible to those passing by. Carved wood and stone associated with the entry gate are usually the only decoration on the exterior of the house.

The principal building of a *zhuangkuo* is placed along the northern wall and made of tamped earth on both ends and wood on the front (Figures 6.18 and 6.19).

Figure 6.19. The large courtyard of a Salar dwelling is surrounded by structures on four sides. Averaging 450 square meters in overall area, each *zhuangkuo* accommodates a single family. Except for the entrance, no other openings puncture the tamped earth wall surrounding the dwelling. [Original photograph used with the permission of Liang Qi.]

Colloquially called "tiger embraces its head" [*hubaotou* 虎抱头], the northern building typically is fronted with an arcaded porch. Interior space is rarely divided by partitions, yet it includes clearly defined areas for reception as well as sleeping. Two *kang*, heated brick beds that are similar to those found widely in northern China, are built along the south-facing wall for family members to enjoy the warmth of the winter sun that comes in through the windows. A large kitchen in the northwestern corner and several bathing areas flank this northern structure. Completing the encirclement of the courtyard are facing side structures that have sleeping rooms for family members and small enclosed areas at the front for storage and for use as a toilet. The flat roofs atop the buildings are made of a thick composition of mud, grasses, straw, and chopped bark. Sloping inward toward the courtyard, the roof is cantilevered to create verandas around the open space. Sections of the roof are reinforced as a drying terrace [*liangtai* 晾台]. Each of the corners of these structures serves a specific purpose: kitchen in the northwest corner, bathing area in the northeast corner, and storage in the southeast and southwest corners. A unique element of Salar dwellings is a well-ventilated subterranean fruit cellar [*guoyao* 果窖] (Liang 1995 178ff).

Dwellings of Xinjiang

More than any other region of China, Xinjiang has always been a dynamic crossroads of Eurasian trade, migration, and invasion that together have contributed to an ethnic diversity that is predominantly Central Asian in origin. As early as the Han dynasty, Chinese garrisons protected the Silk Road, which passed through these western regions along several routes that connected China with the Mediterranean world farther to the west. Imperial control and influence, however, waxed and waned throughout China's history, with only a limited impact on traditional ways of life until relatively recent times. It was not until 1884 that the region was formally incorporated into the imperial administrative system as Xinjiang, or "the New Dominion," the last of China's frontier areas to be consolidated.

With an area of over 1.7 million square kilo-

meters, Xinjiang is larger than Germany, France, Italy, and the United Kingdom combined. Yet with a population of only some 16 million people, most of the autonomous region is virtually empty. Bisected by the 2,500-kilometer-long east-west trending Tianshan range, Xinjiang is divided into two vast basins with distinct climates and landscapes. The alpine meadowed slopes of the Tianshan that pass through the central areas of Xinjiang have been described as "a huge elongated 'wet island' amid the vast expanse of extremely arid deserts" (Zhao 1994, 293), but the temperate Junggar Basin to its north and the bleak Tarim Basin to its south are essentially barren deserts that together represent nearly two-thirds of Xinjiang's total area. Much of what remains are high mountains, such as the Kunlun, Pamir, Karakoram, Altun, and Altai, that effectively isolate Xinjiang from neighboring areas. Capped with glaciers, these fringing wind-chiseled mountains release critical meltwater that has made it possible for downslope settlement to emerge in oases settlements that are spaced along the fabled caravan trails like a handful of pearls on a fragile string.

Most of Xinjiang's population live today in cities and towns. In southern Xinjiang, the bulk of the population resides in towns that were once ancient oases settlements, where water was available along the break in slope between basins and foothills. These oases anchored merchant-oriented settlement and nurtured a pastoral economy based on nearby seasonal pastures, where sun, water, and slope created favorable microclimates. Nearly 62 percent of Xinjiang's population is comprised of thirteen minority nationality groups, with Uygurs and Kazaks dominating. The Han population has increased substantially over the past fifty years and today represents about 38 percent of the region's total. Even though Han still do not exceed the Uygur population (47 percent of the total), Han are more likely than Uygurs to live in concentrated urban settlements. Hui, Mongol, Kirgiz, Tajik, Uzbek, and Xibe principally live among the Uygur and Kazak in well-defined concentrations that have been recognized through the formation of autonomous counties and prefectures in which these smaller minorities predominate.

The largest minority nationality group in Xinjiang, numbering over 7 million, the Uygur have two major centers of settlement. Torrid Turpan (Tulufan in Chinese) in the northeast, with China's highest recorded temperature (47.6EC), and Kashgar (Kashi) in the distant southwest at the edge of the forbidding Taklimakan desert are linked to each other across the vast sun-scorched desert via the oases settlement outposts. Farmland, which totals only 2.5 percent of Xinjiang's total area, is concentrated in those isolated oases areas, which have been favored for settlement either because of natural runoff from mountain glaciers or because they have been reclaimed from sandy or rocky deserts through the extension of irrigation systems.

Wherever Uygur dwellings are located in Xinjiang, they are designed to mitigate the intense heat, wind, and dry desert conditions that are not easily avoided. As in other areas of the world with an arid climate, there is marked diurnal fluctuation from intense heat early in the afternoon to uncomfortably low nighttime temperatures near daybreak. The Uygur solution is quite similar to that achieved elsewhere:

> by use of high heat capacity materials, such as adobe or pisé, mud, stone, and various combinations of these which provide a "heat sink," absorbing heat during the day and reradiating it during the night; by as compact a geometry as possible, which provides maximum volume with minimum surface area exposed to the outside heat; by mutual crowding, which provides shading, and reduces the areas exposed to the sun while increasing the mass of the whole building group, thus increasing the time lag. Heat buildup is avoided by separating cooking, often done outside the house; by reducing the number and size of windows and placing them high up to reduce ground radiation; by painting the house white or some other light color to reflect a maximum of radiant heat; and by minimizing ventilation during the hot time of the day. (Rapoport 1969, 89-90)

The Turpan-Komul (Hami) subregion in eastern Xinjiang, among the hottest and driest areas of the world, was also a strategically important center of urban development in historical times and is an important area today of Uygur rural and town life. The remains of the cities of Yarkhoto (Jiaohe) and Idikot (Gaochang) reveal numerous subterranean rooms, habitats chosen to benefit from the thermal performance of the earth. Further, in an area that rarely experiences rainfall, life would be impossible without *karez*, long underground tunnels that have continued to be used to tap upslope sources of moisture and lead water downslope to areas of settlement. Ancient *karez*, newly dug wells, and canal irrigation today guide settlement and make possible the growing of cotton, fruit such as apricot, melons, and peaches as well as viticulture.

The use of exterior space is an important element of most Xinjiang dwellings. Dwellings with interior earthen barrel roofs that are flat on the outside are common in the Turpan area, a building form found in the nearby urban excavations as well. The building of an adobe barrel arch roof reduces the need for spanning logs. Throughout the Turpan Basin, Uygur dwellings usually include courtyards with an open trellis that supports grape vines with large, shade-producing leaves (Figures 6.20 and 6.21). As overhead shading devices, trellises partially block or filter direct and intense sunlight, in the process reflecting the sun's rays to create softer daylighting. Moreover, loose vines and broad leaves catch passing breezes to cool the area beneath. Sometimes the trellised patio is even linked to a passing stream of cool water in a *karez*, in which case evaporative cooling helps to "air condition" the outdoor space. Interior rooms often have a skylight open to the outside that serves as a flue to evacuate warm air. Sometimes a subterranean or semisubterranean space is dug out for year-round cool storage of vegetables, grain, and fruit. In the grape-growing areas of Turpan, a common feature is the use of a portion of the roof for drying grapes. Since grapes are dried by air rather than by the sun, it is essential that the area, known as a "grape air-curing room" [*qunqe* in Uygur and *putao liangfang* 葡萄晾房 in Chinese], be protected from the sun but be open to the drying wind. A parapet of open brickwork allows air to pass through each *putao liangfang* so that it becomes essentially a perforated room with racks set up to hold the grapes while they air dry beneath a roof that shades them from the sun. While fulfilling a needed role in preserving grapes, *putao liangfang* also ameliorate temperatures in the dwelling below by reducing the absorption of solar radiation during the day and facilitating back radiation of heat at night. Due to local microclimates, some areas of the Turpan-Komul that experience severe summer convectional thunderstorms do not have "grape air-curing rooms" on the roof (Figure 6.22).

At the distant edge of the rain-starved Taklimakan Desert in southwestern Xinjiang is Kashgar, the westernmost and largest of the fabled oasis bazaars along the southern Silk Road. Fed by glacial meltwater from the Pamirs, which loom above the basin, numerous streams split into multiple channels to create

a lush oasis that has drawn significant populations to it over time. The passage of traders from both directions invested this intermediary outpost settlement with a broad range of Central Asian building traditions characteristic of towns. Beijing was a 125 day caravan journey to the east and Ferghana, Samarkand, and Persia lay far to the west, reachable only after traversing difficult high mountain passes and the steppes of Turkestan. As with other oases, there were upslope settlements of nomadic people nearby who enriched the bazaars with their local products and cultural patterns.

Rural dwellings in the Kashgar oasis often are ringed with olivelike oleaster trees to create a windbreak. Houses themselves take many forms but most include a walled garden with dense plantings of deciduous trees and a grape arbor. Shade and evaporative cooling in summer naturally give way to openness in winter for needed sunlight. Sometimes part of the roof is shaded with an arborlike structure, where residents may enjoy the evening breeze. Many dwellings in the town of Kashgar have at their core an *aywan*, a Uygur term meaning "bright garden" or "moon garden" [*ayiwang* 阿以旺 in Chinese transliteration]. An *aywan*, as seen in Figures 6.23 and 6.24, is a sunken open space larger than the skywells, or *tianjing*, found in southern China yet smaller than northern courtyards. *Aywan* are typically wrapped by a compact two-story structure with broad verandas. In this fashion, *aywan* are located at the center of a family's daily life much as are courtyards elsewhere in the

Figure 6.20 (top left). Within the torrid Tulufan Basin, Uygur dwellings are usually compact structures with thick earthen walls. Barrel-arched structures provide substantial insulation and give form to rooms. A walled courtyard usually has several trees and adjacent verandas on the surrounding buildings. [Source: Huang 1996, 52.]

Figure 6.21 (bottom left). Interior view across the courtyard reveals ventilation ports, shaded patios, and recessed verandas. Tulufan, Xinjiang. [Source: Zhang 1995, 143.]

Figure 6.22. "Grape air-curing rooms," *qunqe* in Uygur and *putao liang-fang* in Chinese, are sometimes built atop the flat roofs of Uygur dwellings or at a nearby location, as seen here. Open brickwork lets air pass through to the racks that hold the grapes, which are transformed into raisins as they are dried by the dessicating air. [RGK photograph 1984.]

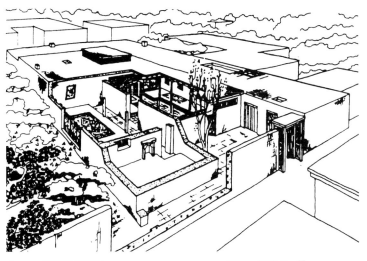

Figure 6.23. As in Tulufan, Uygur dwellings in Kashgar are low and compact and include a shaded courtyard. [Source: Huang Zhongbin 1996, 47.]

Figure 6.24. Dwellings throughout the Kashgar region usually have an *aywan* at their core. *"Aywan"* is a Uygur term meaning "bright garden" or "moon garden" and is a sunken open space larger than the skywells, or *tianjing*, found in southern China but smaller than northern courtyards. [Source: Huang Zhongbin 1996, 50.]

world. High surrounding walls made of earth and without windows act as a barrier to the wind and dust that blow from beyond the oasis. These enclosing earthen walls average 50 centimeters in thickness, wider at the bottom and narrower at the top. Throughout the *aywan*, shaded space is readily available, even if it "moves" as the sun passes across the sky. Local variations in temperature cause the air to stir freely in breezes. Windows facing the *aywan* are normally opened only in the morning and in the evening to exchange air and left closed during most of the day to keep the heat out. Groups of walled houses usually cluster also around a small common open space, a kind of piazza that is also called an *aywan*, that has only one narrow access route to the larger community beyond. Several such isolated dwelling groups and *aywan* have at their hub a larger public square that contains a mosque as well as a public water supply and toilet (Ruxianguli 1993). Whether in town or in the country, the profuse use of vegetation in and around Uygur dwellings creates microclimates that temper the harsh extremes of climate in any season.

Kazaks, a Turkic people with a population of over 1 million, principally live in northern Xinjiang in the Ili Valley and on the northern slopes of the Tianshan mountains as well as in several adjacent parts of Qinghai and Gansu provinces. Although some Kazaks are settled farmers, most are herdsmen who raise horses, sheep, and goats. Kazak herders practice transhumance, as they move with the passage of the seasons in search of pasture. Spring and fall they generally occupy the same lower pasture, while as the mountain snows melt in summer, they move their flocks to grassy open areas on higher slopes. Through this three-season rotation, Kazaks live in collapsible "felt tents" called *kigiz öy* in Kazak and *zhanzhang* 毡帐 or *zhanfang* 毡房 in Chinese, which are rather tall round "yurts" that they transport to and assemble at each location. Among the various pastoral groups, tentlike structures are called "houses" and are distinguished by color as "white houses" or "black houses. "Yurt" is a word of Turkic origin meaning "dwelling" and is appropriate in describing domed tentlike structures in Xinjiang; thus, it will be used throughout this section.

Unlike Tibetan tents, which are often rectangular, Kazak and Mongol yurts, to be discussed later, are round, with a diameter of 4 to 5 meters, although some may reach as much as 15 meters. Kazak yurts, as seen in Figures 6.25 and 6.26, are relatively simple truncated conical structures that can be assembled and dismantled easily. The round shape arises from the simplicity of wrapping the shape with a frame of pliant and braided willow saplings that can be stretched and rolled. The aerodynamic quality of a round shape allows wind from any direction to be deflected around the shape. The wooden poles that are used to weave the individual latticelike wall panels range from 1.8 to 2.5 meters in length and 2 to 3 centimeters in diameter. When the accordionlike frame is fully engaged, each of the side poles is at about a 45-degree angle to the ground. Because the frame and side poles support themselves without needing to be dug into the ground, a yurt can be pitched even where the ground is frozen. The integrity of the circular canopy framework emerges from the lashing together of 2-to-3-meter-long bent wooden ribs that are first tied to the side wall and then extended, gathered, and attached to an elevated 1-to-1.5-meter-diameter ring. To counter the outward thrust of the wooden ribs where they join the woven wall framework, a tension band is woven along the top of the lattice frame in order to pull the forces inward. Once assembled, the frame is then covered with layers of felt made of matted sheep hair that are lashed tightly with cord made of sheep or cattle hair (Chen 1995, 185–187).

Doors of Kazak dwellings generally open to the east, range between 1.5 and 1.6 meters high, and are 70 to 80 centimeters wide. The interior circular floor space of perhaps 20 square meters is typically covered with several rectangular rugs and its use follows a general order (Figure 6.27). Trunks and cabinets typically are lined like chords along the curved wall facing the door and are piled high with blankets and other household items. Here, farthest from the door, is also where the senior generation will sleep. Other family members sleep nearby. Utensils used for cooking are normally kept on the right side inside the door, while riding gear is usually deposited on the left side, where young lambs are also sometimes

Figure 6.25 (top). During a three-season pastoral rotation, Kazaks live in collapsible felt tents that are relatively simple truncated conical structures. The yurt on the left appears less tall because its top covering has been removed. Both yurts have been raised on cement floors, which indicates that the sites are occupied on a perennial basis by at least some family members while others carry portable tents and move their animals from pasture to pasture. Northern slopes of Tianshan mountains. [RGK photograph 1984.]

Figure 6.26 (bottom). Kazak tents, called *kigiz öy* in Kazak, can be assembled and dismantled easily. The outer form is defined by a latticelike frame of pliant and braided willow saplings that can be stretched and rolled. Once the accordionlike frame is fully engaged, the frame is covered on the outside with layers of felt made of matted sheep hair and lashed tightly with cord made of sheep or cattle hair. Tianchi, Xinjiang Uygur Autonomous Region, 1994. [Original photograph used with the permission of Stanley Toops.]

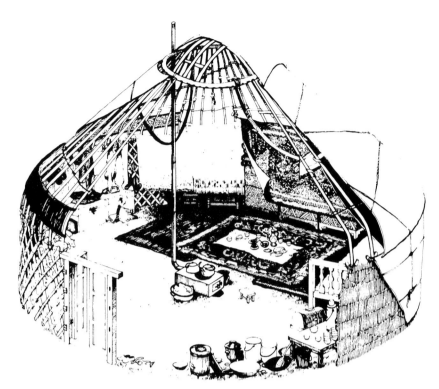

Figure 6.27. This drawing of the structure and furnishings of a Kazak yurt reveals the simple materials used in its construction as well as the ordered placement of interior furnishings. [Source: Chen 1994, 110.]

nursed. When necessary, a stove is lit near the center of the yurt for heat and to keep milk tea warm, placed here at a focal position for all members of the family and to allow the smoke to be evacuated easily through an opening at the apex of the yurt. Since nearby areas outside the yurt are also considered living space, a second cooking stove is often placed just outside the door. The height of the conical interior of a Kazak yurt is substantially greater than that found in either Kirgiz or Mongol yurts, which will be discussed next. It may well be that the elevated roof and aperture at the apex enhances the evacuation of hot air during the summer, a natural condition more likely in areas where Kazaks reside than in those occupied by either Kirgiz or Mongols.

In order to pass the winter, Kazaks traditionally occupy relatively crude huts made of logs, grasses, stone, and mud as temporary quarters. These simple dwellings are called "winter houses" [*kixlik öy*] in Kazak and somewhat pejoratively "winter nests" [*dongwo* 冬窝] in Chinese translation. Often dug into the ground and with thick walls for warmth, winter dwell-

ings are usually placed in locations that are protected from the wind but exposed to the sun (Figures 6.28 and earlier in Figure 3.118). Improved, relatively permanent "winter nests" increasingly have been built in recent years near the spring/fall pasture areas in order to leave the elderly and children there year-round. Those who migrate with their animals in search of pasture and with their yurts borne on the backs of animals return to these fixed encampments for substantial periods of time except during the three months of summer when they are in high pasture areas far from any settlement. Each of the sites chosen for setting up yurts and log huts is determined on the basis of knowledge of favorable microclimatic conditions.

Chinese policy today favors the transformation of transhumant pastoralists into settled ranchers or farmers. In recent years, this has resulted in the building of substantial permanent winter structures, a recasting with obvious implications for traditional Kazak dwellings. Many of these fixed dwellings are made of finished logs or fired bricks. Some are sim-

Figure 6.28. A cluster of crude huts made of stacked logs, grasses, stone, and mud provides temporary winter quarters for Kazak herders on the slopes of Mount Bogda in the eastern Tianshan mountains. Protected from the cold winds by the hill slopes upon which they are built, yet open to the winter sun, these low dwellings are reasonably comfortable during the wintering-over period. With thick walls for warmth, winter dwellings are usually placed in locations that are protected from the wind and open to the sun. Near Tianchi Lake, east of Urumqi, Xinjiang. [RGK photograph 1984.]

ple rectangular structures, while others involve side buildings and courtyards. While it is not surprising that the exterior neither evokes the shape nor materials of a traditional round yurt, the interior accommodates well the rectangular chests, rugs, and wall decorations that often appeared misfitted to the arcuate spaces within yurts. Unlike yurts with their shared and multipurpose spaces, permanent Kazak dwellings, like those of farmers and others, typically have individual rooms for sleeping, reception, cooking, and storage.

The Kirgiz, while practicing animal husbandry like the Kazaks, live principally in the windy mountain nexus linking the Pamir, Karakoram, and Kunlun mountains in southwestern Xinjiang. Under conditions in which summers are merely warm and winters are bitterly cold, Kirgiz yurts stand less tall than do those of the Kazaks. Kirgiz yurts, with their lowered hemispheric roofline closely resembling Mongol yurts that generally do not exceed 3 meters, are better suited to withstanding strong winds than Kazak yurts. Besides differences in profile, Kirgiz yurts often are covered with mats made of grasses as well as white felt with appliquéd patterns. Piled stones are sometimes placed in the direction of the prevailing winds to serve as a windbreak.

Nearly 150,000 Mongols live in eastern and northeastern Xinjiang, with the majority living in the Bayan Nur Prefecture on the Alashan plateau. Here on the edges of the rocky desert and adjacent steppe, Mongols live a pastoral life using yurts similar to those found in Inner Mongolia, which will be discussed in detail in the following section. Some Mongols, however, live on the southern forested slopes of the Altai Mountains in northeastern Xinjiang where Russia, Mongolia, and China join. Where a variety of building materials are available, Mongols build permanent structures of stone, adobe, and logs. Among the interesting forms are yurtlike dwellings of stacked logs. These "round" dwellings usually have ten faces, as seen earlier in Figure 3.120, formed of notched logs that are infilled with a mud and grass nogging. A crude dome is made of piled logs to form an inverted caisson with an aperture at the top that allows smoke to escape. For the most part, the interior layout maintains the plan of traditional Mongol *ger* found elsewhere to the east on the great grasslands of Mongolia.

Dwellings of Inner Mongolia

From the perspective of the cardinal directions, it is a geographical stretch to place Inner Mongolia in western China, since the autonomous region obviously embraces China's northern flank. However, from the perspective of China Proper, the geograph-

Figure 6.29. Building a Mongol *ger* involves first assembling the wooden framework, then wrapping it with felt panels that are strapped together with cords. Inner Mongolia. [Source: Zhongguo kexueyuan 1957, 75.]

ical term used to describe the area within the Great Wall, the broad grasslands of Mongolia are indeed an outlying frontier region with environmental and cultural affinities more like Xinjiang and Tibet than the agrarian civilization that dominates to its south. Chinese cultural geographers make such a distinction, placing Inner Mongolia in western China even though Chinese architects generally do not (Jin 1989, 195-196; Jin 1990, 490-493; Wang 1994, 2). Located at relatively high latitudes in the interior of the Asian continent, the Mongolian plateau's altitude also contributes to a continental climate characterized by pronounced seasonal extremes. Winter is long and severe, summer is short and warm, and precipitation is highly variable throughout the year.

Mongol dwellings are almost always referred to in Chinese as *Menggu bao* [Mongol *bao* 蒙古包] rather than *zhanzhang* [felt tents], the Chinese term introduced earlier for Kazak yurts. Mongols themselves call their tentlike structures *ger*, and it is this term that will be used here to denote the dwellings of Mongol pastoralists rather than the more general "yurt." The origin of the term "*bao*" 包 has been linked to the Manchu word for "dwelling" (Wang 1994, 7), but its etymological lineage indeed may be as convoluted as that of the word "yurt," itself a Russian word borrowed from Turkic languages and used in English to describe the round transportable habitats found throughout the grasslands of Asia.

The use of round shapes for dwellings has a long history in East Asia. That simple round structures were built at neolithic Banpo and that large and complex *tulou* continued to be built by the Hakka in Fujian even in recent times suggest that there indeed are multiple structural, environmental, and social factors that must contribute to the widespread adoption of the round form. No single factor alone determines a particular form. While sociocultural factors must be seen as criti-

cally important in much decision-making that relates to habitat, climate is an extremely important "form generating force," to use Rapoport's term. Just as was discussed earlier for Kazaks and Kirgiz, Mongols and other herding peoples of Asia's steppe regions clearly have employed "minimum resources for maximum comfort" in their development of yurtlike structures (Rapoport 1969, 83). For pastoralists, the need for a lightweight portable housing form that could withstand heavy winds and provide warmth in a region of climatic extremes was a critical consideration. Most yurts can be taken down or reassembled in an hour or so. The combined weight of all of the structural parts, the heavy felt covering, and the household's possessions can range between 300 and 700 kilograms, certainly not an insubstantial load for the pack animals who would carry it but bearable in any case. Systematically and compactly stowed, the structure and the household could be set up again in a matter of hours.

The Mongol *ger*, like the Eskimo igloo and the yurts of other pastoralists, is more than simply a round geometrical shape. All are three-dimensional hemispheres of substantial structural strength that readily deflect strong winds by facilitating the air's passage around them. Especially during periods of howling blizzards, the air carries snow past the surface walls of the domes rather than forcing it to pile up, accumulate, and ultimately bury the structures, a likely condition where wind would encounter a rectangular building. With an aerodynamic hemispheric shape, side walls that reach approximately 1.4 meters high, and a total height of perhaps 2.2 meters, a Mongol *ger* is a rational solution in an environment with limited choices (Figure 6.29). It is likely that the hemispheric shape of the *ger* evolved from earlier conical forms that had roof supports reaching directly to the ground but no "walls." *Ger* may also have evolved from simple hemispherical huts of wicker. There are poetic and artistic representations of *ger*-like structures that reach to the eighth century (Dinsmore 1985, 17–18). Lattimore observed that Mongols even in the 1930s often simply set up the roof sections of their *ger* as they moved about, adding the wall portions only when an encampment was to be relatively long (1938, 9–10).

While there are essential similarities between Kazak "felt tents" and Mongol *ger*, there are certain differences. Both utilize similar expandable multiple latticelike panels to form side walls. Both Kazak and Mongol wall panels pack tightly when closed and are relatively light and portable, but once extended they constitute a remarkably stable framework. Three standardized elements of the structural skeleton of a *ger* are commonly identified: *hana*, wall framework; *wuni*, rafterlike roof supports; and *taonao*, crown opening. Each of these terms is a Chinese transcription from the Mongol language. Between four and eight *hana* 哈那 [Mongol *qana*] are tied together with leather strips, as are the individual *wuni* 乌尼 [Mongol *uni*] ribs that reach upward toward the stabilizing circular hoop called a *taonao* 陶脑 [Mongol *toϒono*]. Wooden portions of the skeleton are generally made today of desert poplar, a lightweight and flexible material, but traditionally willow and larch were used (McColl 1989, 1; Dinsmore 1985, 57, 65). Unlike the roof supports used in Kazak and Tajik yurts that bend about a third of a meter from their end in order to increase interior height, Mongol *wuni* are rather straight. Each roof pole is tapered at the upper end to fit into the roof ring; the lower end has a hole drilled to facilitate securing it to a section of the wall with a braided cord made of horsehair. Mongol *wuni* are usually painted red and green, un-

like those yurts found in Xinjiang, which are left natural.

For all-weather comfort, the entire structure of a *ger* is covered with sheets of felt of various thicknesses made of fluffed, moistened, compressed, and matted animal fibers obtained from their flocks of sheep. (The making of felt is described by Dinsmore, 1985 154–160). Rectangular and semicircular sheets, the number of which depends on the season, are trimmed and finished along their edges in order to reduce disintegration. Sometimes the edging is ornamented. By overlapping the ends and securing them with cords, felt panels provide a versatile material to meet different seasonal requirements. In summer, perhaps only a single or double layer of felt and loose tie downs are used, since the seepage of moving air is somewhat welcomed. In winter, however, more tightly lashed layers of felt are added in order to enhance insulation and maintain warmth. Sometimes a layer of sand is spread between a few of the felt layers to further block heat from escaping (A Jin 1995, 182). The top layer is sometimes oiled in order to shed rainwater. Today, even vinyl, plastic, and canvas are used to facilitate water runoff in summer and block wind in winter. According to some historical descriptions, Mongols who became sedentary in the late nineteenth century sometimes covered their hemispheric frames with a mixture of mud, reeds, and other materials that could not be disassembled, leaving only a felt flap at the apex (Dinsmore 1985, 27–28). To a greater extent than with the yurts of Turkic groups in Xinjiang, Mongol *ger* often have additional colorful covers of various sizes and shapes laid atop the felt panels of the roof.

Chinese historically have applied the term *"tianchuang"* 天窗 [heavenly window or skylight] to the *taonao* aperture at the top of a *ger* to connote the notions of "chimney" and "window." According to one observer, this *taonao*, "the smoke hole that corresponds to the hearth also symbolizes the unity of the family" (Stein 1990, 157). The roof ring that gives shape to the *taonao* aperture usually has holes along its circumference into which the roof ribs are seated. Depending on the size of the *ger* and differing from place to place, the *taonao* vary in complexity. While some may be nothing more than a ring reinforced with several crossing ribs, others are geometrically complex with multiple concentric rings and cross-pieces. Cammann observed in the Ordos area that the roof ring included eight braces and conjectured that this perhaps represented the Buddhist Wheel of Law in an early form as the Sun Wheel (1951, 124-125). Overlapping felt sheets reached across the aperture in a way that flaps could be easily moved open or closed in response to need for light and air. It is normally opened during the day and closed at night.

As with Kazak yurts, the *ger* has only a single entry and no windows, but the entry to a Mongol *ger* typically faces either due south or southeast for maximum early light. Entryways may be nothing more than a flap of felt, a carpet, a reed panel, or single or double panels of wood fitted within a wooden door frame attached to *hana* sections. A door frame is rectangular in shape and held together with leather straps. The lintel must be substantial enough to seat the roof poles. Traditional felt flaps are believed to provide greater winter insulation than other forms that constitute a door cover. Although the thresholds of modern *ger* are nothing more than a cross-piece holding the two jambs together, such apparently was not the case in the past. Dinsmore's study of nineteenth- and early twentieth-century photographs reveals thresholds up to one-third the height of doorways, presumably as a means to reduce drafts (1985, 78-79).

Even though the interior is not subdivided into separate "rooms," those who live within are cognizant of prescribed functions for different areas even though the areas are not marked physically except by the placement of small handwoven rugs. The principal position within is directly opposite the door at a location that can be described as "north" or "back," and it is nearby that religious images and articles are displayed. Also in this inner area, valuables are stored in brightly painted wooden chests. Women utilize the area to the right of the door, actually the eastern or northeastern half depending on the overall orientation. The opposite half is an area for men that is also used to entertain guests. Just as with Kazak yurts, a fire pit or stove that uses cow or sheep dung is placed near the center. By adjusting the size of the entryway and the upper aperture, it is generally possible to promote a draft to re-

Figure 6.30. Beyond the grasslands, in the Ordos desert area of western Inner Mongolia, small fixed settlements comprising a dwelling, a *ger*, a courtyard, and a corral are sometimes found. [Source: Graf zu Castell 1934, 119.]

move most of the smoke. The presence of black soot within many traditional *ger* suggests at least occasional inefficiencies in evacuating smoke from the inside. Riding and hunting gear as well as shears for fleecing are placed just inside the entry on the left in the men's area, while cooking utensils, dippers, buckets, tins of milk, a butter churn, and perhaps a small loom are kept on the right. For the most part, observers have noted that these basic and essential items are found in *ger* of all types, differing only in quality according to the means of the household (Dinsmore 1985, 144-146; Cammann 1951, 63). In order to heat the earth beneath a *ger* in winter, channels are sometimes dug horizontally beneath to contain burning coals or grass that radiate warmth into the interior above.

Both the *wuni* ribs that constitute the roof frame and the circular *taonao* aperture are normally

Figure 6.31. This Han-style five-*jian* house has been built by Mongols adjacent to their *ger*. Hohhot area, Inner Mongolia. [RGK photograph 1986.]

painted red to represent the sun and its radiating heat and light. Blue cloth panels, representing the sky, are often hung along the *hana* frame (A Jin 1995, 182-184). The colors white and green, which are also found on *ger*, are associated with "white food" prepared from milk products and the grass of the steppe.

Before setting up the skeleton of a *ger* at a site, the grass must first be uprooted before the soil is leveled and pounded firm. Sometimes wooden planks are laid to form a floor, but generally only sheets of felt or, if resources permit, finely woven rugs are spread instead. A typical Mongol household, depending on its size, will occupy one to three adjacent *ger*, but larger households may have twice as many. The placement of a group of *ger* may appear rather random, either in a circle around an open area or in a line. Slope, prevailing winds, availability of water, sun, and the need to provide protected areas for flocks are always considered when siting *ger* encampments. Besides individual ger, Mongols traditionally built large movable structures as palaces and lodges and to serve ceremonial purposes. Some reportedly were so complex that they were not disassembled but were lifted as a unit and carted by camels or oxen (Dinsmore 1985, 20).

Throughout the twentieth century, as seen in Figure 6.30, Mongols have built dwellings adjacent to their *ger* wherever a fixed settlement was possible. In recent years in Inner Mongolia as well as Xinjiang, Mongols and other pastoralists have been building stationary *ger*-like structures of modern materials, such as metal and cement, in addition to rectangular houses like those of nearby Han settlers (Figure 6.31). Typically built atop a circular cement platform, modernized *ger* are often a meter or so larger in diameter than traditional ones, have several windows, perhaps a skylight or two, and sometimes a system linked to flues that pass beneath the floor for radiant heating of the interior.

Even tepee-like structures covered with bark, cloth, or felt—similar to those associated with some Native American and Eurasian pastoral peoples—continued to be used by some smaller minority groups on the eastern sections of the Mongolian grasslands and in nearby forested hill slopes well into the twentieth century. The Ewenki and Oroqen originated in the forested areas northeast of the Lake Baikal region of Siberia where they fished, hunted, and herded, subsequently bringing these practices to the upper reaches of the Heilongjiang River valley, where they had ready contact with Manchus and Mongols. Although adopting some dwelling forms of those they came to live among, Ewenki continued to live in simple conical structures made of larch poles that were covered with birch bark in summer and reindeer hides in winter (Figure 6.32). Traditional Ewenki tepee-like structures are rarely seen today as

a result of the reduction of herding and transition to sedentary settlements. While some Oroqen live in Inner Mongolia and in Heilongjiang, most continue to live in forested areas of the Greater Hingan Mountains that separate the Mongolian plateau from the Manchurian plain.

It is more than a curiosity that the efforts to integrate and assimilate minority nationalities in China throughout the twentieth century have also contributed to enhancing ethnic identity. Economic development and the reach of state policies into even remote villages have led in recent years to a general narrowing of differences among minority groups. "Although the 1980s saw a substantial revival of traditions [including those related to vernacular architecture], the overall impact of PRC rule in the 1990s has been to weaken those old patterns of culture and lifestyle which highlighted the differences among the nationalities" (Mackerras 1994, 270). Dwelling types that are no longer being built are now nonetheless visible as reconstructions in folk architecture museums, where the distinctive styles of individual groups are contrasted.

Figure 6.32. Oroqen and Ewenki traditionally built simple conical structures made of larch poles that were covered with birch bark in summer and reindeer hides in winter. As herding and hunting has lessened, more have moved into log dwellings. This is a replica of an Oroqen tepee-like structure in the Chinese Ethnic Culture Park, Beijing. [RGK photograph 1996.]

Part IV

EPILOGUE

CHAPTER 7

Looking Forward: The Future of China's Past

ECONOMIC DEVELOPMENT IN CHINA over the past two decades has been accompanied by an unprecedented construction boom that has led to the wholesale destruction of countless humble as well as fine old dwellings. Throughout even the preceding thirty years, many historic residences, temples, lineage halls, libraries, museums, city walls, and tombs were razed, abandoned, or renovated for alternative uses as a result of a series of calamitous political movements. Particularly noteworthy was the senseless depredation of the Great Proletarian Cultural Revolution (1966-1976), in which hooliganism under the guise of "destroying the 'four olds' and establishing the 'four news'" [*po si jiu, li si xin* 破四旧·立四新—the four olds being "thought, culture, customs, and habits"] wiped out a substantial amount of the material cultural heritage of Han as well as ethnic minorities. With this irredeemable spoliation as prologue, the Chinese public and leadership is now confronting the dilemma of carrying out rapid modernization while securing a place in the country's future for China's past. Issues relating to buildings—China's architectural patrimony—as irreplaceable components of China's cultural heritage are an important component of these concerns. With recent habits and actions exposing a lack of consciousness of and incredible insensitivity to historic preservation, the task is indeed formidable.

Over the past fifty years, China's population swelled from 583 million in 1953 to 1.2 billion as the century ends, an order of magnitude that has overwhelmed the country's supply of housing. With only minimal attention paid to new housing construction during most of the early decades after 1949, existing dwellings and other structures were subdivided to provide mere shelter for increasing numbers of people, leading inexorably to the dilapidation of dwellings throughout the country. It was not until the late 1970s that the Chinese government began to acknowledge a critical housing problem facing people living in rural as well as urban areas and initiated policies that would lead to improvements in living standards for the Chinese people (Knapp and Shen 1991, 1992; Knapp 1996). While the ultimate wherewithal for correcting the problem of substandard housing came less from government than from dramatic increases in income, which made it possible for individual households to carry out capital improvements, the unplanned expansion of new and improved housing has brought in its wake the widespread and indiscriminate destruction of old dwellings.

By 1982, nearly one in three rural households was building a new house or substantially renovating an existing one. New construction included not only the use of traditional styles with familiar materials but also the introduction of designs and materials that broke with tradition (Wood 1987; Knapp 1986, 125-151). In 1984 alone, nearly 50 percent of new housing was of kiln-dried brick and wood frame construction, with only 15 percent of earth and thatch. By 1988, the percentage using higher quality brick and concrete materials increased to 85 percent, and this percentage has remained steady ever since. Shortages of timber and new policies advocating the use of prefabricated concrete materials for floor and roof panels further encouraged these changes. In addition, efforts by planners to reduce the amount of land occupied by housing helped stimulate multistory designs even in areas where they had not been traditionally common. More and better housing indeed was constructed in China's villages between 1979 and 1985 than in the previous three decades. Overall, between 1978 and 1995, the average room area per person in rural China nearly doubled from 10.17 to 20.22 square meters (Guojia tongjiju 1985, 102; 1996, 290). In urban areas, however, where the national target is only 8 square meters per person by the year 2000, changes have been substantial, although not as drastic as in the countryside. The construction and rehabilitation of urban housing remains substantially the responsibility of government and work units, even though the reform of the socialist housing system has increased private market initiatives (Shaw 1997).

This long overdue renewal of housing stock of course has come at a substantial price: the obliteration of not only old and crumbling dwellings of no significant value but also notable structures of historic importance. In addition, the acceptance of new designs and materials has ruptured links with local styles and building conventions, bringing about a striking homogenization of housing in a country once known for the diversity of local traditions. Builders and households have accepted the use of reinforced concrete posts and beams where wood once was used exclusively—a compelling necessity in a country still plagued by a shortage of building timber. Furthermore, new rural settlement patterns involving blocklike residential structures have imposed a monotonous rhythm to building forms in the countryside and in urban areas as well. The impact of large-scale public works projects such as the damming of the Yangzi River Gorges has meant sacrificing notable archaeological and architecturally significant sites. In some cases, such as Dachang, a Ming period village, efforts are being made to relocate a collection of old structures on higher ground but many irreplaceable structures will be inundated. The perennial peril brought by flood, as in summer 1998 when several million families were made home-

less, continues to indiscriminately sweep away old and new dwellings.

Chapter 1 reviewed the tortuous efforts of professionals and amateurs throughout the twentieth century in documenting and preserving the country's architectural patrimony. For all too long and with disastrous consequences, both deliberate actions and apathetic indifference have worked against the recognition and conservation of buildings of all types and the settings in which they are placed. Many unnoticed and unheralded dwellings, it is sad to say, continue to be destroyed because their residents, and others regard them as too ordinary, outdated, and dysfunctional to maintain. Interest in issues of historical preservation have only a limited scope in China, and only a relatively small number of individuals see preserving vernacular structures as important components of protecting China's cultural heritage. As in other areas of the world, the Chinese appreciation of their vernacular built heritage has come about only slowly, a striking contrast with the well-known reverence for their imperial architectural patrimony. Nonetheless, in China today there is an overdue awakening, a slowly growing awareness of the need for historic preservation not only to capture some of the essence of China's great past but also to serve the needs of domestic and international tourists.

Until 1978, tourism in China generally served political rather than economic objectives and only indirectly fostered the preservation of old dwellings. Foreigners visiting China during the Maoist years were commonly viewed as "friends" rather than "tourists," and itineraries focused more on learning about changes under socialism than on understanding China's traditional culture. Visits to factories, communes, and schools complemented obligatory excursions to symbols of the feudal past, such as the Great Wall, Forbidden City, and Tomb of the First Qin Emperor. In some cases, foreign friends traveled to revolutionary sites, as did countless Chinese on pilgrimages, in which traditional dwellings provided mere stages for elucidating Communist doctrine. Prominent among these were Mao Zedong's boyhood home; the tawny caves at Yan'an, Shaanxi, where Mao and his legions lived after the Long March; and the fabled manor complex known as

"Rent Collection Courtyard." Chairman Mao's birthplace in Shaoshan, Hunan, discussed earlier in Chapter 2, became the preeminent revolutionary shrine during the Cultural Revolution as countless zealous Red Guards trekked there for revolutionary inspiration. Today, this modest yet sprawling *sanheyuan*-type dwelling that preserves an example of a late Qing rural dwelling draws nearly 1.5 million domestic and foreign tourists each year and is described in press accounts as a "travel hot spot." "Rent Collection Courtyard" gained fame in the autumn of 1965 when a large set of life-size clay figures were installed in the sprawling residence of Liu Wencai in Dayi *xian*, Sichuan, that became "a museum where the blood crimes of the landlord class are exposed as a lesson for the masses in class struggle." A number of other large traditional dwellings were similarly seconded for revolutionary purposes and thus fortuitously preserved; but far greater numbers were deliberately vandalized or altered to meet the needs of peasant families who moved into spaces once reserved for well-to-do landlord households.

While foreign tourism in China has grown substantially over the past twenty years, changing in focus and intent over time, it is the explosive growth of the domestic tourism industry since the mid-1980s that has had the greatest impact on the restoration of old structures and the re-creation of ersatz historic sites. By 1992, nearly 330 million domestic tourists had already begun to overwhelm the transportation and lodging infrastructure of the country as they visited the limited number of historic sites and natural areas open to the public. Recognizing the potential of domestic tourism as a means to gain wealth, local boosters as well as international investors vied quickly to create facilities to tap this growing demand of mass domestic tourism and reap the benefits of visits by Chinese compatriots from Taiwan, Hong Kong, and Macao.

Homes of personages such as the Peking opera star Mei Lanfang in Beijing, the author Lu Xun in Beijing and Shanghai, the painter Qi Baishi in Hunan, and even religious figures such as the Dalai Lama in Diancai, Ping'an *xian*, Qinghai, have all been designated as "cultural relics" and opened to tourists. Local entrepreneurial boosters all over the country have been able to promote the birthplaces of native sons and daughters, in some cases even the "unique" character of complete "ancient" villages and towns as well as streets that include large numbers of dwellings and other structures from the Ming and Qing dynasties. Alliances with Departments of Architecture at Tsinghua University in Beijing, Tongji University in Shanghai, and Southeast University in Nanjing, among several others, have helped document existing structures with measured drawings and photographs as well as designs for their restoration and accessibility to tourists. Xidi and Hongcun in the Huizhou area of Anhui, Dangjia in Shaanxi, Dingcun in Shanxi, Zhaojiabao in Fujian, Zhouzhuang in Jiangsu, Maoyuan in Jiangxi, the Nanxijiang area of Zhejiang, Yongding in Fujian, Chuandixia, Zhaitangchuan in Mentougou District, Beijing, and Jinzhu in Guangxi are but a small number of the fine examples of traditional built environments the destruction of which has been forestalled by proclaiming them "living fossils" [*huo huashi* 活化石] worthy of preservation and visits by tourists. In an attempt to bring about the conservation of Ming dynasty structures slated for destruction, China's first open-air museum dedicated to residential architecture was created in Qiankou, Anhui, in 1988. Representative houses and ancestral halls, once scattered throughout the region, have been placed together as an ensemble among other elements such as a ceremonial arch, a stone bridge, and a roadside pavilion. Although the ten individual structures are from different places, together they represent China's first attempt to form an authentic "village" like those found commonly as open-air museums in Europe and America. The restoration of these rural projects as well as various urban districts, such as Chengde's Qing Steet, Kaifeng's Song Street, and Liulichang Lane in Beijing, have been the focus of debates over styles and techniques among Chinese architects.

In addition to conserving structures of historic significance, a phenomenon of re-creating traditional buildings in "ethnic minority parks" [*minzu yuan* 民族园] and "folk culture villages" [*minsu wenhua cun* 民俗文化村] has also gained currency in China over the past ten years, providing visitors with tangible links to

China's architectural patrimony. Some of these theme park-like facilities have within them remarkably accurate reconstructions of old dwellings that have been designed by thoughtful architects (Dai 1995), but many are poor and uncreative representations that "cannot match 'real' culture" (Lin Jinghua 1996). "China in a nutshell" is how *China Daily* announced the opening of China Folk Culture Villages in Shenzhen, Guangdong, on October 1, 1991, which includes structures representing twenty-one architectural styles: Bai, Bouyei, Dai, Dong, Gaoshan, Hani, Kazak, Korean, Li, Miao, Mongol, Mosuo, Naxi, Tibetan, Tujia, Uygur, Va, Yao, Yi, and Zhuang as well as Han Beijing-style *siheyuan* and cave dwellings from Shaanxi. The first phase of the Chinese Ethnic Culture Park in Beijing, opened in time for the Asian Games in 1994, represents dwellings of Bouyei, Dai, Dau'er, Dong, Ewenki, Gaoshan, Hani, Hezhen, Jingpo, Korean, Miao, Oroqen, Qiang, Tibetan, Va, and Yi. A second phase with twenty additional ethnic villages is under development. In addition, a China Culture Center representing "the colorful cultures of China's 56 nationalities" has been proposed for construction in Huairou *xian*, sixty kilometers north of Beijing. A 580-hectare complex on the banks of Dianchi Lake in Kunming, Yunnan, called the Haigeng Nationality and Cultural Village has been under construction for some time, with several parts already open to the public. Eventually including twenty-six hamlets showcasing each of the province's ethnic groups, the theme park is viewed by some as being along the same lines as the Polynesian Cultural Center in Hawai'i. At the end of 1996, the first phase of the China Nationalities Grandview Park was opened in the Pudong New Area, Shanghai. This large-scale 73.3-hectare cultural park, according to a press report, "epitomizes the architecture, living habits, clothing, food, handicrafts, wedding customs and festivals, as well as . . . song and dance" and includes attractions such as "horse racing, bull fighting and cock fights, as well as the first large water-screen film in Shanghai." Bohai Folklore Garden opened in June 1997 along the middle reaches of the Mudan River in Heilongjiang province. Centered about a re-creation of an ancient stockaded Manchu village of 1,300 years ago, the site includes replicas of Manchu log dwellings.

Not far from the remains of the neolithic Banpo, an open-air replica museum village was opened in 1994 that, according to a press report, "gives visitors an insight into the lives of the Banpo people who inhabited the area more than 6,000 years ago." Some sets built for period television or film series have been recycled as venues to enjoy Chinese culture of times past: Hancheng for the *Romance of the Three Kingdoms* in Zhenjiang, Jiangsu; A City of *Romance of the Three Kingdoms* in Qingxu, Shanxi; Wu Period Folklore Park in Wuxi, Jiangsu; Jin period Houma Cultural Town in Shanxi; Tang Dynasty City on the banks of Taihu Lake, Wuxi, Jiangsu; Beijing Movie City, which re-creates "the robust lanes of old Beijing;" Cao Xueqin Memorial Temple and Dream Garden with its replicas of Ming and Qing streets for the filming of *A Dream of Red Mansions;* and Beijing Grandview Garden and Shanghai Grandview Garden, both built on the basis of *A Dream of Red Mansions.* Smaller scale sites include Li and Miao ethnic minority villages in Tongshi, Hainan; a Zhuang "theme park" in Nanning, Guangxi; and Mizhenshan village, Liaoning. News reports also tell of a "tourist spot to resemble ancient Beijing" in Xianghe *xian*, Hebei, and folklore museums housed in old manors, such as the Xijiashan Mountain Folklore Museum in Jiangan *xian*, Sichuan, and the Yanshou Exhibition Hall of Folk Beliefs in Qixian, Shanxi. On-location filming of historical dramas has helped bring the public's attention to traditional domestic architecture. Wangcun in Hunan province provided the stage for the making of *Hibiscus Town* in 1986, based on a novel by Gu Hua. With wooden structures and undulating paths paved with stone slabs, Wangcun has become a tourist attraction that provides glimpses of not only prerevolutionary China but also the turmoil of the 1960s and 1970s. Qiaojia *dayuan*, the expansive and splendid mansion of the Qiao family in Qixian, Shanxi, discussed in Chapter 4, was the background location for filming *Raise the Red Lantern*, which was released in 1991.

The production and wide distribution of booklets and books as well as even a series of postage stamps have all helped highlight vernacular architecture. In 1994 a twelve-part television documentary on CCTV focused on old homes all over China, bringing the subject to a mass audience. Directed by Yan Dong, the series emphasized dwellings as mirrors of Chinese society even as techniques of construction, overall layout, and aesthetics were examined.

Much of what has happened in recent decades on the mainland concerning the preservation and re-creation of vernacular architecture was prefigured by earlier actions and attitudes in Taiwan and Hong Kong. Although one might assume that the size of both Taiwan and Hong Kong would facilitate solutions to knotty problems, such has not been the case. Indeed, the intractability of preservation issues, even in such areas with abundant material resources and a high level of education, causes one to pause when seeking solutions at the scale in which they must be addressed on the mainland. The convoluted debate has included many elements over the years: conflicting approaches to preservation by specialists and politicians, availability of craftsmen and conservation techniques, government statutes and designations, sources of funds for project maintenance, irresponsible tourists, and a continuing general lack of concern by the public at large (Lin 1993, 7).

Few structures express better the convoluted process of preservation in Taiwan than the tale of the Lin Antai dwelling. Growing hall by hall and courtyard by courtyard beginning in the Qianlong period (1783–1785) amidst the verdant rice fields in the eastern part of the Taipei Basin, the Lin family residence became an expansive complex housing many generations at the beginning of the twentieth century. By the mid-1970s, due to the accelerating growth of Taipei city, planners had designated that a major road project would pass right through the residence. Early in 1977, when the family was notified that the 200-year-old house was slated for demolition in June, there was ensuing outrage and a degree of political maneuvering (Lee 1977, 20). Proposals were offered for rerouting Tunhua South Road, but ultimately a decision was made to dismantle the house without resolution as to where it would be reconstructed. Working rapidly over two months in mid-1978, the structure was disassembled. Under the direction of architect Li Chung-yueh, measured drawings were completed and each piece of brick, stone, and wood was assessed, numbered, and catalogued. All of the

parts were to be warehoused while discussions continued on determining a location for rebuilding it. An early plan was to move the dwelling to a "folk village" that was to be developed in Nankang, east of Taipei, the site of prestigious research facilities of Academia Sinica. Temporary storage lasted six years before a compromise site was eventually agreed upon: a new park that was to be opened along the elevated Sun Yat-sen Freeway near Yuan-shan in the northern Taipei Basin and just below the path for flights landing at Sung-shan Airport. Over the ensuing years, however, at least 30 percent of the original components of the house had deteriorated due to rotting or breakage and could not be used. What had appeared once to be simply a task of reassembling had now become a more costly project of restoration. Much of the house was reconstructed in Ping-chiang Park in 1985 and opened to the public in 1987 in a western-style garden setting that many find inappropriate. Even though some effort has been made to install appropriate furniture and ornamentation, the rather new-looking red brick structure is sadly a melancholy shell bereft of the activity that once made it a home (Tseng 1988).

Concern about the preservation of folk culture in Taiwan led to a broad-ranging discussion in the late 1970s and early 1980s of ways to preserve individual buildings and blocks of structures *in situ* as well as to establish folk villages to house relocated structures (Chen Chi-lu 1987). Much of this effort was directed toward providing an appropriate traditional-style venue for the preservation of folk crafts and performing arts. Even before these discussions, a folk village of sorts was established by the Atayal tribe on the shores of Sun Moon Lake in the 1960s. Later, this effort was expanded to become The Wulai Aboriginal Culture Village, which emphasizes dance performances, singing, and colorful costumes of Taiwan's nine "high mountain" or Gaoshan minority groups and some re-created examples of aboriginal buildings. Another Nine Tribes Folk Village in Ping-tung, though initiated by Academia Sinica, failed. For the most part, however, these re-creations of material culture provide only hazy glimpses of cultures that have been diluted to the point of extinction as tribal members have been virtually assimilated into the dominant Han culture. More recently, Taiwan Folk Village, located 20 kilometers south of Tai-chung, officially opened in late 1993 and includes not only a 52-hectare village with old dwellings that had been moved from elsewhere on the island but also replicas of dwellings, streets, temples, and other structures. Evidence that the purpose of this folk village is more than to remind visitors of the island's past are the presence of amusement park rides and a shopping center. Scale-model examples of domestic architecture in Taiwan were included in Window on China, opened in Tao-yuan in 1984, with the purpose of showing miniatures of important buildings throughout China. Each of these efforts is more a response to the development of domestic tourism than the desire to preserve heritage.

In the meantime, as efforts were being made to create "authentic" villages as tourist spots, energy was successfully expended on documenting and reconstructing a small number of surviving structures. Notable were the successful efforts to restore the Lin family mansion in Pan-chiao by the architect Han Pao-te, the Chai Hsing Mountain Villa in Tan-tzu, Tai-chung, by the Taipei Architects Association, as well as significant conservation work of historic urban districts in Lu-kang, Taipei, San-hsia, Ta-hsi, Hu-kou, and Tai-nan. A recent visionary attempt at wholesale historic preservation involves the creation of the Kinmen National Park, a cultural complex that embodies several aspects of Taiwan's history during the twentieth century. Also known as Quemoy, Kinmen or Jinmen is part of an archipelago that lies only 2 kilometers off the mainland coast and was, for much of the past half-century, a military redoubt. Because of its strategic value as a forward salient of Taiwan's defences against Communist forces and the fact that most military construction took place underground, the 163 traditional villages on the surface have remained relatively unchanged, actual fossils of more quiescent times and only a short plane ride from Taipei.

Hong Kong is best known as a modern city, characterized by perpetual change that continually is remaking and redeveloping the built landscape. "Looking around Hong Kong," a government publication tells us, "one might think it had no heritage" (Burton 1992,

5). Yet, in the rural New Territories and in urban pockets as well, close observers are still able to note a large number of vestigial remains of times past, including archaeological sites, villages, forts, churches, and important colonial buildings (Hase and Sinn 1995). The meetings and publications of the Royal Asiatic Society, Hong Kong Branch (active from 1847–1859 and then revived in 1959) provided a means to record much of this evidence, but it was only in the mid-1970s that formal procedures were established to legally acknowledge and protect Hong Kong's built heritage. The Antiquities and Monuments Ordinance, passed in January 1976, provided for an office and an advisory board to advise the government on the protection of Chinese and western urban and rural architecture. Over the past twenty years, major efforts have focused on identifying, gazetting, and conserving historical buildings. Increasingly, the office monitors development proposals and actively participates in the rural and urban planning process. The gazetted historic buildings include temples, tombs, railway stations, ancestral halls, post offices, forts, university buildings, study halls, cathedrals, markets, and cenotaphs; rural village complexes such as Kat Hing Wai, Lo Wai, and Kun Long Wai; walled villages; and several traditional dwellings. Notable among this last group are Sam Tung Uk, Sheung Yiu, Tai Fu Tai, and Law Uk. Sheung Yiu, which is operated as a folk museum, and Tai Fu Tai, a fine example of a scholar-gentry dwelling, remain in their quiet country settings and are visited by hikers. Both Sam Tung Uk and Law Uk, virtually swallowed up by high-rise buildings and accessible a few steps from MRT mass transit lines, provide venues as museums of Chinese folk culture. The year 1997 was declared a "Year of Heritage" in order to foster public appreciation. More recently, in spite of significant progress in Hong Kong, successful preservation efforts have been frustrated by lack of coordination by government agencies, inadequate financial incentives for heritage conservation, ineffective ordinances for implementing conservation efforts, and ongoing public apathy (Lung and Friedman 1997; Cody and Richardson 1997)

Efforts at preserving Chinese vernacular architecture by moving it have reached Minnesota and Massachusetts in the United States. In 1996 the Minneapolis Museum of Arts purchased, according to a museum brochure, "what remained of three historical residential structures" in China. Characteristic of Jiangnan architecture in the area near Suzhou, Jiangsu, the buildings were taken apart, reassembled on site once damage was assessed and repairs were made, then carefully packed and sent to Minnesota for reassembling. In addition to an imposing commemorative gate, a late Ming dynasty reception hall, and a study, all dating to 1797, they were reconstructed within the museum and opened in 1998 as galleries, "original settings for the interpretation and display" of the museum's extensive collection of Chinese classical furniture and literati art. Once found in homes of the wealthy in the Jiangnan region, the scholar's study, with its adjacent rock garden, represents a type of contemplative space for painting, reading, writing, and studying antiques, while the three-bay-wide reception hall provides space for formal ritual and receiving guests.

Yin Yu Tang, once the Qing dynasty residence of an Anhui merchant family, was completely dismantled in 1997 with the assistance and approval of the Huangshan municipal government and is being reassembled on the grounds of the Peabody Essex Museum in Salem, Massachusetts. The mission of Yin Yu Tang at the American museum is threefold: to preserve the specific house, its contents, documents, and history; through that preservation to present the house as an example of Chinese architecture and the related traditions of decorative arts and artisanry; and to function as a window into the broader context of Chinese vernacular culture and lifestyles. The rooms in the house will be displayed as they were originally lived in at several distinct time periods and will be furnished with original furniture and household utensils from the house. An interpretive gallery adjacent to the house will present additional material regarding Huizhou architecture, the culture of the region, and the history of the family who inhabited the house for at least nine generations. Nancy Berliner is the curator of the house and accompanying exhibition.

When viewed from a broad academic perspective, there are a number of continuing concerns regarding the preservation of China's vernacular architec-

tural heritage. Specialists and amateurs alike must continue to note old dwellings and other structures, calling attention to their historical significance or even typicality. Whenever it is impossible to save structures, they should at the very least be photographed and documented with drawings so that they can be appreciated in that form. In addition to emphasizing the plans of individual dwellings with measured drawings and architectural details, more attention must be paid to the historical contexts and time periods of common old dwellings. There is a need to use literary and artistic sources for insights into the nature of individual as well as groups of structures. Vernacular architecture needs to be examined at different scales of inquiry, including individual dwellings, ensembles of structures in towns and villages, and regions. Increasingly it is necessary to collect information in a form that facilitates comparisons. Glossaries of building and ornamental terms that speak to regional differences are a priority. Chinese vernacular architecture, as well as other patterns of material culture, is a wide open field of inquiry that is increasingly enriched by cross-cultural and interdisciplinary approaches and insights.

The building traditions for nearly a quarter of the world's population are indeed complex. Much has already been accomplished, yet a significant amount of painstaking fieldwork needs to be done. Imaginative scholarship needs to focus on understanding origins, culture regions, patterns of diffusion, adaptations, acculturation, and shared or unique symbolic motifs across the geographical and temporal vastness of China—the admittedly complex means and sequence by which material cultural forms were diffused across the map of China.

Problems of identification, classification, and nomenclature will continue to frustrate scholars for years to come. The difficulties are monumental and the answers do not come easily. Fred Kniffen, a prominent figure in the articulation of geographers' interest in vernacular architecture stated, "The biologist never finds the tail of a lion grafted to the body of a cow; the classifier of cultural forms has no such assurance. He must judiciously generalize, and he can never be completely objective. Without the necessary historical and comparative data he cannot safely accept apparent genetic relationships. In his morphologic data he must look for central themes, and must temporarily obscure minor variations in individual forms" (1936, 181). While much basic empirical work remains that can be accomplished by individual scholars working alone, the comprehensive study of China's vernacular architecture demands collaborative, comparative, and interdisciplinary investigation. Descriptive and idiosyncratic research will continue, however, even as scholars attempt to bring forward meaningfully systematic analytical frameworks that will help explain the aesthetic and architectonic principles that undergird Chinese vernacular architectural forms.

Today, as in the past, Chinese folk architecture continues to resonate the richness, texture, and complexity of one of the world's great civilizations. Yet, congeries of social, economic, and political forces continue to buffet the Chinese people, their built environments, and natural landscapes. For the most part, Chinese seem to be unsentimental about the loss of traditional architecture, viewing demolition—perhaps even the disintegration of traditional culture in general—as the necessary, if unfortunate, accompaniment of modernization. One young architect recently lamented that "the Cultural Revolution not only destroyed our monuments; it destroyed people's feelings for them" and "killed off the sense of beauty" (Stille 1998, 39). Confounded by the fragmentary awakening of public consciousness concerning the country's vernacular heritage and little popular nostalgia for buildings judged as backward and uncomfortable, it is remarkable that so much has been accomplished by the relatively few, still rather quiet voices that are articulating the cause of historic preservation.

References

A Jin 阿金
    1995   "Nei Menggu chuantong minju—Menggu bao" 内蒙古传统民居—蒙古包 [Traditional vernacular dwellings of Inner Mongolia—Mongol yurts]. In Lu Yuanding 陆元鼎, chief ed. *Minju shilun yu wenhua* 民居史论与文化 [History and culture of vernacular architecture], pp. 182-185. Guangzhou: Huanan ligong daxue chubanshe 华南理工大学出版社.

"Agriculture in Manchuria and Mongolia." *Chinese Economic*
    1927   *Journal* 1:1044-1058.

Ahern, Emily
    1979   "Domestic Architecture in Taiwan: Continuity and Change." In R. W. Wilson, A. A. Wilson, and S. L. Greenblatt, eds. *Value Change in Chinese Society*, pp. 155-170. New York: Praeger.

"Ancient Rock Cave Dwellings." *Beijing Review* 39(42):28.
    1996

Asakawa Shigeo 浅川滋男
    1996   *Unan shō nashi zokubokei shakai no kyojū yōshiki to kenchiku gijutsu ni kansuru chōsa to kenkyū* (1)(2) 雲南省ナシ族母系社会の居住様式と建築技術に關する調査と研究(1)(2) [Research into the residential types and construction techniques of the matriarchal society of the Naxi in Yunnan province]. Tokyo: Jūtaku sōgō kenkyū zaidan 住宅總合研究財団.

Azevedo, J.
    1991   "House Building in Shaanxi, China: A Chronicle of the Technique and Ceremony of Raising the Roof Frame." *Traditional Dwellings and Settlements Review* 11:75-82.

Bennett, Steven J.
    1978   "Patterns of Sky and Earth: A Chinese System of Applied Cosmology." *Chinese Science* 3:1-26.

Berliner, Nancy Zeng
    1986   *Chinese Folk Art: The Small Skills of Carving Insects.* Boston: Little, Brown.

Berliner, Nancy, and Sarah Handler
    1995   *Friends of the House: Furniture from China's Towns and Villages.* Salem: Peabody Essex Museum.

Blaser, Werner
    1979   *Courtyard House in China: Tradition and Present/ Hofhaus in China: Tradition und Gegenwart.* Bilingual ed. Basel: Birkhäuser Verlag. Second enlarged ed., 1995.

Bourton, P. D. W., ed.
    1992   *The Heritage of Hong Kong* 香港文物. Bilingual text. Hong Kong: Antiquities and Monuments Office.

Boyd, Andrew
    1962   *Chinese Architecture and Town Planning: 1500 B.C.–A.D. 1911.* Chicago: University of Chicago Press.

Bray, Francesca
    1997   *Technology and Gender: Fabrics of Power in Late Imperial China.* Berkeley: University of California Press.

Buck, J. Lossing
    1937   *Land Utilization in China.* Chicago: University of Chicago Press.

Cai Jishi 蔡济世
    1995   "Ziyuan xing shengtai yuan tulou" 资源型生态圆土楼 [Resourceful and ecological round *tulou*]. *Jianzhu xuebao* 建筑学报 [Architectural journal] 9:42-44.

Cammann, Schuyler
    1951   *The Land of the Camel: Tents and Temples of Inner Mongolia.* New York: The Ronald Company.

Cao Huaijing 曹坏经
    1992   "Qiangzu juzhu wenhua gaiguan" 羌族居住文化概观 [General survey of the residential culture of the Qiang nationality]. In Lu Yuanding 陆元鼎, chief ed. *Zhongguo chuantong minju yu wenhua, di'er ji* 中国传统民居与文化·第二辑 [China's traditional vernacular dwellings and culture, vol.

2], pp. 68-76. Beijing: Zhongguo jianzhu gongye chubanshe 中国建筑工业出版社.

Cauquelin, Josiane

1987   *Les Buyi, Peuple Thai de la Province du Guizhou dans le Sud-ouest de la Chine.* Paris: Péninsule.

1990   "Les Zhuang, Peuple Thai de la Province du Guangxi." *Les Peuples Thais Aujord'hui.* Bangkok: Pandora.

Chang, Kwang-chih

1980   *Shang Civilization.* New Haven: Yale University Press.

1986   *The Archaeology of Ancient China,* 4th ed. New Haven: Yale University Press.

Chang Wen-jui [Zhang Wenrui]

1976   *Zhongguo minju de fazhan he shigong fangfa* 中國民居的發展和施工方法 [The development and construction methods of Chinese folk housing]. Unpublished Master of Architecture thesis, Department of Architecture, 中國文化大學 Chinese Culture University.

Chard, Robert

1990a   "Folktales on the God of the Stove." *Hanxue yanjiu* 漢學研究 [Chinese studies] 8(6):149-182.

1990b   "Master of the Family: History and Development of the Chinese Cult to the Stove." Unpublished Ph.D. dissertation, University of California, Berkeley.

1995   "Rituals and Scriptures of the Stove Cult." In David Johnson, ed. *Ritual and Scripture in Chinese Popular Religion: Five Studies,* pp. 3-54. Berkeley: Institute of East Asian Studies.

Chavannes, Edouard

1973   *The Five Happinesses: Symbolism in Chinese Popular Art.* Translated by Elaine S. Atwood. New York: Weatherhill. Text originally published as "De l'expression des voeux dans l'art populaire chinois." *Journal Asiatique,* series 9, vol. 18, September-October 1901.

Chen Chi-lu [Chen Qilu] 陳奇祿

1987   "On the Preservation of Folk Culture." In *People and Culture,* pp. 79-88. Taipei: Southern Materials Center, Inc.

Chen Chi-lu [Chen Qilu] 陳奇祿, et al., eds.

1992   *Zhongguo chuantong nianhua yishu tezhan zhuanji* 中國傳統年畫藝術特展專輯 [The art of the traditional Chinese new year print]. Taipei: Guoli zhongyang tushuguan 國立中央圖書館.

Chen Congzhou 陳從周, Pan Hongxuan 潘洪萱, and Lu Bingjie 路秉傑

1993   *Zhongguo minju* 中国民居 [China's vernacular dwellings]. Hong Kong: Sanlian shudian (Xianggang) youxan gongsi 三聯書店(香港)有限公司.

Chen Congzhou 陳從周

1958   *Suzhou jiu zhuzhai cankao tulu* 苏州旧住宅参考 图录 [References of the old dwellings of Suzhou]. Shanghai: Tongji daxue.

Chen Lesheng 陈樂生, Ma Shiyun 馬世雲, and Song Zilong 宋子龍, eds.

1988   徽州石磚雕藝術 [The art of stone carving in Huizhou]. Hefei: Anhui meishu chubanshe 安徽美术出版社.

Chen Lusheng 陈鲁生

1995   *Xixang minju* 西藏民居 [Vernacular dwellings of Tibet]. Beijing: Renmin meishu chubanshe 人民美术出版社.

Chen Moude 陈谋德 and Wang Cuilan 王翠兰

1992   "Zhongguo minju lishi de bowuguan—Yunnan minju" 中国民居历史的博物馆—云南民居 [Historical museum of Chinese vernacular dwellings—Yunnan vernacular dwellings]. In Lu Yuanding 陆元鼎, chief ed. *Zhongguo chuantong minju yu wenhua, di'er ji* 中国传统民居与文化·第二辑 [China's traditional vernacular dwellings and culture, vol. 2], pp. 116-122. Beijing: Zhongguo jianzhu gongye chubanshe 中国建筑工业出版社.

Chen Shouxiang 陳綬祥

1996   *Lao fangzi—Dongzu mulou* 老房子—侗族木樓 [Old houses—timbered structures of the Dong minority nationality]. Nanjing: Jiangsu meishu chubanshe 江苏美术出版社. Photography by Li Yuxiang 李玉祥. English text by Ronald G. Knapp.

Chen Zengbi 陳增弼

1998   "Zhongguo beifang minju yu jiaju" 中國北方民居與家具 [Vernacular dwellings and furniture in northern China]. In *Zhongguo gudian jiaju yu shenghuo huanjing—Lo Kai-yin shoucang qingxuan* 中國古典家具與生活環境—羅啓妍收藏精選 [Classical and vernacular Chinese furniture in the living environment—examples from the Kai-yin Lo collection], pp. 78-89. Hong Kong: Yungmintang 雍明堂. Bilingual text.

Chen Zhendong 陈震东

1994   "Xinjiang qu Hasakezu zhanfang" 新疆区哈萨克族毡房 [Kazak Yurts in Xinjiang]. In Wang Zhili 汪之力, chief ed. *Zhongguo chuantong minju jianzhu* 中国传统民居建筑 [Chinese traditional architecture of residence (sic)], pp. 109-110. Jinan: Shandong kexue jishu chubanshe 山东科学技术出版社.

1995   "Hasakezu minju" 哈萨克族民居 [Vernacular dwellings of the Kazak]. In Yan Dachun 严大椿, chief ed. *Xinjiang minju* 新疆民居 [Vernacular dwellings of Xinjiang], pp. 171-206. Beijing: Zhongguo jianzhu gongye chubanshe 中国建筑工业出版社.

Chen Zhihua 陈志华

1994　"Nan liao xiangtu qing—cunluo, bowuguan, tushuguan" 难了乡土情—村落·博物馆·图书馆 [Hard to bring to an end the affection for the native soil—village, museum and library]. *Jianzhushi* 建筑师 [The architect] 59:47-55.

1997　"Shuoshuo xiangtu jianzhu yanjiu" 说说乡土建筑研究 [Comments on research in vernacular architecture]. *Jianzhushi* 建筑师 [The architect] 75:78-84.

Chen Zhihua 陳志华, Lou Qingxi 樓慶西, and Li Qiuxiang 李秋香

1996　*Zhugecun xiangtu jianzhu* 諸葛村鄉土建築 [Vernacular architecture of Zhuge village]. Taipei: Hansheng zazhishe 漢聲雜誌社.

Cheng Jiyue 程极悦，and Hu Chengen 胡承恩

1980　"Shexian Mingdai juzhu jianzhu 'lao wujiao (ge)' diacha jianbao" 歙县明代居住建築"老屋角(阁)"调查简报 [Brief report on the Ming dynasty houses "Lao Wu Jiao" in Shexian]. *Jianzhu lishi yu lilun* 建筑历史与理论 [Corpus of architectural history and theory] 1:104-111.

Cheu, Rose Y.

1993　"Architecture and Ethnology: The Relationship of the Chinese Family and Kinship to Chinese Vernacular Architecture." Unpublished Master of Arts thesis, Department of Architecture, University of Washington.

Ch'ü, T'ung-tsu 瞿同祖

1965　*Law and Society in Traditional China.* Paris: Mouton & Co.

Clément, Pierre, and Sophie Clément

1988　"Soochow and Venice: Two Cities on Canals." *Mimar: Architecture in Development* 28:10-15.

Clément, Sophie, Pierre Clément, and Shin Yong-hak

1987　*Architecture du paysage en Extrême-Orient.* Paris: Ecole nationale supérieure des Beaux-Arts.

Cody, Jeffrey

1992　"Preservation and Progress in China's Largest Port," *Places* 8(1):73-79.

Cody, Jeffrey W., and James R. Richardson

1997　"Urbanizing Forest and Village Trees in Hong Kong's Sha Tin Valley, 1976-1977." *Traditional Dwellings and Settlement Review* 9(1):21-33.

Cui Yi 崔毅

1992　*Shanxi gu jianzhu zhuangshi tu'an* 山西古建筑装饰图案 [Ornamental patterns of Shanxi's ancient architecture]. Beijing: Renmin meishu chubanshe 人民美术出版社.

Dai Fudong 藏复东

1995　"Beijing Zhonghua minzu yuan" 北京中华民族园 [Chinese ethnic park]. *Jianzhu xuebao* 建筑学报 [Architectural journal] 6:18-24.

Dai Fudong 藏复东, Luo Deqi 羅德啓, and Wu Wenyi 伍文義

1989　*Shitou yu ren—Guizhou yanshi jianzhu* 石頭與人—贵州岩石建築 [Stone and man: rock architecture in Guizhou]. Guiyang: Guizhou renmin chubanshe 贵州人民出版社.

Dai Zhijian 藏志坚

1991　"Fujian Quanzhou minju" 福建泉州民居 [Vernacular dwellings of Quanzhou, Fujian]. In Lu Yuanding 陆元鼎, chief ed. *Zhongguo chuantong minju yu wenhua, di'yi ji* 中国传统民居与文化·第一辑 [China's traditional vernacular dwellings and culture, vol. 1], pp. 163-172. Beijing: Zhongguo jianzhu gongye chubanshe 中国建筑工业出版社.

1992　"Fujian Zhaoan Kejia minju yu wenhua" 福建沼安客家民居与文化 [Dwellings and culture of the Kejia in Zhaoan, Fujian]. In Lu Yuanding 陆元鼎, chief ed. *Zhongguo chuantong minju yu wenhua, di'er ji* 中国传统民居与文化·第二辑 [China's traditional vernacular dwellings and culture, vol. 2], pp. 98-108. Beijing: Zhongguo jianzhu gongye chubanshe 中国建筑工业出版社.

Dali Baizu Zizhizhou chengjianju 大理白族自治州城建局 and Yunnan Gongxueyuan jianzhu xi 云南工学院建筑系, eds.

1994　*Yunnan Dali Baizu jianzhu* 云南大理白族建筑 [The architecture of the Bai nationality in Dali, Yunnan]. Kunming: Yunnan Daxue chubanshe 云南大学出版社.

Davis, Deborah

1989　"My Mother's House." In Perry Link, Richard Madsen, and Paul Pickowicz, eds. *Unofficial China: Popular Culture and Thought in the People's Republic*, pp. 88-100. Boulder, Colorado: Westview Press.

Day, Clarence Burton

1940　*Chinese Peasant Cults: Being a Study of Chinese Paper Gods.* Shanghai: Kelly & Walsh.

De Groot, J. J. M.

1892-　*The Religious System of China.* Leiden: E. J. Brill.
1910

Deng Qisheng 邓其生

1980　"Wo guo gudai jianzhu wumian fangshui cuoshi" 我国古代建筑屋面防水措施 [Ancient measures employed in building waterproof roofs in China]. *Keji wenji* 科技文集 [Collection of the history of science and technology] 5:135-141.

Dillingham, Reed, and Chang-lin Dillingham

1971　*Taiwan chuantong jianzhu zhi kancha* 臺灣傳統建築之勘察 [A survey of traditional architecture of Taiwan]. Taizhong: Donghai daxue zhuzhai ji dushi yanjiu zhongxin 東海大學住宅及都市研究中心.

Dinsmoor, William B., III
1985   "Mongol Housing: with an Emphasis on Architectural Forms of the Ger." Unpublished Ph.D. dissertation, Department of Uralic and Altaic Studies, Indiana University.

Dongnan daxue, Jianzhu xi 東南大学建筑系, and Shexian wenwu guanlisuo 歙县文物管理所, eds.
1993   Tangyue 棠樾 [Tangyue village]. Nanjing: Dongnan daxue chubanshe 东南大学出版社.
1996   Zhanqi 瞻淇 [Zhanqi village]. Nanjing: Dongnan daxue chubanshe 东南大学出版社.
1998   Yu Liang 渔梁 [Yuliang village]. Nanjing: Dongnan daxue chubanshe 东南大学出版社.

Doré, Henry
1917-   Researches into Chinese Superstitions. Shanghai:
1918   T'usewei Printing Press.

Dries-Daffner, Jason
1992   "The Many Faces of Tradition." In Miscegenation of House Form. Traditional Dwellings and Settlements Working Paper Series 39:1-39. Berkeley: Center for Environmental Design Research, University of California.

Duan Zhen 段镇, ed.
1995   Qiaojia dayuan 乔家大院 [Qiao family dayuan]. Qixian, Shanxi: Zhengxie Shanxi sheng Qixian weiyuanhui 政协山西省祁县委员会.

Durocher, Louise
1990   "Traditional Tibetan Houses." Unpublished Master of Architecture thesis, University of Washington.

Dye, Daniel Sheets
1937   A Grammar of Chinese Lattice. Cambridge: Harvard University Press.

Eberhard, Wolfram
1965   Folktales of China. Chicago: University of Chicago Press.
1970   Studies in Chinese Folklore and Related Essays. Indiana University Folklore Institute Monograph Series, Vol. 23. The Hague: Mouton.
1986   A Dictionary of Chinese Symbols: Hidden Symbols in Chinese Life and Thought. London: Routledge & Kegan Paul.

Ebrey, Patricia
1984   Family and Property in Sung China: Yüan Ts'ai's Precepts for Social Life. Princeton: Princeton University Press.
1991a   Chu Hsi's Family Rituals. Princeton: Princeton University Press.
1991b   Confucianism and Family Rituals in Imperial China. Princeton: Princeton University Press.

Fairbank, Wilma
1994   Liang and Lin: Partners in Exploring China's Architectural Past. Philadelphia: University of Pennsylvania Press.

Fan Wei 范为
1992   "Village Fengshui Principles." In Ronald G. Knapp, ed. Chinese Landscapes: The Village as Place, pp. 35-46. Honolulu: University of Hawai'i Press.
1993   "Heaven, Earth and Dwelling—A Comparative Study between Martin Heidegger and Fengshui." Unpublished Master of Science thesis, Department of Architecture and Interior Design, University of Cincinnati.

Fang Jinqi and Xie Zhiren
1994   "Deforestation in Preindustrial China: The Loess Plateau Region as an Example." Chemosphere 29(5):983-999.

Faure, David
1986   The Structure of Chinese Rural Society: Lineage and Village in Eastern New Territories, Hong Kong. Hong Kong: Oxford University Press.

Feuchtwang, Stephen
1974   An Anthropological Analysis of Chinese Geomancy. Vientiane, Laos: Vithagna.

Fitzgerald, C. P.
1941   The Tower of the Five Glories: The Min Chia of Ta Li, Yunnan. London: The Cresset Press.

Flitsch, Mareile
1994   "Manjurische Scherenschnitt-Erzählungen. Bildergeschichten der Künstlerin Hou Yumei." Mitteilungen 6:15-24.

Fong, Mary H.
1983   "The Iconography of the Popular Gods of Happiness, Emolument, and Longevity (Fu Lu Shou)." Artibus Asiae XLIV(2/3):159-199.
1989   "Wu Daozi's Legacy in Popular Door Gods (Menshen) Qin Shubao and Yu Chigong." Archives of Asian Art 42:6-24.

Foshan shi chengxiang jianshe ju 佛山市城乡建设局
1994   "Guangdong sheng Foshan shi Donghuali minju" 广东省佛山市东华里民居 [The Donghuali dwelling in Foshan shi, Guangdong province]. In Wang Zhili 汪之力, chief ed. Zhongguo chuantong minju jianzhu 中国传统民居建筑 [Chinese traditional architecture of residence (sic)], pp. 260-261. Jinan: Shandong kexue jishu chubanshe 山东科学技术出版社.

Franz, Uli
1988   Deng Xiaoping. Boston: Harcourt Brace Jovanovich.

Freedman, Maurice
1966   Chinese Lineage and Society: Fukien and Kwangtung. New York: Humanities Press.

1969 "Geomancy." In *Proceedings, Royal Anthropological Institute of Great Britain and Ireland, 1968*, pp. 5-15. London: Royal Anthropological Institute.

Fu Xinian 傅熹年
1981 "Shaanxi Qishan Fengchu Xi Zhou jianzhu yizhi chutan" 陕西歧山风雏西周建筑遗址初探 [Preliminary examination of the Western Zhou architectural remains at Qishan, Fengchu, Shaanxi]. *Wenwu* 文物 1:65-74.
1984 "Survey: Chinese Traditional Architecture." In Nancy Shatzman Steinhardt, ed. *Chinese Traditional Architecture*, pp. 9-33. New York: China Institute in America.

Fuller, Myron L., and Frederick G. Clapp
1924 "Loess and Rock Dwellings of Shensi, China." *Geographical Review* 14:215-226.

Gao Jiehua 高介华, ed.
1993 *Jianzhu yu wenhuaji* 建筑与文化集 [Architecture and culture collection]. Changsha: Hubei meishu chubanshe 湖北美术出版社.

Gao Zhenming 高钤明, Wang Naixiang 王乃香, and Chen Yu 陈瑜
1987 *Fujian minju* 福建民居 [Vernacular dwellings of Fujian]. Beijing: Zhongguo jianzhu gongye chubanshe 中国建筑工业出版社.

Gaubatz, Piper Rae
1996 *Beyond the Great Wall: Urban Form and Transformation on the Chinese Frontiers*. Stanford: Stanford University Press.

Ged, Françoise, and Feng Yueqiang
1993 "Shanghai's Lilong: Standing the Test of Time." In *Miscegenation of House Form. Traditional Dwellings and Settlements Working Paper Series* 39:55-65. Berkeley: Center for Environmental Design Research, University of California.

Geisler, Timothy C.
1995 "Huizhou mugong" 徽州木工 [Huizhou carpentry]. In *Aspects of Construction*, pp. 63-85. Hong Kong: Chinese University of Hong Kong, Department of Architecture. Bilingual text.

Glahn, Else
1981 "Chinese Building Standards in the 12th Century." *Scientific American* 244 (10):162-173.

Golany, Gideon
1989 *Underground Space Design in China: Vernacular and Modern Practice*. Newark: University of Delaware Press.
1990 *Design and Thermal Performance: Below-ground Dwellings in China*. Newark: University of Delaware Press.
1992 *Chinese Earth-sheltered Dwellings: Indigenous Lessons for Modern Urban Design*. Honolulu: University of Hawai'i Press.

Goldstein, Melvyn, and Cynthia Beall
1990 *Nomads of Western Tibet: The Survival of a Way of Life*. Berkeley: University of California Press.

Graf zu Castell, Wulf Diether
1938 *Chinaflug*. Berlin: Atlantis-Verlag.

Guangxi minzu chuantong jianzhu shilu bianweihui 廣西民族傳統建築史祿編委會
1991 *Guangxi minzu chuantong jianzhu shilu* 廣西民族傳統建築史祿 [A record of traditional architecture of the ethnic groups in Guangxi]. Nanning: Guangxi kexue jishe chubanshe 广西科学技术出版社.

Guangzhou bowuguan 廣州博物館 Xianggang zhongwen daxue wenwuguan 香港中文大學文物館
1983 *Sui-Gang Han mu chutu wenwu* 穗港漢墓出土文物 [Archaeological finds from Han tombs at Guangzhou and Hong Kong]. Hong Kong: Xianggang zhongwen daxue wenwuguan 香港中文大學文物館.

Guangzhou shi wenwu guanli weiyuanhui, ed. 广州市文物管理委員会
1958 *Guangzhou chutu Handai taowu* 广州出土汉代陶屋 [Han dynasty pottery houses excavated in Guangzhou]. Beijing: Wenwu chubanshe 文物出版社.
1981 *Guangzhou Han mu* 廣州漢墓 [Han tombs in Guangzhou]. Beijing: Wenwu chubanshe 文物出版社.

Guo Qinghua 国慶华
1995 "The Structure of Chinese Timber Architecture: Twelfth-Century Design Standards and Construction Principles." Unpublished Ph.D. dissertation, Department of Architecture, Chalmers University of Technology, Gothenburg, Sweden.

Guojia tongji ju, nongcun shehui jingji diaocha zongdui 国家统计局·农村社会经济调查总队
1985, *Zhongguo nongcun tongji nianjian* 中国农村统
1996 计年鉴 [Rural statistical yearbook of China]. Beijing: Zhongguo tongji chubanshe 中国统计出版社.

Hammond, Jonathan
1992 "Xiqi Village, Guangdong: Compact with Ecological Planning." In Ronald G. Knapp, ed. *Chinese Landscapes: The Village as Place*, pp. 95-105. Honolulu: University of Hawai'i Press.

Han Pao-teh [Han Baode] 漢保德
1973 *Banqiao Lin zhai: diaocha yanjiu ji xiufu jihua* 板桥林宅：调查研究及修復計畫 [Banqiao Lin family compound: survey, study, and restoration]. Taizhong: Donghai daxue 東海大學.

1983   *Guji de weihu* 古跡的維護 [The preservation of historic sites]. Taipei: Cultural Buildings Administrative Council.

1992   *The Story of Chinese Landscape Design: External Forms and Internal Visions.* Taipei: Youth Cultural Enterprise Co., Ltd.

Harrell, Stevan

1995   "The History of the History of the Yi." In Stevan Harrell, ed. *Cultural Encounters on China's Ethnic Frontiers*, pp. 63-91. Seattle: University of Washington Press.

Hase, P. H., and Elizabeth Sinn, eds.

1995   *Beyond the Metropolis: Villages in Hong Kong*, pp. 67-75. Hong Kong: Joint Publishing (H.K.) Company Limited.

He Jianqi 何建琪

1991   "Chuantong wenhua yu Chao Shan minju" 传统文化与潮汕民居 [Traditional culture and the vernacular dwellings of Chaozhou and Shantou]. In Lu Yuanding 陆元鼎, chief ed. *Zhongguo chuantong minju yu wenhua, di'yi ji* 中国传统民居与文化 · 第一辑 [China's traditional vernacular dwellings and culture, vol. 1], pp. 65-89. Beijing: Zhongguo jianzhu gongye chubanshe 中国建筑工业出版社.

He Zhongyi 何重义

1995   *Xiangxi minju* 湘西民居 [Vernacular dwellings of western Hunan]. Beijing: Zhongguo jianzhu gongye chubanshe 中国建筑工业出版社.

Heng, Chye-kiang

1993   "Ju-er Hutong: A New Response to the Chinese Traditional Courtyard House." In *Settlements and Resettlements: Issues of Tradition in Development. Traditional Dwellings and Settlements Working Paper Series* 48:40-55. Berkeley: Center for Environmental Design Research, University of California.

1994   "The Role of Ideology in the Making of Chinese Traditional Environment." In *Methods of Traditional Environment Research: Ideology, Philosophy, and Representation. Traditional Dwellings and Settlements Working Paper Series* 65:50-65. Berkeley: Center for Environmental Design Research, University of California.

Ho, Mui

1990   "Vernacular Architecture, Family Hierarchy, and Social Context in Chinese Dwellings." In *Family, Gender, and the Ideologies of Space Interpretation. Traditional Dwellings and Settlements Working Paper Series* 21:10-25. Berkeley: Center for Environmental Design Research, University of California.

1994   "The Chinese Shop-house: An Architectural and Social Model for New Cities." In *Assessing Value in Tradition. Traditional Dwellings and Settlements Working Paper Series* 76:27-38. Berkeley: Center for Environmental Design Research, University of California.

Ho Puay-peng 何培斌

1995   *The Living Building: Vernacular Environments of South China.* Hong Kong: Chinese University of Hong Kong, Department of Architecture.

1996   "Sacred Landscape in a Chinese Village: A Modern Reading." *Tradition: Maintaining Identity in the Face of Change. Traditional Dwellings and Settlements Working Paper Series* 95:93-119. Berkeley: Center for Environmental Design Research, University of California.

1998   "Shiqi shiji de zhaidi—shenghuo huanjing bianzheng guanxi" 十七世紀的宅第—生活環境辯證關係 [The seventeenth century house—the dialectic of the living environment]. In *Zhongguo gudian jiaju yu shenghuo huanjing—Lo Kai-yin shoucang qingxuan* 中國古典家具與生活環境—羅啓妍收藏精選 [Classical and vernacular Chinese furniture in the living environment—examples from the Kai-yin Lo collection], pp. 44-61. Hong Kong: Yungmintang 雍明堂. Bilingual text.

Hommel, Rudolf P.

1937   *China at Work.* New York: The John Day Company.

Hou Jiyao 候继尧

1982   "Shaanxi yaodong minju" 陕西窑洞民居 [The cave dwellings of Shaanxi]. *Jianzhu xuebao* 建筑学报 [Architectural journal] 10:71-73.

1985   "The Architectural Arts about the Cave Dwellings in Shaanxi Province." In *Proceedings of the International Symposium on Earth Architecture*, pp. 107-114. Beijing: Architectural Society of China.

Hou Jiyao 候继尧, Ren Zhiyuan 任致远, Zhou Peinan 周培南, and Li Zhuanze 李传泽

1989   *Yaodong minju* 窑洞民居 [Vernacular cave dwellings]. Beijing: Zhongguo jianzhu gongye chubanshe 中国建筑工业出版社.

Hsu, Francis L. K.

1967   *Under the Ancestor's Shadow: Kinship, Personality and Social Mobility in Village China.* New York: Doubleday.

Hsu Min-fu [Xu Mingfu] 徐明福

1986   "The Origins of Chinese Traditional Architecture." Unpublished Ph.D. dissertation, Department of Architecture, University of Edinburgh.

1990a   *Taiwan chuantong minzhai ji qi difangxing shiliao zhi yanjiu* 臺灣傳統民宅及其地方性史料之研究 [Research on Taiwan's traditional houses and their local historical materials]. Taipei: Hushi tushu gongsi 胡氏圖書公司.

1990b   "Traditional Craftsmen and Local Community in Hsin-pu, Taiwan." *Myth, Ritual, and the Generation of Space. Traditional Dwellings and Settlements Working Paper Series* 20: 1-20. Berkeley: Center for Environmental Design Research, University of California.

Hu Shixian 胡诗仙

1995   "Henan chuantong minju de Zhongyuan dichu tese" 河南传统民居的中原地区特色 [Special characteristics of the Central Plains as seen in the traditional vernacular dwellings of Henan]. In Li Changjie 李长杰, ed. *Zhongguo chuantong minju yu wenhua, disan ji* 中国传统民居与文化·第三辑 [China's traditional vernacular dwellings and culture, vol. 3], pp. 69-77. Beijing: Zhongguo jianzhu gongye chubanshe 中国建筑工业出版社.

Huang Hanmin 黄汉民

1984   "Fujian minju de chuantong tese yu difang fengge, shang, xia" 福建民居的传统特色与地方风格·上·下 [The traditional character and local styles of vernacular dwellings of Fujian, parts 1 and 2]. *Jianzhushi* 建筑师 [The architect] 19:178-203; 21:134, 182-194.

1994a   *Fujian chuantong minju* 福建传统民居 [Vernacular architecture of Fujian]. Xiamen: Lujiang chubanshe 鹭江出版社.

1994b   "Fujian sheng Huaan xian Eryilou" 福建省华安县二宜楼 [Eryilou of Huaan *xian*, Fujian]. In Wang Zhili 汪之力, chief ed. *Zhongguo chuantong minju jianzhu* 中国传统民居建筑 [Chinese traditional architecture of residence (sic)], pp. 364-365. Jinan: Shandong kexue jishu chubanshe 山东科学技术出版社.

1994c   *Fujian tulou* 福建土楼 [The *tulou* of Fujian], 2 volumes. Taipei: Hansheng zazhishe 漢聲雜誌社.

1994d   *Lao fangzi—Fujian minju* 老房子-福建民居 [Old houses—vernacular dwellings of Fujian]. Photography by Li Yuxiang 李玉祥. Nanjing: Jiangsu meishu chubanshe 江苏美术出版社.

1996   "Eryilou de jianzhu tese" 二宜楼的建筑特色 [Special architectural characteristics of Eryilou]. In Huang Hao 黄浩, ed., *Zhongguo chuantong minju yu wenhua, disi ji* 中国传统民居与文化·第四辑 [China's traditional vernacular dwellings and culture, vol. 4], pp. 109-112. Beijing: Zhongguo jianzhu gongye chubanshe 中国建筑工业出版社.

Huang Hao 黄浩, ed.

1996   *Zhongguo chuantong minju yu wenhua, disi ji* 中国传统民居与文化·第四辑 [China's traditional vernacular dwellings and culture, vol. 4]. Beijing: Zhongguo jianzhu gongye chubanshe 中国建筑工业出版社.

Huang Hao 黄浩, Shao Yongjie 邵永杰, and Li Yanrong 李延荣

1990   *Jiangxi tianjing shi minju* 江西天井式民居 [*Tianjing*-style dwellings in Jiangxi]. Jingdezhen: Jiangxi sheng chengxiang jianshe huanjing baohu ting 江西省城乡建设环境保护厅.

1994   "Jiangxi sheng 'San Nan' weizi" 江西省"三南"围子 [*Weizi* of Longnan, Quannan, and Dingnan of Jiangxi province]. In Wang Zhili 汪之力, chief ed. *Zhongguo chuantong minju jianzhu* 中国传统民居建筑 [Chinese traditional architecture of residence (sic)], pp. 335-338. Jinan: Shandong kexue jishu chubanshe 山东科学技术出版社.

1995   "Jiangxi weizi shulue" 江西围子述略 [Brief commentary on Jiangxi *weizi*]. In Lu Yuanding 陆元鼎, chief ed. *Minju shilun yu wenhua* 民居史论与文化 [History and culture of vernacular architecture], pp. 132-140. Guangzhou: Huanan ligong daxue chubanshe 华南理工大学出版社.

Huang Weijuan 黄为隽, Shang Guo 尚廓, Nan Wuyan 南舜熏, Pan Jiaping 潘家平, and Chen Yu 陈瑜

1992   *Min Yue Minzhai* 闽粤民宅 [China vernacular dwelling (sic)—Fujian and Guangdong provinces]. Tianjin: Tianjin kexue jishu chubanshe 天津科学技术出版社.

Huang Yu-mei

1983   "Presto! A 'New' Ancient Landmark." *Free China Review* 34(8):56-63.

Huang Zhongbin 黄仲宾

1996   "Xinjiang weiwuer minju leixing ji kongjian zuhe qianxi" 新疆维吾尔民居类型及空间组合纤细 [Brief examination of the spatial organization of vernacular dwelling types of Uygurs in Xinjiang]. In Huang Hao 黄浩, ed. *Zhongguo chuantong minju yu wenhua, disi ji* 中国传统民居与文化·第四辑 [China's traditional vernacular dwellings and culture, vol. 4], pp. 46-54. Beijing: Zhongguo jianzhu gongye chubanshe 中国建筑工业出版社.

Hui, Desmond [Xu Zhuoquan] 许焯权

1996   "Chaoan gu xiangqu Xiangpuzhai xin minju sheji fangan" 潮安古巷区象埔寨新民居设计方案 [Design proposal for new dwellings in Chaoan's old neighborhood]. In Huang Hao 黄浩, ed. *Zhongguo chuantong minju yu wenhua, disi ji* 中国传统民居与文化·第四辑 [China's traditional vernacular dwellings and culture, vol.

4], pp. 154-160. Beijing: Zhongguo jianzhu gongye chubanshe 中国建筑工业出版社.

Huitu Lu Ban jing 绘图鲁班经 [Illustrated *Lu Ban jing*]

1983   Full original title is *Xinjuan gongshi diaozhuo zhengshi Lu Ban mujing jiangjia jing* 新鐫工師雕鐫正式鲁班木經匠家鏡 [Newly engraved official classic of Lu Ban and artisans' mirror for carpenters and carvers]. Taipei: Zhulin yinshu ju 竹林印書局.

Ji Fuzheng 季富政

n.d.   "Sichuan diaolou minju wenhua zonglan" 四川碉楼民居文化综揽 [Summary observations on the watchtower vernacular dwellings of Sichuan]. Unpublished conference paper.

1993a   "Mingren guju wenhua gouxiang" 名人古居文化构想 [A cultural scheme concerning the ancestral homes of famous people]. Paper presented at the International Conference on Chinese Traditional Houses, August 12.

1993b   "Zhi yu buzhi, jie wei chuangzhi—Sichuan Pengshan Bagua fang bianshuo" 知与不知·皆为创支—四川彭山八卦房辩说 [Knowing and not knowing, all is created—explaining the Bagua building at Pengshan, Sichuan]. Paper presented at the International Conference on Chinese Traditional Houses, Hong Kong, August 12.

1994   "Shouhui Sichuan minju" 手繪四川民居 [Drawings of Sichuan vernacular dwellings]. *Hansheng* 67:1-32.

Ji Fuzheng 季富政 and Zhuang Yuguang 庄裕光

1994   *Sichuan xiao zhen minju jingxuan* 四川小鎮民居精选 [Selected examples of vernacular dwellings in Sichuan's small towns]. Chengdu: Sichuan kexue jishu chubanshe 四川科学出版社.

Jin Obu 金欧卜

1998   *Dui chuantong minju jianzhu yanjiu de huigu he jianyi* 对传统民居建筑研究的回顾和建议 [Review and opinions concerning research in traditional vernacular architecture]. *Jianzhu xuebao* 建筑学报 [Architectural journal] 4:47-51.

Jin Qiming 金其铭

1988   *Nongcun juluo dili* 农村聚落地理 [Rural settlement geography]. Beijing: Kexue chubanshe 科学出版社.

1989   *Zhongguo nongcun juluo dili* 中国农村聚落地理 [Chinese rural settlement geography]. Nanjing: Jiangsu kexue jishu chubanshe 江苏科学技术出版社.

Jin Qiming 金其铭, Dong Xin 董新, and Lu Yuqi 陆玉麒, eds.

1990   *Zhongguo renwen dili gailun* 中国人文地理概论 [An introduction to the human geography of China]. Xian: Shaanxi renmin jiaoyu chubanshe 陕西人民教育出版社.

Jin Qiming 金其铭 and Li Wei 李唯

1992   "China's Rural Settlement Patterns." In Ronald G. Knapp, ed. *Chinese Landscapes: The Village as Place*, pp. 13-34. Honolulu: University of Hawai'i Press.

Jin Yikang 金以康

1991   "Shanxi Jingsheng Ming Qing minju" 山西警升明清民聚 [Ming and Qing vernacular dwellings in Jingsheng, Shanxi]. In Lu Yuanding 陆元鼎, chief ed. *Zhongguo chuantong minju yu wenhua, di yi ji* 中国传统民居与文化·第一辑 [China's traditional vernacular dwellings and culture, vol. 1], pp. 156-162. Beijing: Zhongguo jianzhu gongye chubanshe 中国建筑工业出版社.

Jing Qimin 荆其敏

1985   *Zhongguo chuantong minju baiti* 中国传统民居百题 [One hundred topics concerning Chinese traditional vernacular dwellings]. Tianjin: Tianjin kexue jishu chubanshe. 天津科学技术出版社

1988   *Futu jianzhu* 覆土建筑 [Earth sheltered architecture]. Tianjin: Tianjin kexue jishu chubanshe 天津科学技术出版社.

Jones, Schuyler

1996   *Tibetan Nomads: Environment, Pastoral Economy, and Material Culture.* New York: Thames and Hudson.

Kao Ts'an-jung [Gao Canrong] 高燦榮

1975   "Taiwan minzhai wuding zhi xingtai" 台灣民宅屋頂之形態 (上) (下) [Roof forms on dwellings in Taiwan, vols. 1 and 2]. *Taiwan wenxian* 台灣文獻 26(1):103-126; 26(2):180-211.

1989   *Yanwei, Mabei, Wazhen—Taiwan gucuo wuding de xingtai* 燕尾马背瓦鎮—台灣古厝屋頂的形態 [*Yanwei, Mabei, Wazhen*—the forms of village roofs in Taiwan]. Taipei: Nantian shuju youxian gongsi 南天書局有限公司.

1993   *Taiwan gucuo jianshang* 台灣古厝鑒賞 [An appreciation of Taiwan's old homesteads]. Taipei: Nantian shuju youxian gongsi 南天書局有限公司.

Kawashima, Chūji

1986   *Minka: Traditional Houses of Rural Japan.* Tokyo: Kodansha International.

King, F. H.

1927   *Farmers of Forty Centuries, or Permanent Agriculture in China, Korea, and Japan.* New York: Harcourt, Brace.

Kirby, E. Stuart

1960   *Rural Progress in Taiwan.* Taipei: Chinese-American Joint Commission on Rural Reconstruction.

Knapp, Ronald G.

1977 "The Changing Landscape of the Chinese Cemetery." *The China Geographer* 8:1-13.

1981 "Taiwan's Vernacular Architecture." *Orientations* 12:38-47.

1982 "Chinese Rural Dwellings in Taiwan." *Journal of Cultural Geography* 3(1):1-18.

1986 *China's Traditional Rural Architecture: A Cultural Geography of the Common House.* Honolulu: University of Hawai'i Press.

1989 *China's Vernacular Architecture: House Form and Culture.* Honolulu: University of Hawai'i Press.

1990 *The Chinese House.* Hong Kong: Oxford University Press. Translated into Japanese as *Chūgoku No Sumai* by Hirotsuga Kanno. Tokyo: Gakugei Shuppan-sha Co. Ltd., 1996.

1993 *Chinese Bridges.* Hong Kong: Oxford University Press.

1994 "Popular Rural Architecture." In Wu Dingbo and Patrick D. Murphy, eds. *Handbook of Chinese Popular Culture*, pp. 327-346. Westport, CT: Greenwood Press.

1995a "Chinese Villages as Didactic Narratives" 作为叙述的教化式中国村落 [Zuowei xushu de jiaohua shi Zhongguo cunluo]. English/Chinese text in *Theories of Vernacular Architecture*, pp. 55-64. Hong Kong: Department of Architecture, Chinese University of Hong Kong.

1995b "Zhongguo de jiaodao xing jingguan—minsu chuantong he jianzhu" 中国的教导性景观—民俗传统和建筑 [China's didactic landscapes: the folk tradition and the built environment]. In Lu Yuanding 陆元鼎, ed. *Minju shilun yu wenhua* 民居史论与文化 [History and culture of vernacular architecture], pp. 24-29. Guangzhou: Huanan ligong daxue chubanshe 华南理工大学出版社.

1996 "Rural Housing and Village Transformation in Taiwan and Fujian." *The China Quarterly* 147: 779-794.

1997 "China, North," "China, South," "Jiangxi," "Shandong," and "Zhejiang." In Paul Oliver, ed. *Encyclopedia of Vernacular Architecture of the World.* London: Cambridge University Press, 1997.

1998 "Chinese Villages as Didactic Texts." In Wen-hsin Yeh, ed. *Landscape, Culture, and Power in Chinese Society*, pp. 110-128. Berkeley: Institute of East Asian Studies, University of California, Berkeley.

1999 *China's Living Houses: Folk Beliefs, Symbols, and Household Ornamentation.* Honolulu: University of Hawai'i Press.

Knapp, Ronald G., ed.

1992 *Chinese Landscapes: The Village as Place.* Honolulu: University of Hawai'i Press.

Knapp, Ronald G., and Shen Dongqi 沈冬歧

1991 "Politics and Planning: Rural Settlements in Contemporary China." In Nezar Alsayyad, ed. *Adaptation or Evolution of the Physical Environment: The Politics of Planning. Traditional Dwellings and Settlements Working Paper Series* 29:1-45. Berkeley: Center for Environmental Design Research, University of California.

1992 "Changing Village Landscapes." In Ronald G. Knapp, ed. *Chinese Landscapes: The Village as Place*, pp. 47-72. Honolulu: University of Hawai'i Press.

Kniffen, Fred

1936 "Lousiana House Types." *Annals of the Association of American Geographers* 26:179-193.

1965 "Folk Housing: Key to Diffusion." *Annals of the Association of American Geographers* 55:549-577.

Kwan Hwa-san [Guan Huashan] 關華山

1980 "Taiwan chuantong minzhai biaoxian de kongjian guannian" 臺灣傳統民宅表現的空間觀念 [Traditional houses and folk space concepts in Taiwan]. *Zhongyang yanjiuyuan, minzuxue jikan* 中央研究院，民族學季刊 [Bulletin of the Institute of Ethnology, Academia Sinica] 49:175-215.

Laing, Ellen Johnston

1988- "China 'Tartar' Dynasty (1115-1234) Material
1989 Culture." *Artibus Asiae* 49:73-121.

1989 "The Persistence of Propriety in the 1980s." In Perry Link, Richard Madsen, and Paul Pickowicz, eds. *Unofficial China: Popular Culture and Thought in the People's Republic*, pp. 156-171. Boulder, Colorado: Westview Press.

Lam, Peter

1983 *Sui Gang Han mu chutu wenwu* 穗港漢墓出土文物 [Archaeological finds from Han Tombs at Guangzhou and Hong Kong]. Bilingual text. Guangzhou and Hong Kong: Guangzhou bowuguan 廣州博物館 and Art Gallery, Chinese University of Hong Kong 香港中文大學文物館.

Latham, Richard J. ed.,

1996 *A Spiritual Resonance: The Vernacular Dwellings of China* [Gufeng wujia: Zhongguo chuantong minju xuancui 古风无价：中国传统民居选萃]. Bilingual text. Hong Kong: United Technologies Corporation and Jiangsu Fine Arts Press.

Lattimore, Owen

1938 "The Geographical Factor in Mongol History." *Geographical Journal* 91:1-20.

Lebar, Frank M., Gerald C. Hickey, and John K. Musgrave

1964 *Ethnic Groups of Mainland Southeast Asia.* New Haven: Human Relations Area Files Press.

Lee Chien-lang [Li Qianlang] 李乾朗
1977 "The An Tai Lin Family House." *Echo* 6(6):18–25, 55.
1978 *Jinmen minju jianzhu* 金門民居建築 [A survey of Kinmen (Jinmen) traditional architecture]. Taipei: Xiongshi tushugongsi 雄獅圖書公司.
1980 *Taiwan jianzhu shi* 台灣 建築史 [History of the architecture of Taiwan]. Taipei: Beiwu chubanshe 北屋出版社.
1987 *Banqiao Lin Benyuan tingyuan* 板橋林本源庭園 [The Lin family residence at Panchiao]. Taipei: Xiongshi tushugongsi 雄獅圖書公司.
1995 *Taiwan chuantong jianzhu jiang yi* 台灣 傳統建筑匠藝 [The artistic carpentry of Taiwan's traditional architecture]. Taipei: Yanlou gu jianzhu chubanshe 燕樓建築出版社.
1996 "Taiwan minju ji yanjiu fangxiang" 台湾民居及研究方向 [Research directions and Taiwan's vernacular dwellings]. In Huang Hao 黄浩, ed. *Zhongguo chuantong minju yu wenhua, disi ji* 中国传统民居与文化・第四辑 [China's traditional vernacular dwellings and culture, vol. 4], pp. 8–15. Beijing: Zhongguo jianzhu gongye chubanshe 中国建筑工业出版社.

Lee Chien-lang [Li Qianlang] 李乾朗, Yan Ya-ning 閻亞寧, Shyu Yu-chien [Xu Yujian] 徐裕健
1996 *Qing mo Min chu Fujian damu jiangshi Wang Yishun* 清末民初福建大木匠師王益順 [Wang Yishun, Fujian master carpenter of the late Qing and early Republic periods]. Taipei: Neizheng bu 内政部.

Lee, James, and R. Bin Wong
1991 "Population Movements in Qing China and Their Linguistic Legacy." In William S. Y. Wang, ed. *Languages and Dialects of China*, pp. 52–77. *Journal of Chinese Linguistics, Monograph Series No. 3.*

Lee Sang Hae
1986 "Feng-shui: Its Context and Meaning." Unpublished Ph.D. dissertation, Department of Architecture, Cornell University.

Lewis, Candace J.
1990 *Into the Afterlife: Han and Six Dynasties: Chinese Tomb Sculptures from the Schloss Collection.* Poughkeepsie, NY: Vassar College Art Gallery.
1990 "Tall Towers of the Han." *Orientations* 21(8): 45–54.
1999 "Pottery Towers of Han Dynasty China." Unpublished Ph.D. dissertation, New York University.

Li Changjie 李长杰, chief ed.
1990 *Guibei minjian jianzhu* 桂北民间建筑 [The folk architecture of northern Guangxi]. Beijing: Zhongguo jianzhu gongye chubanshe 中国建筑工业出版社.
1995 *Zhongguo chuantong minju yu wenhua, disan ji* 中国传统民居与文化・第三辑 [China's traditional vernacular dwellings and culture, vol. 3]. Beijing: Zhongguo jianzhu gongye chubanshe 中国建筑工业出版社.

Li Qiuxiang 李秋香
1995 "Zhejiang Xinye cun xiangtu jianzhu yanjiu" 浙江新叶村乡土建筑研究 [Research into the vernacular architecture of Xinye village, Zhejiang]. *Jianzhushi* 建筑师 [The architect] 64:51–70.

Li Rong, Xiong Zhenghui, Zhang Zhenxing, S. A. Wurm, B. T'sou, and D. Bradley, gen. eds.
1988 *Language Atlas of China.* Hong Kong: Longman Group (Far East) Limited.

Li Xiankui 李先逵
1992 "Xinan diqu ganlanshi minju xingtai tezheng yu wenmai jizhi" 西南地区干兰式民居形态特征与文脉机制 [The formative characteristics and mechanisms for the transmittal of *ganlan*-style vernacular dwellings in the southwest]. In Lu Yuanding 陆元鼎, chief ed. *Zhongguo chuantong minju yu wenhua, di'er ji* 中国传统民居与文化・第二辑 [China's traditional vernacular dwellings and culture, vol. 2], pp. 37–49. Beijing: Zhongguo jianzhu gongye chubanshe 中国建筑工业出版社.
1995 "Miaozu minju jianzhu wenhua tezhi" 苗族民居建筑文化特质 [The special character of the architecture of vernacular dwellings of the Miao]. In Li Changjie 李长杰, ed. *Zhongguo chuantong minju yu wenhua, disan ji* 中国传统民居与文化・第三辑 [China's traditional vernacular dwellings and culture, vol. 3], pp. 39–53. Beijing: Zhongguo jianzhu gongye chubanshe 中国建筑工业出版社.

Li Xingfa 李兴发
1992 "Yikeyin de huanjing" 一颗印的环境 [The environment of *yikeyin*]. In Lu Yuanding 陆元鼎, chief ed. *Zhongguo chuantong minju yu wenhua, di'er ji* 中国传统民居与文化・第二辑 [China's traditional vernacular dwellings and culture, vol. 2], pp. 176–186. Beijing: Zhongguo jianzhu gongye chubanshe 中国建筑工业出版社.

Li Xueqin 李学勤
1985 *Eastern Zhou and Qin Civilizations.* Translated by K. C. Chang. New Haven: Yale University Press.

Li Zhen 李浈 and Ye Lin 叶琳
1995 "Jin xibei guyao de fazhan, gaijin he weilai" 晋西北锢窑的发展・改进和未来 [The development, improvement, and future of cavelike dwellings in northwestern Shanxi]. In Lu Yuanding 陆元鼎, chief ed. *Minju shilun yu wenhua* 民居史论与文化 [History and culture of vernacular archi-

tecture], pp. 215-219. Guangzhou: Huanan ligong daxue chubanshe 华南理工大学出版社.

Liang Qi 梁琦

1995 "Qinghai Xunhua Sala minju" 青海循化撒拉民居 [Vernacular dwellings of the Salar in Qinghai]. In Lu Yuanding 陆元鼎, chief ed. *Minju shilun yu wenhua* 民居史论与文化 [History and culture of vernacular architecture], pp. 178-181. Guangzhou: Huanan ligong daxue chubanshe 华南理工大学出版社.

Liang Ssu-ch'eng [Liang Sicheng] 梁思成

1984 *A Pictorial History of Chinese Architecture: A Study of the Development of Its Structural System and the Evolution of Its Types.* Edited by Wilma Fairbank. Cambridge: MIT Press.

Lim, Lucy, ed.

1987 *Stories from China's Past: Han Dynasty Pictorial Tomb Reliefs and Archaeological Objects from Sichuan Province, People's Republic of China.* San Francisco: The Chinese Cultural Foundation of San Francisco.

Lin, Diana

1993 "Saving History Not Easy Task." *The Free China Journal* 43(10):7.

Lin Huadong 林华东

1992 *Hemudu wenhua chutan* 河姆渡文化初探 [Explorations of Hemudu culture]. Hangzhou: Zhejiang remmin chubanshe 浙江人民出版社.

Lin Huicheng 林會承

1984 *Xian Qin shiqi Zhongguo juzhu jianzhu* 先秦時期中國居住建築 [Chinese domestic architecture of the Pre-Ch'in Period]. Taipei: Liuhe chubanshe 六合出版社.

1990 *Taiwan chuantong jianzhu shouce* 台灣傳統建築手冊 [Handbook of Taiwan's traditional architecture]. Taipei: Yishujia chubanshe 藝術家出版社.

Lin Jiashu 林嘉書

1995 *Tulou yu Zhongguo chuantong wenhua* 土楼与中国传统文化 [*Tulou* and China's traditional culture]. Shanghai: Shanghai renmin chubanshe 上海人民出版社.

Lin Jiashu 林嘉書 and Lin Hao 林浩

1992 *Kejia tulou yu Kejia wenhua* 客家土樓與客家文化 [Hakka *tulou* and Hakka culture]. Taipei: Boyuan chuban youxian gongsi 博遠出版有限公司.

Lin Jinghua

1996 "Parks Cannot Match 'Real' Culture." *China Daily* (January 6):3.

Lin Xiaoqi 林小麒 and Li Shaoji 蔡少姬

1991 "Guangdong Nanhai minju yu xiangtu wenhua" 广东南海民居与乡土文化 [The vernacular dwellings of Nanhai, Guangdong and local cul-

ture]. In Lu Yuanding 陆元鼎, chief ed. *Zhongguo chuantong minju yu wenhua, di'yi ji* 中国传统民居与文化·第一辑 [China's traditional vernacular dwellings and culture, vol. 1], pp. 57-64. Beijing: Zhongguo jianzhu gongye chubanshe 中国建筑工业出版社.

Lindqvist, Cecelia

1991 *China: Empire of Living Symbols.* Reading: Addison-Wesley Publishing Company.

Liu Baozhong 刘宝仲

1992 "Dangjia Village, Shaanxi: A Brilliant Pearl." In Ronald G. Knapp, ed. *Chinese Landscapes: The Village as Place*, pp. 129-137. Honolulu: University of Hawai'i Press.

Liu, Cary Y.

1994 "Heavenly Wells' in Ming Dynasty Huizhou Architecture." *Orientations* 25(1):28-36.

Liu Dingkun 刘定坤

1995a "Minju jianzhu zhuangshi jixiang tu'an de xiangzheng zhuyi" 民居建筑装饰吉祥图案的象征主义 [Symbolic meaning of good fortune motifs found in vernacular architectural ornamentation]. Paper presented at the Sixth National Conference on Chinese Vernacular Architecture, Xinjiang, August.

1995b "Xiangtu jianzhu kongjian huanjing zhong de jiaohuaxing tezheng" 乡土建筑空间环境中的教化性特征 [The didactic character of vernacular architectural spatial environments]. Paper presented at the Sixth National Conference on Chinese Vernacular Architecture, Xinjiang, August.

Liu Dunzhen 刘敦桢

1957 *Zhongguo zhuzhai gaishuo* 中国住宅概说 [Introduction to Chinese dwellings]. Beijing: Jianzhu gongye chubanshe 建筑工业出版社.

1993 *Chinese Classical Gardens of Suzhou.* Translated by Chen Lixian and Joseph C. Wang. New York: McGraw-Hill, Inc.

Liu Dunzhen 刘敦桢, chief ed.

1984 *Zhongguo gudai jianzhu shi* 中国古代建筑史 [China's ancient architectural history]. Beijing: Jianzhu gongye chubanshe 建筑工业出版社.

Liu Jinzhong 刘金钟 and Han Yaowu 韩耀舞

1995 "Henan Gongxian yaodong" 河南巩县窑洞 [The *yaodong* of Gongxian, Henan]. In Lu Yuanding 陆元鼎, chief ed. *Minju shilun yu wenhua* 民居史论与文化 [History and culture of vernacular architecture], pp. 114-119. Guangzhou: Huanan ligong daxue chubanshe 华南理工大学出版社.

Liu, John K. C.

1980 "Housing Transformations: A Study of Family

Life and Built Form in Taiwan." Unpublished Ph.D. dissertation, University of California, Berkeley.

Liu Siyuan 劉思源

1989   *Taiwan minzhai* 台灣民宅 [Vernacular residences of Taiwan]. Taipei: Yezhulin 野潴林.

Liu Xin

1996   "Yao—the Cave Dwelling and Everyday Space." Unpublished paper presented at the Landscape, Culture, and Power in Chinese Society Symposium, University of California, Berkeley, March 9.

1998   "Yao: The Practice of Everyday Space in Northern Rural Shaanxi." In Wen-hsin Yeh, ed. *Landscape, Culture, and Power in Chinese Society*, pp. 129-152. Berkeley: Institute of East Asian Studies, University of California, Berkeley.

Liu Zhiping 刘致平

1944   "Yunnan—*yikeyin*" 雲南——一顆印 [Yunnan—*yikeyin*]. *Zhongguo yingzao xueshe huikan* 中國營造學社汇刊 [Bulletin of the Society for the Study of Chinese Architecture] 7(1):63-94.

1957   *Zhongguo jianzhu leixing ji jiegou* 中国建筑类型及结构 [Chinese architectural types and structure]. Beijing: Jianzhu gongye chubanshe 建筑工业出版社.

1990   *Zhongguo juzhu jianzhu jianshi—chengshi, zhuzhai, yuanlin (fu: Sichuan zhuzhai jianzhu)* 中国居住建筑简史—城市・住宅・园林 (附：四川住宅建筑) [A brief history of Chinese residential architecture—cities, houses, gardens (Appendix: residential architecture of Sichuan)]. Beijing: Zhongguo jianzhu gongye chubanshe 中国建筑工业出版社.

Long Feiliao 龍非了

1934   "Xueju zakao" 穴居雜考 [Miscellaneous researches on cave dwellings]. *Zhongguo yingzao xueshe huikan* 中國營造學社汇刊 [Bulletin of the Society for the Study of Chinese Architecture] 5(1):55-76.

Loubes, Jean-Paul

1988   *Maisons Creusées du Fleuve Jaune: L'architecture troglodytique en Chine*. Paris: Editions Creaphis.

1992   "Earth, Water, Grapes: Architecture and Urban Patterns in the Oasis of Turfan, Xinjiang, China." In *Traditional Habitat and Material Culture. Traditional Dwellings and Settlements Working Paper Series* 34:27-75. Berkeley: Center for Environmental Design Research, University of California.

Lu Qi 陆琦

1991   Guangdong minju zhuangshi zhuangxiu 广东民居装飾装修 [The ornamentation and repair of Guangdong's vernacular dwellings]. In Lu Yuanding 陆元鼎, chief ed. *Zhongguo chuantong*

minju yu wenhua, di'yi ji 中国传统民居与文化・第一辑 [China's traditional vernacular dwellings and culture, vol. 1], pp. 90-102. Beijing: Zhongguo jianzhu gongye chubanshe 中国建筑工业出版社.

Lu Shan 陆翔 and Wang Qiming 王其明

1996   *Beijing siheyuan* 北京四合院 [Beijing courtyards]. Beijing: Zhongguo jianzhu gongye chubanshe 中国建筑工业出版社.

Lu Yuanding 陆元鼎

1978   "Nanfang diqu chuantong jianzhu de tongfeng yu fangre" 南方地区传统建筑的通风与防热 [The ventilation and heat insulation of traditional architecture in southern China]. *Jianzhu xuebao* 建筑学报 [Architectural journal] 4:36-41.

1990   "Zhongguo chuantong jianzhu goutu de tezheng, bili yu wending" 中国传统建筑构图的特征・比例与稳定 [Compositional characteristics of traditional Chinese architecture—scale and stability]. *Jianzhushi* 建筑师 [The architect] 39:97-113.

1991   "Guangdong Chaozhou minju zhangganfa" 广东潮州民居丈竿法 [The method of using a rule in Chaozhou, Guangdong]. In Lu Yuanding 陆元鼎, chief ed. *Zhongguo chuantong minju yu wenhua, di'yi ji* 中国传统民居与文化・第一辑 [China's traditional vernacular dwellings and culture, vol. 1], pp. 189-197. Beijing: Zhongguo jianzhu gongye chubanshe 中国建筑工业出版社.

1996   "Zhongguo minju yanjiu de huigu yu zhanwang" 中国民居研究的回顾与展望 [A review and prospect concerning research on Chinese vernacular dwellings]. Paper presented at the Seventh National Conference on Vernacular Architecture, Taiyuan, August 14.

Lu Yuanding 陆元鼎, chief ed.

1991   *Zhongguo chuantong minju yu wenhua, di'yi ji* 中国传统民居与文化・第一辑 [China's traditional vernacular dwellings and culture, vol. 1]. Beijing: Zhongguo jianzhu gongye chubanshe 中国建筑工业出版社.

1992   *Zhongguo chuantong minju yu wenhua, di'er ji* 中国传统民居与文化・第二辑 [China's traditional vernacular dwellings and culture, vol. 2]. Beijing: Zhongguo jianzhu gongye chubanshe 中国建筑工业出版社.

1995   *Minju shilun yu wenhua* 民居史论与文化 [History and culture of vernacular architecture]. Guangzhou: Huanan ligong daxue chubanshe 华南理工大学出版社.

Lu Yuanding 陆元鼎 and Lu Qi 陆琦

1992   *Zhongguo minju zhuangshi zhuangxiu yishu* 中國

民居裝飾裝修藝術 [Art of the ornamentation and decoration of China's vernacular dwellings]. Shanghai: Shanghai kexue jishu chubanshe 上海科學技術出版社.

Lu Yuanding 陆元鼎, Ma Xiuzhi 马秀之, and Deng Qisheng 邓其生

1981 "Guangdong minju" 广东民居 [Vernacular dwellings of Guangdong]. *Jianzhu xuebao* 建筑学报 [Architectural journal] 157:29–40.

Lu Yuanding 陆元鼎 and Wei Yanjun 魏彦均

1982 "Guangdong Chao Shan minju" 广东潮汕民居 [Vernacular dwellings of Chaoan and Shantou, Guangdong]. *Jianzhushi* 建筑师 [The architect] 13:141–162.

1990 *Guangdong minju* 广东民居 [Vernacular dwellings of Guangdong]. Beijing: Zhongguo jianzhu gongye chubanshe 中国建筑工业出版社.

1995 "Guangdong Chaoan Xiangpuzhai minju pingmian goucheng ji xingzhi chutan" 广东潮安象埔寨民居平面构成及形制雏探 [Preliminary discussion of the structure and shape of dwelling plans in Xiangpuzhai, Chaoan, Guangdong]. Paper presented at the Sixth National Conference on Chinese Vernacular Architecture, Xinjiang, August.

Lu Yuanding 陆元鼎 and Yang Gusheng 杨谷生, chief eds.

1988 *Minju jianzhu* 民居建筑 [The architecture of vernacular dwellings]. In *Zhongguo meishu quanji* 中国美术全集 [Complete collection of China's arts, part 5]. Beijing: Zhongguo jianzhu gongye chubanshe 中国建筑工业出版社.

Lung, David Ping-yee 龍炳頤

1978 "Heaven, Earth and Man: Concepts and Processes of Chinese Architecture and City Planning." Unpublished Master of Architecture Thesis, Centre for Environmental Research, University of Oregon.

1979 "Fung Shui, an Intrinsic Way to Environmental Design with Illustration of Kat Hing Wai." *Asian Architect and Builder* 8(10):16–23. Also published in *Journal of Royal Asiatic Society, Hong Kong Branch* 20(1981):81–92.

1991 *Chinese Traditional Vernacular Architecture* 中國傳統民居建築. Bilingual edition. Hong Kong: Regional Council.

1992 *Hong Kong Architecture: Contemporary and Past.* Hong Kong: Joint Publishing.

1993 "What Is Worth Conserving." *History Newsletter* 3:33–35.

1995 "Defensive Architecture of the New Territories." In P. H. Hase and Elizabeth Sinn, eds. *Beyond the Metropolis: Villages in Hong Kong*, pp. 67–75. Hong Kong: Joint Publishing (H.K.) Company Limited.

1997 "Heritage Preservation in a High Density and a Valued Environment—the case in Hong Kong." In *Proceedings Sixth AWPNUC International Symposium*, pp. 89–95.

Lung, David, and Ann Friedman

1997 "Heritage Conservation and Conflicting Community Interests: Heritage Held Hostage in the New Territories and Beyond." Unpublished paper.

Luo Xiaowei 羅小未 and Wu Jiang 伍江, eds.

1997 *Shanghai Longtang* 上海弄堂 [Shanghai neighborhoods]. Shanghai renmin meishu chubanshe 上海人民美术出版社.

Lust, John

1996 *Chinese Popular Prints.* Leiden: E. J. Brill.

Ma Bingjian 马炳坚

1995 *Beijing siheyuan* 北京四合院 [Quadrangles of Beijing]. Beijing: Beijing meishu sheying chubanshe 北京美术摄影出版社.

Ma Ping 马平 and Lai Cunli 賴存理

1995 *Zhongguo Musilin minju wenhua* 中国穆斯林民居文化 [Moslem vernacular architecture in China]. Yinchuan: Ningxia renmin chubanshe 宁夏人民出版社.

Ma Shiyun 馬世雲 and Song Zilong 宋子龍, eds.

1988 *Huizhou mudiao yishu* 徽州木雕藝術 [The art of wood carving in Huizhou]. Hefei: Anhui meishu chubanshe 安徽美术出版社.

Ma Yin 马寅

1989 *China's Minority Nationalities.* Beijing: Foreign Languages Press.

Macgregor, Peter

1985 "A Home for Seven Generations: Chai Hsing Mountain Villa." *Free China Review* 35(11):26–36.

Mackerras, Colin

1994 *China's Minorities: Integration and Modernization in the Twentieth Century.* Hong Kong: Oxford University Press.

1995 *China's Minority Cultures: Identities and Integration since 1912.* New York: St. Martin's Press.

March, Andrew

1968 "An Appreciation of Chinese Geomancy." *Journal of Asian Studies* 27:253–267.

McColl, Robert

1989 "By Their Dwellings Shall We Know Them: Home and Setting among China's Inner Asian Ethnic Groups." *Focus* 39(4):1–6.

McKhann, Charles F.

1989 "Fleshing out the Bones: The Cosmic and Social Dimensions of Space in Naxi Architecture." *New Asia Academic Bulletin* 8:157–177.

1995 "The Naxi and the Nationalities Question." In Stevan Harrell, ed. *Cultural Encounters on China's*

Ethnic Frontiers, pp. 39-62. Seattle: University of Washington Press.

Mei Qing
1996   "Rebuilding Eden: Overseas Chinese Settlements in South Fujian. In *Fluid Traditions: The Immigration of Peoples and Cultures. Traditional Dwellings and Settlements Working Paper Series* 89:45-55. Berkeley: Center for Environmental Design Research, University of California.

Miao Mo 妙摩 and Hui Du 慧度
1993   *Zhongguo fengshui shu* 中国风水术 [The methods of Chinese *fengshui*]. Beijing: *Zhongguo wenlian chuban gongsi* 中国文联出版公司.

Miao Po 缪朴
1989-   "Chuantong de benzhi—Zhongguo chuantong
1991   jianzhu de shisange tedian" 传统的本质—中国传统建筑的十三个特点 [The essence of tradition—thirteen special characteristics of traditional Chinese architecture]. *Jianzhushi* 建筑师 [The architect] 36:56-69; 80:61-69, 80.

Mogi Keiichirō 茂木計一朗, Inaji Toshirō 稲次敏朗, and Katayama Kazutoshi 片山和俊
1991   *Chūgoku minkyo no kūkan o saguru: gunkyo ruijū—"hikari, mizu, tsuchi" Chūgoku tōnanbu no jūkūkan* 中国民居の空間を探る：群居類住—"光。水。土" 中国東南部の住空間 [Chinese vernacular architecture research: types of ensemble architecture—"Light, water, and earth": a discussion of residential spaces in southeastern China]. Tokyo: Kenchiku Shiryō Kenkyūsha 建築資料研究社. Translated into Chinese as *Zhongguo minju yanjiu* 中國民居研究：中國東南地方居住空間探討. Taipei: Nantian shuju youxian gongsi 南天書局有限公司, 1996.

Myrdal, Jan
1965   *Report from a Chinese Village*. New York: New American Library.

Needham, Joseph
1971   *Science and Civilization in China*. Vol. 4. *Physical Technology*. Cambridge: Cambridge University Press.

Oliver, Paul
1987   *Dwellings: The House around the World*. Austin: University of Texas Press.

Oliver, Paul, ed.
1997   *Encyclopedia of World Vernacular Architecture*. Cambridge: Cambridge University Press.

Pai, Chin 白瑾
1989   "Traditional Chinese House Form: The Courtyard House Compound of Peking." *Asian Cultural Quarterly* 17(3):39-56.

Pan An 潘安
1994   "Fangyan, minxi yu difang chuantong jianzhu

fengge" 方言・民系与地方传统建筑风格 [Dialects, ethnicity and local traditional architectural styles]. *Jianzhushi* 建筑师 [The architect] 56:52-59.

1994-   Kejia minxi yu Kejia juju jianzhu" 客家民系与
1995   客家聚居建筑(一)(二)(三)(四) [Hakka ethnicity and Hakka residential architecture, parts 1, 2, 3, 4]. *Jianzhushi* 建筑师 [The architect] 61: 455-468; 62:91-101; 63:50-58; 64:105-112.

1995   "Kejia jianzhu wenhua liuyuan chutan" 客家建筑文化流源初探 [A study of the origin and development of Hakka architectural culture]. In Lu Yuanding 陆元鼎, chief ed. *Minju shilun yu wenhua* 民居史论与文化 [History and culture of vernacular architecture], pp. 63-67. Guangzhou: Huanan ligong daxue chubanshe 华南理工大学出版社.

Peng Yigang 彭一刚
1994   *Chuantong cunzhen juluo jingguan fenxi* 传统村镇聚落景观分析 [An analysis of the landscapes of traditional village settlements]. Beijing: Zhongguo jianzhu gongye chubanshe 中国建筑工业出版社.

Po Sung-nien 薄松年 and David Johnson
1992   *Domesticated Deities and Auspicious Emblems: The Iconography of Everyday Life in Village China*. Berkeley: Chinese Popular Culture Project.

Rao Weichun 饶维纯 and Yu Bing 于冰
1994   "Yunnan sheng Kunming diqu 'yikeyin' minju" 云南省昆明地区一颗印民居 [*Yikeyin* dwellings in the Kunming area of Yunnan]. In Wang Zhili 汪之力, chief ed. *Zhongguo chuantong minju jianzhu* 中国传统民居建筑 [Chinese traditional architecture of residence (sic)], pp. 149-150. Jinan: Shandong kexue jishu chubanshe 山东科学技术出版社.

Raper, Arthur F.
1953   *Rural Taiwan—Problem and Promise*. Taipei: Chinese-American Joint Commission on Rural Reconstruction.

Rapoport, Amos
1969   *House Form and Culture*. Englewood Cliffs: Prentice-Hall.

Ren Naiqiang 任乃強
1934   *Xikang tujing, minsu pian* 西康圖經,民俗篇 [Illustrated record of Xikang, customs]. Nanjing: Xinya xiya xuehui 新亞細亞學會.

Ruitenbeek, Klaas
1986   "Craft and Ritual in Traditional Chinese Carpentry." *Chinese Science* 7:1-23.

1993   *Building & Carpentry in Late Imperial China: A Study of the Fifteenth Century Carpenter's Manual Lu Ban jing*. Leiden: E. J. Brill.

Rural Architecture in Hong Kong
1979   Hong Kong: Government Information Services.

Ruxianguli 茹先古丽
1993   "Traditional Houses in Kashgar and the Distinctive Features of the City." Paper presented at the International Conference on Chinese Traditional Houses, Guangzhou, Guangdong, August 12.

Samuels, Carmencita Mariano
1986   "Cultural Ideology and the Landscape of Confucian China: The Tradition of the *Si he yuan*." Unpublished Master of Arts thesis, Department of Geography, University of British Columbia.

Shan Deqi 单德启
1984   "Cunxi, tianjing, matouqiang—Huizhou minju biji" 村溪, 天井, 马头墙—徽州民居笔记 [Village streams, *tianjing*, gable walls—notes on the vernacular architecture of Huizhou]. *Jianzhu shi lunwenji* 建筑史论文集 [Treatise on the history of architecture] 6:120-134.
1992   "Hongcun Village, Anhui: A Place of Rivers and Lakes." In Ronald G. Knapp, ed. *Chinese Landscapes: The Village as Place*, pp. 119-127. Honolulu: University of Hawai'i Press.
1995   "Xiangtu minju he 'yexing siwei'" 乡土民居和 "野性思维" [Vernacular dwellings and 'wild thinking']. *Jianzhu xuebao* 建筑学报 [Architectural journal] 3:19-21.

Shan Shiyuan 单士元
1981a   "Hangtu jishu qiantan" 夯土技术浅谈 [Summary talk on earth-tamping techniques], *Kejishi wenji* 科技史文集 [Collection of the history of science and technology] 7:119-123.
1981b   "Zhongguo wuwa de fazhan guocheng shitan" 中国屋瓦的发展过程试探 [Tentative research into the development of Chinese roof tiles], *Jianzhu lishi yu lilun* 建筑历史与理论 [Corpus of architectural history and theory] 2:1-4.

Shang Guo 尚廓 and Yang Lingyu 杨玲玉
1982   "Chuantong tingyuan shi zhuzhai yu diceng gaomidu" 传统庭院式住宅与低层高密度 [Traditional courtyard style houses and the high densities of ground floors]. *Jianzhu xuebao* 建筑学报 [Architectural journal] 5:51-60, 72.

Shaw, Victor N.
1997   "Urban Housing Reform in China." *Habitat International* 21(2):199-212.

Shemie, Bonnie
1996   *Houses of China*. Toronto: Tundra Books.

Shen Hua 沈华, chief ed.
1993   *Shanghai lilong minju* 上海里弄民居 [Vernacular dwellings of Shanghai's neighborhoods]. Beijing: Zhongguo jianzhu gongye chubanshe 中国建筑工业出版社.

Shi Min 石敏
1995   "Mengguzu minju" 蒙古族民居 [Mongol vernacular dwellings]. In Yan Dachun 严大椿, chief ed. *Xinjiang minju* 新疆民居 [Vernacular dwellings of Xinjiang], pp. 273-296. Beijing: Zhongguo jianzhu gongye chubanshe 中国建筑工业出版社.

Shih Tien-fu [Shi Tianfu] 施添福
1991   "Taiwan Zhuqian diqu chuantong daozuo nongcun de minzhai: yige renwen shengtaixue de quanshi" 臺灣竹塹地區傳統蹈作農村的民宅: 一個人文生態學的詮釋 [Traditional houses in rural Taiwan: a human ecological approach]. *Shida dili yanjiu baogao* 師大地理研究報告 17:39-62.

Si Xinzhi 斯心直
1992   *Xinan minzu jianzhu yanjiu* 西南民族建筑研究 [Studies of national architecture of Southwest China]. Kunming: Yunnan jiaoyu chubanshe 云南教育出版社.

Skinner, R. T. F.
1958   "Chinese Domestic Architecture." *Journal of the Royal Institute of British Architects* 65:430-431.

Smith, Richard J.
1991   *Fortune-Tellers & Philosophers: Divination in Traditional Chinese Society*. Boulder: Westview Press.

Song Zilong 宋子龍 and Ma Shiyun 馬世雲, eds.
1990   *Huizhou zhuandiao yishu* 徽州磚雕藝術 [The art of brick engraving in Huizhou]. Hefei: Anhui meishu chubanshe 安徽美术出版社.

Spencer, Joseph E.
1947   "The Houses of the Chinese." *Geographical Review* 37:254-273.

Starikov, Vladimir Sergeevich
1967   *Material'naja Kul'tura Kitajcev Severo-Vostochnch Provinciij KNR*. Moscow: Izd-vo Nauka.

Stein, Rolf A.
1990   *The World in Miniature: Container Gardens and Dwellings in Far Eastern Religious Thought*. Translated by Phyllis Brooks. Stanford: Stanford University Press.

Steinhardt, Nancy Shatzman
1990   "East Asia: Architectural History across War Zones and Political Boundaries." In Elisabeth Blair MacDougall, ed. *The Architectural Historian in America*. Hanover and London: National Gallery of Art and the University Press of New England.

Steinhardt, Nancy Shatzman, ed.
1984   *Chinese Traditional Architecture*. New York: China Institute in America.

Stille, Alexander
1998   "Faking It." *The New Yorker* 74 (June 15):36-43.

Sugimoto Hisatsugu 杉本尚次, ed.
1984   *Nihon no sumai no genryū: Nihon kiso bunka no*

tankyū 日本のす まいの 源流：日本基層文化 の 探究 [The origin of Japanese folk dwellings]. Tokyo: Bunka Shuppankyoku 文化出版局.

Sun, Paul

1982   "Underground Houses." *Mimar: Architecture in Development* 3:41–46.

Sung Ying-hsing [Song Yingxing] 宋应星

1966   *T'ien-kung k'ai-wu: Chinese Technology in the Seventeenth Century.* Translated by E-tu Zen Sun and Shiou-chuan Sun. University Park: Pennsylvania University Press.

1983   *Tiangong kaiwu* 天工開物 [The creations of nature and man]. Taipei: Taiwan shangwu yinshuguan 臺灣 商務印書館.

Tanaka Tan 田中淡

1995   "The Symbolism of the Roof in Chinese Architecture." In *Form and Symbol*, pp. 63–74. Hong Kong: Chinese University of Hong Kong, Department of Architecture.

Tao Fu 陶复

1984   "Jianzhu kaogu sanshi nian zongshu" 建筑考古 三十年综述 [Survey of architectural archaeology of the past 30 years]. *Jianzhu lishi yu lilun* 建 筑历史与理论 [Corpus of architectural history and theory] 3/4:13–52.

Tao Fuhai 陶富海

1992   "Shanxi Xiangfen Dingcun minju" 山西襄汾丁 村 民 居 [Vernacular dwellings of Dingcun, Xiangfen, Shanxi]. *Wenwu* 文物 [Cultural relics] 6:53–62.

1993a   "Dingcun Ming Qing minju shizuo yishu" 丁村 明清民居石作艺术 [The artistry of stonework on Ming-Qing dwellings in Dingcun]. *Wenwu jikan* 文物季刊 [Journal of Chinese antiquity] 2:73–78.

1993b   "Dingcun Ming Qing minju muzuo yishu" 丁村 明清民居木作艺术 [The artistry of woodwork on Ming-Qing dwellings in Dingcun]. *Wenwu jikan* 文物季刊 [Journal of Chinese antiquity] 4:67–71, 89.

1995   "Dingcun Ming Qing minju jianzhu gaishu" 丁 村明清民居建筑 概述 [An introduction to the Ming-Qing domestic architecture of Dingcun]. In Tao Fuhai, ed. *Pingyang minsu congtan* 平阳民 俗丛谭 [Collection of folk customs concerning Ping-Yang]. Taiyuan: Shanxi guji chubanshe 山 西古籍出版社.

Thorpe, Robert

1983   "Origins of Chinese Architectural Style: The Earliest Plans and Building Types." *Archives of Asian Art* 36:22–39.

1984   "The Architectural Heritage of the Bronze Age." In Nancy Shatzman Steinhardt, ed. *Chinese Tra-* ditional Architecture, pp. 60–67. New York: China Institute in America.

1986   "Architectural Principles in Early Imperial China: Structural Problems and Their Solution." *Art Bulletin* 68(3):360–376.

1992   "'Let the Past Serve the Present': The Ideological Claims of Cultural Relics Work." *China Exchange News* 20(2):16–19.

Tseng Li-ling

1988a   "Architect as Preservationist." *Free China Review* 38(12):48–53.

1988b   "Cultural Values in Wood and Stone." *Free China Review* 38(12):36–47.

Unger, Jonathan

1997   "Not Quite Han: The Ethnic Minorities of China's Southwest." *Bulletin of Concerned Asian Scholars* 29(3):67–78.

von Glahn, Richard

1987   *The Country of Streams and Grottoes: Expansion, Settlement, and the Civilizing of the Sichuan Frontier.* Cambridge: Harvard University Press.

von Poseck, Helena

1905   "How John Chinaman Builds His House." *East of Asia Magazine* 4:348–355.

Waldron, Arthur

1990   *The Great Wall of China: From History to Myth.* Cambridge: Cambridge University Press.

Waley, Arthur, trans.

1937   *The Book of Songs.* New York: Grove Press.

Wan Younan 万幼楠

1995   "Gannan weiwu ji qi chengyin" 赣南围屋及其成 因 [The *weiwu* of southern Jiangxi and the reasons for their origin]. In *Haixia liangan chuantong minju lilun qingnian zhuanjia xueshu yantaohui lunwenji* 海峡两岸传统民居理论青年专家学术研 讨会论文集 [Proceedings of the youth and specialist symposium on the theory of traditional vernacular dwellings on both sides of the Taiwan Straits], pp. 68–72. Guangzhou: Huanan ligong daxue jianzhu xi 华南理工大学建筑烬 .

Wang Cuilan 王翠兰 and Chen Moude 陈谋德, eds.

1993   *Yunnan minju xubian* 云南民居续编 [Vernacular dwellings of Yunnan, continued]. Beijing: Zhongguo jianzhu gongye chubanshe 中国建筑 工业 出版社.

Wang Enyong 王恩涌

1993   "Minju zhong de qiji—Fujian de tulou" 民居中 的奇迹—福建的土楼 [Wonders among vernacular dwellings—Fujian's *tulou*]. *Renwen dili* 人文 地理 8(1):8–12.

Wang Han-ch'ing

1981   "Feng-shui and Traditional Chinese Domestic Architecture." Unpublished Master of Science thesis, Department of Architecture, Cornell University.

Wang, Joseph Chuo 王綽

1991   "Zoufang guzhen Zhouzhuang: jingguan Zhongguo shuixiang zhi mei" 走訪古鎮周庄：靜觀中國水鄉之美 [A visit to old village Zhouzhuang: the tranquil beauty of Chinese watertowns]. *ARCH* 6:121-134.

1992a   "A Chinese Village in Transformation." *Places* 8(1):12-22.

1992b   "Heritage: Watertown Zhouzhuang." *Mimar: Architecture in Development* 42:28-33.

1992c   "Zhouzhuang, Jiangsu: A Historic Market Town." In Ronald G. Knapp, ed. *Chinese Landscapes: The Village as Place*, pp. 139-150. Honolulu: University of Hawai'i Press.

1998   *The Chinese Garden.* Hong Kong: Oxford University Press.

Wang Qijun 王其均

1991a   "Shanzhai cang gulou, Ming zhai yun qihuan" 山寨藏古楼, 明宅蘊奇幻 [Mountain strongholds contain old structures, Ming dwellings contain strange illusions]. *Jianzhushi* 建筑师 [The architect] 43:92-99.

1991b   *Zhongguo minju* 中国民居 [China's vernacular dwellings]. Shanghai: Renmin meishu chubanshe 人民美术出版社.

1993a   *Minjian zhuzhai jianzhu: yuanlou yaodong siheyuan* 民间住宅建筑：圆楼窑洞四合院 [The architecture of vernacular dwellings: *yuanlou, yaodong, and siheyuan*]. Beijing: Zhongguo jianzhu gongye chubanshe 中国建筑工业出版社.

1993b   *Zhongguo chuantong minju jianzhu* 中國傳統民居建築 [China's traditional vernacular architecture]. Taipei: Nantian shuju youxian gongsi 南天書局有限司.

1994   *Lao fangzi—Shanxi minju* 老房子—山西民居 [Old houses—vernacular dwellings of Shanxi]. Photography by Li Yuxiang 李玉祥. Nanjing: Jiangsu meishu chubanshe 江苏美术出版社.

1995   "Minsu wenhua dui minju xingzhi de zhiyue" 民俗文化对民居型制的制约 [Folk cultural factors underlying the typological organization of traditional dwellings]. In *Society, Culture and Architecture*, pp. 38-59. Bilingual text. Hong Kong: Chinese University of Hong Kong, Department of Architecture.

1996a   *Zhongguo gudian jianzhu meishu congshu—Chengzhen minju* 中国古典建筑美术丛书—城镇民居 [Chinese classical architectural art collection—vernacular dwellings of cities and towns]. Shanghai: Renmin meishu chubanshe 人民美术出版社.

1996b   "Minsu wenhua dui minju xingzhi de zhiyue" 民俗文化对民居型制的制约 [Formative conditions affecting folk culture and vernacular dwellings]. In Huang Hao 黄浩, ed. *Zhongguo chuantong minju yu wenhua, disi ji* 中国传统民居与文化·第四辑 [China's traditional vernacular dwellings and culture, vol. 4], pp. 67-74. Beijing: Zhongguo jianzhu gongye chubanshe 中国建筑工业出版社.

1996c   "The artistry of Chinese Vernacular Dwellings" [Minjian zhuzhai de yishu tezheng 民间住宅的艺术特征]. In Richard J. Latham, ed. *A Spiritual Resonance: The vernacular dwellings of China* [Gufeng wujia: Zhongguo chuantong minju xuancui 古风无价：中国传统民居选萃]. Bilingual text. Hong Kong: United Technologies Corporation and Jiangsu Fine Arts Press.

1998a   "Tingtang yiyun zhi goucheng 廳堂意蘊之構成 [The main hall—nucleus of the Chinese home. In *Zhongguo gudian jiaju yu shenghuo huanjing—Lo Kai-yin shoucang qingxuan* 中國古典家具與生活環境—羅啓妍收藏精選 [Classical and vernacular Chinese furniture in the living environment—examples from the Kai-yin Lo collection], pp. 90-96. Bilingual text. Hong Kong: Yungmintang 雍明堂.

1998b   *Lao fangzi—Beijing siheyuan* 老房子—北京四合院 [Old houses—Beijing *siheyuan*]. Photography by Li Yuxiang 李玉祥. Nanjing: Jiangsu meishu chubanshe 江苏美术出版社.

Wang Shixiang

1986   *Classic Chinese Furniture.* Hong Kong: Joint Publications.

Wang Shucun 王树村

1985   *Minjian nianhua* 民间年画 [Folk New Year's prints]. Beijing: Renmin meishu chubanshe 人民美术出版社.

1992a   *Paper Joss: Deity Worship through Folk Prints* 中国古代民俗版画 [Zhongguo gudai minsu banhua]. Beijing: New World Press 新世界出版社.

1992b   *Zhongguo jixiang tu jicheng* 中國吉祥圖集成 [Collection of Chinese auspicious prints]. Shijiazhuang: Hebei renmin chubanshe 河北人民出版社.

Wang, Sung-hsing

1974   "Taiwanese Architecture and the Supernatural." In Arthur P. Wolf, ed. *Religion and Ritual in Chinese Society*, pp. 183-192. Stanford: Stanford University Press.

Wang Weijen 王維仁

1987   "Penghu heyuan zhuzhai xingshi ji qi kongjian jiegou zhuanhua" 澎湖合院住宅形式及其空間結構轉化 [Prototype and transformation of courtyard houses in Penghu]. *Guoli Taiwan daxue jianzhu yu chengxiang yanjiu xuebao* 國立 臺灣大學建築與城鄉研究學報 [Bulletin of architecture and city planning, National Taiwan University] 3(1):87-118.

1993   "The Typological Evolution and its Social Dominance in Jinmen." In *Miscegenation of House Form. Traditional Dwellings and Settlements Working Paper Series* 39:40-54. Berkeley: Center for Environmental Design Research, University of California.

Wang Zhili 王之力, chief ed.

1994   *Zhongguo chuantong minju jianzhu* 中国传统民 居建筑 [Chinese traditional architecture of residence (sic)]. Jinan: Shandong kexue jishu chubanshe 山东科学技术出版社.

Wang Zhongshu

1982   *Han Civilization*. Translated by K. C. Chang and collaborators. New Haven: Yale University Press.

Wang Zhunqin 王准勤

1991   "Tigao beifang minju re shushixing de yanjiu" 提高北方民居热舒适性的研究 [The improvement of thermal comfort in rural houses in north China]. In Lu Yuanding 陆元鼎, chief ed. *Zhongguo chuantong minju yu wenhua, di'yi ji* 中国 传统民居与文化·第一辑 [China's traditional vernacular dwellings and culture, vol. 1], pp. 238-244. Beijing: Zhongguo jianzhu gongye chubanshe 中国建筑工业出版社.

Wei Guanglai 魏广来 and Li Huimin 李惠民

1986   *Nongcun jianzhu jianming shouce* 农村建筑简明 手册. Taiyuan: Shanxi renmin chubanshe 山西 人民出版社.

Wei Yanjun 魏彦均

1991   "Guangdong qiaoxiang minju" 广东侨乡民居 [Vernacular dwellings of the overseas townships in Guangdong]. In Lu Yuanding 陆元鼎, chief ed. *Zhongguo chuantong minju yu wenhua, di'yi ji* 中国传统民居与文化·第一辑 [China's traditional vernacular dwellings and culture, vol. 1], pp. 121-133. Beijing: Zhongguo jianzhu gongye chubanshe 中国建筑工业出版社.

1992   "Yuebei Yaozu minju yu wenhua" 粤北瑶族民居 与文化 [Yao nationality dwellings and culture in northern Guangdong]. In Lu Yuanding 陆元鼎, chief ed. *Zhongguo chuantong minju yu wenhua, di'er ji* 中国传统民居与文化·第二辑 [China's traditional vernacular dwellings and culture, vol. 2], pp. 90-97. Beijing: Zhongguo jianzhu gongye chubanshe 中国建筑工业出版社.

Wei Yicao 魏挹曹, Fang Xianfu 方咸孚, Wang Jikui 王齐 凯, and Zhang Yukun 张玉坤, eds.

1995   *Xiangxi chengzhen yu fengtu jianzhu* 湘西城镇与 风土建筑 [The vernacular architecture of the cities and towns of western Hunan]. Tianjin: Tianjin daxue chubanshe 天津大学出版社.

Weng Li 瓮立, chief ed.

1994   *Beijing de hutong* 北京的胡同 [Hutongs of Beijing]. Bilingual edition. Beijing: Beijing meishu sheying chubanshe 北京美术摄影出版社.

Williams, C. A. S.

1932   *Outlines of Chinese Symbolism and Art Motifs*. Shanghai: Kelly & Walsh.

Wong Shiu Kwan

1970   *Macao Architecture: An Integrate of Chinese and Portuguese Influences*. Macao: Imprensa Nacional.

Wood, Francis

1987   "Style in Rural Domestic Architecture: the *yang-fang*." In Rosemary E. Scott and Graham Hutt, eds. *Style in the East Asian Tradition, Colloquies on Art & Archaeology in Asia No. 14*, pp. 217-227. London: University of London, School of Oriental and African Studies.

1996   "Domestic Architecture: Historical Development." In Jane Shoaf Turner, ed. *Macmillan Dictionary of Art*, pp. 684-693. London: Macmillan.

Wu Liangyong 吴良镛

1994   *Beijing jiu cheng yu Ju'er hutong* 北京旧城与菊儿 胡同 [The old city of Beijing and Ju'er lane]. Beijing: Zhongguo jianzhu gongye chubanshe 中国 建筑工业出版社.

Wu, Nelson [Wu Nosun]

1963   *Chinese and Indian Architecture: The City of Man, the Mountain of Gold, and the Realm of the Immortals*. New York: George Braziller.

Wu Qingzhou 吴庆州

1993   "Xiangtian, fadi, faren, faziran—Zhongguo chuantong jianzhu yijiang fahui" 象天·法 地·法人·法自然—中国传统建筑意匠发微 [Heavenly portents, earthly laws, laws of men, and natural law—the abstract conceptualization of Chinese traditional architecture]. *Huazhong jianzhu* 华中建筑 [Huazhong architecture] 11(4):71-76.

1994   "Zhongguo minju jianzhu yishu de xiangzheng zhuyi" 中国民居建筑艺术的象征主义 [The symbolic meaning of Chinese vernacular architectural ornamentation]. Paper presented at the Fifth National Conference on Chinese Vernacular Architecture, Chongqing, Sichuan, May.

Wu Xinghan 吴兴汉

1980   "Huizhou diqu Ming Qing jianzhu de xingcheng ji qi leixing" 徽州地区明清建筑的形成 及其类型 [Development and form of Ming and Qing dynasty Huizhou architecture]. *Anhui wenbo* 安徽文博 [Anhui culture] 1:61-67.

Xu Minsu 徐民苏, Zhan Yongwei 詹永伟, Liang Zhixia 梁支厦, Ren Huakun 任华堃, and Shao Qing 邵庆, eds.

1991　*Suzhou minju* 苏州民居 [The vernacular dwellings of Suzhou]. Beijing: Zhongguo jianzhu gongye chubanshe 中国建筑工业出版社.

Xu Ping

1990　"Feng-shui: A Model for Landscape Analysis." Unpublished Dr.Des. dissertation, Graduate School of Design, Harvard University.

Xu Yinong 许亦农

1989- "Zhongguo chuantong fuhe kongjian guannian"
1990　中国传统复合空间观念—上·中·下 [Composite space concepts in traditional Chinese architecture, parts 1, 2, 3]. *Jianzhushi* 建筑师 [The architect] 36:68-87; 38:71-37; 39:67-82.

Yan Dachun 严大椿, chief ed.

1995　*Xinjiang minju* 新疆民居 [Vernacular dwellings of Xinjiang]. Beijing: Zhongguo jianzhu gongye chubanshe 中国建筑工业出版社.

Yan Jichen 颜记臣, Yang Ping 杨平, and Zhang Liuzhu 张留柱

1994　"Shanxi sheng Qixian Qiaojia dayuan" 山西省祁县乔家大院 [Qiaojia manor, Qixian, Shanxi]. In Wang Zhili 汪之力, chief ed. *Zhongguo chuantong minju jianzhu* 中国传统民居建筑 [Chinese traditional architecture of residence (sic)], pp. 115-117. Jinan: Shandong kexue jishu chubanshe 山东科学技术出版社.

Yang Changming 杨昌鸣

1993　"Ganlan jianzhu yanjiu santi" 干栏建筑研究三题 [Three research topics regarding *ganlan* architecture]. *Jianzhushi* 建筑师 [The architect] 51:77-103.

Yang Chunfeng 杨春风

1993　"Architectural Colors of Tibetan Houses." *Proceedings of the International Conference on Chinese Traditional Houses*, pp. 191-195. Guangzhou: South China University of Technology.

1995　"Xizang chuantong minju jianzhu huanjing secai wenhua" 西藏传统民居建筑环境色彩文化 [Colorful culture of the traditional vernacular architectural environment in Tibet]. In Lu Yuanding 陆元鼎, chief ed. *Minju shilun yu wenhua* 民居史论与文化 [History and culture of vernacular architecture], pp. 80-84. Guangzhou: Huanan ligong daxue chubanshe 华南理工大学出版社.

Yang Gusheng 杨谷生

1995　"Weizi, baozi yu dugang loudian" 围子·堡子与都纲楼殿 [Fortresses, forts and urban halls]. In Lu Yuanding 陆元鼎, chief ed. *Minju shilun yu wenhua* 民居史论与文化 [History and culture of vernacular architecture], pp. 19-23. Guang-zhou: Huanan ligong daxue chubanshe 华南理工大学出版社.

Yang Hongxun 杨鸿勋

1980a　"Hemudu yizhi mugou shuijing jianding ji caoqi mugou gongyi kaocha" 河姆渡遗址木构水井鉴定及早期木构工艺考察 [Identification of the timber structure well at the Hemudu site and inspection of the technology of early timber structure]. *Kejishi wenji* 科技史文集 [Collection on the history of science and technology] 5:63-70.

1980b　"Zhongguo zaoqi jianzhu de fazhan" 中国早期建筑的发展 [Development of early architecture in China]. *Jianzhu lishi yu lilun* 建筑历史与理论 [Corpus of architectural history and theory] 1:112-135.

1981　"Xi Zhou Qiyi jianzhu yizhi chubu kaocha" 西周歧邑建筑遗址初步考查 [Preliminary examination of the Western Zhou Qishan architectural remains]. *Wenwu* 文物 3:23-33.

Yang Shenchu 杨慎初, ed.

1993　*Hunan chuantong jianzhu* 湖南传统建筑 [Traditional architecture of Hunan]. Changsha: Hunan jiaoyu chubanshe 湖南教育出版社.

Ye Qishen 叶启燊

1992　*Sichuan Zangzu minzhai* 四川藏族民宅 [The vernacular dwellings of Tibetans in Sichuan]. Chengdu: Sichuan minzu chubanshe 四川民族出版社.

Yin Yongda 殷永达

1996　"Huizhou Chengkan gucun ji Ming zhai diaocha" 徽州呈坎古村及明宅调查 [Investigation of the Ming dynasty dwellings found in Chengkan old village in Huizhou]. In Huang Hao 黄浩, ed. *Zhongguo chuantong minju yu wenhua, disi ji* 中国传统民居与文化·第四辑 [China's traditional vernacular dwellings and culture, vol. 4], pp. 113-117. Beijing: Zhongguo jianzhu gongye chubanshe 中国建筑工业出版社.

Yongding tulou bianxiezu 永定土楼编写组, ed.

1990　*Yongding tulou* 永定土楼 [Yongding *tulou*]. Fuzhou: Fujian renmin chubanshe 福建人民出版社.

Yoon, Hong-key

1990　"Loess Cave-Dwellings in Shaanxi Province, China." *GeoJournal* 21(1-2):95-102.

Yu Hongli 俞宏理

1994a　*Huizhou minjian diaoke yishu* 徽州民间雕刻艺术 [The art of Huizhou vernacular carving]. Beijing: Renmin meishu chubanshe 人民美术出版社.

1994b　*Lao fangzi—Wannan minju* 老房子—皖南民居 [Old houses—vernacular dwellings of Southern Anhui]. Photography by Li Yuxiang 李玉祥.

Nanjing: Jiangsu meishu chubanshe 江苏美术出版社.

Yunnan sheng sheji yuan 云南省设计院, ed.

1986   *Yunnan minju* 云南民居 [Vernacular dwellings of Yunnan]. Beijing: Zhongguo jianzhu gongye chubanshe 中国建筑工业出版社.

Zeng Wuyue 曾五岳

1992   "Zhongguo yuanlou yanjiu" 中国圆楼研究 [Research on Chinese *yuanlou*]. *Jianzhushi* 建筑师 [The architect] 46:70-76.

Zhang Bitian 张壁田 and Liu Zhenya 刘振亚

1993   *Shaanxi minju* 陕西民居 [Vernacular dwellings of Shaanxi]. Beijing: Zhongguo jianzhu gongye chubanshe 中国建筑工业出版社.

Zhang Dingxiong 张定雄, general ed.

1994   *Yongding xianzhi* 永定县志 [Gazetteer of Yongding *xian*]. Fuzhou: Zhongguo kexue jishu chubanshe 中国科学技术出版社.

Zhang Guangshan 张广善

1993   "Gaoping xian Yuan dai minju" 高平县元代民居 [Yuan dynasty vernacular dwellings in Gaoping *xian*—the Ji residence]. *Wenwu jikan* 文物季刊 [Journal of Chinese antiquity] 3:29-33.

Zhang Liangnie 张良臬

1994   *Lao fangzi—Tujia diaojiaolou* 老房子—土家吊脚楼 [Old houses—overhanging houses of the Tujia nationality]. Nanjing: Jiangsu meishu chubanshe 江苏美术出版社.

Zhang Shengyi 张胜仪

1995   "Xinjiang de Hanzu minju" 新疆的汉族民居 [Han vernacular dwellings in Xinjiang]. In Yan Dachun 严大椿, chief ed. *Xinjiang minju* 新疆民居 [Vernacular dwellings of Xinjiang], pp. 155-170. Beijing: Zhongguo jianzhu gongye chubanshe 中国建筑工业出版社.

Zhang Sijie 张嗣介

1993   "Gannan Kejia weilou de wenhua beijing" 赣南客家围楼的文化背景 [The cultural background of Kejia *weilou* in Gannan]. Unpublished paper.

Zhang Yuhuan 张驭寰

1985a   *Jilin minju* 吉林民居 [Vernacular dwellings of Jilin]. Beijing: Zhongguo jianzhu gongye chubanshe 中国建筑工业出版社.

1986a   "Wo guo minjian juzhu fangwu yi pie" 我国民间居住房屋一瞥 [A glimpse at China's folk dwellings]. In Shanxi sheng gu jianzhu baohu yanjiusuo 山西省古建筑保护研究所, ed. *Zhongguo gu jianzhu xueshu zuotan wenji* 中国古建筑学术座谈文集 [Proceedings of the symposium on China's ancient architecture], pp. 201-210. Beijing: Zhongguo zhanwang chubanshe 中国展望出版社.

Zhang Yuhuan 张驭寰, chief compiler

1985b   *Zhongguo gudai jianzhu jishu shi* 中国古代建筑技术史 [History of China's ancient architectural technology]. Beijing: Kexue chubanshe 科学出版社.

1986b   *History and Development of Ancient Chinese Architecture.* Beijing: Science Press.

Zhang Yukun 张玉坤 and Song Kun 宋昆

1995   "Pingyao chuantong minju jianxi" 平谣传统民居简析 [Brief analysis of traditional dwellings in Pingyao]. In Lu Yuanding 陆元鼎, chief ed. *Minju shilun yu wenhua* 民居史论与文化 [History and culture of vernacular architecture], pp. 108-113. Guangzhou: Huanan ligong daxue chubanshe 华南理工大学出版社.

Zhang Zhaoji 张肇基, ed.

1995   *Beijing siheyuan* 北京四合院 [Quadrangles of Beijing]. Chinese/English bilingual edition. Beijing: Beijing meishu sheying chubanshe 北京美术摄影出版社.

Zhang Zhongyi 张仲一, Cao Jianbao 曹见宝, Fu Gaojie 傅高傑, and Du Xiujun 杜修均

1957   *Huizhou Mingdai zhuzhai* 徽州明代住宅 [Ming dynasty houses in Huizhou]. Beijing: Jianzhu gongcheng chubanshe 建筑工程出版社.

Zhao Songqiao

1994   *Geography of China: Environment, Resources, Population, and Development.* New York: John Wiley & Sons, Inc.

Zheng Guangfu 鄭光復

1993   *Lao fangzi—Jiangnan shuixiang minju* 老房子—江南水乡民居 [Old houses—vernacular dwellings of Jiangnan]. Nanjing: Jiangsu meishu chubanshe 江苏美术出版社.

Zhongguo gudian jiaju yu shenghuo huanjing—Lo Kai-yin

1998   *shoucang qingxuan* 中國古典家具與生活環境羅啓妍收藏精選 [Classical and vernacular Chinese furniture in the living environment—examples from the Kai-yin Lo collection]. Bilingual text. Hong Kong: Yongmingtang 雍明堂.

Zhongguo jianzhu jishu fazhan zhongxin, jianzhu lishi yanjiusuo 中国建筑技术发展中心·建筑历史研究所

1984   *Zhejiang minju* 浙江民居 [Vernacular dwellings of Zhejiang]. Beijing: Zhongguo jianzhu gongye chubanshe 中国建筑工业出版社.

Zhongguo kexueyuan tumu jianzhu yanjiusuo and Qinghua daxue jianzhuxi 中国科学院土木建筑研究所·清华大学建筑系, joint eds.

1957   *Zhongguo jianzhu* 中国建筑 [Chinese architecture]. Beijing: Wenwu chubanshe 文物出版社.

Zhou Lijun 周立军

1992   "Heilongjiang sheng chuantong minju chutan" 黑龙江省传统民居初探 [Preliminary examination of the traditional vernacular architecture of Heilongjiang province]. In Lu Yuanding 陆元鼎, chief ed. *Zhongguo chuantong minju yu wenhua, di'er ji* 中国传统民居与文化·第二辑 [China's traditional vernacular dwellings and culture, vol. 2], pp. 140-147. Beijing: Zhongguo jianzhu gongye chubanshe 中国建筑工业出版社.

Zhou Weiquan 周维权
1987   "Zangzu jianzhu" 藏族建筑 [Tibetan architecture]. *Jianzhushi* 建筑师 [The architect] 28:103-120.

Zhou Zhenhe
1991   "Migrations in Chinese History and Their Legacy on Chinese Dialects." In William S. Y. Wang, ed. *Languages and Dialects of China*, pp. 21-49. *Journal of Chinese Linguistics, Monograph Series No. 3.*

Zhu Baotian
1989   "A Preliminary Account of Ji-nuo Long-houses." *Thai-Yunnan Project Newsletter* 6:13-19. Translated by Irene Bain.

Zhu Fuyi 朱馥艺
1996   "Dongzu jianzhu yu shui" 侗族建筑与水 [Dong architecture and water]. *Huazhong jianzhu* 华中建筑 [Huazhong architecture] 14(1):1-4, 19.

Zhu Liangwen 朱良文
1988   *Lijiang Naxizu minju* 丽江纳西族民居 [Vernacular dwellings of the Lijiang Naxi]. Kunming: Yunnan keji chubanshe 云南科技出版社.

1992a   *The Dai, or the Tai and their Architecture and Customs in South China.* Bangkok: D. D. Book House.

1992b   "Yunnan minju zhong de bankaichang kongjian tanxi" 云南民居中的半开敞空间探析 [An analysis of semiopen spaces in Yunnan vernacular dwellings]. In Lu Yuanding 陆元鼎, chief ed. *Zhongguo chuantong minju yu wenhua, di'er ji* 中国传统民居与文化·第二辑 [China's traditional vernacular dwellings and culture, vol. 2], pp. 123-132. Beijing: Zhongguo jianzhu gongye chubanshe 中国建筑工业出版社.

1994   "Yunnan Yizu shanzhai—jinggan jiegou you cun" 云南彝族山寨—井干结构犹存 [Yi nationality mountain villages in Yunnan—*jinggan* structures still present]. Paper presented at the Fifth National Conference on Chinese Vernacular Architecture, Chongqing, Sichuan, May.

Zhu Qiqian 朱啓鈐
1930   "Inaugral [sic] Address: The Society for the Research in Chinese Architecture, February 16, 1930." *Zhonguo yingzao xueshe huikan* 中國營造學社彙刊 [Bulletin of the Society for the Research in Chinese Architecture] 1(1):1-10.

Zhuang Yuguang 庄裕光
1994   "Ba Shu minju yuanliu chutan" 巴蜀民居源流初探 [A brief discussion of the origin and development of vernacular dwellings in Ba and Shu]. Paper presented at the Fifth National Conference on Chinese Vernacular Architecture, Chongqing, Sichuan, May.

Zou Hongcan 邹洪灿
1993   "Taiwan Gaoshanzu minju" 台湾高山族民居 [Dwellings of Taiwan's Gaoshan tribes]. *Nanfang jianzhu* 南方建筑 [Southern architecture] 51:49-55.

Zou Ying 邹颖 and Gao Yilan 高亦兰
1994   "Jianzhu xingtai, shehui wenhua xinli, jianzhu wenhua" 建筑形态·社会文化心理·建筑文化—晋中南地区四合院研究 [Architectural form, sociocultural psychology, architectural culture: research into *siheyuan* in south central Shanxi]. *Jianzhushi* 建筑师 [The architect] 59:4-19.

Index

References to illustrations are in **boldface**.

ABOUT THE AUTHOR

RONALD G. KNAPP IS SUNY Distinguished Professor of Geography at the State University of New York at New Paltz, where he has taught since 1968. He is the author or editor of eight books, including *China's Traditional Rural Architecture: A Cultural Geography of the Common House* (1986); *China's Vernacular Architecture: House Form and Culture* (1989); *Chinese Landscapes: The Village as Place* (1992); and *China's Living Houses: Folk Beliefs, Symbols, and Household Ornamentation* (1999), which is a companion volume of this book.